W9-ACI-208

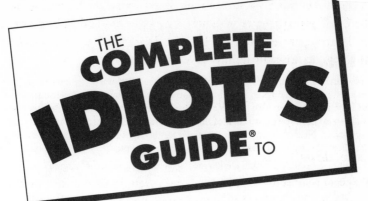

THE
COMPLETE IDIOT'S GUIDE® TO

Understanding Buddhism

Second Edition

by Gary Gach

ALPHA

A member of Penguin Group (USA) Inc.

To the well-being of all beings.

Copyright © 2004 by Gary Gach

All rights reserved. No part of this book shall be reproduced, stored in a retrieval system, or transmitted by any means, electronic, mechanical, photocopying, recording, or otherwise, without written permission from the publisher. No patent liability is assumed with respect to the use of the information contained herein. Although every precaution has been taken in the preparation of this book, the publisher and author assume no responsibility for errors or omissions. Neither is any liability assumed for damages resulting from the use of information contained herein. For information, address Alpha Books, 800 East 96th Street, Indianapolis, IN 46240.

THE COMPLETE IDIOT'S GUIDE TO and Design are registered trademarks of Penguin Group (USA) Inc.

International Standard Book Number: 1-59257-277-4
Library of Congress Catalog Card Number: 2004108626

06 05   8 7 6 5 4 3 2

Interpretation of the printing code: The rightmost number of the first series of numbers is the year of the book's printing; the rightmost number of the second series of numbers is the number of the book's printing. For example, a printing code of 04-1 shows that the first printing occurred in 2004.

Printed in the United States of America

Note: This publication contains the opinions and ideas of its author. It is intended to provide helpful and informative material on the subject matter covered. It is sold with the understanding that the author and publisher are not engaged in rendering professional services in the book. If the reader requires personal assistance or advice, a competent professional should be consulted.

The author and publisher specifically disclaim any responsibility for any liability, loss, or risk, personal or otherwise, which is incurred as a consequence, directly or indirectly, of the use and application of any of the contents of this book.

Most Alpha books are available at special quantity discounts for bulk purchases for sales promotions, premiums, fund-raising, or educational use. Special books, or book excerpts, can also be created to fit specific needs.

For details, write: Special Markets, Alpha Books, 375 Hudson Street, New York, NY 10014.

Publisher: *Marie Butler-Knight*
Product Manager: *Phil Kitchel*
Senior Managing Editor: *Jennifer Chisholm*
Senior Acquisitions Editor: *Randy Ladenheim-Gil*
Development Editor: *Michael Thomas*
Production Editor: *Megan Douglass*
Copy Editor: *Ross Patty*
Illustrator: *Jody Schaeffer*
Cover/Book Designer: *Trina Wurst*
Indexer: *Heather McNeil*
Layout/Proofreading: *Becky Harmon, John Etchison*

Contents at a Glance

Part 1:   **Buddha, Showing the Way**   1

1 Why Is This Person Smiling?: The Life of the Buddha   3
*The Buddha is his teachings, embodied in his life. Still alive
today. Take and make real in your own life as much as you
need. A little goes a long way. Just this story of one person has
changed civilizations. A smile that's gone around the world.*

2 Different Flavors, One Taste: The Teachings
Travel to Different Lands   19
*How the news spread, by foot and by ear ... and how it trans-
formed and was transformed by each country it touched. The
ripples still ring out ...*

3 What Might an Italian Buddha Look Like?:
Western Buddhism   35
*Buddhism's latest chapter is still being written ...
by cabbies and dentists, stewardesses and stevedores.
Buddhism's definitely destined to remain part of our culture.*

4 Different Travel Agents, Same Destination?: Interfaith   51
*No matter your outlook, there's room for Buddha. There are
Zen Judaists ... Benedictine buddhas ... Sufi Muslim buddhas ... atheists and agnostics and pagans. (All roads lead
to Om.)*

Part 2:   **Dharma: Truth, and the Way to Truth**   67

5 The Treasure and the Teachings: Jewels of Refuge
and Ennobling Truths   69
*Here's a Buddhist Pledge of Allegiance: taking refuge
in the Three Jewels. The ABCs. And the Four Noble Truths,
four-square like a table. Of such simplest of statements come
profundity you can rely on. Like a rock.*

6 Buddha's Way: The Eightfold Path   85
*Count them on your fingers. These eight steps lead to wisdom
and compassion ... liberation from fear and suffering ...
awakening to deep peace and lasting joy.*

7 Conscious Conduct: Precepts for a Path with a Heart   99
*Five variations on the Golden Rule, with a Buddhist twist.
These blueprints for happiness guide our steps to freedom.*

8   Take Karma, Make Dharma: Essential Ideas   115
    Dotting the i's and crossing the t's. Here are the fine points
    that make everything click. Everything ... and nothing.

Part 3:   Sangha: Joining the Path   133

9   How's Your Practice?: Getting Set   135
    Why read about it when you can find out for yourself? Here's
    how to get started ... and keep at it.

10 Meditation: Base Camp   151
    The mind at rest is the greatest human achievement. You can
    achieve that anywhere, all the time. Walking, sitting ...
    driving, or washing the dishes. Welcome to base camp!

11 Look Within, and Know: Insight Meditation   169
    What's with all these spiritual metaphors about seeing
    (enlightenment, illumination, insight)? Well, they're all
    about clarity, seeing clearly and deeply ... and so attaining
    understanding ... understanding life, and your own life ...
    with calm, wisdom, and boundless love—as you shall see ...

12 See? Words Cannot Express: Zen   187
    What can I tell you that you don't already know? This very
    moment is a complete manifestation of the entire universe ...
    utter buddhahood ... and you're absolutely intertwined with
    it. (And you don't need cable to enjoy it!)

13 True Devotion: Pure Land   205
    The simplest and largest path of Buddhism has been the least
    known (outside its numerous followers) ... until now. But,
    then, sometimes we learn the simplest things last.

14 Diamond Way: Tibetan Buddhism   223
    The most recent school to awaken the West claims the most
    evolved teachings of the Buddha, and the most complete. We
    can't promise to take you to enlightenment, but we certainly
    bring you to the Gates.

Part 4:   Buddhism in Action: Applications in Everyday Life   241

15 Bringing It All Back Home: Mutual Relations   243
    No one is an island. Rather, we're stories. Intertangled, and
    continuing. Here are Buddhist perspectives on life's most basic
    stories, from cradle to grave, and all the juicy good stuff in
    between.

16　Food for the Heart: The Meal of Life　　　　　　　259
*At least once or twice a day, seven days a week, we encounter
the whole universe: through food. The ingredients are all
there. We only need to stop to give thanks ... and all of life
comes into view.*

17　Working as if You Didn't Need the Money:
Right Livelihood　　　　　　　　　　　　　　　273
*Chop wood, carry water. Or do you chop wood thinking you'd
rather be carrying water? Is a job just to pay the rent, or can
work fulfill us? See how Dharma is a sound investment in
meaningful success.*

18　Everybody's Doing It: Buddhism and Popular Culture　285
*There's Buddhism in the crack of a bat hitting a ball ... the
twang of a guitar ... a Saturday afternoon matinee. Come
one, come all. The Buddha's highway is easy and wide.*

19　New Ways of Seeing and Being: Buddhism and Fine Arts　303
*Who says art or enlightenment dwell in worlds apart from
us? Not Buddha! Here are arts of awakening you can enjoy
... and practice yourself.*

20　Within and Without: Buddhism and the Sciences　321
*Buddhism has been mapping inner and outer space for mil-
lennia. Discover how breakthroughs like neuroimmunology
and holography, fractals and the Butterfly Effect, are shedding
new light on ancient wisdom, as a new mind-set re-evaluates
everything from psychology and physics ... to prayer.*

21　Happiness Is Not an Individual Matter: Engaged
Buddhism　　　　　　　　　　　　　　　　339
*In its unique way, Buddhism is responding to the challenges of
the modern world. Quality of life. Human rights. Democracy.
The environment. Buddhism in action can be a chance to
assist ourselves and others, in mutual care.*

Appendixes

A　The Unfolding of the Lotus: A Chronology of
the Timeless　　　　　　　　　　　　　　　355

B　Buddhism in a Nutshell: A Quick Reference　　　363

C　The Vocabulary of Silence: A Glossary　　　　　367

　　Index　　　　　　　　　　　　　　　　　373

Contents

Part 1: Buddha, Showing the Way   **1**

1 Why Is This Person Smiling?: The Life of the Buddha   **3**

Are You Ready?: Waking Up to Yourself, Waking Up
to Buddha 4
The Birth of a Sage, Siddhartha Gautama 5
   The Life of a Prince 6
   Reality Bites: The Four Signs 6
Going Forth, the Buddha 8
   Into the Forest: Finding Out 9
   The Middle Way 10
   Enlightenment 11
After Enlightenment: Teach! 13
Tales Heard Around Buddha's Campfire 15
   Beyond the Dualism of Words: Silence, and Parables 16
   The Final Teaching 17

2 Different Flavors, One Taste: The Teachings Travel to Different Lands   **19**

Mother India 20
   King Ashoka—Servant of the Dharma 21
   Camps and Schools: Don't Sweat Over Any Isms or Schisms 22
   The Buddha Has Left the House 24
Original Buddhism: The Wisdom of the Elders 25
Before the Internet: The Spice and Silk Routes 26
The Middle Kingdom: China 28
   China's Golden Age: The T'ang 29
   What Goes Up Must Come Down 30
Blossoms in Other Gardens 30
   Korea: The Land of Morning Calm 30
   Japan: The Land of Eight Islands 31
   Meeting Place: Vietnam 32
At the Roof of the World: Tibet, Land of Snows 32
Continuing Buddha's Way in Asia Today 33

3 What Might an Italian Buddha Look Like?: Western Buddhism   **35**

Preparing the Ground: Mulching the Cultural Soil 36
Seasons and Lunar Phases Conducive to Growth 36
   The Flames of War and the Phoenix from the Ashes 37
   Give Peace a Chance: The Sixties and Beyond 37

Gardeners in the Fields of the Buddha 38
  Pilgrims to the Western Lands 39
  Advance Scouts: Journeys to the East 40
  Living Dharma from Living Teachers 41
  Interpreters, Translators, and Scholars 42
Stay Tuned: Topics to Watch in Years to Come 44
  East? West? West Meets East in the West, and Vice-Versa 44
  Women Buddhas: Of Course! 46
  The Cherry Blossom Grafted onto the Hickory Branch:
   Buddhist Democracy 46
  Integration into Ordinary Workaday Life 47
  Diversity, a Tapestry of Many Threads 48
  Nonsecularism: Buddha at the Salad Bar 49

4 Different Travel Agents, Same Destination?: Interfaith   51

Beyond Exclusivity: Oneness 52
  Do Buddhists Necessarily Believe in God? 53
Roots: Buddha Was Born a Hindu 54
  The Hindu Matrix 55
  The Buddha's Unique Emphases 56
China's Version 1.0: Buddhism + Taoism 57
Benedictine Buddhists, Zen Judaists, Sufi Yogis 59
  Christian Followers of the Way: Onwards! 59
  A Personal Note 61
  JuBus: Where Mt. Sinai Meets Mt. Sumeru 62
  Make Room for Rumi 64
  Indigenous Spirituality: Everything's (a) Relative 65

Part 2: Dharma: Truth, and the Way to Truth   67

5 The Treasure and the Teachings: Jewels of Refuge and Ennobling Truths 69

The Triple Gem 70
Safe Harbor: Taking Refuge 71
  In Everyday Life 72
  Different Schools, Different Spins 73
  From the Ultimate Dimension 74
The Teaching: Four Noble Truths 75
  The First Fact of Life 76
  The Second Fact of Life 76
  The Third Fact of Life 78
  The Fourth Fact of Life 80
Theme and Variations 81

6 Buddha's Way: The Eightfold Path **85**

The Path 86
Connecting the Dots *87*
Perfect View: You See!? *90*
Perfect Thought: We Are What We Think *91*
Right Action: Good Karma *92*
Say the Word and It Will Happen: Perfect Speech *93*
More Than a Job: Wholesome Work *93*
Proper Effort: Just Do It *94*
Complete Mindfulness: Intelligent Alertness *94*
Total Concentration: Hitting the Nail on the Head *96*

7 Conscious Conduct: Precepts for a Path with a Heart **99**

To Not Kill: Reverence for Life 100
Every "Shalt-Not" Has Its "Shall" *101*
Vegetarianism *101*
Abortion *102*
To Not Steal: Trustworthiness and Generosity 103
Sexual Restraint: Respect, Intimacy, Trust, and
   Responsibility 105
To Not Lie: Deep Listening and Loving Speech 106
Bearing Witness *106*
Loving Speech *108*
Mindful Consumption: Proper Diet for Transformation 109
Altered States? Or Altered Traits? *109*
The Eightfold Path Meets the Twelve-Step Program *110*
So What's Your Addiction? (Precepts as Meditation) *110*
Media Consumption: We Ingest Words and Images, Too *111*
Practicing the Precepts 111
Precepts: A Mindfulness Meditation *112*
Making the Precepts Your Own *114*

8 Take Karma, Make Dharma: Key Concepts **115**

One Thing Leads to Another: Karma 116
This Depends on That: Interbeing 117
Different Mind-Sets, Different Worldviews *119*
Don't Sweat the Terminology *119*
The Stamp of Reality: The Three Dharma Seals 120
It Was That, Now It's This: Impermanence *120*
It's Neither This nor That: Selflessness *122*
You're IT: Nirvana *Now* 124

It Is and It Isn't: Emptiness (Infinite Openness) 125
   Emptiness, Unique and Full: Suchness 126
   No Thing: Even Emptiness Is Empty 128
Living It: Meditations in a Floating World 129

Part 3:   Sangha: Joining the Path   133

9 How's Your Practice?: Getting Set   135
Getting Started: Beginner's Mind 136
There's No Time Like the Right Time, and the
   Right Time Is: Now 138
   The Time It Takes Is the Time You Make 138
   A Retreat Doesn't Always Mean a Step Backward 139
   Dharma Has All the Time in the World for You 139
Buddha's in the House 140
   Setting Aside Some Breathing Room 140
   Altars: The Buddha Within and Without 141
Stocking Up on Gear: Clean Socks, and What Else? 142
Joining in Community of Practice: Friends Along the Path 143
As Much or as Little as You Like: The Choices Are Yours 144
   Picking and Choosing Wisely 144
   Don't Sweat the Isms 145
   When the Student Is Ready, the Master Appears 145
   Go as a Sangha 146
Viewless View and Effortless Effort 147
   Road Sign: Perfect View Begins Here 147
   Effort Can Be Effortless 149

10 Meditation: Base Camp   151
Be a Buddha and Sit Like a Buddha: Posture 152
   Ears over Shoulders: Basic Posture 153
   Giving Body Language a Hand: Mudras 154
   Getting Down to Earth: Prostration 155
Doing No Thing: How Relaxing! 155
   What if I Froze Like This?: Warm-Up Stretches 156
Why Not Breathe: You're Alive! 157
   Having a Gut Feeling That the Nose Knows 159
   Making Each Breath Count 160
   Words to Meditate by: Mantras and Gathas 160
   Slow, Deep, Calm Release: Peace Is Every Breath 161

Turning Off the Radio: Quieting the Mind 162
  Notice What You Notice *164*
  Note Sounds (Plink!) *as Well as Silence ( )* *164*
  Be Mindful and Compassionate Toward Yourself *165*
Meditation in Action: Mindful Walking 165
First-Aid Kit for Beginners' Problems 167

11 Look Within, and Know: Insight Meditation   **169**
Stopping and Seeing Deeply: Tranquil Concentration
  and Insight 170
Noting the Itch, Without Scratching 172
  Tips for Noting *173*
  Internalizing the Practice *174*
Material Meditations: The Wisdom of the Body 176
  The Body Scan: A Clean Sweep *176*
  Where's Self?: It's Elementary *178*
Here Today, Gone Tomorrow: Impermanence Meditation 179
Medicine for a Healthy Heart: Loving Kindness (*Metta*) 180
  Sublime States: The Four Brahmaviharas *180*
  Things Go Betta with Metta *181*
  Tips for Practice *183*
Stop: In the Name of Love 184

12 See? Words Cannot Express: Zen   **187**
Look, Where's Buddha? 188
A Few Drops of Zen 189
  Zen Is Meditation Right Here, Right Now *189*
  Zen Is Emptiness in Action, as Natural as Pie *189*
Just Do It! 190
Lineage: Direct from the Buddha to You, with Love 191
  The First Zen Patriarch: Kasyapa's Smile *191*
  The First Chinese Zen Patriarch: Bodhidharma *192*
  The Illiterate Sixth Patriarch: Hui Neng *194*
Now Why Not You? 195
Universal Participation: The Bodhisattva Vow 196
Without a Trace Along an Untrod Trail 198
Expressing the Inexpressible Without Words 200
  I Swear This Is True: "I Am a Liar" (Koans) *200*
  Who's on First?: Mondo *203*

13 True Devotion: Pure Land   205

The Story of Pure Land 206
  In the Land of the Buddha: Say His Name, and You'll Be Free 206
  Transferring Merit: Instant Karma? 208
The Primal Vow Is Universal Compassion 210
Three Keys: Faith, Vows, and Practice 211
Saint Shinran 212
  Other Power 213
  Self and Other: No Dualism 215
The Story of Deities: Room for Interpretation 215
A Simple, Universal Method, Alone or in Combination 217
Pure Land in Daily Life 218
  Giving Chants a Chance: Recitation 219
  Further Pure Land Paths 220
Other Schools 221

14 Diamond Way: Tibetan Buddhism   223

Tibetan Buddhism in 500 Words or Less 224
Vajrayana Is Mahayana with a Tantric Twist 226
Lamrim: Step-by-Step Stages Along the Path 227
Connecting with a Teacher 228
Empowerment: Initiation into Tantra 230
Body, Speech, and Mind as One: Some Essential
  Tantric Practices 231
  The Path Is the Body 232
  Say the Word: Speech Vibrations Can Set Great
    Things in Motion 233
  Seeing with Your Mind's Eye: Mandalas and Deities 233
Skillful Means of Ritual and Symbol 237
The End of the Road 238

Part 4: Buddhism in Action: Applications in Everyday Life   241

15 Bringing It All Back Home: Mutual Relations   243

The Way of Relation: Interrelation 244
  The Buddha's Own Family: Back to the Shakya 244
  If Emily Post Met the Buddha: Treating All Beings as
    Created Mutual 245
Cultural Relatives 246
Happily Ever After? How About "Happily Ever
  Here"? (Love) 246

Would You Promise to Be Mindful of the Present
  Moment with Your Beloved? (Marriage) 248
Nobody Does It Better 249
Mama Buddha, Papa Buddha, and Baby Buddha (Parenting) 251
  Parenting as Practice *251*
  Family Sangha, and Dharma for Kids *252*
  What's Your "E.Q."?: Emotional Intelligence *253*
Welcome to the Club: Rites of Passage 253
Learning How to Learn: Buddhist Education 254
Good Life: Good Death 256

16 Food for the Heart: The Meal of Life   **259**
Food as Food for Thought 260
You Are How You Eat: Heart Nourishment 260
  Thanksgiving's Every Day *261*
  Mindful Meals *262*
  Lifting an Elbow Together *264*
  Food Awareness *265*
Do You Hunger and Thirst?: Food Issues 267
  Mindless Food *268*
  Meat, Chewing It Over *268*
  Mindful Food *269*
Take Tea and See: The Tea Ceremony 269

17 Working as if You Didn't Need the Money: Right Livelihood   **273**
The Middle Way Between the Greatest Good and the
  Greatest Goods 274
Inter-Office Memo: "Less Stress!" 275
The Practice: Right Livelihood 276
Price or Value: How Do You Measure Wealth? 278
  "Small Is Beautiful": Economics from the Heart *279*
Dharma at Work: Zentrepreneurs and Tantrapreneurs 280

18 Everybody's Doing It: Buddhism and Popular Culture   **285**
A Gift from a Flower to a Garden 286
  Flower Power: By the Flowers, of the Flowers, and
  for the Flowers *286*
  Saying It with Flowers *287*
  Ooh, Ooh, Ooh! What Just Five Rocks Can Do *289*

Physical Culture Is Culture 290
  Martial Arts Are an Art 290
  Way of the Warrior: Zen Swords and Arrows 291
  Maximum Performance: Go, Sangha! BE the Ball! 292
Play It Again, Samadhi!—Musical Meditation 294
  Giving Buddhism Its Chants 294
  Blowing Your Mind the Buddhist Way 295
  Country 'n' Eastern, and Other Soundtracks 296
Mind Mirror: Buddha at the Movies 297
  Now Playing: Film as Buddhist 297
  Is Gone with the Wind *About Impermanence?: Buddhist Films* 300

19 New Ways of Seeing and Being: Buddhism and Fine Arts   303
But ... Is It Art? And ... Is It Buddhist? 304
Words for the Wordless: Buddhist Literature 307
  Some Picks for a Buddhist Reading Group 307
  One-Breath Meditation: Haiku 309
  How to Haiku 311
The Eye in the Heart of the Heart 311
  Drawing Attention: Drawing the Buddha 312
  The Way of the Brush: Zen Eye-Openers 312
Art as Life: Life Is Art 315
  Soundscape Without Horizon 316
  No Borders to Erase 318

20 Within and Without: Buddhism and the Sciences   321
New Physics and Ancient Eastern Thought 322
  Holism: Keep Your Eye on the Doughnut AND the Hole 322
  Middle-Way Logic, Fractal Buddhas, and Dharma Systems:
    Fuzzy, Chaos, and Complexity 326
  Chaos: There's a Method in the Madness 326
  Complexity: It's Basically Simple 328
Infinite Healing: Dr. Buddha 329
  Body Dharma: Healing the Whole Person 329
  Different Schools, But All Heal 329
Do Feelings Have a Mind of Their Own?:
  Buddhist Psychology 331
No Matter, Never Mind: Mind/Body Connections 333
  Mapping the Ineffable: Cognitive Science 333
  Gut Feelings: Neuroimmunology 333

Imagine, Just Imagine: Mind to Mind (Heart to Heart) 334
  Indra's Net: A Scientific Paradigm for Mind 335
  Neither Here nor There: Nonlocal Phenomena 336

21 Happiness Is Not an Individual Matter: Engaged Buddhism   339
What Is Engaged Buddhism? 340
Historical Engagement 341
  Knowing a Better Way to Catch a Snake 343
Service: One Big Circle of Giving 343
  Paradigm Shift: The Butterfly Effect 344
  Living Dying: Service in Hospices 345
  Doing Time: Prison Dharma 347
Seeing Like a River, Thinking Like a Tree: Deep Ecology 348
Wide Horizons: Humanity Is Our Sangha 349
  Female Buddhas (Continued) 349
  Colors of Compassion: Dharma Pluralism 352
Peace! 353

Appendixes

A The Unfolding of the Lotus: A Chronology of the Timeless   355

B Buddhism in a Nutshell: A Quick Reference   363

C The Vocabulary of Silence: A Glossary   367

Index   373

Foreword

The complex and varied cultural and textural manifestations of Buddhism are bewildering to many modern Western readers. A living religion that has spanned half the globe over 2,500 years is not easy to encapsulate. You may feel like a complete idiot when confronted by the variety of forms and teachings of one of the world's great religions. All of the different strands of Buddhism are simultaneously being introduced to the West at this very moment. A trivial example is the color of Buddhist robes. In southeast Asia, Saffron robes are worn; in the Tibetan traditions, red; Korean Buddhists wear gray; those from the Japanese tradition wear black.

The need for a guide through this vibrant thicket is clear. Gary Gach has taken up this difficult challenge in *The Complete Idiot's Guide to Understanding Buddhism, Second Edition*. Pointing out the similarities and differences in the complex weave of teachings of the cultures and practices called Buddhism, he puts them into a comprehensive context. It may be a guide for the complete idiot in that it assumes little, yet it avoids the traps of oversimplifying and dumbing down the subject. The book explores and presents simply and creatively the practical and theoretical, the mundane and the sacred, of Buddhism.

I suggest that you keep in mind the following words of Eihei Dogan, the twelfth-century founder of Soto Zen in Japan, from his famous essay, *Genjo Koan*, when trying to come to grips with Buddhism:

> To study Buddhism is to study the self
> To study the self is to forget the self
> To forget the self is to be awakened by all things
> And this awakening continues endlessly

You can study Buddhism as an external object, but it is also an internal exploration. "To study Buddhism is to study the self." Not the study of old and antiquated artifacts, but of something alive and kicking. "To study the self is to forget the self." When you study the self, Buddhism as a separate object disappears. When you study and focus on yourself as a discrete object, the self loses its boundary. "To forget the self is to be awakened by all things." To let go of your habits and preconceptions is to experience things as they are, not as you have grown to expect them to be. "This awakening continues endlessly." By letting go of your conditioning, awakening is present in each moment. Thus, wisdom and compassion naturally arise.

I would like to close with an old Zen caution: "Don't mistake the finger for the moon." Buddhism, Zen, Christianity, Islam, Taoism, Judaism, Confucianism, and so on are all useful fingers. Teachings that point the way to fully actualizing ourselves and benefiting others are pointers, but not the end itself. All religious teachings are about what is, but if we focus on the teachings as objects we miss the point. Enjoy this book, and allow your natural light to inform your reading.

Michael Wenger

Michael Wenger has practiced since 1972 at the San Francisco Zen Center, where he is currently Dean of Buddhist Studies. A Soto Zen lineage holder, he is the author of *33 Fingers: A Collection of Modern American Koans* and editor of *Wind Bell: Teachings from the San Francisco Zen Center 1968–2001*, and, with Mel Weitsman, of *Branching Streams Flow in the Darkness* by Shunryu Suzuki.

Introduction

It is a great honor, indeed, to present the message and practice of Buddhism to you. And it's a particular honor to do so in the time-tested *Complete Idiot's Guides'* format. A few people may scoff that this is sacrilegious, or something. I don't know. I can think of no better reply than the words of British writer G. K. Chesterton, when he said, "Angels can fly because they take themselves lightly." Not that my heels are more than an inch off the ground, mind you.

Now, if you're already a fan of *Complete Idiot's Guides*, like me, you'll know they're highly organized, which was one reason I thought it a perfect fit for introducing Buddhism, which is itself a highly organized system. So the book covers a whole lot of territory, and in a very developmental, step-by-step manner. Presenting the story and teachings of the Buddha in this way, I only hope you find them no less stimulating and rewarding … and sacred … than they have continued to be for me, and hundreds of millions of others. Becoming enlightened by a mere book might be asking a bit much, but I think you might find yourself thinking about things in ways you might not have done before.

Enjoy the journey. I think you'll find the merits of Buddhism penetrate beyond the intellect. People who practice Buddhism notice less stress in their lives, for one thing. Sharper concentration and attentive focus are also common features of the path. Dealing with each encounter more fully is another by-product. Living in closer intimacy with life.

Buddhism tends to allow people to accept and not cling, and so experience their life with greater calm and insight. Kindness is another common factor, kindness to others, but also to oneself. You might find difficult emotions easier to handle. You might also notice other people giving you nicer vibes than before. If they remark that you have a halo, or a brighter aura, well, I don't know. These are all already yours from birth.

See for yourself.

How to Use This Book

If you were to learn only four essential Buddhist things, they'd be about …

1. *Buddha*, the awakened.
2. *Dharma*, the teachings of the Buddha, and all they pertain to.
3. *Sangha*, the practice and practitioners of the teachings.
4. Seeing Buddhism in daily life.

The first three elements—called the Three Jewels—are the nitty-gritty of Buddhism. So, along with a fourth, I've made them the blueprint for this book. Part 1, "Buddha, Showing the Way," looks at the Buddha and the spread of his teachings. Part 2, "Dharma: Truth and the Way to Truth," explores the essence of his teachings (the Dharma). Part 3, "Sangha: Joining the Path," introduces the practice of Buddhism and surveys primary communities of practice (the Sangha). Part 4, "Buddhism in Action: Applications in Everyday Life," shows the possibilities and value of putting Buddhism into practice in further perspective.

Buddhism is amazing. It's composed of utterly simple things. Put them together, they're a whole greater than the sum of their parts: equal to life itself. (Plus, approximately equal to this book, as well.)

In **Part 1, "Buddha, Showing the Way,"** we start out with a biographical short story: the life of the Buddha. Then I sketch the fascinating history of how the Buddha's teachings have spread and adapted to different lands. To sharpen the point on that, we'll zero in next on Buddhism in the West. This may be the most interesting phase of Buddhism's history yet. (We're living inside of it, so like fish swimming through water, it's hard to see. And it will take decades before it takes shape. But I point out some directions this process is already headed.) To sum up, we'll compare and contrast Buddhism with major religions. It's compatible with them all, actually, as well as atheism.

Next, having laid the scene, who Buddha was in history, we'll explore what he taught. In **Part 2, "Dharma: Truth and the Way to Truth,"** you'll find the essence of the teachings in plain, everyday language. Here's the core, beginning with the Three Jewels: Buddha, Dharma, Sangha. Then comes the Buddha's primary philosophy, the Four Noble Truths, four holy Facts of Life succinctly delineating his unique approach. The last truth opens up into a path which we'll tour step by step. Please don't skip the subsequent chapter on conscious conduct, even if its contents might sound familiar at first glance. They're vital. As a capper, we'll survey key concepts of Buddhism and explore their unique wisdom.

We've now paved the way for putting all this into practice. In **Part 3, "Sangha: Joining the Path,"** I'll introduce you to meditation, in two chapters devoted to setting up a basic practice. Then I'll spotlight four major schools of practice in the West, another unique feature of this book. While I don't want to make Buddhism seem like a supermarket ("Attention, shoppers! Zen bread-tasting in Aisle 4!"), one of the unprecedented aspects of Western Buddhism, particularly American, is the variety of schools coexisting and co-evolving side by side for the first time. You'll hear about a couple other schools besides Insight Meditation (*Vipassana*), Zen, Pure Land, and Tibetan (*Vajrayana*)—but these four are kind of like basic food groups. And, as in a balanced meal, there's healthy interchange between them.

From there, you might consider the book's last part, the entire second half, a kind of buffet: a broad, salad-bar selection of ways in which the Way can be tested and tasted in the world at large. In **Part 4, "Buddhism in Action: Applications in Everyday Life,"** we'll survey real-world interchanges with Buddhism, starting with our primary relations—from cradle to grave. Then two more aspects of everyday life enriched by Buddhist views: food and work. Two more chapters explore Buddhism and the arts, popular and fine, including sports, gardening, music, movies, writing (your own, even), and life art. Then we see how Buddhism harmonizes with the shift in view (paradigm) taking place in the sciences. These realms hold exciting possibilities for a renewed importance of Buddhism. Our final chapter shows ways in which volunteering to serve others can enrich your own practice, plus spotlights modern issues which Buddhism is addressing in its own gentle, transformative way.

Throughout the book, you'll find meditations and tips you can try out for yourself. And there's a short and longer Table of Contents at the front, and a glossary, chronology, and reference page at the back, plus our Buddhist Bulletin Board sprinkled throughout.

Our Buddhist Bulletin Board

Part of the added value and fun of any *Complete Idiot's Guide* are the boxed notes in the margin, called sidebars. (Until I wrote this book, I always thought they were called "little doohickeys.") For your reading pleasure, I'll incorporate four little doohickeys:

Leaves from the Bodhi Tree

A tree sheltered the Buddha during the meditation that led to his supreme enlightenment, and its descendant still grows today. This sidebar is for leaves from that tree, anecdotes and meditations illuminating aspects of the vast living organism that is Buddhism. (Like, did you hear the one about the priest, the rabbi, and the guru …?)

This Is

… highlights and defines key words and phrases. Don't mistake a finger pointing to the moon for the moon itself. Or, as semanticist W. I. Korczybyski put it, "The map is not the territory." Meaning: A word can leave you at the gates but can't bring you across; it's up to you to make it real.

> **Hear and Now**
>
> … is for listening to notable folks who illuminate some gist or pith. However distant their origin, they speak to us as contemporaries, here and now.

> **Along the Path**
>
> … is reserved for various and sundry sayings and thoughts commenting on the text, like violets doodled in the margin. Often they mingle different traditions, or East and West. All roads lead to Om.

Quick Reference

This is a handy summary of essential points along the Way. There's no one regimen. The Way of the Buddha can be understood, realized, and expressed through the most subtle or simple concept or fact. Putting just one into practice can eventually lead to all the others.

Acknowledgements

I am humbly grateful to my parents, family, sangha, teachers, and friends. The following people were particularly invaluable in making my efforts even better: my indefatigable editor Randy Ladenheim-Gil, now twice as special, plus Michael Thomas, Christy Wagner, Ross Patty, and Megan Douglass, patient, cheery, brilliant production pals, all a great honor to work with; as always, gentleman literary representative Jack Scovil; and all the genius artists and photographers. Special thanks to Chungliang Al Huang for playing with Eastern and Western imagery in the 1980s in a book called *Quantum Soup*, from which I cannot help but light my candle with his permission; to Annapurna; bbear; Margery Cantor; Terry Yee Carlson, Chinatown Branch, San Francisco Public Library; Swami Chaitanya; Cindy; Aaron Fagerstrom; Iftekhai Har; Wendy Johnson; Maxine Hong Kingston; Jack Kornfield; Arnold Kotler and Therese Fitzgerald, Dharma Friends; Rev. Ryuei Mike McCormick, Nichiren Buddhist Temple of San Jose; Travis Masch, Parallax Press; Reference Desk, Mechanics' Institute Library; Susan Moon, Buddhist Peace Fellowship; National Japanese American Historical Society; Tipu Shardar, Colour Drop; Ven. Shih Ying-Fa, CloudWater Zendo; Miriam Solon; Daishin Sunseri, GMBS (Gay Men's Buddhist Sangha of San Francisco); Stephen Toole; and all the readers writing me with feedback.

Additional inexpressible gratitudes to Wes Nisker, for his review of the chapter on Vipassana, and then some; Reverend Ken Tanaka for comments on my section on Pure Land; Prof. Janis Willis and Peter Wood for their expertise on Vajrayana; and Prof. Lewis R. Lancaster and Michael Wenger, for their infallible encouragement and sweet support from first to last. Actually, Michael's name now comes up along with mine in my Web search for this title, which may be about right. Any residual errors remain wholly my own.

"Dream Deferred" by Langston Hughes, from *The Collected Poems of Langston Hughes*, copyright 1994 by The Estate of Langston Hughes. Used by permission of Alfred A. Knopf, a division of Random House, Inc.

"The Red Wheelbarrow" by William Carlos Williams, from *Collected Poems 1909–1939*, Volume 1, copyright 1938 by New Directions Publishing Corp. Reprinted by permission of New Directions Publishing Corp.

Best efforts have been made to locate all rights holders and clear necessary reprint permissions. If any acknowledgments have been omitted, or any rights overlooked, it is unintentional and forgiveness is requested. Any oversights will be rectified for future editions upon proper notice.

Special Thanks to the Technical Editor

The Complete Idiot's Guide to Understanding Buddhism was reviewed in its previous edition by an expert who not only checked the accuracy of what you'll learn in this book but also provided valuable insight to help ensure that it tells you everything you need to know about Buddhism. Our special thanks are extended to Professor Lewis R. Lancaster.

Prof. Lancaster was born in Virginia, and earned his B.A. from Roanake College, his M.Th. from USC-ST, and his Ph.D. from the University of Wisconsin. Since 1967, he has been affiliated with the University of California, Berkeley, in a number of key positions, notably as cofounder of its Buddhist Studies program, as well as serving on committees for numerous programs and departments, including the Program in Religious Studies, the Center for Chinese Studies, the Center for Korean Studies, and the Department of East Asian Languages. He also serves on the adjunct faculty of the Graduate Theological Union and the Institute of Buddhist Studies (both also in Berkeley), and Hsi Lai University (Los Angeles). Advisor and consultant to a number of nonprofits, he's a renowned speaker at national and international panels, workshops, conferences, and symposia.

Editor of nine scholarly Buddhist books and of the Berkeley Buddhist Studies Series, his essays have been published in dozens of anthologies and journals. Most recently, he's been a pioneering contributor to the electronic publication of six CD-ROM collections of such definitive texts as 45 volumes of the Pali Canon, 11,000 pages of Sanskrit texts, 70 Chinese Zen texts with bibliography, 8,000 pages of archival materials on Korean Buddhist history, and an interactive database on Korean Buddhist thought. In addition to his research, lecturing, and writings, he currently devotes a considerable amount of his time to the Electronic Cultural Atlas Initiative (www.ias.berkeley.edu/ecai), an unprecedented international collaboration that will open new dimensions of scholarly research. That he's taken time from such endeavors to focus such considerable expertise and care to this book is an immeasurably great honor and aid.

Trademarks

All terms mentioned in this book that are known to be or are suspected of being trademarks or service marks have been appropriately capitalized. Alpha Books and Penguin Group (USA) Inc. cannot attest to the accuracy of this information. Use of a term in this book should not be regarded as affecting the validity of any trademark or service mark.

Part 1

Buddha, Showing the Way

Let's start our tour by asking "Who?" Such is the beginning of various primary questions, as "Who wrote the book of love?" "Who's in charge here?" and "Who am I, really?" (And "So who wants to know?")

In this case, our "who" is the Buddha. The Original Teacher. The one who shows us the way in this world. The Awakened One. I'm talking about the historical person here, who also embodied his teachings ... and about the buddha within. Within you, me, and everyone.

No matter what your religion, your country, or your car, the Buddha has something necessary to show you. So without further ado, it's a great privilege and pleasure for me to introduce to you everyone's good old buddy ... the Buddha.

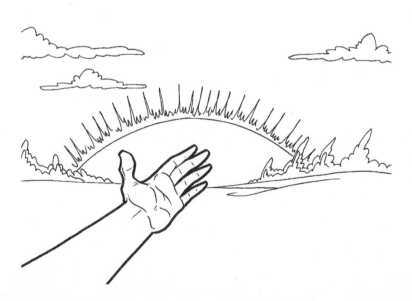

Why Is This Person Smiling?: The Life of the Buddha

In This Chapter

- ◆ The life of the Buddha
- ◆ The Four Signs
- ◆ The Great Renunciation
- ◆ The Middle Way
- ◆ Supreme Enlightenment
- ◆ Then what?

We humans are curious. We're curious about ourselves and we're curious about other humans—hence diaries, memoirs, and unauthorized biographies. Our own life is, of course, the world's greatest story, for sure; the one where we're most curious to find out what happens next. ("Tune in again tomorrow!") We're also inspired by others: Dante, Black Elk, Helen Keller, Babe Ruth, _____ (fill in the blank). Everybody has their favorites. Some of these fellow human beans we designate as role models. We even set aside national holidays so we can contemplate their accomplishments. The life of the Buddha has been just such a great event in the life of humanity;

his teachings a glorious gift we all can appreciate as a valuable part of our common heritage. I invite you to sit back and share in that splendor.

Over millennia, the Buddha's life story has been used as a tale for teaching, mingling biographical fact with legend, even myth. Taking myth as sacred story, Joseph Campbell has said, "The closest we have to planetary mythology is Buddhism. In it all things are potentially Buddha things." It's no surprise some cherish Buddha's teachings so much they worship him. Along these lines, some say the historical Buddha whom we're about to meet was but one of myriads of other buddhas, past and present and future, throughout the universe.

Here, we'll take as our basis a humanist view. That is, there was a human being with a birth date and death date like you or me—and whose gifts to us remain profoundly vital today. "Obviously, I think his is a story everyone should know. If you've never heard it before, just think … the life of the Buddha is known to over one third of humanity. Join the club.

Are You Ready?: Waking Up to Yourself, Waking Up to Buddha

Once there was a man who discovered a priceless, commonsensical guide to happiness. *The Complete Idiot's Guide to Happiness*, if you will. This discovery, he also found, is available to every human being. Right in front of their face. But, as he would also discover, something so simple might not be for everyone. Why not? Well, for one thing, the Buddha only said he discovered something that worked for him, and invited others to try it and see for themselves. He was a guide but not a god, and some people prefer to wait for God or priests to tell them what they can find out for themselves or intuitively know already. (Might this be you?)

Moreover, some people prefer to imagine their happiness will last forever. (Could *this* be you?) Others have a hard time letting go of the accumulation of wounds and labels that have stuck to them throughout life, tenaciously clinging to sorrows, as if for ballast rather than letting go and sensing the innate, ineffable lightness of life; rather than appreciating the luminous blue sky, solid brown earth, and tender green plants, always present for enjoyment. (Is *this* you?) If you can see yourself in this portrait gallery (and who can't?), then "Welcome to the club!" It's commonly called The Human Condition. Right there, in a nutshell, you have it. We spin around in our self-created rat cage when all along the cage door is unlocked.

But so long as there are people living their life as if sleepwalking through a kind of depressing bad dream, there'll always be a chance for awakening. That's what *Buddha* means, in essence. Some one or even some thing that awakens, and awakens us. Thus it might be said that anything is a buddha, if it wakes us up, mentally and spiritually, as well as physically. Really awakens. It could be the sound of a bird. Or the look of wonder and unconditional love on a baby's face. Pause, right now, be attentive, listen and look: A buddha voice or buddha sight will probably appear. Now, if all things are potentially buddha, then we have great reason to consider and learn from, if not honor, the original Buddha.

The Buddha once said, "If you want to really see me, then look at my teachings." The reverse is equally true. That is, his life is itself a teaching, or series of teachings.

The Buddha teaches that becoming intimate with life, becoming awake, is to awaken to ourselves, to our fullest potential as human beings, to the buddha within all of us. It's as important as life and death, and as easy as drinking a cup of tea.

Though his story has become one of the most multilayered of all time, throughout it all there remains the Buddha's ineffable smile, beyond words. You'll see. It starts like this ...

> **This Is**
>
> **Buddha,** derived from the Sanskrit root *budh,* to awaken, is a title, not a name; like King, or Christ. As such, it means Awakened One Supremely Awakened. (There are degrees of awakening. Just 'cos your eyes are open doesn't mean you're awake.)

The Birth of a Sage, Siddhartha Gautama

One full-moon night in May, around 560 B.C.E., a woman on a journey gave birth. Her name was Mahamaya, and she'd been headed from her home to her father's house, about 50 miles away, to lie in waiting, as was the custom in India in those days. So she returned home to the foothills of the Himalayas, on the border between what's now India and Nepal, to present her husband his son. This would be no ordinary son. Mahamaya was a queen, married to King Suddhodana, the ruler of the Shakya people. Her son would be prince of their small but prosperous kingdom. They named him Siddhartha, meaning "a wish fulfilled" or "aim accomplishment."

> **Along the Path**
>
> Sometimes it seems like this one guy had a string of aliases. Here's the lowdown. Gautama (*goh-tah-mah*) was his family clan name, and Siddhartha was his personal name. He's also sometimes called Shakyamuni, meaning the sage of the Shakya tribe. Interestingly, he's called Buddha from the time of his going forth on his quest.

According to the custom of the day, a soothsayer made a prediction at birth. A Brahmin of the highest caste foresaw Siddhartha would rule over all the land, but only if he were kept from the reality of decay and death. Otherwise, he'd be a great mystic saint.

The Life of a Prince

The king adored his son and wanted him to inherit and rule over his kingdom and so kept him cloistered within the strong, high palace walls—not unlike the way we cloister ourselves in our set ways and go about our lives unquestioningly. Moreover, some say the father went so far as to create an environment as artificial as a Hollywood soundstage, wherein sick people, the elderly, even dirt and withered leaves were all whisked from view. But, as the story reveals, the truth is always out there, for the persevering seeker to discover.

Anyway, the king brought the finest tutors to teach his son to be a warrior king. The prince was a prodigy; he soon knew more than his teachers. He was unequalled in literature and math. He surpassed everyone in swimming and running, archery and fencing. One legend has it that it was in a huge athletic competition that he won the hand of one of the most beautiful of maidens, Yashodhara (Keeper of Radiance), who became his bride. He could strategize, command respect, and win any battle.

Not only a whiz kid and a champ, he got along with everyone and proved a compassionate and loving husband. The mark of success was upon him. Naturally, his father was delighted. He gave Siddhartha and his bride three different palaces, one for each of India's three seasons, hot, cool, and wet. There, the prince was lavished with beautiful attendants, fleets of horses, endless fun and games, fabulous feasts, live concerts at the snap of his fingers, the whole bit. But Siddhartha started to champ at that bit.

Reality Bites: The Four Signs

Siddhartha wanted to know about the world outside the palace walls, the real world. So does anyone who wants to lead an authentic life. To keep his son happy, the king granted his wish, yet made sure everything outside was as controlled as it had been inside.

Everywhere Siddhartha went, he saw prosperity and happiness until, somehow, a decrepit form passed through all the young, healthy people the king had arranged for him to see. Siddhartha asked his servant Channa "What is this!?" The faithful servant told him that although he had white hair down to his knees, this was a man, an old man, using a staff to walk, and this is what happens to everyone eventually. All the way back to the castle, Siddhartha brooded, and when the king heard about this, he increased the budget for Siddhartha's lavish lifestyle.

A second time, however, on another trip to the country, Siddhartha chanced upon a maimed fellow with bloodshot eyes, groaning through a frothy mouth. "What is this!?" Siddhartha asked, and was told by his faithful servant that this was a person who'd become ill, but that Siddhartha needn't worry since the prince ate a good diet and exercised. Siddhartha returned home brooding, and so the king plied him with even more opulent luxuries.

A third time out, reality bit yet again. On another outing, Siddhartha chanced upon a funeral procession, mourners sobbing and waving their arms in all directions, while at the head of the procession a body was being carried, utterly still, as if sleeping. Siddhartha saw and faithful servant Channa explained what death is—that nothing could be done for it, and that it happens to everyone. No point in worrying, he said, just hope for a long life.

What a shock! Old age and sickness were bad enough. But now this, their final resolution! The ultimate, inevitable destination of us all. Is there anyone for whom the first encounter with death isn't one of the most unforgettable, difficult moments of their life?

Each of these encounters were but glimpses, but perhaps their having been withheld for so long made them even more of a revelation. In any event, Siddhartha saw they were a matter of his own life and death, and, by extension, of everyone he loved—and indeed, all mortals. Was there no way out?! Meanwhile, when the king saw his beloved boy brooding more darkly than ever before, and found out why, he despaired. He didn't want to lose his only beloved son and heir. But did he level with him? No, he pampered him all the more. Yet life as it really is broke through the walls again, a fourth and final time.

Journeying outside the palace walls, Siddhartha happened to see a man with shaven head, clad only in an orange sheet the color of liquid sunshine, walking slowly, holding only an empty bowl, his entire manner radiating majestic tranquility and serene joy. "What is this?" Siddhartha asked, and was told that this was a monk, who'd renounced the world in search of spiritual truth. This silent monk seemed to be telling him, yes, there is an answer to the questions burning inside him since he'd so starkly witnessed human suffering for himself. An answer he'd never find as long as he numbed his mind with endless sensual indulgence. Well, when all this got back to the king, he was beside himself.

Just then, as fate would have it, Siddhartha's bride bore a child. Siddhartha probably was torn, as we can see from the name he gave his son, Rahula, which means "chain." The king took the occasion to stage a blowout celebration to keep Siddhartha close to hearth and home. But after the sumptuous feast, as Siddhartha was being entertained by the finest dancing girls in all the land, he yawned, laid down on his cushion, and

Dream Deferred

What happens to a dream
  deferred?
Does it dry up
Like a raisin in the sun?
Or fester like a sore —
And then run?
Does it stink like rotten meat?
Or crust and sugar over —
like a syrupy sweet?
Maybe it just sags
like a heavy load.
Or does it explode?

—Langston Hughes

closed his eyes. No point entertaining someone who isn't paying attention, so the dancing girls stopped, laid down, too, and napped. When Siddhartha opened his eyes again, he saw these women who just moments ago had been the quintessence of beauty, now sweaty, sprawled in awkward positions, once lovely faces now drooling or gnashing their teeth in their sleep. So much for the pleasures of the material world! And what a cue for an exit!

Stealthily, he got up and tiptoed out. Passing by his wife's chambers, he took one last lingering look at his sleeping beloved ones, and then was gone—gone in search of an answer to the human riddles of disease, decay, and death, in search of the ultimate meaning of life.

Going Forth, the Buddha

Time out. Before we follow Siddhartha on his quest, we might pause for a moment to consider his break with his past, his renunciation. For one thing, it was extreme: a prince renouncing the wealth and power that was his birthright. In today's terms, he could have been a trillionaire. Actually, though, it was respectable for noblemen of India to investigate ultimate truth, but only in their retirement, *after* they'd fulfilled their family and social obligations. For Siddhartha, however, the truth couldn't wait.

Plus, Siddhartha would be walking away from his responsibilities as a father as well as a prince. He was aware of the pain he'd cause others by leaving, but suffering seemed the ever-present essence of this ultimate riddle he intended to resolve, once and for all. Once he'd found the answer, Siddhartha vowed to return, bringing it back home to his people and all the land.

So we acknowledge the courage of Siddhartha, the fearlessness necessary to stand up for his dream, his ideals, his quest, to seek sovereignty over his own life rather than over a kingdom. It's also interesting to notice that Siddhartha was leaving behind inherited ideas, as well as inherited privilege. A message here, I think, for all of us is to look at life with our own two eyes, regardless of what Simon says, without asking "Mother, may I?"—seeing for ourselves, beyond the high, strong palace walls of what we've learned to call self.

Into the Forest: Finding Out

So Siddhartha gave his royal robes and jewels to his faithful servant. Before giving him his sword, he shaved his head (an act repeated by those who become Buddhists monks and nuns today), leaving only a top-knot, severing his ties with his family and caste. And he set out for the forests.

Now, in those days, India's wild forests and mountains were dotted with various seekers after truth. As many as 63 different schools prevailed. Siddhartha studied under one renowned forest teacher after another. In relatively no time, he learned all his teachers knew and was even offered jobs carrying on their work, but that wasn't what he was looking for. True, he'd learned to transcend his senses and thoughts, his materiality, and even his own consciousness. But while these techniques transcended reality, they didn't unlock it. They didn't resolve the riddle of birth and death. They offered temporary bliss, but not permanent peace. They couldn't answer the pain still resounding in his heart.

Siddhartha's achievements had drawn to him a handful of companions. With them, he tried the *ascetic* path of self-denial to the point of self-mortification, as a means of attaining self-control and liberation. He lay on a bed of nails. He progressively reduced his diet until he was down to one grain of rice a day. Soon, overachiever that he was, he came to the brink of self-annihilation.

Just skin and bones. This sculpture depicts Buddha's extreme asceticism. His veins bulge over his ribs, through his blackened and withering skin. If he rubbed his tummy he could feel his spine. His eyes stare from their sockets like stale water from a deep well.

From Sikri, Pakistan (Gandhara). Second century C.E. 83.8 cm. Lahore Museum.

> **This Is** _____
>
> **Ascetic,** from Greek, originally meant "hermit," such as a person practicing austere self-discipline for religious purposes. Besides seclusion, common forms of *asceticism* are fasting, celibacy, and poverty. These self-disciplines are believed to sharpen the mind, heighten awareness, and free the practitioner from mundane attachments.

The Middle Way

At this point, a young girl from the village passed by with food her mother had given her as an offering to the forest gods. She saw Siddhartha, nearly unconscious, and put some rice-milk to his lips, and he drank. By so doing, he renounced not only asceticism but also extremism.

There are two things going on here worth noting. First, there's the wonderful recognition of the importance of our bodies and their relationship to our happiness! So many spiritual paths have trod on the body as evil. Siddhartha realized he couldn't achieve his goal if his mind was in a trance and his body too weak to grasp and carry on the truth. Indeed, realizing the mind-body connection, he saw he couldn't have a sound mind without a sound body.

Moreover, he realized something simple yet sublime, now known as the *Middle Way*. We all meet with varying forms of extremism in ourselves and others. The Buddha would say to listen to all sides, then find a harmonious middle road. Don't tear the ground out from under your feet, nor chase after a spring dream. If the guitar string's too taut, it snaps; too loose, it won't play. Find the mean and, *Ping!*, it sings.

> **This Is** _____
>
> The **Middle Way** is a profound yet practical expression of the Buddha's nondualist outlook. That is, dualism divides everything: good vs. evil, self vs. other, mind vs. body, either/or, all or nothing. Buddhism embraces all sides, seeing their interrelatedness, and seeks the mean. (A whole school of Buddhism developed dedicated to studying the Middle Way, called *Madhyamika*.)

So he realized self-denial didn't free him from attachments, and also came to see self-denial as but another kind of attachment, another attachment to self, no different from his princely self-indulgence. Looking deeper, he began to truly wake up to how identification with "self" is always a set-up for ultimate disappointment, since it implies a dualist opposition: self and its desires ("in here") vs. world and its rewards ("out there"). This *versus* That. So no attachment to self, no dualism.

Well, meanwhile, his eating food blew his credibility with his five self-appointed disciples, for sure. They wandered off before he could explain his realization. And so he went at it alone. At some point, we all must. But the girl returned and offered him food every day. With the recovery of his health came fresh perceptions, which led to new insights, which would lead to wisdom. And, ultimately, enlightenment.

Enlightenment

Meditating in a healthy body allowed him to look at things around him with clarity. Whether looking at the food the girl offered before he ate it, or just sitting under a tree and looking at one of its leaves, he saw that each of these things was not independent. Food might come from a leaf. And the leaf? The leaf came from the sun in the sky, from the earth beneath him, and from the water in a cloud. And where did each of these come from? They were all interconnected. Interdependent. Interacting and inter-reacting. He saw now that self-denial could never liberate him from the intricate, vast web of life. Nor was the web of life at fault. Indeed, there was no fault, anywhere.

Looking further, he saw that nothing in life lasts. Nothing is permanent. The cloud passes away in the sun. The leaf falls to the earth. Similarly, he, too, was part of not only the interdependence but also the impermanence of all life. Meditating clearly now, these realizations made him appreciate each moment to the fullest. And why not? Why not live each moment to the fullest when each moment occurs only once, and when each instant potentially contains the whole of life?

Now he felt he was really getting somewhere. Now he was cooking! The meaning of suffering and death was becoming clear at last. Before sundown, looking at the evening star beside the full moon of May, he felt that tonight he'd make his final, ultimate breakthrough.

Sitting beneath the sheltering leaves of a fig tree (the Indian *banyan* variety), he endured thunderstorms, some say even demonic temptations, lead by Mara (embodiment of death). First Mara surrounded the Buddha with the most seductive women imaginable, but the Buddha remained composed. Then Mara unleashed the most bloodthirsty warrior demons upon him, but he had no fear. Finally, Mara tried to tempt him away from his meditation by challenging his motives, saying, "Aren't you really doing this for selfish reasons? What right have you, anyway? And if you've transcended this realm, then why don't you just leave? And even if you did attain enlightenment, who'd believe you?" Whereupon the Buddha looked at Mara and touched the ground with his hand, taking the earth as his witness, all of creation. Mara admitted defeat.

With his right hand, the Buddha calls upon the earth as witness of his enlightenment.

Sukhothai school, fourteenth or early fifteenth century. Bronze; 101.6 cm. National Museum, Ayuthya.

Oblivious to all distractions, gazing deeper and deeper into his mind and the mind of creation, the heart of life. In the darkest night, he penetrated the enigma of life, that we are born to die, thus inevitably bound to suffer. Mortality leads to cravings that can never be fulfilled—and perpetuates false mind-sets of self that only produce more suffering. He saw clearly now the jail in which we entrap ourselves and which we ourselves police.

He understood that what we call our life is but a wave, not the ocean. He became one with that ocean, and all the rivers and raindrops that feed it. He became enlightened. He saw the morning star in the sky as if for the first time, his mind as clear now as a mirror, and his heart, as wide now as the world, was overbrimming with understanding and love. The bright, keen, joyous starlight matched the smile on his lips. This was it. He had found out. Now he was fully awake.

Buddhaship attained.

After Enlightenment: Teach!

So imagine Siddhartha sitting there, at the culmination of a seven-year quest, now the most fully self-realized being ever in human history, so happy!, finally having found complete freedom from all mortal suffering. He'd experienced great awakening and attained supreme enlightenment. That means he directly perceived ultimate reality, free of all limitation, his compassionate awareness and sublime wisdom one with all that is.

After some time, he stood up and took his first steps, just walking lovingly around the tree that had sheltered him. He felt the solid earth supporting his bare feet, the fresh wind caressing his cheek, as if he and the world had been born together just now. When the young girl brought food that day, she could feel his transformation in her own heart.

It's interesting to consider how he might have remained beneath the tree in perfect nirvana for the rest of his days. Yet his enlightenment showed him how the seeds of enlightenment are within the hearts of everyone. His love for all beings and compassion for their needless suffering was bound up, part and parcel, with his awakening to life's ultimate meaning. So he returned to the companionship of his fellow human beings.

Now when his five former followers saw Siddhartha coming, they turned their backs. They remembered him as having copped out on the rigors of the ascetic path. But as he drew nearer, they could recognize in their own hearts that he was transformed. Supreme Enlightenment was evident just from his presence. They let go of their judgments and preconceptions, and welcomed him. They could see he merited being called "Buddha."

That night he gave his first talk, known as "The Turning of the Wheel of Truth." Explaining his discovery, he introduced four premises, known as the *Four Noble Truths* (discussed in Chapter 5), defining the origin of and liberation from suffering, with a practical, personal program for such liberation, known as the *Eightfold Path* (discussed in Chapter 6). While some were mulling it over, one of the companions got it and awoke on the spot. Nothing to memorize or take on faith, instead he awoke to the truth resounding within himself.

Buddha was a traveling teacher (peripatetic), on a perpetual pilgrimage. Thus did his teachings spread by foot. The traditional topknot of his hair is elongated to represent his enlightenment. His fingers are tapered to symbolize his ability to reach deep within. His gesture of one hand up means "Have no fear"; the other hand offers a boon. The design displays an amazing balance of motion and rest.

Sukhhothai, 3.53 cm × 2.35 cm.

And it was decided that these teachings would be called "*Dharma*," the path. Those on this path would be called "*Sangha*." And Siddhartha would become known as "*The Buddha*," the one who shows others the path in this world. Thus began the Buddha's course of teaching—to whomever would listen, as well as to his growing band of disciples, as he walked around the vast delta of the Ganges River, with an annual retreat during India's three-month heavy rains. All told, it was to be a journey lasting the next 45 years.

> **This Is** _____
>
> **Dharma,** from Sanskrit (Dhamma, Pali), has a number of meanings, depending on the context: teachings, doctrine, system, path, reality, and truth (also virtue, law, standard, and cosmic order). Here we can say it refers to truth, and the way to the truth; the Buddha's teachings and that to which they pertain (everything in life).
>
> **Sangha** means "assembly, host." Generally, it refers to the Buddhist community; more specifically, to its monastic order, one of the oldest in the world.

Tales Heard Around Buddha's Campfire

The Buddha's life itself is his teachings. So of all the statues of him, I love best the ones of him walking. We see him on the move, dynamic, and thus his teachings as nothing fixed. Later, people wrote down his talks (called _sutras_). The entire next part of this book is devoted to a tour of the Buddha's basic teachings. Meanwhile, just a couple stories from this phase of his life shed light on his method and thought.

Buddha's persuasiveness can be judged not only for the truth of his message but also the simplicity, inclusiveness, realism, and care with which he would present it. For example, a woman named Kisa Gotami came to him, clutching in her arms the body of her only child, who'd just died. She'd heard he'd transcended the bonds of death and, weeping, implored him to restore her daughter to life. He could see she was in shock. Nothing he could say would get through to her. (If you were the Buddha, what would you do?)

The Buddha smiled compassionately, giving her hope. She felt reassured in his warm, calm presence and trusted the lucidity of wisdom. "Before I do anything," he told her, "go to the nearby village and bring me a handful of mustard seed. But, please, make sure the seed comes only from a home where death is unknown." And so Kisa Gotami hurried to the village, believing the Buddha would save her daughter, and knocked on the first door. When the owners of the house saw her, clutching her dead child, they invited her in and said they'd be glad to give her some mustard seed. But when she added the Buddha's stipulation, the woman of the house wiped away a tear as her husband told her of the death of his father. Second house, third house: same thing. Eventually, she'd knocked on the doors of the entire village. Kisa Gotami returned to the Buddha's enclave in the forest, buried her child, and asked to learn the Dharma.

Amazing story. He hadn't told her to learn to forget and be happy. No, he showed her a way to reach deeper into her grief, a way that also enabled her to see something larger than her own loss, something in which she could take refuge: the universality of impermanence.

Along the Path

In Asia, "Buddhism" is an alien term, because to them it merely refers to reality, "Buddha Dharma." What to call it? Because the Buddha wouldn't address certain basic metaphysical questions, his path isn't technically philosophy. Likewise, because his teachings aren't built around God or an afterlife, they aren't precisely a religion. And his teachings about self as an illusory construction makes it tricky to categorize as psychology. Some people prefer to call it a science, an education, or a way of life. A path.

Beyond the Dualism of Words: Silence, and Parables

Other times, the Buddha answered with silence. Such was the case when asked questions typically not open to direct, personal experience, and so whose answer really didn't matter. "It does not further," he might say, at best (meaning "time is too precious to go down that path"), when asked is space infinite, is the universe eternal, is the soul immortal, are body and mind identical. Had the Buddha heard of stand-up comedy, he might have replied with one-liners, like Woody Allen: "If man were immortal, just think of what his laundry bills would be!" Ba-dum!

The Buddha wasn't necessarily nonreverential about the ineffable, but he sure didn't try to catch the wind. Some say that, being omniscient, the Buddha actually knew the answers to questions of infinity and eternity, divinity and immortality, but kept silent realizing how the rest of us would get tangled up in words and views, wanting to argue all night but never getting anywhere. Rather, he's like a noble fireman who doesn't debate the metaphysics of the origin of fire with people caught in a burning building.

Sometimes Buddha answered about profound imponderables with a parable. He'd say, for example, that asking where the universe began was like the man struck by a poison dart, who won't allow himself to be taken to a doctor until he knows exactly who fired the dart, just what poison he used, precisely how the dart was made, and so on.

Parable is a favorite tool of great teachers and mystics, and the Buddha is no exception. His most famous is yet another of his responses to questions that "do not further"— and more particularly the dogmatism arising with them. He'd been called to deal with some intellectuals debating some unprovable philosophical matter, who were now practically ready to come to blows. He told them the story of a king who'd entertained himself by assembling some local blind men and then leading an elephant into their midst. One man felt its leg and declared it was a pillar. One man touched the end of its tail and said it was a broom, whereas another who held the tail itself said it was a rope. One man touched the side and swore it was a wall. Another touched its ear and called it a basket for winnowing grain. Yet another felt the tusk and yelled that he was touching a plowshare. The king watched with amusement as they began arguing, each having seen only one aspect of the whole and insisting that his was the only reality. Like the elephant, truth has elements of different views, yet it's also really something unto itself.

Furthermore, egalitarianism was inherent in his approach, which contradicted the social order of India. If India were a body, the peasants were the feet; the merchants and craftsmen were the legs; the warrior and noble class, from which the Buddha hailed, were the arms; and the priestly Brahmins were the head. But when Siddhartha shaved his head and went forth, he not only renounced his own caste but the whole hereditary caste system as well. The Buddha and his disciples taught whomever they met, young and old, rich and poor, male and female. He even touched the so-called untouchables, the outcasts below the peasant class. But nirvana knows no borders.

The Final Teaching

The end was unexpected. Some food he'd been given as alms was bad. Eventually, he had to lie down. Just as he'd taught meditation while sitting, standing, and walking, now he taught while on his side. (See the first picture in Chapter 21.) Naturally, many in the community feared they couldn't go on without him, but he reassured them it wasn't necessary for him to be there personally for them to practice his teachings for themselves. "The Dharma is the best teacher," he said.

"Even if I were to live for aeons," he told them, "I'd still have to leave you because every meeting implies a departure, one day." With his faithful disciples by his side, he died the way he'd lived for nearly 50 years, an exemplary spiritual teacher beyond compare. It is said that, as with his birth, and his enlightenment, his final nirvana (extinction) was on the night of a full moon, in May.

And that's a quick sketch of the tapestry that is the Buddha's life: a life that is, itself, a teaching. From the very first, the Buddha, and each of us, was born with the capacity for a life of tranquility and joy. Harmony and love. Clarity and truth. Excellence. This ability is a gift. And it is yours.

The Least You Need to Know

- The Buddha realized the Middle Way: finding the nondual, practical mean between extreme positions.
- The Buddha sought the meaning of life and death, and found it. Becoming one with all creation, with wisdom and compassion, he realized suffering's origin and its end. Just as he could attain enlightenment, so can we.

♦ We experience degrees of awakening. Buddha's awakening is called enlightenment, and the state of supreme enlightenment is nirvana. It's more useful to
think of it in terms of an evolutionary process than as a thing, more a way of
enlightened living.

♦ The Buddha was nondogmatic and nonauthoritarian—more like a guide than a
god. Pragmatic and scientific, he invites us to come and see for ourselves.

♦ Extensively, buddha can mean whoever or whatever awakens us to greater intimacy with life.

♦ When asked about God, Heaven, and the immortality of the soul, the Buddha
simply remained silent, because these theoretical matters didn't affect his teachings. Buddhism isn't about belief, but rather firsthand experience.

2

Different Flavors, One Taste: The Teachings Travel to Different Lands

In This Chapter

- ◆ Life after Buddha's death
- ◆ An awakened king
- ◆ Adoption and adaptation in various lands
- ◆ Evolution of camps and schools
- ◆ Modern times, and an overview

Truth (dharma) is everywhere. It doesn't spread; rather, people awaken to it. As they do so, their own recognition, understanding, and realization of it resonates with their individual background and temperament. And this is as true for countries as for people.

The teachings of the Buddha have traveled and are now practiced in every major continent on the planet, where they take on the colors of various cultures. In this respect, Buddhism's like tofu. It picks up the flavor of the food around it while retaining its own subtle taste: the taste of freedom.

After his ultimate nirvana, the Buddha remains present in his teachings. It's interesting to look back at the history of that unfolding over time.

Mother India

The Buddha designated no single heir, no centralized religious structure, no Head Office. Instead, he'd left a map of the Path, and said, "Listen up, everyone. Here's the Way. Mindfully work on your enlightenment."

His community (*Sangha*) of monks (*bhikkhus*) and nuns (*bhikkhunis*) was a gathering of those who'd vowed to follow his teachings (the *Dharma*) and become *arhats* (those who free their mind through perfect understanding, attaining union with ultimate reality). The Sangha formed one of the world's first monastic communities, pledged to a life of simplicity, meditation, and teaching.

The core sangha had no other day jobs than meditation, teaching, and monastic upkeep. But their door was open to people who did work, the laity. Many were close to cities, which were now forming under rulers keen on territorial and economic expansion. Sympathetic merchants and noblemen might not become "full-timers," joining the monastic order, yet partook of the teachings plus donated money or land. Monasteries formed in some of the capitals of big new kingdoms, such as Vaisali in Kosala and Rajagaha in Magadha, whose kings sought out the Buddha for advice.

Buddhism offered a culture and set of values to the newly emerging urban civilizations, and one more tolerant of diversity than the Brahman religion, which was arcane and whose demand for animal sacrifices strained both city-dwellers and farmers. Monks were sometimes requested to establish monasteries in cities and play a role in the community, not only as spiritual teachers but also educators and even physicians. By the time of the Buddha's death, the Dharma had been heard over some 50,000 square miles, spanning some seven nations of central India. Considering that Buddha and his followers traveled on foot, this was no mean feat (no pun intended).

After the Buddha died, a council of 500 arhats assembled for a summit conference. They recited from memory all he'd said, to agree on his teachings and the codes of monastic discipline. If such a prodigious feat of memory seems extreme today, bear in mind that oral culture and the art of memory were highly developed in pre-modern civilizations not yet organized around writing. (And it helped that the Buddha used bullet points and numbered lists, creating a very cohesive, complex system out of very simple elements.)

Further councils of elders were convened, such as the second one a century later, in 383 B.C.E., to clarify such practices as the use of money (though they knew that *change* must come from within). By this time, money had become a common medium of exchange, enabling long-distance trade. Monasteries were often close to trading posts, and some merchants investing in caravan expeditions were Buddhist.

Along the Path

The Buddha is a prominent example of a general period of world history that marked the beginnings of humanity as we know it today. This pivotal era, dubbed the *Axial Age* by Karl Jaspers, spanning from roughly 800–200 B.C.E., included also the Upanishads and the Jain religion in India; Confucius and Lao-tzu in China; Homer, Heraclitus, and Socrates in Greece; Zarathustra in Persia; and the Hebrew prophets.

King Ashoka–Servant of the Dharma

One man was pivotal in Buddhism's evolution toward a world community. Two centuries after the Buddha's death, the Sangha remained small and little known. But within a mere 50 years more, thanks to a king named Ashoka, the Dharma took hold in a big way. (We were taught about Alexander when I was a boy, but why not King Ashoka?! Such a hero! What a human being!)

Reigning from 272 to 236 B.C.E., Ashoka held vast power in his hands, ruling from the southern tip of the Indian subcontinent on up to part of Persia. After a long but victorious battle, revulsed by the enormity of the violence he'd witnessed firsthand, he hung up his sword and soon took up the Dharma, which he'd learned from a disciple of the Buddha.

Ashoka replaced his former hunting expeditions with pilgrimages; military parades now became devotional processions. A tree-hugger, he ordered forests be preserved. He not only had hospitals built but saw that animals had medical care as well. Wells were dug along roads so that travelers wouldn't thirst. Egalitarian, his citizenry could call on him anytime, day or night, whether he was on the throne or in his carriage, in the dining room, or in the boudoir. Buddhism now appealed to the common people, emulating their emperor.

He also sent envoys to teach the Dharma all around the Indian subcontinent and beyond, as far as Syria, Egypt, and Macedonia. Following the Buddha's example, these ambassadors of Dharma didn't try to convert anyone, only inform. No censorship, no inquisition, rather the demonstration of truth-force, with gentle, loving example. Spreading Buddha's truth (Buddha-dharma) would be rather like telling someone that the sum of the angles of a triangle equals 180°. And if the speaker had a good vibe, a nice aura, people would likely want to check out where he or she is coming from. Thanks to the enlightened patronage of King Ashoka and King Kanishka (78–123 C.E.), Buddhism flourished in India for a millennium, and the Buddha ultimately became a worldwide influence, not a mere footnote to history.

Camps and Schools: Don't Sweat Over Any Isms or Schisms

Another factor in the transmission of Buddhism was education. In the fifth century B.C.E., Buddhist monastics established the world's first university, in the city of Nalanda. Along with Buddha-Dharma, courses included the primary spiritual texts of the time (*Upanishads* and *Vedas*), medicine, grammar, logic, philosophy, and politics. The library housed an estimated nine million scriptures, not to mention the texts on these other subjects. Providing free tuition and residence, it attracted thousands of teachers, and students from all over the country and Asia, as far east as China and Korea, as well as neighboring Tibet and Sri Lanka. Its average peak enrollment was 10,000 students. The complex continued for seven centuries, until destroyed by Bakhtiar Khilji, and was said to burn for months.

With the tragic destruction of Nalanda University, we pause to spotlight another important factor in the history of Buddhism: schools of practice. Consider this: Buddhism is what *you* make of it. It's a personal affair. There's no one-size-fits-all "Buddhism," to take home, plug in, and awaken you. There are as many "Buddhisms" as there are people.

It is said that 10 years after the Buddha's death, there were 16 schools of practice, and more than 500 by the first century C.E. Overall, there seemed to be two collections of schools. Sorting this out today, it's useful to think of them not so much as different Buddhisms, different truths, as rather different approaches (a theme you'll find throughout this book). Traditionally, the two branches are typified as "Old School" and "New School," but branches of the "Old School" were formed well after those of the "New School." And it is also quite possible that divergence was essentially present from the beginning of the Sangha.

On the one hand, there were those who emphasized the Buddha's first, original teachings as central. Their ideal was the individuated, monastic *arhat*. And, on the other hand, there were those who also sought enlightenment, but emphasized the ideal of the *bodhisattva*, whose aspiration for enlightenment is, from the very beginning of practice, for the benefit of all beings.

This Is _____

A **bodhisattva** ("bodhi," Sanskrit awakened, wisdom, and way; "sattva," essence, or being) means literally an "enlightened being" or "essence of the Way." A bodhisattva's enlightenment, whether attained or aspired to, is for the benefit of all. And not just all people but all sentient beings; some even define "sentient beings" to include all beings (period), since every body and every thing is sacred, imbued with innate *Buddha nature.*

For a moment, let's call the camp emphasizing the bodhisattva approach the Great Vehicle ("great" as in inclusive). Historically, it reflected various factors. Laypeople, for example, who'd often donated quite a share, deservedly wanted more representation. And fewer people aspired to arhatship. Laypeople weren't intrigued by the idea of monastic life and wanted a more immediate sense of kinship between themselves and the Buddha. This led to inclusion of deities embodying the Dharma, approachable and active in daily life. Plus, doctrinal aspects of the traditional teachings seemed to call for clarification.

Interestingly, the Great Vehicle evolved in those Indian regions with the most foreign influences, and so it became highly adaptable for export. Indeed, this approach to Buddhism would prevail in China, Korea, and Japan to the east, and Nepal, Tibet, and Mongolia to the north. The more traditionalist schools, on the other hand, developed in regions in the south that were relatively isolated.

So what to call them? The names themselves often reflected factionalism. First, it was the "elders" and the "majority" or "great vehicle." (Sound like any political camps you know?) The latter became known as *Mahayana* ("Great Way"), "yana" meaning "way," or "path." And Mahayana called the other camp *Hinayana,* "Narrow Way." But "narrow" had a decidedly pejorative spin; as in "lesser," "inferior," even "dirty." We shall say *Theravada* ("tair-ah-vah-duh," meaning "teachings of the elders"), without implying that others were newcomers or naive.

A factor that further dampens any rivalry between Buddhist camps came from the Mongols. Though short-lived, the Mongol Empire had a deep impact. Following their encounter with the Mongols, Southeast Asian nations adopted a "new Theravada." This new Theravada not only had no nuns, but no arhats as well. So if Mahayana accuses Hinayana of only being interested in arhatship (individual attainment), it no longer pertains, since the latter hasn't produced any arhats for a thousand years. But the distinction can get murkier when considering such instances as Vietnamese Buddhism, where the two coalesced, and Tibetan Buddhism, which said it was uniting the two within a third, Vajrayana ("Indestructible Path").

You might hear about different practices, and our approach is to focus on what's widely practiced here in the West. The most common Western Theravada practices are called *Vipassana* (pronounced *va-PAH-sa-na*, literally "insight"). Our leading Mahayana practices are *Zen* and *Pure Land* (in treating the latter, we'll also distinguish it from the more recent *Lotus Sutra schools*, such as *Nichiren-shu* and *Soka Gakai*). And though it could have a category of its own, called *Vajrayana*, Tibetan Buddhism can be thought of as "Mahayana with a tantric twist," as we'll see in Chapter 14. But, like I say, don't fret over any schisms or isms. We'll fill you in on the basics common to them all, as well as the different twists, and let you decide how you wish to put it all together.

> **This Is** _____
>
> The word **sutra**, from Sanskrit, means "a thread," such as for stringing jewels, or prayer beads, perhaps. It also carries the connotation of "story," the way we hear "tale" in the word "yarn." It comes from the same root from which we derive the word "suture," meaning to sew; to connect; and to heal wounds.

The Buddha Has Left the House

Back to Mother India. Buddhism became one of her greatest exports to all of Asia and beyond. Yet it's interesting that, until recently, Buddhism as a distinct path all but died out in its country of origin. How did this happen? For one thing, the destruction of Nalanda was like a blow to the head. Nalanda was as much of a central leadership as Buddhism ever had, and with that much of the Sangha destroyed, the practice never quite recovered. But the body itself had already been weakened by blows from Hun marauders from the Steppes, about eight centuries earlier. And we might note how Hinduism, on the other hand, survived both these attacks, and prevailed.

Hinduism had always been integrated into the lives of common people, throughout the villages, whereas Buddhism had relied more solely on royal and aristocratic patronage. When the raids of the Huns ended the Gupta Dynasty, funding for Buddhist monasteries evaporated. Moreover, by the time of the destruction of Nalanda, Hinduism had reasserted itself as the dominant religion. Buddhism had always drawn the ire of the priests for its rejection of rites and of the caste system. Moreover, its critique of Hindu philosophy helped spark a new, self-critical, revitalized reformulation of Hindu tradition, known as Advaita (non-dualism), related to Vedanta, which became the dominant religion, with popular devotional rites that Buddhism lacked.

So the Buddha's teachings were ultimately reabsorbed into the Hindu matrix from which they spring. Today, King Ashoka's lion is part of the national emblem of India, and the Buddha's wheel of the Dharma is on the flag. The Buddha is still visible in Hinduism as an incarnation of Vishnu. And it has reemerged in India as a distinct path, comprising about 15 percent of the population, fueled in part by the conversion of a million former *dalits* ("untouchables"). And the influx of Tibetans is creating renewed dialogue. The Dharma proves to be a living law.

> **This Is**
>
> **Hinduism** refers to the indigenous spirituality of the Indian people originating between 1700 and 500 B.C.E. (though the orthodox date it as far back as 7000 B.C.E.). Defined sects didn't appear until around the time of the Buddha. The word "Hinduism" itself is a modern, Western invention, though universally accepted. More correct would be the "Brahmanic traditions," referring to a common belief in *Brahman*, God; or "Vedic traditions," referring to primary teachings (*Vedas*); or *"Sanantana Dharma"* (Eternal Way). Familiar in the West are techniques for physical and mental cultivation that are a part of **yoga**.

Original Buddhism: The Wisdom of the Elders

Much of what we now call Southeast Asia was once referred to as "Further India" by the Indians who'd colonized it. Commerce with "central" India brought an interchange of cultures and creeds as well as goods.

The tropical island of Ceylon, now known as Sri Lanka, has enjoyed the oldest continuous Buddhist tradition in the world. In 250 B.C.E., Ashoka's prince and princess, Mahinda and Sanghamitta (both arhats), personally introduced Buddhism to Ceylon's King Tissa. Besides establishing a monastery and nunnery there, they brought a sapling from the bodhi tree, which still grows today.

A century and a half later, Buddhist scripture was committed to writing here, in a language called Pali, similar to Sanskrit. (In the Buddha's time, India had no single common language.) The canon became known as the *Tripitaka* ("three baskets"), around a hundred volumes, each about 600 pages long. The three baskets are:

- Buddha's talks (*sutras*). Beginning with his explanation of the Dharma to his five ascetic companions at the deer park, there are now a couple of hundred sutras and several thousand volumes of commentaries.

- Ethical monastic conduct (*vinaya*). Ethical rules were established in the Buddha's Sangha on a case-by-case basis, as various situations arose. So the *vinaya* illustrates each rule with the story of its origin.

- "Special dharma" (*abhidharma*), including in-depth cosmology, natural science, philosophy, and psychology, plus a thesaurus.

(Don't worry, you won't be quizzed. Buddhists aren't "people of the book.") The Tripitaka guided the Theravadin tradition of southeast Asia—branching through Ceylon (Sri Lanka) to Siam (Thailand), Burma (Myanmar), Cambodia, and Laos. By the tenth century, the Ceylon monastery conferred kingship; only a Buddhist could be king, up until the nineteenth century. Thus Buddhism in Ceylon adapted to social and political as well as religious life.

Burma originally had a mix of Hinduism, Mahayana, and esoteric practices. But when Anawrahta became the first Burmese king, in 1044, he conquered the neighboring Mon country and brought Theravadin monks and books back as part of his booty. With Theravada the dominant religion, he then had *thousands* of monasteries and temples built in Pagan, his capital (still present today), earning the nickname "Land of Pagodas" for his country.

The Mon people of Siam practiced Buddha's way ever since Ashoka sent missionaries, and continued to as the Thai people of southwestern China were driven in by the armies of Kublai Khan. As a national kingdom evolved, Buddhism became the state religion. In some Thai Buddhist temples, you might see some traces of Hinduism as well as *animism* (the belief that all things have souls). While there are temples in cities and towns, many practitioners still study in the caves and tropical forests, perpetuating the forest tradition of Buddha's own time.

Before the Internet: The Spice and Silk Routes

Just as sheer information has become a hot item these days, along with the means of getting it (such as TV, wireless phone, Internet, and, oh yes, books), back in the Buddha's days the hot item was silk, and the means to get it. Just as folks of late have developed a yen to have a pager, Chinese silk was the big status item of the day, as far west as Rome and Egypt. Even Cleopatra had to have it.

Not too far from the Buddha's stomping grounds emerged a zone just north of India, south of Central Asia, and west of Tibet that was a hotbed of interchange. Present-day Afghanistan (then Greek Bactria) forms part of this fertile crossroads of the world, as well as Pakistan and China's Xinkiang region. In this relatively small niche, a mix of people settled: Tokharians, Kapisans, Soghdians, Bactrian Greeks who'd come with Alexander, and also Kushanas (Indo-Scythians). From this emerged a robust culture of international trade.

Thousands of years before FedEx and UPS, there evolved a 6,000-mile road now known as the Silk Route. Silk left China along this route, through Central Asia, passing from way station to way station. Meanwhile, from the other direction, caravans with gold, silver, and wool rode in. Always an exchange; roads travel in two directions.

And along for the ride came Nestorian Christians … and Buddhist scholars and monks. Thus did Buddhism make its way across Central Asia and on to Russia, and east to Mongolia and China. Eventually there were Buddhist outposts at way stations, with not only monastic centers, but also libraries and schools, as well as hotels and hospitals.

Word gets around.

Map: Gary Gach

Alternatively, there was transport by ocean, between India and the Arabian peninsula, along what would become known as the Spice Route. Merchant sailing expeditions often invited Buddhist monks along, a good luck charm as well as a calming influence during storms. Borderless, the Spice Route probably saw even more trade than the Silk Route, but traffic across watery ways leaves no traces.

The Silk Route also furnished another potent vehicle for the Dharma: art. Previously, the only devotional images were abstract, such as a wheel, or footprints or an empty throne ("the Buddha has left the building"). Now, Hellenism (devotion to Greek culture) had taken root in Northern India, following Alexander the Great's campaign there (fourth century B.C.E.). Under the influence of Greek art, sculptors made bas-reliefs of Buddhist patrons and of the Buddha. One early example looked like Apollo in a toga accompanied by female lute players and floating cherubs. On the other hand, the Buddhist paintings in the caves of Dun Huang (a Silk Route terminal to outermost China) display a mix of styles—from semi-abstract graffiti to elegant, visionary frescoes. And so we come to China herself, as two great civilizations of Asia encounter each other, in part because of their smiling mutual friend, the Buddha.

The Middle Kingdom: China

The Silk Route gave Buddhism the horse (or camel) power to get past the blazing, barren deserts and perilous, precipitous peaks, from India to China. But there was another mighty obstacle to overcome: culture. Indian culture had more in common with Europe than with China. Plus there's China's strong national identity and insular culture—just consider the Great Wall! (In calling herself "Middle Kingdom," ancient China implied she's the center of the world.) Indeed, if Buddhism could make it here, it could make it anywhere.

Two lucky similarities played out in favor of the Buddhists. One, Buddhism seemed to answer questions that *Confucius* couldn't. Two, Buddhism clicked with a revival of *Taoism* that happened to be brewing. And, curiously, both Confucius and the father of Taoism, Lao-tse, were born roughly around the same time as the Buddha, and all three were, at bottom, key reformers of old ways.

This was a lucky break, since the Tao and Confucianism composed the double helix of Chinese culture. Confuciansm, like Buddhism, can be seen as more of an educational system than a religion. And, since Buddhism and Taoism explored similar themes (and words, like "the Way"), monks took the opportunity to translate Buddhist terms in Sanskrit with Chinese words already in vogue through Taoism. Plus, since Taoism's chief proponent, Lao-tzu, had, in old age, headed west fairly recently and never come back, the notion arose that this Buddhism was the result of Lao-tzu's teachings abroad, his "conversion of the barbarians." That works! And this way China wouldn't be importing something foreign into the culture—merely welcoming back a native tradition they'd exported in the first place.

This Is

The Tao (pronounced *dow*) means "the Way." Its chief writer was Lao-tzu (b. 604 B.C.E.). **Taoism** holds that 1) what's really real is that which never changes, and 2) we're each a part of this reality, through our innate, individual character. **Confucianism** is an ethical and social system. Lao-tzu seems a carefree, terse mystic next to Confucius (K'ung Fu Tzu, 551–479 B.C.E.), a deep-thinking, wide-ranging humanist force who became China's "philosopher king" (his philosophy becoming imperial ideology).

So China adapted Buddhism, making it theirs kind of the way kids customize their cars. Emperor Ming (58–75 C.E.) invited Buddhist envoys in 67 C.E. During the political chaos from 221 to 589 that came with the collapse of the Han Dynasty, Buddhism started to become a strong presence in China. Monasteries and temples were permitted and flourished across the land, and Buddhism integrated itself into daily life.

The Chinese often concocted their own mix of Confucianism, Taoism, Buddhism, ancestor worship, and folk cults. Chinese religion thus often resembles a salad bar, or a menu in a Chinatown restaurant: "Pick one from *Column A* or two from *Column B*." And if there are enough people, you get a big lazy-susan-type revolving table, and everyone can pick what they like. In general, Chinese religion tends toward the practical over the philosophical. Whatever works.

China's Golden Age: The T'ang

It's not uncommon for the history of an Asian nation's development to intertwine with its adoption of the Buddha's way. China was already highly developed when Buddhism arrived. Yet Buddhism's peak years in China roughly coincided with its Golden Age, the T'ang Dynasty (618–906) (pronounced "tong"). Of the major Buddhist schools prominently studied or practiced then, *Pure Land* would become the most popular school in China, Japan, and Vietnam today. Emphasizing faith in the boundless love of the bodhisattva, the Pure Land school practices recitation of the name of Amida Buddha. The school most widely known in the West is *Zen* ("*Ch'an*" in Chinese), which literally means "meditation," had incubated and was refined in China. Indeed, it's been said that Zen is a synthesis of India and China. Certainly, it's proven to be the most historically resilient.

Two general, influential developments in China are worth noting. China (cleverly) transformed the Buddhist embodiment of compassion, from India, a formerly genderless deity named Avalokiteshvara ("Ah-vah-loh-key-teh-shvah-rah"), into a female, named *Kwan Yin*. Not only simpler to pronounce, this drew women practitioners to the Path in great numbers. Kwan Yin would become like Buddhism's Virgin of Guadalupe (patron saint of Mexico).

Besides commissioning translators to render Sanskrit into Chinese, China also printed Buddhist books. In 868, monks disseminated copies of the Diamond Sutra hither and yon, via the first printed book, sharing the Dharma and earning merit thereby. Indeed, Buddhism influenced the development of printing. (Korea was printing Buddhist texts with movable type two centuries before Gutenberg. It was then just a matter of time before the printing of *Complete Idiot's Guides*. China became a hub of Buddhism in the East. As some countries would learn Latin to learn of Jesus, others were learning Chinese to learn of Shakyamuni Buddha.

What Goes Up Must Come Down

Members of the Chinese elite had, from the very get-go, lifted an eyebrow at the sight of Buddhist monks who hadn't any sons to perpetuate the honor of their parents, contrary to Confucian values. And now you didn't need an abacus to see the strain on the economy the temples were causing. By the middle of the ninth century, China's Buddhist monasteries were richer than the Emperor's court. Indeed, the empire looked with alarm at the possible economic crash this could cause. Farmers were leaving the fields to help construct monasteries. (Who'd feed the country?) Buddhist monks produced no revenue. (Who supported them? Members of the royal court and wealthy aristocrats, who could've been underwriting Imperial projects instead.) And what value had gold or silver now that those ores were being used to cast Buddhas and other accoutrements of this foreign craze? So the empire struck back.

Monasteries and temples were shut down or choked off under strict government supervision. State Confucianism was encouraged instead. Here, as elsewhere in Asia, Zen survived adversity. During the T'ang dynasty, Zen was still the most influential form of Buddhism in the land, and continued so through the subsequent Sung dynasty (960–1278).

Blossoms in Other Gardens

From China, Buddhism went further east to Korea and Japan, and south to Vietnam. In each land, it mixed with various local practices.

Korea: The Land of Morning Calm

Many people aren't aware that Korea adopted Buddhism from China in the fourth century. This had led Korea to learn Chinese in order to know about Buddhism; almost half their vocabulary today is Chinese. Yet, over time, Korean Buddhists would attain such mastery that China would send emissaries to study with them, for clarification and guidance as to fine points.

Leaves from the Bodhi Tree

Korean monk Wonhyo (617–686) set out for China to study Buddhism. On the road one night, he took shelter in a cave. He found a gourd of pure water which he drank, and he fell asleep, content. At dawn, he awoke startled to discover he'd spent the night in a tomb and that he'd drunk putrid water from an old skull. It came to him in a flash that "mind creates all things, all things are products of the mind alone." Realizing this, he turned around, as there was no longer any need to study in China. He studied his own mind instead and went on to become one of Korea's greatest Buddhist teachers and scholars.

Korean Buddhism blended with the indigenous religion of the time, *shamanism.* Shamanism dates back to the Neolithic. This ancient religion of animism and nature worship believes human beings as well as natural forces and inanimate objects all possess spirits or are gods. A shaman contacts and mediates with supernatural forces, combining duties of priest, doctor, psychologist, psychic, weatherman, and family counselor. Buddhism doesn't conflict with rites of nature worship.

Monasteries were often built on mountains patronized by an immortal old man no one ever saw, accompanied by a tiger deity from heaven. Buddhism became the basis of national ideology for a millennium, lasting through two dynasties: the Silla (668–935), under which the peninsula's three kingdoms were unified, and the Koryo (1140–1390), a golden age from which Korea takes its name. Korean Zen ("*Son*") emerged as the dominant practice. As with China, beginning in the thirteenth century institutional Confucianism took the upper hand in the royal court and the power of Buddhism waned. For two centuries, no monk or nun could so much as set foot in any major city. But following a vacuum in the nineteenth and twentieth centuries, Buddhism there is strong again. A recent development is a simple and practical school called Won, having only a large circle for its symbol.

Japan: The Land of Eight Islands

After Koreans brought Chinese Buddhism to Japan, Japan later sent emissaries to China and eventually learned all the Chinese schools. Buddhism here mingled with or formed alliances with local beliefs, such as the indigenous Shinto cults. Japan developed its own version of Vajrayana, the Buddhist esoteric school (intended only for initiates), which they called *Shingon*, and its own versions of Pure Land sometimes known as *Amidism*.

Zen emerged in Japan during the Kamakura Era (1185–1333). Seizing power from a decadent imperial aristocracy, the military elite (*samurai*) established a military government (the *Shogunate*) at Kamakura. Imagine a well-heeled, swashbuckling soldier of fortune strutting down the street and encountering some mere monk on his path, sitting in open-eyed meditation. The samurai draws his

This Is

In Japan, the indigenous religion is **Shinto,** centered on the spiritual essence (*kami*) present in gods, human beings, animals, and even inanimate objects. "Shinto" is an umbrella term for hundreds of different customs, and was coined in the sixth century when Japan felt it needed to distinguish its own native beliefs and practices from new foreign concepts such as Confucianism and Buddhism.

sword and bellows, "Out of my way, wretched dog, or I'll test this new blade on your bald scalp!" (and those swords could slice through flesh and bone like so much cheese)—and the monk looks up with an unflinching, implacable expression of "So!?" as if merely brushed by a breeze. Totally present to each instant, and nothing else. Naturally, the samurai wanted such absolute fearlessness for themselves and so studied Zen.

When Kublai Khan sent two envoys to Japanese soil, dictating terms of surrender, *Kwaaatz!*, they were beheaded on the spot by samurai Zen swordsmen. Soon thereafter (1281), these Zen warriors defeated the Khan's attack by sea, one of the largest naval forces in history, about 100,000 men. Little wonder that Zen temples were given the finest plots of land, and the finest teachers imported from China to coach them. Today, there's hardly a branch of Japanese culture untouched by her many forms of Buddhism.

Meeting Place: Vietnam

Vietnam is somewhat equidistant from China to the north and India to the West, and has been enriched by both cultures. As Vietnamese Buddhist teacher Thich Nhat Hanh relates the history, Buddhism came from India, in the first century C.E., via the Spice Route, as merchants often took monks along for luck. Subsequently, Vietnam brought Buddhism to parts of southern China, and was later enriched by Mahayana Buddhism from China. As befitting its geographical position, Theravada and Mahayana practices became unified in Vietnam.

At the Roof of the World: Tibet, Land of Snows

Buddhism didn't reach Tibet until 1,300 years after the Buddha. Though close to India, Tibet is separated by the Himalayas, plus different climates. (India's subtropical, Tibet's 12,000 feet above sea-level. Indian civilization is largely agricultural; Tibet's, pastoral.)

Moreover, there was also a wall of cultural resistance from the indigenous shamanist religion called *Bon*. Furthermore, the country wasn't unified. But when King Songtsan Gampo inherited a newly centralized authority, he traveled around his new nation and brought back a bride from over the border, in Nepal, who was Buddhist. Eventually, he made Buddhism a state religion. But Bon put up strong opposition. Then in the eighth century, King Trisong Detsan enlisted Padma Sambhava ("Lotus-Born") from Nepal to aid him.

Besides overcoming Bon magic with his own Buddhist mojo, Padma Sambhava translated the Dharma for the common Tibetan. Interestingly, Tibet had been pre-literate but devised an alphabet in order to learn the Buddha's way. Like India of Siddhartha's time, Buddhism helped unify a patchwork into a cohesive nation. Buddhism went on to be more than a state religion, becoming a theocracy (rule by divine sanction), or more properly a Buddhocracy, and in the sixteenth century, became the first country in the world with a monk on the throne, the *Dalai Lama* (meaning "teacher whose wisdom is as great as the ocean").

The Buddhism that made its way up to Tibet from India bore elements called *tantra* that were diffusing throughout both Hinduism and Buddhism in India at that time. (When China tried exporting Buddhism to Tibet, it clashed with tantra, and the Chinese were expelled from Tibet near the end of the eighth century.) Called *Vajrayana* ("diamond path"), some consider it a third camp, alongside Theravada and Mahayana, while others view it as a branch of Mahayana with a tantric twist. (More later, when we explore Tibetan Buddhism.)

The original school was called Nyingma (meaning "Ancient Ones"), from which comes *The Book of the Dead*, and *Dzogchen*, a form of practice recently becoming popular in the West. After Nyingma became established, and following the pillaging of monasteries in India by the Huns, Indian Buddhist adepts brought texts to Tibet for preservation. Since Buddhism had developed further in India by then, Tibetan Buddhism amassed the world's largest collection of Buddhist scripture. Two more schools then arose in 1000. One new school was Sakya ("Grey Earth"), a scholarly group that unified teachings of the sutras and tantras. Another school was called Kagyu, which counted among its ancestors such celebrated teachers as Naropa (1016–1100), Marpa (1012–1097), and Milarepa (1052–1135).

The fourth major school, established in the fourteenth century, is called Gelug, "Way of Virtue." Gelug was a reformist movement combining elements of the other three schools, while returning to original Indian sources. The Gelug became the largest school and initiated the office of the Dalai Lama. Among other schools, a modern development is *Rime* ("ree-may"), with allegiance to no one particular school, drawing from each.

(*Note:* Readers considering travel to any of the lands discussed here might wish to visit our Dharma Door's online itinerary: http://awakening.to/pilgrimage.html.)

Continuing Buddha's Way in Asia Today

Buddhism has adapted to modern times as well as to foreign lands—weathering such upheavals as invasions, wars, revolutions, and exile. For example, many Asian lands have been spiritually developed but materially underdeveloped. (The phrase "underdeveloped nations" depends on your perspective.) Thus many took to socialism or communism to advance themselves materially, with the result that Buddhism was often repressed—Karl Marx (1818–1883) having branded religion "the opiate of the people." (An ex-Communist friend of mine once laughed when he saw the graffiti "Revolution is the opiate of the people," but that's all another story.) So the Buddha has had a paradoxical bedfellow in the military regime of the Buddhist nation of Myanmar.

Overall, has the transmission of Buddhism been worthwhile? Well, Buddhism has educated and even enlightened masses of human beings, fueling literacy, self-reliance, and tolerance, as well as helped peacefully to establish or unify nations and empires. And when each nation looks to its past, it often finds its greatest historical periods coinciding with Buddhism's flourishing. Buddhism has touched all of Asia and is one common heritage uniting the peoples of Asia today. (What else? Well, rice!)

The Middle Way's culture has fostered the development of medicine and other sciences; sparked such agents of change as the printed book with movable type; established a precedent for interfaith understanding, if not world religion and, no less, a world community. The promise of all these gifts, above, remains yet to be absolutely fulfilled, but then history is a golden book whose next chapter is always awaited with steadfast anticipation.

Our own next chapter will turn to the most recent development in Buddhist history. For the first time in over a millennium, the Lotus has opened a new petal.

The Least You Need to Know

♦ Buddha's teachings (Dharma) are common to all of Asia, and continue to flourish through its growing community (Sangha).

♦ Buddhism adapted to the different cultures of various lands. But all its forms have a fundamental essence—the taste of freedom.

♦ Two main branches, or collections of schools, developed: Theravada and Mahayana. In the West, Theravada's most popular manifestation is Vipassana ("Insight Meditation"); Mahayana's are Zen and Pure Land, plus the more recent Lotus Sutra schools.

♦ Tibetans speak of three branches of Buddhism: Theravada, Mahayana, and Vajrayana, though the latter might also be considered Mahayana.

♦ Buddhism has played a part in nation-building, and its flourishing has coincided with the golden ages of many nations.

♦ Tolerance has been one of Buddhism's leading social characteristics. (Quick, how many Buddhist wars can you name?)

What Might an Italian Buddha Look Like?: Western Buddhism

In This Chapter

- ◆ Buddhism and modern thought
- ◆ Conditions conducive to East-West interchange
- ◆ Western Buddhist teachers, translators, scholars, etc.
- ◆ Issues and themes in Western Buddhism

Everything we've seen thus far may seem well and good … for Asia. But can Buddhism survive in a land where the greatest good is oft equated with the greatest goods? Selflessness, in a culture that glorifies self? Or is it better suited here than we might casually think?

Actually, eighth-century China was in many ways more different from India than were many of its neighbors to the west, all sharing a common *Indo*-European language family, for one thing. Yet China adopted Buddhism, which remarkably transformed its culture. And, like the West, that culture was already highly developed at the time.

Toward the end of his life, noted historian Arnold Toynbee (1869–1975) was asked to single out the most significant event of his times. Out of all the things he'd seen, he remarked, "The coming of Buddhism to the West may well prove to be the most important event of the Twentieth Century." Indeed, now, for the first time in more than a millennium, the lotus of the Dharma is opening a new petal. On Western shores. And it has proven itself definitely here to stay, happy to grow in our soil.

It will take some time before we can say how this will all shake out. Meanwhile, why wait? Tune in and see for yourself! Here's our story up to now …

Preparing the Ground: Mulching the Cultural Soil

Dharma, like gardening, is a living process. Cultivate soil. Plant seeds at the right time. Nourish them. New life emerges. It's very nice. And the transplant, transformation, and thriving of Buddhism here in the West is the story of just such a process.

Since the Renaissance, the evolution in the West of secularism (nontheism) has been crucial to philosophy, society, and government as we know them today. This secular evolution can be seen as more and more conducive toward learning about and understanding Buddhism, a nontheistic outlook. Fast-forwarding now to the dawn of the twentieth century, we see modernism shifting the focus away from divinity, fixity, and permanency, transferring attention instead to the worldliness, fluidity, and transience of reality and the many ways we can interpret it. Modernism likewise ripened conditions for the seeds of Buddha's teachings to take root and flower in the West and take their place alongside other Western cultural tall trees.

Four textbook figures unglued conventional notions of the universe and self, helping to pave the way for both modernism and Western Buddhist thought. Einstein spoke of the universe as a process; Freud, of the self as an interplay. Darwin contradicted the image of humans as a predetermined goal in a linear progression, redefining the model for living change. And Marx's global idealist vision further deconstructed world and self as being interdependent. Hearing the Buddha's teachings in dialogue with such figures thus enables his ancient path to be considered as a very modern way of thought.

Seasons and Lunar Phases Conducive to Growth

National cultivation of Buddhism is like individual cultivation on a larger scale. The seeds of awakening are present within us all; they just require proper conditions and care. Time and timing thus enter in …

The Flames of War and the Phoenix from the Ashes

Ashes of war have fertilized the soil, enabling flowers of peace to bloom. This is not paradoxical. Everything is interdependent. Peace is composed of nonpeace elements. The first Buddhist king, King Ashoka, turned toward Buddhism after waging his bloodiest battle.

Buddhism's development in the West can partly be seen as a phoenix arising out of ashes. When we consider the large number of Jews practicing Buddhism, for example, disproportionate to the general Western population, we must factor in the second World War. One third of all Jews in the world were systematically mass-murdered, leaving the souls of many survivors deeply scarred. And of those destroyed, more than 80 percent were rabbis and teachers of an ancient oral tradition. Buddhism has provided access to spirit and healing to many descendants of survivors.

And the War extended to Asia. Many Asian women, who happened to be Buddhist, married Western soldiers and brought their traditions to their new homes. Many veterans who'd never seen chopsticks before entered newly forming Asian studies programs on their G.I. Bill. In the aftermath, lawyer Christmas Humphreys went to Japan to serve on the International War Crimes Tribunal, and Philip Kapleau traveled there as a reporter covering the trials. Humphreys would become a major propagator of Buddhism in the West. Kapleau returned to Japan and studied Zen for 13 years. His book *Three Pillars of Zen* (1965) presented the gateless gates of living Zen for more than a million Westerners.

Other foreign political upheavals have also played a role in Western Buddhism. Vipassana teacher S. N. Goenka, for instance, left Burma due to the 1960 socialist coup, which in turn gave him an unexpected audience in the West. Venerable Masters Hsuan Hua, Hsing Yun, and Sheng-yen left China following the Communist Revolution. Living in France in political exile from his native Vietnam, pacifist Zen master Thich Nhat Hanh likewise never intended on becoming a spiritual teacher in the West. And numerous Tibetan teachers in exile have come West where Tibetan Buddhism is developing a large following. Indeed, since his exile, Tenzin Gyatso, His Holiness (HH) the fourteenth Dalai Lama, unexpectedly became the unofficial Ambassador of Buddhism in the West.

Give Peace a Chance: The Sixties and Beyond

From the ashes of war come flowers of peace. As our chronology (Appendix B) partially reflects, change in the 1960s was clicking like a Geiger counter near uranium. Major topics were civil rights, feminism, Earth Day, holistic health and organic food, martial arts, popular psychology, quarks … and the East, including Buddhism. Curiously, while China was experiencing its cultural revolution, so was the West. Yet subtler spiritual transformations were eclipsed by more mediagenic "poster children": sex, and drugs, and rock 'n' roll. Upon reflection, these three could be seen as outcroppings of a deeper seismic shift of worldview taking place. Women, for example, who could take control of their bodies with the availability of the contraceptive pill, as well as take charge of their own income, could also more viably undertake a quest for enlightenment.

Rock 'n' roll and spirituality? For the first time, American youth was suddenly thrust into the role of consumer, and rock captivated a global audience. So when the Beatles followed George Harrison on a spiritual pilgrimage to India in 1976 and announced they'd become disciples of Maharishi Mahesh Yogi, suddenly anything Indian was "in"—incense, patchouli oil, sitar music, Transcendental Meditation, yoga, and ... on quiet feet, Buddha.

Like rock, drugs were part of marginal subcultures that went big-time. One survey found more than half of white baby-boomer Buddhists had come to the path following chemical experimentation, post-hippies now ready to discipline themselves to access their minds without psychedelics. (*Psychedelic* means "mind manifesting.")

Consider how many Buddhist meditation temples opened during this period. Only two percent of the thousand or more flourishing in America today were in existence before 1964. In the next decade, by 1975, the number had multiplied fivefold. No longer were there more Buddhas in glass cases in museums in the West than actual practitioners. One last note about the sixties. In 1965 the national quota system for immigrants was cast aside. This quietly signaled the beginning of what would become a steady inflow of Asian newcomers to America that continues today. Starting with these pilgrims, let's review the seminal work contributing to the Buddha's national park without borders, in the West, then survey some topics to watch in coming years.

Gardeners in the Fields of the Buddha

A transplant needs tending. Here's a look at footprints of some gardeners of Western Buddhism: pilgrims in the form of pioneers from the East and advance scouts from the West; living teachers; and interpreters, translators, and scholars. All part of the Western Buddhist Gardening Crew.

Leaves from the Bodhi Tree

Among numerous cases of "discovery" of North America before Christopher Columbus (headed for India), we might consider Buddhist monk Hu Shen, who sailed here from China in ... 499 C.E.! He named our continent "Fusheng" after the Chinese name for the maguey plant (agave). He stayed 40 years, trekking through forests and across mountains and deserts and even seeing a huge canyon with bands of color along its sides and a river at the bottom (the Grand Canyon?). Was he a fluke, or might there have been other similar explorers from the East, unrecorded?

Pilgrims to the Western Lands

Buddhist practice took hold in America earlier than in Europe. At the gates of that huge train station known as New York stands the Statue of Liberty, proclaiming "Welcome to Hotel California!" China had its own nickname for the U.S.: "Gold Mountain," after the Gold Rush of 1848. In 1853, they established America's first Chinese Buddhist temple, in San Francisco. Imagine: Over in New England, Emerson and Thoreau were waxing rhapsodic about Eastern spirituality they'd never even seen firsthand, while literally hundreds of active Chinese temples were springing up in California like mushrooms after a good rain, some with Buddhist priests, others with Taoist masters or Confucian scholars. Then America passed the Chinese Immigration Exclusion Act in 1882, denying any further immigration of Chinese workers. In 1888, the Act was extended to include Chinese women except merchants' wives. Gold Mountain suddenly became steeper than Mt. Everest.

Entrance to Kuan-yin Temple, Spofford Street, Chinatown, San Francisco, on a summer day sometime between 1895 and 1906— already second-generation Eastern spirituality in the West. (Note: One gentleman wears a traditional hat while others on the scene sport various snazzy Western brims.)

Photography: Arnold Genthe

In 1899, two Japanese priests came to support the Buddhists among the 10,000 Japanese immigrants in America, many resistant to conversion to Christianity. These two became America's first permanent resident Buddhist clergy. (They were ordained in the Jodo Shinshu Pure Land tradition, and it should be noted that their order was renamed Buddhist Churches of America after the Second World War. Following Pearl Harbor, Buddhists priests, suspected of being spies, were among the first Japanese Americans to be interned and placed in prisoner-of-war camps. Eventually the majority of Japanese Americans were interned in civilian camps during the war, and over half were Buddhists, mostly Jodo Shinshu. Some, forbidden to return to the west coast, established temples on the east coast. The new name is an affirmation of their American identity.)

In 1924, a national immigration act limited the annual quota of immigrants from any country to 2 percent of the number of individuals born in that country and resident in the United States in 1890. These restrictions were relaxed in 1965. Immigration from Thailand, Laos, and Kampuchea, for example, increased roughly a hundredfold in just three decades. Thus, some rural North Americans discovered acreage adjacent to their farms being bought and settled by monks in orange robes. Of the three to four million Buddhists estimated in America at the dawn of the twenty-first century, a minority 800,000 were white, plus or minus.

Advance Scouts: Journeys to the East

Early Western pilgrims to the East were like advance scouts returning to our campfires to tell us what they'd seen over the mountain ranges. Here are a few examples. Russian noblewoman Madame Helena Blavatsky (1831–1891) teamed up with Colonel Henry Steel Olcott (1832–1906) and founded the Theosophical Society in 1875. They traveled in south and southeast Asia from 1879 to 1884. In Ceylon, in 1880, she and Olcott became the first Europeans to formally take vows of Theravadan Buddhism. It wasn't until 1966 that the Theravada tradition would have a home in America, with the establishment of the Washington Buddhist Vihara, in the District of Columbia. All good things all in good time.

In 1923, Alexandra David-Neel (1868–1969), well-versed in Sanskrit, became the first European woman to enter Tibet's forbidden city of Lhasa. She stayed in Tibet for 14 years. Her subsequent books helped somewhat to dispel the romantic myths spun by the fiction of James Hilton, Talbot Mundy, and H. Rider Haggard. One of her visitors there, Ernst Lothar Hoffmann, stayed in Tibet, India, Ceylon, Burma, and Sikkim, as Lama Anagarika Govinda, later becoming a venerated teacher in the West. But it would take another half-century before Tibetan teachers would establish their own bases in the West.

Following World War II, a few priests in Japan were surprised to discover white pilgrims coming to their temples requesting instruction in Zen, such as Philip Kapleau and poet-ecologist-anthropologist Gary Snyder.

In the late 1960s and early 1970s, veterans of the U.S. Peace Corps returned from south Asia, sharing their inspiration with their peers, and fueled a subsequent wanderlust for trekking to India, Burma, Thailand, and Ceylon. Daniel Goleman, Joseph Goldstein, Jack Kornfield, Ram Dass, Wes Nisker, Sharon Salzberg, and Lama Surya Das are just some of the pilgrims to the East who became first-generation pale-faced teachers of Buddhism in the West.

Living Dharma from Living Teachers

Living teachers nourish the Dharma in contemporary soil. Up to the dawn of the twentieth century, Buddhism in the West had been mostly based on book learning. A watershed turning point was the World Parliament of Religions, held in 1893 in conjunction with the Chicago World's Fair. It was the first formal gathering of representatives of Eastern and Western spiritual traditions, as well as a milestone in global interfaith dialogue (a topic awaiting in the next chapter). Anagarika Dharmapala, founder of the Maha Bodhi Society, from Ceylon, showed Buddhism in practice. Zen Master Soen Shaku also taught, accompanied by D.T. Suzuki, Nyogen Senzaki, and Shaku Sokatsu, each to become important Western Buddhist pioneers. And there were representatives of Jodo Shinshu, Nicheren, Tendai, and Shingon schools, as well as Hindu Jains and Vedantists. Former abstractions now had a human face. Along with Buddha and Dharma, the West was learning the value of Sangha: the living, contemporary expression of the teachings.

Founder of the San Francisco Zen Center and of the first Zen monastery in the West, and author of Zen Mind, Beginner's Mind, *Shunryu Suzuki Roshi (1904–1971) has been arguably the single most influential figure in the adoption of Zen practice in America. Maybe his smiling face will begin to tell you why.*

Photo: Robert S. Boni

Eastern teachers arrived in three waves in the twentieth century. First, the 1920s marked the rise of insight (Vipassana) meditation in the West. Zen's popularity began in the early 1960s; Tibetan Buddhism's, a decade later. The "big sky mind" to which the Buddha points has come alive beneath the wide open skies of Europe and America. Now with former Western students of teachers in the East returned to Western soil, new generations of Western seekers don't necessarily have to cross the great waters for training. Moreover, teacher and student can now speak the same language. This brings up the interesting question of *translation*, which we'll explore next.

Would you buy a used car from this man? I sure would, only he's not selling anything. (No thing!) His name's Robert Aitken Roshi (Roshi meaning Zen Master), a patriarch of Western Buddhism—and timeless.

Photo: Tom Haar

Interpreters, Translators, and Scholars

We've noted how translation of Buddha's teachings was so important in the dissemination of Buddhism throughout Asia, spreading Chinese as well as Sanskrit and even leading to adoption of whole writing systems. Translation's equally essential for Westerners, who often can't read a foreign menu without a trained diplomatic interpreter (also known as a waiter).

Thoreau officially published the first American translation of a Buddhist sutra in 1844, giving the wheel another turn West. Sir Edwin Arnold (1832–1904) gave the wheel a big spin. He penned a book-length retelling in Victorian verse of the life and teachings of the Buddha titled *The Light of Asia*. Published in 1879, it went through 80 editions, selling upward of a million copies, helping make Buddhism a household word.

It wouldn't be until after World War II that American universities would include serious programs for intensive study in Chinese and Sanskrit. Some compare the influence of Chinese and Sanskrit studies to the impact the rediscovery of Greek and Roman art had upon the European Renaissance.

We may indeed be experiencing the beginning of such a second renaissance (or an inevitable continuation of the first). A 1995 survey of over 675 faculty members at over eleven academic institutions revealed 59 proficient in Sanskrit and 43 in its cousin Pali; 49 proficient in Japanese, and 37 in Chinese; 33 know Tibetan, and 2 Korean. I remember learning, when I received my own baccalaureate degree, how the cap and gown carried traditions that hailed from thirteenth-century monks. Buddhist scholars in academia today might thus be considered a contemporary Western Buddhist monastic tradition of sorts ("Buddhology," if you will). By 1997, at least 850 academic dissertations and theses were on file dealing with Buddhism, (including this very topic of Western Buddhism). And there are now such private schools as California Institute of Integral Studies, Hsi Lai University, Institute for World Religions, Naropa Institute, and Soka University of America.

The Buddha traveled by foot, teaching eye-to-eye. Today, the Dharma is now digitized, available for keyword search, random access, or cross-indexing with other databases. The Electronic Cultural Atlas Initiative website, for example, is using maps as a springboard for accessing layers of cultural heritage including text, photos, audio and video files—all contributed from and shared by scholars collaborating around the planet.

Hear and Now

"… looking deep, he saw … / How lizard fed on ant, and snake on him, / And kite on both; and how the fish-hawk robbed / The fish-tiger of that which it had seized; / The shrike chasing the bulbul, which did chase / The jeweled butterflies: till everywhere / Each slew a slayer and in turn was slain, / Life living upon death. … / The Prince Siddhartha sighed."

—*The Light of Asia*, Edwin Arnold (1892)

Along the Path

Compare this quote from the Buddha, and a contemporary update:

Words are just like a man carrying a lamp to look for his property, by which he can say: This is my property.

—The Buddha, Lankavatara Sutra

Seeking Perfect Total
    Enlightenment
is looking for a flashlight
when all you need the flashlight
    for
is to find your flashlight.

—Lew Welch, Difficulty Along the Way

Stay Tuned: Topics to Watch in Years to Come

Buddha's roots are more than two and a half millennia old. They've spread like that fig tree beloved for sheltering the Buddha in the forest. A fig tree grows broad roots that support long branches. And it renews itself by planting those long branches in the soil and using them as new roots. The branches now reach every major continent. Conditions for Buddhism's flowering in the West have, as we've just seen, proven very, very good: fertile soil, receptive environment, and loving gardeners tending shoots and sprouts of the new roots.

It's far too soon to predict what the outcome of all this might be. But Western Buddhism has thus far manifested at least six interesting, distinguishing issues and themes: acculturation, feminism, egalitarianism, integration into daily life, ethnicity, and ecumenism (the movement for greater dialogue and cooperation between religious groups, in this case within Buddhism itself). As is customarily the case in Buddhism, no component stands alone; chunks overlap.

East? West? West Meets East in the West, and Vice-Versa

To survive, Buddhism has always adapted to native conditions, finding the Middle Way between tradition and change. It's interesting that the path traditionally associated with preserving the original teachings (Theravada) is in the West the one most likely to incorporate teachings of different schools, and having the greatest latitude as to their lineage. Zen in the West is allowing adaptation of its tradition, but gradually, generation by generation. Pure Land has a much longer tradition in the West, largely Asian-based until now, and is confronting how it wants to proceed. And Tibetan Buddhism keeps its traditions the most intact.

Acculturation raises a commonly asked question: Can Westerners adapt to an Eastern practice? So while we speak of oneness, it's always important to realize differences count, too. For example, someone once said all human beings basically see the same world the same way. So someone else conducted a study to test this out. They set up a decorative fish tank and showed it to some Westerners, then some Easterners, and asked each to write about what they saw. The Westerners began by describing the fish. The Easterners began by describing how much water there was, the rocks that lined the bottom, etc. Yet eventually each got the whole picture. There are just different ways of getting at it, with different emphases.

So is it difficult for Westerners to follow an Eastern path? Hardly. Frankly, I'm a complete idiot when it comes to knowing where East ends and West begins. (Or vice-versa.) In just whose backyard is it? In between Ankara and Constantinople? Or Buda and Pest? I find "karma" and "guru" in my *American Heritage Dictionary*. And there are now white American Buddhists, "Dharma brats," born and raised at Buddhist monasteries in the West, for whom "Eastern thought" isn't applicable to anything; to them, it's Western. Without implying stereotypes, Michael Wenger has noted that up until now the East has looked to the past, and the West toward the future. As East and West come together now, we arrive fully at the present moment. So in this wonderful moment, we're seeing how much really is universal, and what's unique.

In defining Euro Dharma and New World Dharma, it's good to question whether there's an attraction to a pasture seemingly greener on the other side of the fence, the mango as more exotic than the apple. Exoticism can be as much of an illusion as attachment to ego. But Buddha shows there's no fence, no "other," no dualism. So why not a Buddha in a baseball cap? Or a beret?

> ### Along the Path
>
> "Many Westerners have gotten involved in the chopsticks, tatami mats, flower arrangements, green tea, etc., thinking them to be Zen. This is a terrible shame. The Japanese made use of their own forms to express meditation, and there is just as much Zen in golf or car driving or jogging … We must let Zen permeate our daily lives, not graft on a foreign artificial lifestyle. Remember the Buddha did not eat with chopsticks and never in his whole life chanted in Japanese."
>
> —Jitsudo Baran and Isan Sacco

How much dogma and foreign ritual is necessary? Even though she was formally ordained as a Zen Master by Roshi Philip Kapleau in a lineage that traces itself back to the Buddha, Toni Packer decided to sidestep all the ritual and trappings. So, rightly, she calls her work "meditative inquiry" rather than Zen. American Buddhist monks and nuns at Shasta Abbey, on the other hand, eat on tables instead of on the floor, replace the Japanese tea ceremony with English tea, and chant Gregorian-style rather than in Japanese. Out in the world, they wear Christian ecclesiastical robes. Yet they bow in the Asian manner.

Historically, we've noted that the West met living teachers of Eastern spirituality for the first time in any big way at the Parliament of World Religions. Now, you might not think anything similar could be presented in the East. Yet representatives of Western civilization assemble in the East quite frequently, only they're called business summits. So while the West has been playing catch-up with Eastern holistic thought and spiritual cultivation, the East has been doing likewise as to Western individualism and materiality. (That's why I've never liked the term "underdeveloped country," because it depends on what the criteria for "development" are.)

Footprints travel in two directions. Consider this—Thoreau was influenced by the East, and his writings influenced … Mahatma Gandhi, who in turn influenced … Martin Luther King, Jr., whose speeches have also been studied around the world (all of which are separate stories in themselves). So an intriguing aspect of Western Buddhism is the effect our adaptations can have, in turn, on the East, because of the West's influence today. Consider women, for example.

Women Buddhas: Of Course!

For Buddhism to take hold in the West, it absolutely has to accommodate certain basics Westerners come to expect of their own culture. Women's rights, for example. If you read that the Buddha was wary of this topic, I think you're getting something filtered through the ingrained sexism of its author, not the Buddha. Old habits die hard.

In the Buddha's time, it was forbidden for women (and slaves) to read Hindu scriptures; nor could women even pray on their own. In defiance of the Brahmins, the Buddha ordained nuns, starting with his own stepmother and then his former wife. His order of nuns is one of the earliest women's associations in the world. Today, there are dozens of Western women Buddhist priests and teachers. This is certainly good, and has been hard-won. And since it hasn't always been this way, many eyes in Asia are turned toward the various ways Buddhism adapts in the West, including Buddhist women in Asia lobbying for full ordination. (There's more on female buddhas in our final chapter.)

Women also seem to have a great eye for picking up on social imbalances, perhaps in part due to their historic exclusion from so many situations of power themselves. Women priests have often replaced hierarchical models with more communal approaches, sharing power with a free flow of responsibilities and roles back and forth from periphery to center. Which brings us to democracy.

The Cherry Blossom Grafted onto the Hickory Branch: Buddhist Democracy

The premise of democracy is that everyone can make their own choices about their lives. Buddhism is similarly based. All beings carry the seeds of their own enlightenment. (Consider that when Thomas Jefferson wrote "All beings are endowed with inalienable human rights to life, liberty, and the pursuit of happiness," in 1776, he'd originally written "property," before changing that to "the pursuit of happiness." So Thomas Jefferson said you have a right to study Buddhism.)

It's a good match. That is, the Buddha fits in really well with the Yankee spirit. After all, he's a do-it-yourself self-starter. (When I think of self-reliance, not only Emerson's essay of the same name comes to mind, but also Frank Sinatra saying, "Don't tell me—suggest it to me!") The Buddha was the kind of pragmatic, no-nonsense, can-do, no-limit guy that appeals to Americans. What he said, essentially, was "Hey! I tried this! Worked for me. But don't take my word for it. See for yourself." That emphasis on independence and personal experience is at the heart of America's most cherished ideals.

We're still tinkering with our translation and interpretation, which is fine because, like us, the Buddha was used to reinventing himself, so to speak. It will be interesting to see how Buddhism plays out in a couple of decades on Western shores. For example, what organizational forms will there be? Buddhism balances a dynamic between authority (the teachings) and egalitarianism (the community). Asian conditioning has become familiar with "gentle authoritarianism," emphasizing the teacher. While some people may want to all face one master, others will prefer to all face in the same direction, teaching and learning from each other. We'll continue awakening, whether in formal temples or in a neighbor's living room, which brings us to the next element …

> **Along the Path**
>
> "In Europe, intellectualism takes precedence over tradition; in the East it is the reverse. In Dharma terms, the European has an excess of *panna* (intelligence) over *saddha* (faith), and he tends to reject what he cannot understand even if it is true; the [Asian] has an excess of *saddha* over *panna*, which leads him to accept anything ancient, even if it is false."
>
> —Nanavira (1963)

Integration into Ordinary Workaday Life

Another key characteristic of Western Buddhism is that it's primarily lay, rather than primarily monastic as in the East. This means that many Western sanghas allow a member to hold an outside job and pay rent, plus bypass celibacy and maintain a family life, while still undergoing a full course of training of a monk or nun.

And why not? Well, monastic tradition ensures stability. This might be one reason why many lay Buddhist centers pack up their tents and fold, lacking a strong succession of teachers and administrators. There's a lesson here for "convert" Buddhists (European Americans) to learn from "ethnic" Buddhists (Asian Americans). Asian-American sanghas are entering their second century in America. Though many have no monastic orders, one reason for their stability is their emphasis on community and continuity, which European Americans are often still discovering.

Another upshot of the lay emphasis in Western Buddhism is its concerns for "worldly" affairs. The whole last chapter of this book, in fact, is devoted to this important trend, generally known as "engaged Buddhism" (being engaged with the world), although we're touching on some of those issues here, such as the rights of women, and …

Diversity, a Tapestry of Many Threads

A sure sign that Buddhism has truly arrived in the West is awareness of diversity. As a litmus, we might look to the most racially diverse Buddhist organization in the West, Soka Gakkai International, where there might be one or two white people in a sangha, composed of members from Hispanic, Latino, and Asian heritage. Race matters. It offers another opportunity to think outside our self. (There's more on this idea in our final chapter.)

Consider "ethnic" Buddhism. "Born-again" white Buddhists didn't exactly discover Buddha. This divide has partially kept Pure Land, the most widely practiced school in Asia, from being more widely appreciated in the West, until now. And Pure Land temples, conversely, are re-examining their tradition in the West in terms of opening it up more to others.

Koreans aren't Japanese. And Asian Americans are Americans. Bridge-building and dialogue is evolving between those for whom Buddhism is new to their heritage, and those for whom it is integral. As long as there appears to be sides at all, then one might say Buddhism has yet to be completely successful. An evolving Western Buddhism will necessarily be nourished by the cultural traditions of Buddhists of any color and culture, red, white, yellow, and brown. And purple! What we have in common is our diversity.

As Buddhism develops into a mainstream religion in America, it draws forth a diversity of trailblazers. The first African American Indo-Tibetan scholar, Jan Willis, has personal insight into Buddhism's answers to the challenges of diversity and its potent medicine for healing the wounds of race. Like a Buddha, she offers her findings to all who need.

Photo: Marlies Bosch

Nonsecularism: Buddha at the Salad Bar

In the East, a corner store might stock a bar of soap by Kleenexes and batteries. A Western supermarket displays seven brands of soap on a big shelf. For better or worse, so, too, here with spirituality: ("Attention, shoppers! Krishna's playing flute in Aisle 9!" "Macrobiotic food samples next to the Vitamin Bin!") In Asia, religious pluralism can be as rare as an overweight postman. In the West, this is one of the most dynamic and exciting aspects of Buddhism. Vipassana teacher Joseph Goldstein calls it One Dharma.

For the first time, different schools of Buddhism that might never even know about each other back home in Asia are now rubbing elbows, opening new possibilities as to what it might mean to follow the path of the Buddha. Indeed, this book is a tangible example of the trend (if I may toot my own horn), as the first to survey and spotlight different major paths of practice all within the same covers. (Who woulda thunk it? Or why did it take so long to happen!) A gray-robed Korean Buddhist monk might have never seen a saffron-robed Sri Lankan one, much less studied such other culture's practice, in translation. It's a striking difference between East and West.

This ecumenical approach is important to recognize, too, in terms of Western living teachers, who're naturally more inclined to embody a pluralism within their approach. Stephen Batchelor, for just one example, is an Englishman who'd lived in Asia and studied Tibetan Buddhism for nine years, then Korean Buddhism for four. In retrospect, he's said his Korean trainings enabled him to drill straight down within himself, vertically, as it were, while his Tibetan trainings covered the terrain in a more horizontal expanse through separate rituals. He's now co-founder of Sharpham College, inspired by, but independent of, all traditions. And he's coined the phrase "Buddhism without beliefs" for his own teachings. (True enough, Buddhism's not a religion about dogma or beliefs, but about what's in front of your face, right now. Thus, Christianity or Judaism asks us to believe their tenets, whereas the Buddha asks us to practice his findings.)

Hear and Now

"In the final analysis, there is no entity called 'Buddhism' which travels from one culture to another. The insights and values of Buddhism are transmitted solely through their being realized in and communicated through the lives of individual women and men. And we can no more create a Western form of Buddhism than we can manufacture a fairy tale or a myth. For Buddhism achieves its cultural expressions in a mysterious and unpredictable way over many generations; in a way that no one of us can possibly foresee."

—Stephen Batchelor

Study different teachings. The second Bodhisattva Vow reminds us that Dharma doors are endless, inviting us to enter them all. They're all different doors to the same goal. (We'll pick up this theme directly in the next chapter.)

No new petals had blossomed from the Lotus for a thousand years, until now. Buddha the Gardener has had his passport stamped, headed West, and is hoeing his row over here. This is a wonderful time.

The Least You Need to Know

♦ The impact of the Buddha upon the West can be seen to equal that of Marx, Einstein, Darwin, and Freud.

♦ Western Buddhism is a fascinating and vital evolution of Buddhism. It's destined to remain here, though it will take generations before we can say in exactly what shape.

♦ Western Buddhism includes practitioners of European heritage and Asian immigrants, plus many other ethnicities, all of whom have much to teach and learn from each other.

♦ Western Buddhism brings a number of additional issues to the table, such as acculturation (adaptation), feminism, organization, integration into everyday life, pluralism, and ecumenism (different schools).

4

Different Travel Agents, Same Destination?: Interfaith

In This Chapter

- ◆ Oneness (not sameness)
- ◆ Buddha and God, atheism, or agnosticism
- ◆ Buddhism, Hinduism, and Taoism
- ◆ Buddhism and the children of Abraham
- ◆ Buddhism and other creeds

King Ashoka had his edicts inscribed on monumental stone pillars still standing today. We see from them that his India was a model for spirituality without borders: "There should be growth in the essentials of all religions .... Whoever due to excessive devotion praises one's own religion and condemns others only harms one's own religion."

His words ring true today. When I was a lad, "interfaith" meant maybe comparing Genesis 15 with Luke 1, Sarah and Mary, or, more practically, accommodating for marriages between Christians and Jews. Today, interfaith has come to mean a spiritual dialogue between ourselves and others, and within ourselves. Given how interconnected our diverse global village has become, we're all coming to find ourselves enrolled in its course of study.

Compared to the variability of culture, and even statecraft, religion is a more stable factor of history. All religions maintain perennial values at their core. Neglect of these core values appears to be a direct cause of the illnesses now polluting families, cities, the world. Let's see how Buddhism figures in the religious mix. It's an exciting time to be alive. Healing and holy resources both new and old are flourishing, cross-fertilizing each other, and revitalizing what it means to be human.

Beyond Exclusivity: Oneness

You know what the Buddhist said to the hotdog vendor? "Make me one with everything."

Buddhism is certainly responsible in part for a relatively recent, general reawakening to the oneness of all that is. But the Buddha's truth can be found in any spiritual tradition, really. (What religion is God?) It's not an exclusive contract nor a one-course diet. Once you awaken to the Buddha, his oneness can enable you to see this truth in your own religious roots, and appreciate how these roots support your growth. So adding a few drops of the Dharma to your Christian, or Jewish, or Moslem roots (or whatever they might be), can be like gaining an extra pair of wings. And if, after that, you still feel Buddhism is your way, then fine. It's excellent through and through.

In my book, all religions preach the Golden Rule. Period. Don't do to anyone what you wouldn't have done to you. When you observe carefully, I think you'll see it's deeply true how people treat others as they'd like to be treated themselves. So why can't religions do likewise? Well, naturally, religions, like people, tend over time to develop chauvinist tendencies; we look out for number one, ourselves, and think our way is the best. The problem is when one path wants to harm another.

Let's do some basic Interfaith Math. Judaism says God is one: *Adonai echad.* Christianity says the Father, the Son, and the Holy Spirit are one in God. Islam says *La illaha il'allah:* There is no God but God. Hinduism says our *Atman* (innermost self) is one with *Brahman* (the eternal essence of the universe, equivalent to God). Don't these all boil down to the same destination, only with different travel agents? (One has a connecting flight from The Cosmic Dream to The Eye of the Heart with a layover in Silence; another takes you through The Phantom Flux of Life with a sleeper coach.)

> **Hear and Now**
>
> "Aware of the suffering created by fanaticism and intolerance, we are determined not to be idolatrous about or bound to any doctrine, theory, or ideology, even Buddhist ones. Buddhist teachings are guiding means to help us learn to look deeply and to develop our understanding and compassion. They are not doctrines to fight, kill, or die for."
>
> —The Order of Interbeing. First Mindfulness Training: Openness

Certainly it's your personal means of approach, as well as companions, crew, and scenery, which mold the journey. Differences matter. (Oneness isn't sameness.) And to appreciate difference, we must experience commonality, nondualism. Otherwise, we're like the blind men confronting an elephant, each insistent that his point of view is the only one.

Some religious leaders, even Buddhist, might tell you to shun all other paths. I think this is like a hospital asking your religion before surgery; kind of scary. (I like Joe Gould's answer: "In the summer, I'm a nudist; in the winter, I'm a Buddhist.") My question to myself is, instead, the very first thing when I wake up in the morning: "Who am I?" And the answer that invariably comes is that I don't know, but I'm awakening. (And the second thought? It's a good day. Be happy!)

Continuing a medical metaphor, consider how many different *kinds* of remedies people turn to these days. It's not uncommon to find an herbal extract alongside a pharmaceutical in a medicine cabinet. So it can be with the spiritual path. When people warn that a variety of traditions makes a salad out of spirituality, the answer is, "So what's wrong with salad?!" The danger is like digging a number of shallow holes in the ground when you're trying to reach water. A well requires boring down. So whatever you practice, practice it all the way.

Hear and Now

"It seems to me that the world's religions are like siblings separated at birth. We've grown up in different neighborhoods, different households, with different songs and stories, traditions and customs. But now we've been reunited, and, having found each other after so many years apart, we look into each other's faces and can see the family resemblance. We're back together again, and it's very good."
—Rev. Richard Watts

Do Buddhists Necessarily Believe in God?

The question of God isn't part of the teachings of the Buddha. This makes it interesting to treat Buddhism in the context of religion, since God is central to other religions. (Buddhist folksinger Suzanne Vega asks, "Did you hear about the agnostic dyslexic insomniac who lies awake at night wondering if there really is a dog?")

Buddhism doesn't ask for belief. Its gold standard for truth isn't theoretical but experiential, and useful; what you can observe and experience yourself and test in your own life. This may be one reason Buddhism *is* so popular today. Of all the sayings of the

Buddha, his most commonly looked-up quotation on the Internet is from his talk to some citizens known as the Kalamas, when he tells them, in effect:

> "Don't believe a teaching just because you've heard it from a man who's supposed to be holy, or because it's contained in a book supposed to be holy, or because all your friends and neighbors believe it. But whatever you've observed and analyzed for yourself and found to be reasonable and good, then accept that and put it into practice."

Both the Buddha and the Bible say, "O taste and see!" This fits in squarely with what's been an open secret since the end of the last century, namely, the mass movement of people adopting practices to make real for themselves their relation to the sacred, rather than repeating what they've learned by rote.

Indeed, Buddhism may never be universally popular precisely because it doesn't necessarily require anyone to believe anything. And that ain't easy for many folks. But the nuts and bolts of the Buddha's teaching boils down to one thing and one thing only: personally understanding the human condition—why we suffer and how to be free.

Along with this Buddhist practice, you can believe in God. Or gods. You can be an atheist, or agnostic. It doesn't hinge on any of these. There's no story about the divine origin of the universe, no divine messengers. If you wish, B.Y.O. (bring your own).

Me, I've had a Buddhist outlook as long as I can remember. So when a dear rabbi with whom I was once studying would call God "The Most High," I went along with this, taking it as a place marker signifying the highest anyone can conceive of when on the highest peak of awareness. (Worked for me.) If your experience in practicing Buddhism confirms your belief in something divinely sacred, then fine. Buddhist meditation puts you in touch with the heart of creation; whether or not that's the same as the heart of your creator is up to you.

Roots: Buddha Was Born a Hindu

The Buddha's motherland was India. Indian culture is like being Jewish or Italian—as hard to change as a zebra its stripes. So naturally his teachings have deep affinities with Indian culture, which is like a long, wide, deep river. For instance, we know that on his way to Enlightenment, the Buddha practiced yoga (which includes meditation as well as postures and ethics). But the formal codification of the branches of yoga by a man named Patanjali didn't take place until centuries later. So today no one can say with surety which elements are borrowed from the Buddhists, and which the Buddhists borrowed. Reviewing Buddhist and Hindu thought as two neighboring trees from the same soil, let's compare then contrast them and thus better understand each.

The Hindu Matrix

Ethics, and a keen sense of the impermanence and needless suffering of life, are aspects of Hindu culture which the Buddha's teachings naturally inherited. Indeed, he shares with Hindu spirituality common aspects of *dharma*, truth, the natural way of the universe, reality—such as karma, the round dance of life, and interconnectedness of life. *Karma* is a kind of moral cause and effect. Everything we do (or say or even think) has its effect, causing something else in turn, all bound up in an interactive web. But don't think it's fatalistic. If you hear someone saying that you're the product of all the karma of your past, or past lives, and meanwhile you can't even remember what you had for breakfast, then maybe that might as well have been a past life. (You might thus speak of *rebirth*, a continual metamorphosis, rather than *reincarnation*, which pinpoints a self that gets reborn.) The point the Buddha taught is that we're all responsible for our own destinies. Our reality is a result of our karma. As ye sow, so shall ye reap.

Another related quintessential Indian cultural concept that influenced the Buddha is the circularity of life. A typically Western approach is to think linearly, "1-2-3," naturally predisposed to mechanistic thinking, "insert big toe into Slot B and twist," therefore and thusly. Primal Western symbols of life include the procession, the ladder, the chain, and next month's credit card bill. In India, the wheel is an archetypal symbol, reflecting cyclic rather than rectilinear thinking. A seed that becomes a flower will decay into mulch so as to fertilize a new seed. Round and round we go, as with a merry-go-round or a spinning top. And it makes for playful thinking.

While Western traditions view the universe as a measurable thing—God's *creation*, signed in the lower right-hand corner—in Indian culture the universe is more of a play. The deity Shiva, for instance, is often depicted in a dance that simultaneously creates, maintains, and destroys the universe, while also waving grace to his devotees plus also concealing and revealing all of it. (*Olé!*) Life's a ballroom, and we and everything around us are part of a never-ending cosmic pageant of energies called gods boogying with themselves and us intermingled. A big square dance with light shows, where dancers get mixed and reshuffled, do-si-do your partners. Hide-and-seek: peek-a-boo! In a sense, it's like the limitless, undifferentiated God of the Bible creating our universe and us humans so that He might know Himself in us. (And, now and then, a word from our sponsor …) Except we and He have been One throughout all eternity, once we see through the dance of illusion to the unchanging truth.

This makes for interconnectedness, as seen in the Hindu *advaita* (nondualist) motto "Thou Art That." Short, sweet, and a mighty concept to contemplate. We're all part of a cosmic dance or dream of the gods, thus everything we see is but foam and wave of the same vast ocean of which we're all made. So although we identify with our masks and roles in the stirring pageant (or soap opera) we call life, we're also part of a greater, cosmic unfoldment—the universe playing peek-a-boo with itself. This theme crops up again with the idea that we're all buddhas, only we don't know it yet (such idiots we mortals be!), until we wake up to our place in the process of truth. Another variant you'll also hear is that everyday reality mirrors cosmic reality. An ordinary radish is a manifestation of the cosmos, and so are you.

The Buddha's Unique Emphases

As noted in Chapter 2, what's now called Hinduism ultimately appropriated and incorporated enough of Buddha's influence—and vice-versa (particularly in Tibetan Buddhism)—so that the idea of separating the two today might be like a couple married sixty years filing for divorce. But it's good to see Buddha's unique twist. For one thing, Hindu spirituality at the time of the Buddha had its head in the clouds, so to speak, and the Buddha brought its idealism down to earth. Nonattachment is all well and good, but if it means saying good-bye to my body or my desires, then no thank you.

Moreover, Buddha Dharma was a striking spiritual reaction to the caste system. Tradition said the castes were God's plan. If you were born into a lowly caste, that was due to your unresolved bad karma in a previous life. (That didn't explain, however, why the elite could pass their caste along to their children.) When Siddhartha shaved his head and went forth, he not only renounced his own caste but the whole caste system as well. As he'd discover, the seeds of enlightenment are innate in everyone. What he'd experienced for himself anyone else could, too, through self-discipline rather than external ritual. Same thing when the Buddha criticized the Brahmans' practice of animal sacrifice as superstitious and a waste of precious life. He was saying *all* life is precious. And so he'd read from the Vedas to his followers, rather than creating an exclusive school. But that was as inspiring poetry rather than anything to be studied according to one sole interpretation, such as laid down by elite Brahmin priests.

Furthermore, the Buddha gave a special twist to the search for ultimate identity. The Hindu path seeks to realize the inherent union (*yoga*) between a person's core, inner self (*Atman*) and the Overself—the transpersonal, timeless Self (*Brahman*), the supreme source and essence of reality. Self is the universe using you as part of its nervous system, as it were, as Dr. Deepak Chopra might say. It is only the Self that can realize itself because that's all there is. However, the Buddha instead affirmed "*an-atman*"—"*an*" in Sanskrit being like our prefix "un" or "non." No eternal self. In terms of interfaith, the Buddha's teachings on the illusory nature of self, in fact, are unique in the history of ideas. And if he rejected Atman, he certainly didn't preach about Brahman or any creator deity whatsoever.

But, as we've seen, he's deeply rooted in his native soil. He shares with yoga the insight that small self (me me me) stands in the way of seeing reality. Such self is a fiction, called ego, our getting caught up in and identifying with our moment in the soap opera. Addicted to the drama. ("Don't touch that dial! We'll be back with scenes from next week's all-new episode—starring … you!") Let it go.

On a practical level, in the West you might find yogis sliding across the hall to Buddhist meditation workshops, to open their wisdom eye (that is, to see deeply and understand). And many Buddhists practice yoga postures (*asanas*) as warm-up for meditation. After all, when we see the Buddha sitting in the lotus position, it's a basic yoga position (*padmasana*). And just as yoga offers meditation on breathing (*panayama*), so does the Buddha devote an entire sutra to breathing. (And whose faith is breath?)

China's Version 1.0: Buddhism + Taoism

A keystone of ecumenical, interfaith awareness is the *Tao Te Ching* (pronounced *dow deh jing, The Book of the Way*), a mere 5,000 words in Chinese. It's a simple but profound account of how to be in harmony with the unchanging amidst the 10,000 things of whatever's happening at any given moment. ('Twas ever *thus*. Like this: just so.) As we've noted, there's a fundamental link between Tao and Zen. It's as if Zen is born of the marriage of Indian philosophizing and Chinese practicality. Both are imbued with the spontaneity and playfulness of a newborn kitten, the intuitive wisdom of finding the light switch in the dark, the commonplace simplicity of a glass of water, and the completeness of swallowing the whole world in a single gulp.

Like Buddhism, Taoism says we're each embedded in what's ultimately real, that one thing beyond realms of contingency and form (called the Tao, the Way), through our innate, individual character. One way to realize our connection to the Tao would be through *tso wang*, sitting with blank mind, forgetting our transient self, and finding *hsin tsung*—the heart within the heart, the mind of the mind, the still point within the turning world, the ground of our consciousness within the cosmic processes. There's a similarity here to the idea of perfecting the self through selflessness, the Hindu yoking (*yoga*) of *Atman* and *Brahman*, and the actual technique is very similar to the Buddhist practice of sitting meditation to enrich our innate "buddha nature."

Like Zen, the Tao is beyond words, and any attempt to pigeonhole it is to miss the point. To speak of the Tao is not the Tao. Or as Louis Armstrong said of jazz, "If you got to ask, you'll never get it." Yet it has a very instructive symbol, the *tai chi* yin-yang. A Taoist map of the Middle Way.

This Chinese symbol of the Ultimate Principle of All Things (often referred to as "yin-yang") seems to resemble two fish each forever trying to catch the other's tail in its mouth. (Ain't life like that?!) They represent all polarities, and each contains its opposite within its own heart.

Here we see the origin of all polarities—male and female, light and dark, outer and inner, self and other, chocolate and vanilla ice cream, hot and cold—and also their unity. While the two are clearly distinguishable, they're clearly interdependent. One defines the other. There's no buying without selling, no selling without buying. There's no me without you, and this book is proof: no writers without readers. The more extreme my position is, the more it embraces my worst enemy's. The more I try to control and pin everything down with labels, the more everything turns to goo. And the more I let everything just flow, the more everything reflects an uncanny, inherent order—like the fractal formula for the pattern of a seashore which matches that for the outline of a cloud, discovered in Chaos Theory.

The Middle Way isn't some statistical mean, but a very dynamic process. Within the heart of the darkness there's a bright spot; and vice versa. But the most direct path between the two isn't necessarily a direct line (it's nonlinear). Try and walk across this map via any "straight narrow path" and you step in black and white equally. The contact between the two equal halves isn't fixed or static (like a fence, or words) but fluid and flowing (like a dance, or a river).

Here's a fundamental difference between Buddhist and Christian worldviews, between Eastern and Western mind-sets. The Western mind-set is typically *dualistic*, the self split asunder from the world (in order to, say, put up a parking lot), body separated from soul, self from the cosmos, humanity from God. The Eastern mind-set, on the other hand, sees humanity and the cosmos as *interconnected*, intertwined (see the Mu Chi landscape reproduced in Chapter 12 for an example).

But if you say yin-yang is a symbol of two things, you're wrong, because it's one picture. If you say it's one picture, you're wrong again, because it clearly shows two different things. Buddhism recognizes heads and tails as two sides of the same coin—without attachment to either the one-ness of the coin, nor the two-ness of the sides. Zen says: "Not one, not two." So here again we reach the One, via a different road map.

Leaves from the Bodhi Tree

Who can judge good from bad? In a Taoist story, a farmer's horse once ran off into foreign lands. The neighbors all said this was terrible, but the farmer shrugged, "Maybe, maybe not." Later, the horse returned with a foreign horse of fine breed. The neighbors all said this was wonderful, but the farmer shrugged, "Maybe, maybe not." The horses mated, and the farmer eventually became a wealthy horse trader. One day his only son was riding and fell and broke his hip. The neighbors all said how horrible, but the man shrugged, "Maybe, maybe not." Next year, foreigners invaded. All able-bodied young men were drafted. Almost all died in battle. The army had taken all the man's horses, but his son, because of the broken hip, was spared.

Benedictine Buddhists, Zen Judaists, Sufi Yogis

In the last chapter, we noted the majority of American Buddhists being of Asian heritage. Newcomers from, say, Jewish or Christian or Islamic heritages typically look to Buddhism for one of two things: new roots, because the spiritual tradition of their parents had become inaccessible to them—or, they'd been raised in an active, vibrant spiritual heritage, which Buddhism further vitalizes and strengthens. A good fit, either way.

Christian Followers of the Way: Onwards!

What religion was Jesus? (Was he a Christian?) What religion was Shakyamuni? (Was he a Buddhist?) Had Jesus and Shakyamuni met, I know they'd be two good buddies. Some even say that Buddhists from the Silk Route were present in Galilee during Jesus' time, so maybe their minds met. Buddha and Christ are still conversing today, and the ongoing dialogue is making for many good hearts. Amen.

Jesus said, "I am the Way." The Buddha said, "Here is the Way." Lest we forget, both were inviting us to emulate their teachings ourselves, to live their meaning—to *be* the Way, ourselves—rather than lose our way by studying their words like a lawyer. Yet it is interesting how their teachings tabulate, in divine double-entry bookkeeping fashion. Seek and ye shall find, the Buddha said. Jesus said, "He who would may reach the utmost height, but he must be anxious to learn." And Jesus once said, "Regard the lilies of the field" … and the Buddha once gave a sermon in which he just held up a flower.

Students of the apocrypha have noted how Jesus in the Gospel of Thomas speaks in terms of illusion and enlightenment rather than sin and redemption. Scholar Elaine Pagels notes how in this text "he comes as a guide who opens access to spiritual understanding. But when the disciple attains enlightenment, Jesus no longer serves as his spiritual master: the two have become equal—even identical." Lists of Buddhist-Christian correspondences are lengthy, though the real places of convergence aren't in books but in living hearts and minds.

Different paths can lead to a common destination. These images of Buddha and Christ seem to have been drawn by the same person, though one was made by a Tibetan artist, the other by a Russian. From 1981 to 1992, these images hung on the sign outside the School of Sacred Arts in New York City, the Buddha facing east, Christ facing west.

Buddha by Tupten Norbu   *Christ by Vladislav Andreyev*

As we saw with Vedanta, a model in our time for Buddhist interfaith is revitalization of roots. If you're a Christian, you might find yourself being "a better Christian" by adding a few drops of Dharma to your ordinary faith. A Tibetan Buddhist meditation called *tonglen*, for example, enables a practitioner to literally love one's enemy as one-self. And Buddhist recitation—be it Buddha's name or the Sanskrit syllables *Aum Mani Padme Hum* ("the jewel in the lotus")—resonates with early traditions of Christian prayer, such as recitation of *Kyrie Eleison*, and the Jesus Prayer (*Hesychasm*) still practiced by Eastern Orthodox Christians. The similarity between Christian and Buddhist rosary beads is another reminder that spirit knows no boundary.

Now, through meditation of mindful breathing, for example, many Christians are rediscovering what St. Paul meant by praying without ceasing (1 Thessalonians 5:17). Buddhist meditation also parallels what Paul had spoken of as *kenosis* (emptying out), an active recognition of the utter mystery of God; also referred to in Christianity as "the cloud of unknowing," this parallels the "Don't-Know Mind" of Zen discipline.

For Simone Weil, a Jewish Catholic who also studied Buddhism, prayer is nothing other than paying attention. (Listening to God in silence, we hear God also listening, in silence.) Honorary Catholic bodhisattva St. Francis said "Preach the Gospel always, and use words if necessary."

Along the Path

"Be still and know that I am God." (Psalm 46) "'Be still' means to become peaceful and concentrated. The Buddhist term is *samatha* (stopping, calming). 'Know' means to acquire wisdom or understanding. The Buddhist term is *vipassana* (insight or looking deeply). When we are still, looking deeply, and touching the source of our true wisdom, we touch the living Buddha and the living Christ in ourselves and each person we meet."

—Thich Nhat Hanh

A Personal Note

The interfaith dialogue breaks down isolation. In my own experience, growing up Jewish, I'd felt distanced from Christianity. When my Hebrew school made a field trip to the Catholic church across the street, it seemed, alas, mostly a lesson in deportment. Interestingly, for me, it was through Buddhism that I came to deeply understand and appreciate Jesus.

When I understood the Buddha's teaching on the inevitability of suffering and how to deal with that as instrumental in finding true happiness, I began to understand how Christians could worship an image of a human being suffering so horribly, on a cross; the ultimate sacrifice and universal redemption. Both Buddha and Christ offer a message of love having participated in the sorrows of the world, out of compassion for the human condition. (Those who mark the difference between the physical agony of the crucifixion and the mental anguish of leaving one's own wife and child will miss my point.)

When asked to pick up Jesus' cross for myself, I'm touched to recognize my own sorrows, and transform them into fertilizer for my own flowers of peace, and to bear witness to the needless sorrows of others. In the bodhisattva ideal, pain is overcome by bearing it for others, with others. Vowing to save all beings. (Those who try to split the hair of difference between enlightenment and salvation will miss my point.)

When I'd touched "the peace that passeth understanding" for myself, through my Buddhist practice, and experienced how it's available at any time, all the time, then I understood the Kingdom of Heaven within reach of all. The seeds of enlightened living are within all of us. The Quakers ask, "Where shalt thou turn if not to the light within?"

JuBus: Where Mt. Sinai Meets Mt. Sumeru

Today there are Jews who bring Buddhism into their Jewish practice, and full-time Buddhists who are Jewish on their parents' side. However you slice it, there are proportionately more Jews found along the Buddha's way than Christians. In America, for example, Jews comprise less then 3 percent of the population, yet make up at least 15 percent of non-Asian Buddhists. Certainly this reflects strong spiritual devotion.

> ### Leaves from the Bodhi Tree
>
> A Jewish mother traveled to Nepal to seek an audience with a guru. When she arrived at the monastery, she was told that she could have an audience with him but visitors could only utter five words to him. So she passed through the outer doors and entered the inner sanctum. She approached the guru, putting down her bags, and said, "So Sheldon, come home already!"

Buddhism and Judaism share much in common. This-worldly rather than otherworldly, they're based in the here and now. The garden is always available to us. To reconnect with that fact, Jews traditionally go on a weekly spiritual retreat called *shabbos* (Sabbath), which a Buddhist would call a day of mindfulness.

Monotheist, Judaism is a path of unity; to be a Jew is to be one with the source of creation and see a day's various encounters as opportunities to realize that oneness. The Bible speaks of our separation from the garden, from oneness, as our fall. For the Buddha, the sword that divides us from oneness is our identification with a separate self, the cause of our suffering.

And, as with Buddhism, there's no head office to Judaism either, so there's a kindred dynamic here, too, between tradition and adaptation. Like Buddhism, or any spiritual path, Judaism's not an object on a shelf, but rather a living tradition, and a process of perpetual renewal is built into its worldview. In our time, Buddhism has provided impetus and grist for major Jewish renewal no different from the model we've already seen. So, for instance, when such Jewish sages as Rabbi Zalman Schachter and Shlomo Carlebach saw Jewish kids flocking in droves to Hindu and Buddhist meditation in the '60s, they realized the need for Judaism to renew its meditative paths, a need now addressed by a movement called Jewish Renewal. The traditional bar for entry to Jewish meditative traditions had always been high, a topic not even to be mentioned until after the age of 40; and never available to women. Now Dharma rain has been nourishing roots of Jewish mystical and contemplative traditions that had been lying dormant and making them available to all.

The renewal of Hasidism, like Buddhism within Hinduism, and Sufism within Islam, emphasizes each person's innate powers of directly accessing the sacred in everyday life. The utter devotion of Hasidic Jews who don't doubt the Messiah could come riding into town tomorrow on a donkey resonates with the Buddhist Pure Land school.

In recent years, too, there's been a rediscovery of the Jewish meditation of silent communion and union with God (*hitbodedut*), quite similar to the Zen practice of *shikantaza* (just sitting). There's a tradition in Jewish mysticism of restoring oneness to the world (*tikkun ha'olam*), by participating in the co-creation of the universe, not unlike the bodhisattva path. And along with an emptying of self in Jewish wisdom traditions, there's an interplay between something and nothingness similar to the Buddhist equation of phenomena (form) and blank essence (emptiness); after all, divine creation brought something out of nothing. (Such a deal!)

Hear and Now

"By detachment from appearances, abide in real truth. I tell you, thus shall you think of all this fleeting world: a star at dawn, a bubble in a stream ... a flash of lightning in a summer cloud ... a flickering lamp, a phantom, a dream."
—Buddha, Diamond Sutra 32

"All flesh is grass, and all its beauty is like the flowers of the field. Grass withers, flowers fade, when the breath of the Lord blows upon them .... But the word of our God will stand forever."
—Isaiah 40:6–8

In its worldly wanderings and travels Judaism has always been in dialogue. Interestingly, when Abraham Maimonides, son of one of Judaism's greatest commentators and philosophers, Moses Maimonides (1138–1204), began studying the mystical Islamic path of Sufism, Moses wrote that any Jew who did so needn't be formally initiated back into the fold since the two paths were monotheistic and not that strange to each other. (And Moses himself had learned much of his Aristotle through Arabic sources.)

Interchange is never one-sided. (The Silk Route traveled in two directions, remember?) In 1990, for example, the Dalai Lama invited eight Jewish scholars and rabbis for a Tibetan-Jewish dialogue. Throughout the summit a key question was the "Jewish secret" of survival in exile. As one such Jewish guest later reflected, it was "... a reasonable question, even if it's the first time anybody ever asked us."

*Rabbi Zalman Schachter-
Shalomi responds to a question by the Dalai Lama
about angels.*

Photo: Rodger Kamenetz

Make Room for Rumi

Muslims are no doubt glad the rest of the world is having dialogue with them, and after so much misunderstanding and misrepresentation, for so long. And we all can learn in the process. Actually, Buddhists and Muslims share a long history of dialogue. For example, in the southeast Asian country of Java, predominantly Islamic, there's a strong spiritual tradition called *Kejawen* (meaning "the state of being Javanese), which mixes Buddhism and Hinduism with Sufi-influenced mystical Islam. Java is also home to a Buddhist temple called Borodubur, one of the wonders of the world, where local Jesuit priests use the sculptures on its walls as topics for interfaith dialogue.

In southwest Asia, architects from India helped build Baghdad, in the eighth century, when the Islamic caliphs made it their capital. Buddhist as well as Hindu translators came along and practiced there, learning the local language and rubbing elbows with the local Christians, Zoroastrians, and Jews, as well as Muslims. So it's no shock to hear that the Buddhist Pure Land school inherits some influence from Persia (now Iran).

Hear and Now

When we are face to face with truth, the point of view of Krishna, Buddha, Christ, or any other prophet, is the same. When we look at life from the top of the mountain, there is no limitation; there is the same immensity.

—Hazrat Inayat Khan (1887–1927)

Indigenous Spirituality: Everything's (a) Relative

The Buddha's way and the spiritual paths of indigenous peoples can concoct powerful, healing medicine together. A common theme between the two is an appreciation of our place in the world, forming a respect for all life forms. Some Buddhists say the Bodhisattva Vow of awakening with and for all encompasses not just human beings and animals and vegetables, but all things. As an indigenous American shaman expressed it, "Everything that is, is alive." Or as San Francisco Native American psychologist Leslie Gray said to me recently, "Well, didn't Buddha get enlightened by a *tree!?*"

Shared wisdom also includes a vision of the interconnectedness of all things, and their impermanence. Many are familiar with the 1854 speech of Suquamish Chief Seattle, affirming all things being part of a web of life, of which we are but one strand. "Whatever we do to the web we do to ourselves. All things are bound together. All things connect." And to survive all things must change. Chief Flying Hawk, an Oglala Sioux, testifies: "If the Great Spirit wanted men to stay in one place, he would make the world stand still; but He made it to always change, so birds and animals can move and always have green grass and ripe berries, sunlight to work and play, and night to sleep; always changing; everything for good; nothing for nothing."

To my knowledge, the Buddha hasn't been translated into Kiswahili nor Creole … yet. Yet I already see viable correspondences between Buddhism and African spiritualities. But I've already said too much about Buddhism and too little about everything else. (Or is it vice versa?)

This part has put our feet on solid ground, introducing ourselves to the Buddha—his life, and the spread of his teachings, and their relationship to other teachings. But, wait! What exactly are his teachings? Well, when we continue (continue to begin), in Part 2 we'll apply what we've seen to find out what the Buddha taught—and continues to teach, in fact, in every moment, every atom: the Dharma.

The Least You Need to Know

- Interfaith dialogue is one of the most crucial topics of our times, and Buddhism converses well with all other faiths.

- Buddha was part of the culture of his time and place. So Hindu practices such as yoga are a natural part of his heritage. And his teachings are found within Hinduism today.

- When Buddhism came to China, the confrontation was made easier by the pre-existence of the Taoist religion, which in turn influenced Zen.

- Europeans usually come to Buddhism with a Judeo-Christian background. Buddhism has a mutually rewarding dialogue with both, as well as with Islam.

Part 2

Dharma: Truth, and the Way to Truth

The Buddha taught for nearly 45 years. Yet all his teachings comprise One Dharma. One Truth. One Love. One Taste. Their taste is that of freedom. Here's both freedom from, and freedom to. Freedom from needless suffering, from repeating the same-old same-old. Freedom to be genuine, to be on intimate terms with life. To live to the fullest. (*Yum!*)

And the Buddha tells us the seeds of awakening to freedom are inherent within us all. They're our innate capacity. Our birthright. It only takes waking up to it. (You'd recognize the Truth if you saw it, right?)

Nothing to be learned by rote, or be taken on faith. Rather, seeing and making real for yourself. Here's the essential harvest of the Buddha's teachings about life. The Dharma. The Way …

The Treasure and the Teachings: Jewels of Refuge and Ennobling Truths

In This Chapter

- ◆ The Triple Gem
- ◆ The nature of refuge
- ◆ The Four Noble Truths
- ◆ Liberation from suffering

What's important?

In prehistoric times, human life harmonized with the universe. Our ancestors might have pictured the universe as a giant buffalo, if buffalo was the animal that provided them with hide for clothing and shelter, meat for food, bone for tools. And they knew to take no more than they needed. But now buffalo are nearly extinct. Gone too is a simple, common frame of meaning for why we're alive. Contemporary life's typically out of balance, fragmented, incoherent. (Press "5" for more options.) Sometimes it's hard to find any meaning except what we bring to the table.

Did the Buddha leave us with an answer? Yes! Only, he intentionally left no central church, and nothing was written down. He trusted the autonomy of each person to listen to his teaching, and select, test, and self-actualize its truth for herself or himself. Since this led to a diversity of schools, and adaptations to various cultures, we might still ask if there's any bedrock to Buddhism.

The answer is, again, yes! And it's really quite simple …

The Triple Gem

The first three parts of this book are structured around three elements (with a fourth part surveying various applications in the world around us). Let's review them once more. Known as the Three Treasures, the Triple Gem, or the Three Refuges, the three are:

- **Buddha.** From the Sanskrit root *budh*, to awaken. This is the title given Siddhartha, because he attained enlightenment. More generally it could refer to any self-realized being.

- **Dharma.** Sanskrit for virtue; law; cosmic process; discipline; reality; truth. It refers to the teachings of the Buddha. More generally, it can also refer to all that the teachings pertain to, and all that leads to the truth, as a falling leaf teaches impermanence.

- **Sangha.** Sanskrit for aggregate of particles; gathering; assembly. It refers to the monastic order established by the Buddha, plus lay followers; communities of practice. By extension, it also means the practice of the Way.

This Is

The Tibetan language has no word for **"Buddhist"**—using instead *nangpha,* meaning, roughly, a person who looks within. In fact, "Buddhism" isn't used in Asia. The closest word is *"Buddha-Dharma,"* meaning roughly "facts of an enlightened life," "awakened life-truth." The nature of reality as Buddha pointed out. It's at our feet here and now.

We've imagined the historical origin of these three words. Words probably failed to express the influence, if not the light, which five former followers of Siddhartha saw when he'd come to them from the bodhi tree. A certain peaceful lightness in his step. An all-inclusiveness in his glance. A majesty, a simple splendor in his presence. After he spoke to them, they all declared themselves to be Sangha, a community, a body of seekers and teachers along the path. "Dharma" became their word for the path itself. And "Buddha," the one who'd found and shows that path, became the example for others to follow for themselves.

Why jewels? Jewels don't quite evoke the power they did 2,600 years ago. (Things change.) But we're not talking about synthetic diamonds nor healing crystals. The meaning also goes beyond a beautiful adornment (which these are) to include being rare … priceless … flawless. As gold once was, these jewels are—a touchstone, a standard of value. Unlike the stock market, their worth never fluctuates.

A slang for jewel is "rock." Here it has the connotation of the solidity missing from a life adrift. Here's the rock of Buddhism … the diamond dormant in a lump of coal … the bedrock underlying everything. As being given a rare jewel might lift us out of material want, so can these jewels liberate us spiritually. Some think of a magic gem, a wish-fulfilling jewel for their deepest aspirations.

And just like wishes and other good things come in threes, so are only three jewels enough. Touch one deeply, you touch all three. One truth. One heart. One mind.

Next question: What relation could you or I have to the Triple Gem?

> **Hear and Now**
>
> "I've given Buddhism another name. I don't call it Buddhism. What do I call it? I call it People-ism (the religion of the people). Why? Because people become Buddhas. It isn't that the Buddha becomes a person, but the people can become Buddhas. So Buddhism can be called People-ism."
>
> —Venerable Tripitaka Master Hsüan Hua

Safe Harbor: Taking Refuge

The Triple Gem is something in which Buddhists *take refuge*. Taking refuge means affirming one's appreciation of and trust in them. Using the analogy of healing, the Three Jewels are like a doctor's *care*. The mere existence of some medicine or a doctor or a hospital doesn't guarantee health. That is, if your doctor gives you a prescription but you haven't taken the medicine yet, then you still haven't taken refuge in his or her care. Taking refuge in the Three Jewels means you've evaluated them and decided they're good healing. The Buddha's like a doctor; the Dharma, his medicine; and the Sangha, the hospital staff. You can put your life in their hands.

There are many manifestations of taking refuge. Drivers sometimes keep an image of a saint on their dashboard. If you were on a ship, lost at sea, in a high storm, the light from the Triple Gem is the North Star by which you'd steer; your rudder. Our mother's womb was our refuge when we were but tiny buds. Refuge is our true home.

In Everyday Life

You can appreciate *Buddha* and *buddha nature* in your everyday life without having to formally take refuge. Meditation, for example, is a link to the Buddha, deepening with practice. We explore meditation in detail in Part 3, but, meanwhile, here's a meditation. Author and teacher Franz Metcalf came up with a wonderful mantra (a phrase to say to yourself to keep your mind focused on a positive energy). He saw a book titled *What Would Jesus Do?* and decided to write one of his own titled *What Would the Buddha Do?* It's a question you can ask all the time, any time. In a crisis or at calm. "What would the Buddha do?" The more you think of Buddha, the deeper your understanding and bond will grow. The more you think of the Buddha, the more you'll think like a Buddha.

Similarly, you can appreciate the presence of *dharma* in your everyday life without formally taking refuge. I take refuge in it whenever I find it. It might not be capital "D" Dharma, something the Buddha said specifically, but—you never know. The Buddha never took a bus but his Great Vehicle carries us all. Just yesterday, in fact, I was waiting at a bus stop during the after-work rush hour. The bus was very late, and a large crowd had formed, growing anxious and tense. When the bus finally arrived, it was already like a sardine can, crammed with people who'd accumulated in the long wait at previous bus stops.

> **Hear and Now**
>
> "Associations with wise and compassionate people help sustain the practice. To reflect on the *Sangha* of past, present, and future can give further inspiration. We develop appreciation for this expansive network that contributes to living with love. The *Sangha* has no particular religion, no dogmatic standpoints, no flavor of being a cult or sect. It is found inside and outside religion. Wherever we find wisdom and compassion, we find the *Sangha*."
>
> —Christopher Titmuss

At the front of this palpably uncomfortably crowd I saw a lady, of rather large girth. I mean, we're talking big. Very big. She'd undoubtedly seen her share of trouble in life, including boarding crowded buses. The driver, way behind schedule now, opened his doors and, completely out of patience, yelled at us all, "Hurry up! C'mon, get on! C'mon, c'mon, move to the rear of the bus!" But the woman just stood there and waited. No one could get past her, right in front of the open door. So we all waited. Finally, the driver sensed something was happening outside his bus and turned and saw her standing there. When he'd finally made eye contact with her, she just said one thing to him: "Please! Please don't make me get angry at you. Because then we'd be liable to say or do something for which we'd *both* be sorry!" The driver lifted his hands from the wheel and bowed his head in apology. Everyone calmed down, inside and outside the bus. People very kindly made room for us. The drive was otherwise uneventful.

The dharma of the story?

◆ It takes two to fuel anger. Fighting anger with anger only generates more anger. If one person refrains then the other might, too.

◆ Awakening of mind can happen anywhere. Not just in a temple. Dharma is where you find it. A teacher doesn't have to hold beads or wear robes. The voice of the Buddha is always clear, if you have ears to hear.

◆ A Buddha waiting for a bus once taught this dharma to the Rush-Hour Sangha of life. And sangha is where you find it. Right now, you're a member of *The Complete Idiot's Sangha*—you and me and all fellow readers of this book past, present, and future. Thank you.

Actually, we all embody the sangha of the universe through the earth in our bones, the wind in our lungs, the ocean in our bloodstream and cells, and the fire in our metabolism. When I sit in meditation, I do so with the whole universe. And the whole universe does so with me.

Hear and Now

"We take refuge in the Buddha because he is our teacher. We take refuge in the Dharma because it is good medicine. We take refuge in the Sangha because it is composed of excellent friends."
—Dogen (1200–1253)

"To realize the very heart of essential nature is to take refuge in the Buddha. To cultivate the garden of realization is to take refuge in the Dharma. To share the fruits of the garden is to take refuge in the Sangha."
—Robert Aitken

Different Schools, Different Spins

The major currents within Buddhism complement and reinforce each other in how they emphasize the Three Jewels. Traditionally, Theravadins refer to Buddha as the historical Buddha; the Dharma, as the Pali canon, the Tripitaka, recording his teachings; and the Sangha, as those who've attained enlightenment, and more generally the monastic community, plus the wider community of lay practitioners.

Mahayana perspectives are typically interpretive and innovative. For example, if you prefer, the Buddha is realization, Dharma is truth, and Sangha is being in harmony. Members of the Zen Peacemaker Order take refuge in:

♦ Buddha, the awakened nature of all beings

♦ Dharma, the ocean of wisdom and compassion

♦ Sangha, the community of those living in harmony with all Buddhas and Dharmas

With the Three Jewels, Mahayana Buddhists often take refuge in the path of the Bodhisattva, vowing to liberate all needless suffering. With the Three Jewels, Tibetan Buddhists take refuge in an additional triplet (called "the refuge tree"), consisting of the *lama* (*guru*, teacher, living embodiment of the Buddha), *yidam* (personal deity, an enlightened being whose attainment we wish to emulate), and dharma protector (similar to a guardian angel).

And *The Complete Idiot's Guide* simple spin is: The Three Jewels are the firm, basic handshake we make between ourselves and the universe when we've begun to appreciate, understand, and live the path of the Buddha in the twenty-first century.

From the Ultimate Dimension

I'd said, "One thing Buddhists agree on is the Three Jewels"—even though this one thing appears to be three. No contradiction. Not unlike the Christian trinity, they form a unity. Indeed, early Western interpretations of the Three Jewels reflect the interpretation of Christian missionaries. The Buddha was called the Savior, the Dharma was called the Scripture, and the Sangha was called the Church. But with or without any Christian overlay, the Three Jewels are so interconnected as to be one. And each contains all the others.

The Buddha is his teachings, the Dharma. After all, the Buddha's teachings are what enabled him to become Buddha. The Dharma is thus the essence of the Buddha. And Sangha depends on Buddha and Dharma to show people the way. Conversely, if the Buddha hadn't established the Sangha, then his teachings wouldn't ever have been preserved and kept alive. Buddha and Dharma depend on Sangha to be actualized. If there were no people, there'd be no Buddhism.

So Buddha, Dharma, and Sangha are ultimately one. One love.

The Teaching: Four Noble Truths

The Three Jewels are the root structure of Buddhism. The root teaching of the Buddha, the turn of the wheel he set in motion, is known as the *Four Noble Truths:*

1. Suffering (*duhkha*)
2. Attachment (*trishna*)
3. Liberation (*nirvana*)
4. The path of liberation (*marga*)

The Buddha said he had but one thing to teach—the nature of suffering, and freedom from suffering. Here is that teaching.

In 25 words or less: 1) "There's the fact of suffering." 2) "There's a cause to suffering." 3) "There's an end of suffering." 4) "There's a way to end suffering."

You do the math. You don't have to be a rocket scientist to see that putting these four propositions at the forefront of your awareness, understanding what they mean, and testing them out could change your life—for the good. All the rest of the Buddha's teachings could be seen as elaboration. These four interlocking sayings can teach us to grasp the human enigma of life and death … recognize the origin of and cure for human anguish … and awaken to life's sublime perfections.

This Is

The Sanskrit word **trishna** can be translated as desire. It's the root of our word for thirst. Like the thirst of a person all alone in a desert, it seems unquenchable. It can also be translated as attachment. Another good translation, in this context, would be clinging, grabbing. In modern, colloquial terms: being hung up, having a hang-up.

Four facts of life. "Truths" as in a proclamation: "We hold these truths to be self-evident." "Noble" because they can ennoble us. Revealing the nobility of what it means to be a human being. In Chinese, they're called the Four Holy Truths. Another translation might be Four Worthy Hypotheses.

The teaching, shoehorned into 75 words or less, is: 1) we'll inevitably reach a point where we'll say life sucks. Why? From 2) craving after stuff, or clinging to thoughts, which can never truly satisfy … born of unrealistic images of life … life being impermanent, and interconnected, yet we try to make out that it isn't. Nevertheless, 3) everyone can free themselves from continual disappointment. How? By 4) recognizing the life's truth we resist facing, and personally taking steps to understand and actualize that truth in our daily lives. Okay, now let's look deeper.

Leaves from the Bodhi Tree

Following his enlightenment, the Buddha adapted his teachings to the capacity of his listeners. Thus it is said that during his 50-some years of traveling and teaching, the Buddha taught dharma in 84,000 different ways. This led to the expression, "There are 84,000 dharma doors," meaning there are 84,000 different paths (or doors) to the truth. (This humble *Complete Idiot's Guide* is but one.)

Now imagine that raindrops could be classified, and the tally came to 84,000 drops, and all drops fall equally, but big trees lap up more water, and dead trees can't absorb any at all. So there are 84,000 different kinds of trees, all absorbing rain differently. And different kinds of people, all absorbing dharma. And different kinds of schools of Buddhism, adapted to different needs. And so we see how the *ultimate dimension* reflects the *relative dimension*, and vice versa.

The First Fact of Life

It began with the young prince's stark confrontation with the facts of life: sickness, old age, and death. No one gets out pain-free. Oh, maybe you're lucky: Perhaps your body doesn't send you pain signals when something's wrong, your old age will be a bed of roses, and you'll die in your sleep when you least expect it. Even so, let's face it, because your life span will ultimately end you'll never be able to have it all. (And even if you could, where would you put all of it?!) And so you're bound to be disappointed, you're bound to try some seeming solution that really only perpetuates suffering. (Unless you wake up to life's truth.) Call it Fact Number One:

Life will always be a bumpy road.

The Second Fact of Life

It's common wisdom that recognizing a problem is the hardest part of dealing with a problem. Pains are inevitable, but we don't have to experience needless suffering. We can identify the root of our suffering.

Needless suffering comes from trying to hang on to life, which is impermanent, ever changing. Like trying to catch the wind. And since we *are* life, trying to hang on to life is like trying to bite your teeth. (*Exercise:* Take a deep breath, then hold it. Notice how that builds up anxiety and cuts you off from natural process. That's a problem.) Even our pleasure can cause suffering, if we try to hang on to it.

When the Buddha discovered the Middle Way, he attained great understanding. Suffering is not enough. That's just another form of *attachment*. His self-hate and self-love were two names for the same thing: attachment to self. What is *self*? A construct we create to avoid suffering. A separation of our experience from the oneness of life. Seeing the waves, but not the ocean.

He let go of attachment. Once he took food, his health came back and he could see and think clearly again. And no longer being so hard on himself allowed him to feel a little compassion for himself. And for all beings.

Mystic poet William Blake epitomized the Buddhist definition of attachment when he wrote, "He who binds himself to a joy, does the wingèd life destroy." And he continues, "But he who kisses the joy as it flies, lives in eternity's sunrise."

Recognition of the Buddha's second fact clarifies his first. Life is truly suffering *because* we try to run away from its inevitability. The ways we try to scheme and bargain with life's infirmities and impermanences are all bound to fail—and bring us further needless suffering. Like trying to hold our breath. We seek alternative illusions, building up more of the same under different names, rather than let go of our faulty viewpoint.

The second truth locates the cause of suffering in *trishna*, craving—craving, maybe wanting the right things but in the wrong way, or wanting what's beyond our grasp— a misplaced sense of values. So since we can't change life, we *can* change our values, our way of going about the business of living. Instead of trying to hang on to life, why not become one with it, instead?

This grotesque creature's called a "hungry ghost" (Sanskrit, preta; *Chinese,* li mei), *this one being of the Japanese variety called* gaki. *Its belly is immense, because of its ravenous hunger, but its throat's only as wide as a soda straw or sometimes only the eye of a needle. And so it's emaciated because it can't get enough food to nourish itself, let alone slake its enormous appetite. It symbolizes human craving for more than it can ever have. (When's the last time you felt in a somewhat similar shape?)*

Drawing: Gary Gach

The Third Fact of Life

The third fact looks even deeper, toward the end of the whole affair. Since we bring pain onto ourselves, we can end doing so. The candle that has us so hypnotized is in our own hands. We can blow it out and step out into the plain light of day. It's a matter of our choice. Period. The rest is theme and variations. We can stop trying to clutch, as if life or our happiness were a thing. As if happiness comes in a box tied up in a red ribbon with a neat little bow that we can just order off a shelf, and that we'll be unhappy if we can't get it. We can end such delusions.

We can't end sickness, old age, or death, but we can stop setting ourselves up for a fall. We can stop investing in an unrealistic outlook on them. We can face the fact that we won't live forever. Accumulating more and more stuff won't prevent that final day when we'll have to give it all back. (And if we *were* immortal, just imagine what our Visa bill would be!)

The only place we have in which we can live is *now*. The present is the only place that's ever available to us—and contains within it everything, if we let go and live it fully. Reality is staring us in the face, only we're too busy chasing rainbows to see it.

We can clear up two common stereotypes about Buddhism here:

- The Buddha didn't say all life is suffering. (What a drag that would be.) Rather, he got at the inevitability of suffering in such a way that to really understand it would enable anyone to be free of it.

- The Buddha didn't say anyone should cease desiring. As living beings we'll always desire water and air, comfort and kindness. What he did say was not to hang on to our desires, and thus get hung up. Rather, live life to the fullest. Find out thus what's important. And let be.

The Buddha taught a simple truth that isn't always easy to accept. We're like spiders caught in our own web. The Buddha taught that we can recognize the Three Poisons that fuel our running round and round in our self-created rat cage: greed (clinging desire), anger (thwarted desire), and delusion (ignorance of the way things are, which forms the basis of the other two and also gives birth to fear). Perhaps the ultimate delusion is that our happiness exists outside of ourselves, as if we're separate from the oneness of life. When we recognize and understand these are poisons we cling to, and then step aside, we find the door to the cage is open. Freedom is just a step away.

Remember Kisa Gotami, clutching her dead child to her breast, thinking it could still live. So, too, do we clutch our suffering to our own breast as if that's our identity, rather than awaken to what's unborn and will never die, our true nature.

Poor guy, seems like he'll just never learn. He's laboring under a common misconception that Buddhism means eliminating desire. But desires are a natural part of being alive. The Buddha said, "Don't hang on to them, and thus get hung up." Meanwhile, this poor dunce tries to learn this fact by repeating the words, rather than understanding their true meaning for himself, and living it. (When's the last time you felt like this?)

Drawing: Robert Crumb

The Buddha likened our delusion to a small child, home alone, playing with toys while the house is burning down. He invites us to stop and see the source of the fire and extinguish it, rather than feed it by clinging. Blowing out the candle of clinging to illusory concepts and seeing reality directly is called *nirvana*.

This Is

Nirvana represents the state of ultimate perfection, beyond dualism, beyond words. The Sanskrit word literally means "extinguishing": the extinction of duhkha, difficulties, pain; extinction of the three fires (or poisons) of ignorance, greed, and anger; liberation from **samsara,** the wheel of endless rebirth based on the karma of our actions; end of ignorance and delusion. Sometimes called "the other shore," it's attainable, here and now.

Rather than playing with sandcastles or doll's houses, we can face our pain, duhkha, realize its needlessness, and also forgive ourselves for having clung to it anyway. Then move on. It takes work, but we have only the rest of our lives to rediscover how precious each moment really is. To look at the world with the freshness and wonder of a child again, now with the maturity of a responsible adult—what a wonderful opportunity!

Hear and Now

"It is the nature of life that all beings will face difficulties; through enlightened living one can transcend these difficulties, ultimately become fulfilled, liberated, and free…. The way to realize this liberation and enlightenment is by leading a compassionate life of virtue, wisdom, and meditation. These three spiritual trainings comprise the teachings of the Eight-Fold Path to Enlightenment."

—Lama Surya Das

We're mature enough to know true happiness doesn't lie in our job title, nor our married name. Nor are we nothing, either. We're the unique crossroads of all the happenings within and outside us, of which we're unaware when we identify ourselves with our personal hang-ups. When we get all wound up and bound up in "self," we make a very small package. Awakening to our true nature, we find what vast luminosity we really are. The inherent buddha nature all beings innately possess. Our birthright. Holy Fact Number Three: Awakening, enlightenment, *is* possible. And Holy Fact Number Four: There *is* a path (*marga*, in Sanskrit).

The Fourth Fact of Life

We all can enjoy the true happiness called freedom. It's in our very being. But somehow, somewhere along the way, we forget, actually choose to forget. Buddha's here to remind us, showing us the way.

I live on a one-way street, and sometimes a car turns onto it, facing the wrong way. It's a great image of the first truth, duhkha. Then I see them turn around, when they notice the cars all pointing the other way, and sometimes even before another comes headed their way. This turning around, this awakening of mind, is like the fourth truth, the beginning of the Path. If Buddha were a road sign, he'd be "Stop. Look Around. Change Your Mind." The fourth and final Holy Truth is a guided tour of the way of harmony and love. The Path.

The Buddha blazed a trail for us. The fourth noble truth points to that trail. (And its map is entirely the subject of the very next chapter.) To some, it might seem at first glance like a tall order. Venturing into freedom might seem like stepping off a 10,000-foot pole. Only a complete idiot would do that, some might say. Yet others could argue that only a complete idiot would've gotten up on that pole in the first place.

This fourth holy fact reminds me of the monk Siddhartha saw, following sickness, old age, and death. The monk said nothing to him. Yet to the prince it was as if the monk were telling him, "You are not alone in your quest for truth. Come and see. There is a way." (Indeed, no one on a quest for awakening walks alone. The whole universe yearns for enlightenment.)

The Buddha ultimately found that different path. Not esoteric, but one anyone could travel on. Instead of the arduous pain of asceticism, one with self-discipline of body, spirit, and mind. "After trial and error," he tells us, "*this* is the path I've found. I say it's correct, and beneficial from start to finish. Please, come and try it and see for yourself."

It is up to each of us. You must take the path yourself in order to really see it. Over time, you might even be it.

Theme and Variations

Four facts of life not all of us learned as kids. Four truths to renew the nobility of our lives. Here are some variations on ways of appreciating their meaning, so you can begin to understand and apply them to your daily life. (This section is also a model for expanding on other doctrines throughout this book, on your own.)

Objective, scientific, and compassionate, like a good doctor, the Buddha made this compact list:

1. *Symptom:* duhkha, suffering

2. *Diagnosis:* trishna, ignorance, attachment

3. *Prognosis:* nirvana, liberation is possible

4. *Prescription:* marga, the Eightfold Path

Short and sweet. Like something jotted on those little prescription pads doctors use. Only it doesn't require anything external, like a drug. Rather, it's something to take home to study and use to cultivate our own natural curative powers.

We compared the Sangha to a clinic, where Dr. Buddha prescribes medicine (Dharma). Here, the Fourth Holy Truth (the Eightfold Path) prescribes a *whole* plan of treatment, for healing, not unlike the way a doctor might recommend a balanced diet, enough exercise, and rest. Otherwise, prescribed medication or surgery may not have a lasting effect.

Another way to embrace the Buddha in our own lives is to consider the teachings in terms of active verbs rather than static nouns. (Actually, Sanskrit words can work as verbs as much as nouns.) Buddha's a verb: to awaken; Dharma's being in harmony with what is; Sangha is gathering to follow the Way.

Yet another approach might be to phrase the four truths as questions. If you're familiar with the contemporary mystic Byron Katie, you'll hear how the four truths asked as questions resonate with the Work she teaches. Questions are really just a form of seeking. Once we've grown up, we forget how questions were such a reality to us as children. Some of that reality, we learn, is unprofitable craving. "Can I have that red car?" "Can I eat just dessert?" They're like the metaphysical questions that the Buddha wouldn't answer because they didn't further. But other kid questions are really profound, like, "What is that?" And "Who says?" Questions are a wonderful way of finding what's overlooked, of amplifying what's really juicy, and of bringing forth answers already within us. Indeed, another synonym for the Way, besides self-realization, is self-inquiry (same difference). Ask yourself:

Am I suffering? What's the situation? (Be brief.)

What keeps me from being happy? What am I attached to about my suffering? How do I identify myself with it? Is it real? Does it have a life of its own? Is it physically present here and now? Is it in my mind? Is it permanent?

What if I let go of my attachment to the situation that's not immediately present, and the self-image I identify with that situation? Would I be happy then?

How can I cultivate a better way of living that doesn't let me fall into the same trap I fell into all over again?

Self-inquiry is an essential method for making the teachings real for you. Try writing your answers; really process them within yourself. And have fun with it. One fun method is called Jukebox Mind. Think about song lyrics echoing the four truths. Can't get no satisfaction? (*Duhkha* is often translated as "unsatisfactory.") You try and you try? (Unless you get to the root, dissatisfaction will keep cropping up.) You can't always get what you want (by craving for stuff), but if you try (remember the teachings and test them in your own life) you can get what you need (nirvana). And there are jokes. *(Question:* Why don't Buddhists vacuum in corners? *Answer:* They don't have any attachments!) Whatever makes it real for you.

As Venerable Maha Ghosananda says: Slowly, slowly, step by step. As my grandmother would say: Get started, and keep at it.

> **This Is**
>
> The Sanskrit word **duhkha** (say *doo-kah*) means an axle that doesn't quite fit into the hub of a wheel. It's usually translated as suffering, but could also be "bumpy road." Or sour, unpleasant, or unsatisfactory. Also applicable are difficulty, pain, frustration, disturbed emotions, stress, anxiety, anguish, angst. *Ick!* (The grimace is extra.)

Why are these two people smiling? Maybe the Mona Lisa can't help but smile in the Buddha's presence. Each seems to have looked deeply into the heart of life and to invite us to do likewise. Each, in their own way, reminds us, "We've all known suffering. True happiness is the goal, the real accomplishment. Find it."

Leonardo da Vinci, Mona Lisa *[c. 1505–1514]. Paris, Musée du Louvre*. Buddha in Meditation, *Gongxian style. Grey limestone. Northern Wei Dynasty [386–535]. 95.3 cm. Honolulu Academy of Arts, Gift of Mrs. Charles M. Cooke, Sr. 1930 [3468].*

The Least You Need to Know

♦ Most all Buddhists agree on the core value of the Three Jewels and the Four Noble Truths.

♦ The first is the basic structure of Buddhism. The second is the basic teaching of Buddhism.

♦ The Three Jewels are the Buddha, the Dharma, and the Sangha.

♦ They are so valuable and solid, timely and true, we can take refuge in them.

♦ The Four Noble Truths deal with 1) the existence of suffering, 2) the origin of suffering, 3) the cessation of suffering, 4) the way to live without suffering.

Chapter 6

Buddha's Way: The Eightfold Path

In This Chapter

- Touring Buddhism as a path, the Middle Path, step by step
- Putting theory into practice for awareness, happiness, and well-being
- Joining body, spirit, and mind through conduct, wisdom, and meditation
- Understanding and practicing all eight aspects of the Path

The whole wheel of the Buddha's teachings, the complete pizza, is summed up in the Four Noble Truths and the Eightfold Path. The truths lay out his doctrine for you to understand. The path outlines his discipline, for you to practice.

In the neat way the Buddha interlinked the last Noble Truth and the first step on the Path, both theory and practice can inform and refine each other. Here's a path we can follow for ourselves right now. So we turn next to Buddha's thought in action—that we may activate it for ourselves, and learn by doing, and apply those insights. The simple awareness the path teaches can make us each a Buddha.

The Path

Sometimes a journey of 10,000 miles begins with a leaky tire or a broken fan belt. Sometimes it begins with just one step. The way of the Buddha has eight aspects— each an integral part. Each leads to all the others. Slowly, slowly, step by step.

Hear and Now

"The spiritual journey does not consist of arriving at a new destination where a person gains what he did not have, or becomes what he is not. It consists in the dissipation of one's own ignorance concerning oneself and life, and the gradual growth of that understanding which begins the spiritual awakening."

–Aldous Huxley

The Path is:

1. Right View

2. Right Thought

3. Right Speech

4. Right Action

5. Right Livelihood

6. Right Effort

7. Right Mindfulness

8. Right Concentration

"Right" is the traditional translation of what's literally "perfect" in Sanskrit, but I vary the interpretation in the chapter headings to encourage you to feel them for yourself. Here "right" doesn't imply that there's also a "wrong." Buddhism is not that judgmental. No dualities, remember? Good and bad still apply, but Buddhism also uses the words "skillful" and "unskillful," referring to *skillful means* that are, in themselves, conducive toward enlightenment. For example, recall how skillfully the Buddha taught Kisa Gotami when she brought her dead child to him. Perfect. Right on.

I've always liked "right" as a verb, as in "to restore." (This is vaguely akin to how a certain author I once knew used to reply when asked what he wrote: "I right wrongs.") Besides verbs, you could frame the eight steps as questions. "Am I viewing correctly? How would the Buddha view [such-and-such a situation]?" However you read them, they're yours to claim, own, and practice.

This may be the only teaching the Buddha ever wrote down, perhaps sketching it in the dirt with a stick and eight pebbles. A wheel is a very skillful means of traveling along. The spokes can be memorized in linear sequence, but the wheel is circular, with no top, no bottom. No beginning, no middle, no end. All eight spokes are needed to navigate the whole journey.

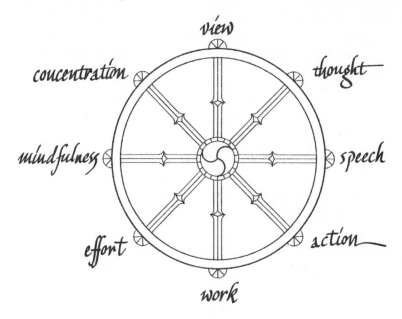

Likewise, you can write the steps down, as a personal memo to yourself. Memorize them, just eight words. *Exercise:* Take a blank sheet of paper and fold it into eighths. (Fold it in half, then in half the other way. Then fold it in half yet again. Voilà!) Unfolding it, you have eight little boxes, into which to write the name of each step of the path. Then fold the paper back up, and put it in your wallet or purse. Throughout the day, whenever you find yourself in a situation where one of the steps might present itself to you, write down a key word, a hindrance or an aid, a habit or a goal. For example, under "speech" you might write "gossip," or under "concentration" you might write "one-pointedness: getting to the bottom of things." Soon you'll see all eight in your everyday life. *Tip:* Each aspect of the Path isn't so much a destination "out there" somewhere, for us to align ourselves to, as innate abilities to cultivate, already within ourselves.

Tip: You'll notice the circle in our illustration has three subdivisions at the center. Integrating mind, body, and spirit, as one, the path can be broken down into *wisdom* (view and thought), *ethics* or "conscious conduct" (speech, action, work); and *meditation* (effort, mindfulness, concentration).

Connecting the Dots

Starting out, the path can be easily memorized as a series forming a step-by-step progression. First off, there's the introduction of this path already given in the Four Noble Truths: "There is a path." Like a doorway or hinge, the Fourth Noble Truth invokes the Eightfold Path. Reciprocally, the first step of the path, *view*, is a re-view of the Noble Truths—did we understand them? (View can also be translated as *understanding*.) The Four Truths are simple, yet the more we study them the more aspects of the Buddha's wisdom we can see in them.

Now, we could understand the Four Truths intellectually, without putting them into practice in order to change how we act in and perceive the world. So we must also have willingness and commitment to really take the journey. More like our conscious *intentions* than intellectual work, this link is called *thought*. (These first two links focus on the wisdom of the Path.)

What's next? Well, to put wisdom into practice in our lives, we need to conduct ourselves well. It's counterproductive to proceed with the best perspective and intentions, while still *saying* things that contradict the wisdom of our intent. Similarly, it's not skillful if we can express our wisdom perfectly but don't *do* what we say. So *word* and *deed* are important steps. Plus, at the end of the day, it matters how we put a roof over our heads and bread on the table. As followers of the Way, our job is to maintain our practice through our *work*; making a living, as they say. (These links focus on ethics, or conscious conduct.)

Okay. But a road doesn't travel on its own. So it takes diligence to follow through. My grandmother used to call it "elbow grease." With such *effort*, we can access the Buddha's teachings deep within ourselves through our meditational practices, be they Insight or Zen, Pure Land or Tibetan, a mix-and-match of traditions or a school with no name. So meditation means rolling up your sleeves and sticking to the task at hand, even if it's a labor of love, effortless effort. And meditation is a balance—between *mindfulness* and *concentration*, which are like a beam of light and a lens, respectively. It brings us tranquility and contentment, and lets us see clearly and deeply.

And so we come full circle again. Meditation grounds our wisdom from personal experience, which better informs our conduct—on and on, keeping the wheel turning round.

Tip: Take your time. Slowly, slowly, step by step. Don't feel you have to dive in and put in an eight-hour day spending an hour on each element. If your doctor recommended eight ways to change your diet—for instance, no salt, less caffeine, no fried foods, less red meat, and so on—you'd modify your diet gradually, so as not to throw your metabolism into a state of shock. (Spiritual as well as physical crash-courses might result in a kind of adrenaline rush at first, but without sustained benefit.) Instead, by gradual adjustment, all steps eventually become integrated and second nature.

The Buddhist medical model is *holistic*. We'll explore this further in Chapter 20, but for now we can note how, in medicine, a drug or surgery might make a symptom vanish but may not necessarily eradicate the root cause. Holistic medicine looks at the root. And it's found that with a balance of stress reduction, exercise, diet, meditation, and medication, each of these things can have a *synergistic* effect. Synergy means that in interaction each element has a greater power than each would acting alone.

This Is

Holistic health treats the whole person–body, mind, and spirit. A holistic outlook focuses on patterns interacting to form a whole, rather than breaking things down into parts and ana-lyzing each piece separately (the mechanistic outlook). The word "holistic" shares a common Old English root with "hale," "heal," "health," "holy," and "whole."

Wisdom. (On the left, a block-style version; a more flowing, cursive version on the right.) One interpretation of the Chinese word sees the upper component as a broom, the middle as a hand, taking hold of the broom, sweeping the heart, below. In this view, understanding or wisdom isn't an accumulation of knowledge, but rather the shedding of ignorance. A clean-ing and clearing away. A clean sweep; an open mind.

Calligraphy: Kazuaki Tanahashi

We saw a Buddhist outlook on holism in the previous chapter, when we considered how the Three Gems inter-reflect each other. So, too, your practicing just one single step of the Way fully is to ultimately come to practice the others. Let's now look at each a bit deeper.

This is the character for "heart" in Chinese and Japanese. It depicts a human heart, with chambers and aorta. It's also the character for "mind." So here we see mind and body as one. The equivalent word in Tibetan has this sense, as well. (On the left, a block-style version; a more flowing, cursive version on the right; both straight from the heart.)

Calligraphy: Kazuaki Tanahashi

Perfect View: You See!?

There is a sense of mind in this step and the next, and throughout Buddhism, requiring a word of explanation. When the Buddha speaks of *mind*, he isn't referring to intellect. As the calligraphy here conveys, our mind is one with our heart. When you experience a change from a dark mood to a light one, and ask yourself what changed, I think you might agree it's a change of mind.

Hear and Now

"Mind is forerunner of action, foremost of deeds. Everything's made up of mind. If your mind is polluted, sorrow will follow, as the wheels trail the heels of an ox …. If your mind is pure, happiness will ensue, the way your shadow trails along wherever you go."

–The Buddha

The French author Marcel Proust wrote, "The real voyage of discovery consists not in seeking new landscapes, but in having new eyes." Thoreau echoes this when he says, "Only that day dawns to which we're awake." Are we just looking, or seeing attentively? Is our mind awake? How's our *view?* Viewing ourselves and our impact in the world aright, having a proper outlook on life, means seeing things as they are. Not as we might wish, imposing our conditions and projections, but unconditionally, *without attachment,* to concepts or preconceptions. Starting out, at the gate, the Buddha shows us the Four Noble Truths: but do we understand?

The Four Noble Truths cleanse us of ignorance, and enable us to experience What Is. Just being in the moment. Attentive. The noble truths open our eyes, and the eightfold path trains them—that we may see with the wisdom of a sage, the compassion of a beloved grandparent, and the wonder of a child. If we understand and maintain a wholesome outlook we'll have a perfect view. Every seat is the best seat in the house.

> ### Along the Path
>
> Take a blank sheet of paper and write on it with big, clear letters, "Are you SURE?" Tack it up to a wall where you'll see it regularly, such as at work. If the ringing of your phone sounds like an alarm, then you might answer nervously. Are you sure it's a danger signal? Prevent unnecessary anxiety and pain by examining your attitude, again and yet again. Less stress.

Perfect Thought: We Are What We Think

Thought here carries the sense of motive, intention, attitude, mind-set, as well as commitment. How we think about our path will color our journey. (Please check in your mental luggage at the door before you embark upon the Path.)

For example, consider the brain as both a transmitter and a receiver. It sifts and interprets sense data about the world, and coordinates our actions within that world, which actions in turn help to shape it. This creates a circular feedback loop. As computer programmers say, "Garbage in, garbage out." And, conversely, a positive outlook multiplies the good in life.

People understand this who follow the stock market, which rests on people's perceptions. Events create perceptions. And perceptions, in turn, cause people to react and create new events. For a real dark example, consider paranoia. Like a self-fulfilling prophecy, if I walk around with a look of suspicion, sure enough, folks will lift their eyebrows, looking at me askance, and so I'll start muttering to myself, which behavior causes people to talk about me behind my back, and you see it's a needless, self-created bummer. True, we're all interconnected; paranoia looks at that fact through the wrong end of the telescope. The same holds for fear, anger, jealousy, and the whole nine yards of ways we get in our own way.

We suffer because we *think* we'll be happy by possessing things we lust after, but which only create more dissatisfaction, because they never change our misdirected thought patterns. Thoughts traditionally to be avoided are greed (want want want), ill will (aversion), and fear (ignorance). Pure poison. Similarly, if we think Buddhism will provide an escape from commitment, or a magic bullet, or a means of getting back at our parents, then forget about it. Yet we all come to the path with our residue of pain, so it takes continual self-examination to put out the fires and embers of suffering. To free ourselves, we check our mind-set, reevaluate our motives, and see what works, continually. It's a wise model for growth.

Thought as attitude. You can almost hear the cogitation in the Rodin sculpture, thinking with every muscle and fiber right down to his very toes. The Buddha or bodhisattva sits straight, enjoying his breathing. Whatever thought comes is welcomed, like hearing the chirp of a happy bird.

Auguste Rodin, The Thinker *(1880). 79″ × 51¼″ × 55¼″. The Rodin Museum, Philadelphia: Gift of Jules E. Mastbaum.* Bodhisattva Maitreya in Pensive Pose. *Korean National Museum, Seoul. Silla Period. Early seventh century. Gilt bronze. 90.8 cm.*

Tip: From time to time, we stop and return to the fundamental wisdom of understanding our motive for Buddhism. We might catch ourselves "seeking enlightenment," which is a set-up for a fall: a conceptual dualism separating "self" from "enlightenment," as if we didn't have innate Buddha nature already.

Attitude is all. While my ultimate goal *is* enlightenment, I can only attain it by dis-identifying myself with concepts, conditionings, and cravings, no attachments to them, so that enlightenment may happen of itself. That is, I can't enlighten myself any more than I can surprise myself. Rather, through the discipline of the path I am laying a strong foundation, with ample space and wholesome conditions for that chance to take place. Only then can I discover that I've already arrived.

Right Action: Good Karma

The traditional definition of right action is a series of road signs, traditionally known as precepts, as we'll explore in depth in the next chapter. Right action means acting out of love, not causing suffering by our acts. For now, we might observe three things about action.

First, the Buddhist values of action aren't based on any code handed down from on high. Nor are we being judged from a celestial throne. Rather, morality here is a matter of what can skillfully further the awakening of mind, the opening of the heart; and what doesn't. At the core of this sense is the notion of moral cause and effect, called karma, which is a personal responsibility. Your yesterday affects today and what you do today affects tomorrow. Karma includes speech as well as deeds, and even thoughts and feelings. Scientists have zeroed in on the physics of thought so finely they can rig up a prosthetic limb that can be operated by mere thought. Thought equals action, whether we act on it or not.

Second, we're free to act, but we're not entitled to the fruit of our action. That is, if we're really present to ourselves and what's in front of our nose, in the moment, we do each thing fully, without clinging to any outcome. Hit each nail on the head, blam!, then move on.

And, third, it might be more useful to think in terms of enlightened actions rather than of enlightenment as any concrete thing. Everything's a perpetual process, a work-in-progress. So action is as much a factor of enlightenment as are meditation and wisdom.

Say the Word and It Will Happen: Perfect Speech

As noted, *speech* is considered an action. The Buddha asks us to listen as we speak. Traditional habits to watch and learn to refrain from include:

- Lies
- Slander
- Harsh words
- Frivolous speech

How often do we put people down, or put people off, or put people on hold through our speech? How often do we gossip about things for which we don't have any first-hand evidence? I believe words can create thunderstorms and earthquakes, as well as cool breezes and clear summer days. (Just say the word.) We'll explore speech in more depth in the next chapter.

More Than a Job: Wholesome Work

We put our money where our mouth is by our *work*. We can become a monk or nun, and learn to circulate other people's money. Or we can earn our own bread. Professions traditionally deemed unsuitable for Buddhists include trading in:

- Arms
- Human beings (slavery, prostitution)

- ◆ Flesh (breeding animals for slaughter)

- ◆ Intoxicants and poison

Today we might say, "Don't harm the ecosystem, don't exploit nature or people." But the choices in modern times haven't gotten any easier. For example, is it breeding an animal for slaughter when animals are used for medical experimentation which might save lives? Such complexity of contemporary transactions can make us even more aware of traditional values. (More on work follows in Chapter 17 as well as the next chapter.)

Proper Effort: Just Do It

When laid out on the wheel, *effort* is directly opposite from thought. In that context, intent's where we're coming from, effort's where we're going. It's our direction, our pole star—and keeping at it. A sangha and teacher are important, but effort starts with us.

I've seen people who've quit the practice after a year and a half, saying, "No hard feelings, but nothing happened." Well, a plant won't grow just by holding some roots against a rock. Besides the right conditions, it takes effort and follow-through, which sometime require active intuition and so seem effortless effort. Case in point: Martine Bachelor, now a founding teacher at Sharpham College of Buddhist Studies and Contemporary Enquiry, had studied at a Buddhist monastery in Korea for ten years. When she went for her regular visit to a great Zen master, and asked him how best to practice, he said, "I think you already know." Well, this non-answer wasn't at all what she'd wished for. But when she got back to her room, and sat, and meditated, she realized she did know. She knew what she had to do and followed through.

Like winning the grand-stakes lottery, Buddhism has tales of people who become totally enlightened—*Shazam!*—at the drop of a coconut. More often than not, out in the world rather than in a temple. But it usually takes preparation. The Buddha sat for six years in the wilderness. The elimination of self-torture wasn't a cue for spiritual laziness. Remember, among the Buddha's last words were "Seek your enlightenment *with diligence*." (Meaning: "You can do it, too—so get busy!") And if the Buddha were alive today, he'd be that person sitting way over in the back and to one side in the meditation hall … still sitting, practicing …

Complete Mindfulness: Intelligent Alertness

Awareness is a primary characteristic distinguishing us from animals; we're warm and aware we're warm, hungry but also aware of it, feeling sexy and aware of it, and so on. In the evolution from slime to worm to ape, you could imagine awareness as an extra fillip, a little doodling or filigree that nature tossed into our human makeup. A jazzy extra resonance, as author-sage Alan Watts once pointed out, like singing in the shower to hear our voice echo off the wet tiles that may serve no utilitarian purpose but is fun to do anyway. But being aware of our awareness is a major evolutionary leap—as author and meditation teacher Wes Nisker spryly puts it, "mindfulness is the opposable thumb of consciousness." That is, we can aim our awareness (and evolution) toward a direction, and change our course. Our intelligent self-awareness composes what Buddha called *mindfulness*.

When the Buddha quit fasting and began to look at himself in relationship to his environment with clearer vision, he focused on each of his natural activities, like breathing, with mindfulness. When breathing, he concentrated his mind on his breath and nothing else. Not trying to change it, as in yoga, just observing. As he did so, he became aware in finer detail of the many minute processes that make up "breathing," and saw how his clinging caused duhkha, suffering. (Try holding your breath.) Letting go, and letting his breath simply be, he saw how, in and of itself, it was perfect. Nirvana. He'd been too tied up by tight self to notice.

> **This Is**
>
> The Sanskrit word for **mindfulness,** *smriti,* means "to remember." We become intimate with life when we remember to be aware; to be here and now. Mindfulness is being fully attentive to things as they are, in and of themselves, moment to moment. And if this awareness feels splendid, even miraculous, remember it's your birthright.

We're all aware in varying degrees. To be mindful means our minds are fully focused on what's at our feet. Right now, if I stop writing I can be more aware of my posture, the clothes I'm wearing, sounds outside the window, my breathing, thoughts coming and going, and so on. (I only imagine my editor's eagle eye over my shoulder, or what readers might look like.) If I just focus my awareness on one thing, like sounds, for example, I feel my innate awareness grow as I become aware of the phenomenal, rhythmic, continuous symphony of life's natural, unnoticed soundtrack, moment to moment. I might notice, too, how my mind might be drawn toward some sounds and repelled by others. "Birds, good! Garbage truck, bad!" (Actually, they're both quite interesting.) Or not hearing others because I've branded them neutral, like the faint hum of room tone. In so doing, I'm also noticing my mind, and can apply the Four Noble Truths to look deeper into how my mind makes knee-jerk judgments and in so doing colors my world. We'll come back to this technique of observation in more detail in Chapter 11. But here's a bit more foundation.

Buddha taught a method of building a strong practice of meditation, in his sutra called the Four Establishments of Mindfulness (*Satipatthana*). He asks us to shine the light of mindfulness in the following directions:

1. Body
2. Feelings
3. Mind
4. Phenomena (objects of mind)

At any given time, whatever we're doing, *without judging*, we can be mindful of our body (comfort or discomfort, being in motion or at rest, quality of in-breath, out-breath), grounding our practice. Centering. We can be mindful of sense impressions and feelings (pleasant, unpleasant, happy, sad, angry, joyous), and no longer be swept away by their tide but, rather, sit on their banks, watching them flow out to sea. And we can make our mind the focus of our mindfulness (noticing if it's calm or craving "stuff," caring or angry, opinionated or open) as well as the phenomena to which our mind relates (such as the object of our care or craving, opinion or openness). Awareness of pure awareness is ... a taste of nirvana.

Leaves from the Bodhi Tree

A passing stranger encountered some Buddhist monks in a forest. He asked what they were doing. A monk stopped to explain that they were Buddhists and that he and his fellow monks were cutting wood. "Wait. I cut wood, too, for my fire," said the man. "I don't see anything extraordinary about that." Well, sir," the monk replied, "when we cut wood, we know we're cutting wood. We don't cut wood in order to build a fire. We cut wood in order to cut wood." The monk smiled, and added, "If we can't cut wood, how then can we build a fire?" Then he resumed his work, and the man went on his way.

Total Concentration: Hitting the Nail on the Head

Just as wisdom is a balance of attitude and understanding, meditation is a balance between mindfulness and *concentration* working in tandem. Concentration is like a lens lit by a powerful light; mindfulness observes an object through the lens. Attention and awareness.

To Westerners, concentration normally implies Rodin's thinker: furrowing your brow, beads of sweat run off the bridge of your nose, and so on. The Buddhist meaning of total concentration is, rather, nondualist awareness. The practitioner might begin by concentrating his or her mind on an object, as if threading a needle, but object and mind (and concentration) become fused at a common center, a single point.

Hear and Now

"Concentration and mindfulness go hand in hand in the job of meditation. Mindfulness directs the power of concentration .... Concentration furnishes the power by which mindfulness can penetrate into the deepest level of mind .... Too much awareness without calm to balance it will result in a wildly over-sensitized state similar to abusing LSD. Too much concentration without a balancing ratio of awareness will result in the 'Stone Buddha' syndrome."

–Venerable Henepola Gunaratana

Buddhist concentration is often described as "one-pointed." Like a hammer hitting the nail on the head, this one-pointed attention is fixed on neither hammer nor nail but the concentrated *thwack!*, straight through in a single stroke. Hammering a nail while thinking about dinner, on the other hand, can be an invitation to a swollen thumb. The Sanskrit word for concentration, *samadhi*, implies a bit more than focus: it contains mindfulness, a steadiness and equanimity that can also be described as *peace*.

And the Way awaits. You *are* the path.

One foot on the path opens it everywhere, all around, and within. Enjoy the journey.

The Least You Need to Know

♦ Buddhist practice (the Eightfold Path) and Buddhist theory (the Four Noble Truths) mutually support each other.

♦ The eight steps are easy to memorize, and can be grouped in three. *Wisdom:* view (or understanding) and thought (or intention, motive). *Conduct:* speech, action, livelihood. *Meditation:* effort, mindfulness, concentration.

♦ Meditation is only one aspect of Buddhist practice, along with wisdom and conscious conduct (ethics). They both build upon and feed into each other.

♦ You needn't practice the steps in any order, nor all at once. Develop each element gradually but steadily.

♦ Each step is an end unto itself. Indeed, in everything you do, just do that—fully aware of your doing that and nothing else. And enjoy!

Chapter 7

Conscious Conduct: Precepts for a Path with a Heart

In This Chapter

- ◆ Reverence for life
- ◆ Trustworthiness and generosity
- ◆ Sexual respect
- ◆ Loving speech and deep listening
- ◆ Mindful consumption
- ◆ Your personal precepts

To live the loving Middle Way of the Buddha of full attention all the time, wouldn't you want to have guidelines for carrying on the practice in the world? Well, the early Buddhists laid down a set based on their own experiences, for daily, active cultivation, called the precepts. The precepts reveal how deeply interwoven we are with our environment. As an ethical framework they lead to enlightenment: to enlightened ways of living.

As we've just seen, meditation and wisdom can change the way we go about our lives. Conscious conduct can, in turn, further illumine our meditation and the wisdom we gain thereby, and furnish them with a solid basis in experience. Since the time of the Buddha, the precepts have preserved the continuity and vitality of the sangha. Indeed, initiation into many Buddhist sanghas, the beginning of formal practice, occurs through transmission of the precepts. You take refuge in them, along with the Three Jewels. And you don't have to sign up for them all at once, just the ones you're comfortable with. Anyway, just practicing one deeply will lead you eventually to all the others.

Actually, for monastics there are 254 precepts. Some schools have 58, for everyone; others, 16. So there are different ways to cut up the ethical pie. You could boil them all down to one, the Golden Rule. These precepts are cast from that same gold. The basic principles underlying them resonate with those of any religion, yet you might notice different emphases you could apply to your own root tradition. Learn them. Practice them. Meditate on them. And see for yourself. They're the foundation of a path with heart.

To Not Kill: Reverence for Life

This precept applies to not only other human beings but all beings. Such reverence for life, manifesting in myriad life forms, isn't unique to Buddhism. It's essential, for example, to Native American spirituality, exemplified by its wealth of marvelous tall tales starring coyotes, otters, spiders, salmon, eagles, and bears, as well as two-leggeds. By broadening the horizon to embrace all creation, the negative tense of "not-killing" subtly flips to positive: what a missionary physician stationed in Africa named Albert Schweitzer termed "reverence for life."

This Is

Central to Buddhist, Hindu, and Jain spirituality is the concept of **ahimsa** (Sanskrit, meaning "to do no harm; reverence for life"). Jain followers take great lengths to observe ahimsa. Monks filter water so as not to consume microbes. Priests wear white gauze masks so as not to breathe an insect in, and don't walk at night so as not to step on a worm.

Look: A lion with a lamb, a leopard and a cow, living together so peaceably! This is the first of many paintings of the peaceable kingdom prophesied by Isaiah (11:6–9). It was rendered by a gifted Quaker minister and visionary named Edward Hicks. In this, his first of many versions, its creatures are the most playful, its sky the most luminous.

Edward Hicks, American (1780–1849), The Peaceable Kingdom. Oil on canvas, 47.6 cm × 59.7 cm. © The Cleveland Museum of Art, 2001, Gift of the Hanna Fund, 1945.38.

Every "Shalt-Not" Has Its "Shall"

Seeing not-killing rephrased as reverence for life, we might pause to consider this range of potential to all the precepts. The precepts offer both a negative and a positive response to the human condition. Do's and don'ts. One reason they're phrased restrictively recognizes that humanity is prone to and already has a head start on bad habits. Yet, though they may sound like restrictions, they promote freedom. A positive outcome results If I refrain from harmful behavior, everyone will be much happier, myself included.

Eliminate negatives? Accentuate positives? Embrace the fuzzy in-betweens of the Middle Way! The path begins with our using our natural capacity for mindful awareness. While every "Shalt Not" has its "Shall," there aren't any preprinted road maps. Each is up to you to determine.

Vegetarianism

Food is so important, it has a chapter of its own in this smart person's guide. Suffice it to say for now that Buddhists are often vegetarians for ethical reasons (reverence for life). If you eat mindfully, attentively, communing with a beet or carrot, for example, it tells you what it means to live inside the dark earth, growing so moist, compact, and sweet. And that it had no mother or father who'll miss it if you eat it.

But it may be impossible to eat meat as mindfully on a consistent basis, unless you have a health need (in which case you might consider fish, or chicken). Perhaps you might leaven the fact by choosing the healthiest meat, allowed to range and feed instead of supermarket cattle, pumped full of chemicals, cramped up in a pen. Killed compassionately, instead of being chained on an assembly-line kill floor, sensing its fate, adrenaline of fright flooding its bloodstream. In so doing, you might learn how animals are raised, killed, and processed these days, reading John Robbins or Eric Schlosser, either of whom might make you reconsider the whole deal.

Abortion

Sooner or later, abortion comes up in any extensive discussion of the first precept. Dharma can compassionately see the suffering either way. Japanese Buddhists have evolved a very interesting and unique practice. Many Japanese Buddhist temples will conduct a funeral service for an aborted or stillborn fetus (in Japanese "water baby"). Zen master and teacher Robert Aitken notes, "It's given a posthumous Buddhist name, and thus identified as an individual, however incomplete, to whom we can say fare-well. With this ceremony, the woman is in touch with life and death as they pass through her existence, and she finds that such basic changes are relative waves on the great ocean of true nature which is not born and does not pass away."

Jizo is the Japanese Buddhist patron saint of children and travelers. These stone Jizo images in Chichibu, Japan, are accompanied by umbrellas, shawls, and toys to express compassion for deceased children and the unborn, as well as prayers for their well-being in the world beyond.

Photo: William R. LaFleur, from Liquid Life: Abortion and Buddhism in Japan *(Princeton University Press, 1992)*

To Not Steal: Trustworthiness and Generosity

This precept is also very simple and forthright. And we can also see its awareness pervading many things we might not have considered, and in new ways.

You don't have to be a thief to consider the precepts in your own life. Imagine you're at an airport to see your best friend off. All flights are running late. The area where you've been waiting has filled with people, then emptied out, then filled up again. You notice that aluminum suitcase someone's parked in the seat next to you is still there, and the owner's never come back. Okay, your friend is curious—and the brass tabs don't seem to be locked.

Imagine your surprise as you open it up and see the suitcase is packed with neat stacks of $100 bills. You close it, quickly, and look around to see if anyone else saw. Sure, it's a perfect setup for a nail-biting suspense thriller—but what would *you* do? Give it all away at the airport, on the spot? Give it to Lost and Found, leaving the temptation to them?

> **Hear and Now**
>
> "Where you did not sow, do not reap."
>
> —African proverb, Igala (Nigeria)
>
> "Because what is yours is not yours, how then can you regard what is not yours as yours?"
>
> —Talmud

Or would you split it with your friend? Say you found out it wasn't counterfeit. Would you still wonder about its karma? Maybe it was payment for some black-market transaction. Or blackmail … or a ransom … or a bribe …. What if you and your friend decide to split it in thirds, giving a third to a charity? Which charity? Do either of you have a charitable cause? Have you examined charities to find one where your donation will be put to good use, without it greasing bureaucratic wheels or lining somebody else's pockets? And so the uncertainty widens even further, and the money still sits there, like radioactive plutonium. (Would a lawyer be the solution?)

Fiction; make-believe. Yet don't we encounter similar situations every day, implicated in an invisible nexus of property and poverty, credit and cash, without even thinking? To drive the point home, here's one more example. As I write, there's an apple on my desk. Because I have this apple, you don't. Very simple.

But maybe you do happen to have an apple right now. What then? Well, there must be other people who don't have the apples that you and I do—the whole world, in fact. So, like I say, if you have an apple, I don't. Suddenly, world hunger stares us straight in the face. We have apples; they don't. The problem is simple: The poor don't have enough—and the rich have more than enough. It's interesting how money and property make the interconnectedness of all things more vivid to our imagination. Given the awareness, the challenge is to live simpler, consuming less needless stuff, cherishing what one already has, and being generous.

I know, all this might imply that everyone should immediately donate their posses-sions to the poor. That might even be true. But if we give all our things away then the poor would have things that everyone else would no longer have, and the cycle of poverty wouldn't be broken. That would violate the Middle Way of harmony and bal-ance. So we learn to not take more than we need, and not to take what's not ours, and to share what we have with those who don't, without going in want ourselves.

This means "recycling sta-tion" or "recycled product." The three arrows represent Recycle, Reuse, and Reduce waste.

These are timeless truths, but the world seems to be presently suffering from amnesia. What's Buddhist, here, is emphasis on …

◆ Compassionate awareness of property's potential for suffering or happiness.

◆ Consideration of the karma created by the use to which things are put.

◆ The interconnectedness of all deeds.

What matters is weighing pros and cons, and finding your Middle Way. For example, if we stop and consider the potential political correctness or incorrectness of all our purchases, it seems hard to do anything except to stay at home and count our fingers. But, as we've seen, thoughts are deeds. And with consciousness can come consciousness raising, the next step in any tipping of the scales of karma. When I use a computer, for instance, I'm aware of how its miraculous silicon chips are often manufactured under very harsh conditions, often by immigrant women. And it results in toxic waste byproducts. What can I do? I don't condone suffering or potential environmental degradation, yet I am mindful of the suffering that is still part of my landscape. And now you know, too. (More on these questions when we get to the last precept.)

Sexual Restraint: Respect, Intimacy, Trust, and Responsibility

All religious orders are vulnerable to human fallibility. Hence precepts. We come now to one fallibility that has invariably generated scandal, cover-ups, and further scandal, in all religious orders: sexual irresponsibility. Is it any surprise, given the power of priesthood, the trust in taking refuge, the intimacy of meditation, and the joyful friendliness of spiritual community, that sexual abuse should be of concern? Which is to say that abused sexuality is no less unconscionable when it occurs within such conditions, and can take generations for the wounds it inflicts throughout the community to heal.

Pardon my French, but in the common parlance of today the Thou Shalt Not here means to not screw around. That is, don't mess with the sexual surge that shaped us and throbs within us still. It's an elemental force comparable to the intertwining of yin and yang. Daily, we interact with physical reality and energy fields in ways that are sexual although we don't usually call them such. This precept, then, acknowledges the fundamental yin-yang dance of male and female and calls us to focus our mindfulness upon it, to let that energy flow skillfully.

Our society's obsessed with sexuality, as you'll see from flipping through the tabloids at supermarket checkout stands. Look, too, at today's ads. In our consumer culture, sex sells—everything from face cream to cars. Since advertisers aren't known for hiring models that look like my Aunt Ida in Jersey, some American women have starved themselves silly to emulate shadow-thin models. And sometimes when a husband and wife look at each other in bed and don't see dream models, they roll over and lick their wounds of suffering self—and, presumably, go out the next day and invest in something unessential, to fill that void. The fact of the matter is, superficial social conventions can't fully answer the complexities of life, and so suffering inevitably continues.

Hear and Now

"… our social conception has managed to supply shelters of every sort, for, as it was disposed to take love-life as a pleasure, it had also to give it an easy form, cheap, safe and sure, as public pleasures are…. For one human being to love another: that's perhaps the most difficult of all our tasks, the ultimate, the last test and proof, the work for which all other work is but preparation."

—Rainer Maria Rilke

Love is not a toy. Respect is key; respecting Self and Other as really no different. No dualism. With that foundation comes true intimacy. This is a core experience in Buddhism. Respecting life, all life forms, we enter into the heart of creation, enjoying a greater intimacy with life. When two people have a long-term commitment to each other, then sexual intimacy can be one of life's most profound human experiences.

To Not Lie: Deep Listening and Loving Speech

The Ten Commandments don't directly address lying, per se, but rather false witness. Yet it's there. The Talmud (Hebrew books of biblical commentary) say that no one should talk one way with his or her lips and think another way in his or her heart. This is so universal it hardly sounds any different in, say, Taoism: "Do not assert with your mouth what your heart denies."

To lie is to automatically be dishonest about everything—to be indifferent to the truth. The Buddha is very clear about this. (Ready?) He says, "A person is born with an axe in his mouth. He whose speech is unwholesome cuts himself with an axe." Talk about having a sharp tongue! Putting someone else down, we put ourselves down. But the reverse is true, too. That is, when we say "love" in all sincerity, we actually bring love into the world.

True, Buddhism is aware of the inability of words to describe the truth we *are*. Yet, from a nondualist approach we can find our Middle Way between speech and silence. I've expressed this third precept in terms of both listening and speaking. So if some people say silly things, you might say they've forgotten how to listen—to themselves and others. Are you a good listener? Consider the depth of active engagement truly implied in the act, through the Chinese word for listening, combining four components: eyes as well as ears, plus undivided attention, and heart-mind. Listen …

Bearing Witness

There's no secret to the craft of writing: it's reading as well as writing. I began by reading what others had written, to get a sense of my own voice. And now I re-read what I've written, and rewrite what doesn't sound right to me; then I show it to other readers for feedback, then editors, and so on. So words always imply two activities: writing and reading; listening as well as speaking. Plus an audience (a word that comes from "audio," to hear).

And the other trick is knowing an intention will be transformed during the act of writing, and so being open to listening to that happening. Another word for it might be "bearing witness": not writing to tell someone what you already know, but doing so to see what you think.

To *bear witness* is a form of deep listening, leaving behind preconceptions or expectations. As a person who uses words yourself, you're probably aware of your Inner Judge, right? You know, the one who says, "Who *is* this guy?! What's he asking *me* for? Sheesh! Let's get on with the show!" This voice judges everything, makes lists of likes and dislikes, and never forgets. Meanwhile, life awaits us, unconditionally.

To turn down the volume on your internal Judge Jim or Judge Judy, you only need to become aware of that inner soundtrack; roof-brain chatter. You're constantly sifting through your experience (we all do), commenting on it like a movie reviewer talking to his- or herself in a theater ("Liked that: two thumbs up!" "Now why'd that happen? That was all wrong!" and "Uh-oh! Boring part coming up!"). And it's always past or future, reviewing or rehearsing, never present tense.

This Is _____

"When you go to **bear witness,** it means that you go with no preconceived notions about what you'll see and what will happen…. Bearing witness means to have a relationship…. Out of bearing witness, out of that relationship, a healing arises. In what form, through what activity or event, through what person, I have no idea."

—Bernie Glassman

One way to be in the present without judgment is to just witness it. Right now, I pause to look out my window, and bear witness to how the misty morning fog makes the buildings look more vivid. I bear witness to the unseen bird in the tree outside my window, its song mimicking the morning's mood and my own. I bear witness to life. Try it yourself, anytime. Stop and *listen* to the life where you're living, as all of life, right now. What keeps us from being aware 360° all around is our inner narrator, who fades down only when we shift attention from everything being our story to the more expansive reality of What Is—things as they are, in and of themselves—seemingly without limit.

Sometimes when I overhear two people talking, I get the impression they're playing verbal tennis. The rules are: Person A speaks for three minutes, then Person B gets to speak for three minutes, then it's A's turn again. Talking *at* each other, they're listening with their mouth, not their heart. I once participated in a workshop in which Joan Halifax Roshi introduced an exercise in bearing witness which provided a healthy, potent alternative. We broke up into twos and sat facing each other. My job was to make myself as transparent as I possibly could, dropping all my masks and just manifesting my deepest, truest nature to my partner. As I did so, my partner did the same for me. In silence, looking into each other's open face, we gave our undivided attention to the Buddha nature we sensed. Then we each took turns telling the other what we experienced, with the same awareness. Then we took turns telling the group, and listening to everyone else. There was a common feeling of compassion and mutuality.

It is said that Kuan Yin, the bodhisattva embodying compassion, can *see* the sounds of human suffering. Kuan Yin's Chinese name has two components: "gaze" (regard) and "sound." It is said she became enlightened through hearing.

If you believe in God, try imagining sometime you're a spy from heaven, acting as God's eyes and ears. Some Christian sects have maintained that life as we know it is what the Creator sees when looking into us. If the beginning was the Word, rather than argue over the wording, we might begin to hear It—whatever it happens to be, right now, clear as a bell. (The word is … love.)

Loving Speech

Speech invites listening. They both create karma. I think of Claude Anshin Thomas, a helicopter crew chief during the American war in Vietnam, and his karma, for example. Now a Zen priest, in 1998 he embarked on a peace pilgrimage across America. By foot. In some cities, he and his companions were about to be run out of town until dialogue began, and then they were invited to dinner instead. Midway in his journey, a media photographer approached him and asked, "If you don't mind, I'd like you to stand beside that tree so I can shoot you." Without a word, Claude just walked away. I hope the photographer eventually heard within himself why. (The prize word was "shoot.")

It's interesting to stop and notice how the very words we use imply certain values and color our views. When we become mindful of all the baggage we carry around, it's useful to smile at these assumptions and realize how they've been along for the ride, too. Doing so would be practicing Right View.

In my own profession, I pause and try to substitute "due date" instead of the word "deadline." (During the Civil War, at Andersonville, a borderline was formed of prisoners who'd tried to run away and were shot.) Nor do I wish for my writing to knock my audiences dead. (I'd prefer my readers might just levitate an inch or two off the ground now and then.) Another speech temptation my profession's prone to is gossip: who's up, who's down, who fired who, etc. Maybe you've indulged in it, too. Gossip's a common red flag indicating that loving speech is absent. My dictionary defines gossip as trivial *rumor*. Even positive gossip can be secondhand information, and usually about someone not present in the moment. Loving speech is here and now, or else it's nowhere—which makes it a meditation (effortless effort, one-pointed concentration, mindfulness), as are all the precepts. The opportunities occur daily. Yet a recent survey found, alas, that working couples spend four minutes a day talking to each other with concentrated attention; a typical parent and child engage in meaningful conversation for only 20 minutes a week.

Language is the oldest form of human technology, and reveals our connection to the entire universe. Speech can be a great meditation. Listening to … and saying … each … word … with … love.

Mindful Consumption: Proper Diet for Transformation

In a strict Theravadin sense, this precept means no alcohol. Period. Alcohol can not only interfere with the practice, by releasing inhibitions while clouding the mind, it could lead a practitioner to then proceed to break all the other precepts—killing, rape, and so on.

Where's the Middle Way here? Recognition that abstinence forgoes pleasures on the one hand, but harmful possibilities, on the other. Thus awareness of karmic implications. If I drink just a drop at dinner, then I'm acting as a role model for others, some of whom might not be able to stop at just a drop, or unable to "hold their liquor." It's like the opposite of the minimal amount of food the Buddha first ate following his asceticism. Here just a few drops may not nourish but rather destroy.

Altered States? Or Altered Traits?

In San Francisco, back in the mid-1960s, invariably somebody high on LSD from the Haight-Ashbury neighborhood would think they'd attained *satori*, Zen enlightenment, and so would trek down to the newly-opened Zen monastery nearby, knock on the door, demand to see the abbot, and try to engage in some verbal Dharma dueling, for which Zen is famous. (Such as "All things return to the One. So what does the One return to?") A later survey found over half of white baby-boomer Buddhists had come to the path following chemical experimentation, post-hippies now ready to discipline themselves to access their minds without psychedelics. (*Psychedelic* means "mind manifesting.") Even today, some people pack recreational drugs for a Buddhist retreat.

Are drugs helpful or harmful to the Way? This question's still being debated in the Western Buddhist community. Some say that intoxicants means only toxic substances. A very useful distinction to make here is between altered states and altered traits. That is, even if a drug could externally induce an enlightened state, it wears off. (And the come-down can take its toll.) It's like someone who attends a weekend retreat and comes back with a new hair-do, a new name, and says they're a totally new person. Only time will tell. Self-transformation takes daily discipline. It's a process, not a thing, like a pill. It's integral, not external. And it's spontaneous, not at-will.

The Eightfold Path Meets the Twelve-Step Program

Alcoholism is an addiction, not a disease as was once thought. To paint the damage in primary colors, in just one year at the end of the century the United States spent an estimated $150 billion on illnesses, premature deaths, car crashes, and crimes all caused by alcohol.

Whatever story of ruined lives alcoholism tells, it's but the manifestation of deeper causes, of which it's only a symptom. Buddhism is not an alternative for those in real medical need, yet can naturally be beneficial. The precepts, mindfulness, or Pure Land practice all provide healthy substitutes for suffering. For people who have a hard time with God and higher powers in general (the eleventh step of Alcoholics Anonymous), and judgmental, patriarchal mind-sets in particular, Buddhism can provide a welcome relief, for forgiving one's self with compassion, rather than play the Blame Game of shame or guilt.

Addiction sets up a separate self, identifying with one's craving, a denial or delusion that Buddhism addresses: a denial of our unity with each other and the universe; our unity with the perfection of the present moment. Delusion is one of the three poisons (also called fires), along with greed, so graphic in the craving of addition. *Tip:* Just as the recovery movement is steering away from the phrase "self-help," neither should Buddhism be considered self-help, a quick-fix. To consider it as a therapeutic system risks minimizing its infinite essence. Then even Buddhism can become an addiction.

So What's *Your* Addiction? (Precepts as Meditation)

The precepts require personal consideration. For example, what if you smoke? In the Buddha's time, people knew of camels but never smoked them; there's nothing in the precepts about tobacco. But we know tobacco is toxic. So smoking would fit into the Fifth Precept defined as "no intoxicants."

More generally, we might recognize we live within an addictive society. You can divide any roomful of people into two groups: those in recovery, and those in denial. (Denial is more than a river in Egypt.) Food binges, gambling, shopping sprees, noise—what's your addiction/compulsion? There's a recovery group for each (and hence such words as "workaholic"). Whether addiction or compulsive behavior, at the root is craving (trishna, gotta gotta gotta have it) that continues despite the consequences of suffering. Your exercise for meditation here is to consider your compulsive behavior, your addictions, and possible negative consequences.

Recognition of suffering is the beginning of transformation, and a lifelong process. What actions, and ideas, are you addicted to? Addiction is, by definition, self-perpetuating;

from a Buddhist view, it perpetuates an illusory self. When we understand this, we come to see how the Buddha's Four Noble Truths are really one. Understanding the nature of suffering, its root and its arising, we see the way out.

Media Consumption: We Ingest Words and Images, Too

Consider media as consumption: TV programs, magazines, books, films, CDs, websites. Buddhists say when we ingest media they, too, become part of our make-up. Their cynicism and violence affect our consciousness. Toxins cause damage.

I confess. I'm an accredited member of the media (in recovery). Sure, today's papers tell useful things like the date, weather, and tides (along with crimes du jour, scandals, and other sensationalism). But the news seldom reports the good news, the three million other stories happening each day. But the Golden Rule is: "He who owns the gold rules." And so, to spike circulation and make stockholders happy, a common motto (besides "Sex Sells") is "If it bleeds, it leads" (leads, as the Number-One Story). And so we're stuck with this Frankenstein monster of media on steroids. *Crash! Boom!!* (splat!)

And it's interesting to recognize how it's programmed. When HH the Dalai Lama was in America once, he'd been in a room where a TV was on. Glancing over at the screen, he'd see a pretty image, like children dancing in a field of flowers. He'd looked away, but when he looked back just a moment later, there was a terrible image, such as a man threatening a woman with a chainsaw. Positive image, then negative image, he discovered, and so it went, on into the night. He concluded that watching TV must make Americans really exhausted!

Of course, we don't notice how we're being manipulated—that's part of the agreement. We either develop antibodies or grow numb to the strain. But consider this: By the time an average American is 18 years old, they'll have seen 16,000 simulated murders, plus 200,000 other acts of violence. (Ever have to remind yourself, or your kids, "It's only a movie!"?)

I'm not proposing a ban or crusade. We ourselves hold the switch, on or off. Why else do you think they call TV a "plug-in drug"? ("Don't touch that dial! We'll be right back!" "Are you talking to *me?!*") Ask yourself: Does it make me happy? What really does make you happy?

Practicing the Precepts

As Venerable Master Hsing Yun points out, we might consider three aspects to practicing the precepts: *form, practice,* and *spirit.* Form means grasping the idea. But once you understand the words, you must put them into practice yourself. Then you'll see the inner spirit of the precepts, and can internalize them for yourself, and see how they're integral to meditation and wisdom.

Step by step. Taking refuge only in those precepts with which you're comfortable. This is in accord with the Buddhist tenet of weighing everything against your own life experience. Use your intuition. Listen within. And, as mentioned, to touch just one precept deeply is to touch the others. Lying (denial) can lead to addiction, such as addiction to sexuality, which can lead to violence, and violence to greed, greed to disrespect for life, and all of this to unhappiness. Reverence for life leads to generosity and consideration for others, which makes for happy relations, and peace.

To practice *all* the precepts might seem to require monasticism. Yet you can follow them and still carry on with regular, rent-paying everyday life. That seeming impossibility, however, is important to note. It's an aspect of another Buddhist tenet that asks us to consider the seemingly impossible … a snowball of purity in a blazing furnace … the sound of one hand … what the One returns to. (If that seems "illogical" it's only to our dualistic mind-set.) Such is a Zen approach.

Zen recognizes three levels to the precepts. The first level is *straightforward:* Don't do harmful things, such as killing. The second level asks us to recognize that we're killing *all the time* (crushing microbes, blowing out flames, eating vegetables, and so on). Being aware of this keeps us from being too *self*-righteous. The third level asks us to recognize the *impossibility* of killing. Matter is never created nor destroyed. Destroy something here, and it pops up in another form elsewhere. This threefold approach applies for all the precepts.

Precepts: A Mindfulness Meditation

In my own experience, the precepts reinforce my mindfulness, and my mindfulness illuminates my understanding of the precepts. A beautiful coexistence. Within your ordinary mind is buddha mind, as you discover when you do one thing at a time, mindfully. This takes discipline, and inspires it. The precepts cultivate conditions to further that goal. It's not an imposition from the outside but rather a means of realizing that no one owns your mind but you, an opportunity of learning how to live that freedom well.

Building upon an insight meditation exercise taught by author and Vipassana teacher Jack Kornfield, I'd like relay (in my own words) his wonderful invitation for you to make this Precept Mindfulness Month. (Actually, a five-week month.) For one week, just notice the influence of the first precept in your life. Vow to bring *no harm* to any living creature through word, deed, or thought. Yourself included. Notice all the living beings in your world you might normally ignore. Weeds poking up through pavement. Bugs. Birds. Cultivate a sense of care and reverence for them. Houseplants are buddhas, too. Stones, too.

Next week, observe the *material things* in your daily life, including money. How do you handle objects that cross your path—yours and others? Do you recycle? Do you waste water in the shower? Are you energy efficient? Are you tempted by what's not yours? And you might practice random acts of spontaneous kindness. Act on your friendly, benevolent impulses. At the end of the week, measure your wealth in non-material terms. How many sunsets or dawns did you watch? How many times did you play with kids? Did you smile enough?

During Week Three, notice how often *sex* arises in your consciousness. Each time, ask yourself what it's associated with. Power? Loneliness? Compassion? Stress? Self-esteem? Pressure? Pleasure? You might be surprised. You can extend this into an additional week of observing your sensuality, sensing your senses, and seeing what pulls you in. Yet another week could be devoted to relationships. Do you view others as objects? Where do you withhold, where do you yield? Where do you respond as an equal?

Hear and Now

At first, precepts are a practice. Then they become a necessity, and finally they become a joy. When our heart is awakened, they spontaneously illuminate our way in the world. This is called Shining Virtue. The light around someone who speaks truth, who consistently acts with compassion for all, even in great difficulty, is visible to all around them. Better than perfume, its fragrance rises to the gods."

—Jack Kornfield

Next, devote a week to *deep listening* and *loving speech*. Listening, see if you can completely give yourself over, without preconception or judgment. Listen with an open mind, an open heart. Are you … trying to show what a good listener you are … or rehearsing what you'll say? Speaking, listen to yourself. Do you see and mean each word? Try envisioning every noun, verb, and adjective in your mind's eye. Note how often you make frivolous, cynical, and negative comments. And how often do you speak of things about which you really don't know firsthand?

Last, spend one week observing what you *consume*. Do you consume only things that promote health? When you have an urge to consume a little dose of poison, see what motivates your impulse. Refrain from smoking, drinking, or using any drugs. See how much caffeine or sugar you consume. Notice your addictions and observe what beliefs they satisfy. Remember, habits are habit-forming.

Making the Precepts Your Own

If you're already practicing with a sangha, then you already have its set of precepts to live by. Some adapt and personalize the precepts. This doesn't mean you make up your own. Don't act like your own defense attorney. Rather, hear them deeply, within yourself, as your own inclinations worthy of bringing out through mindful conduct. Thich Nhat Hanh's extended sangha, the Community of Mindful Living, for example, call the precepts "mindfulness trainings," since "precepts" can sound daunting and judgmental.

It's up to each person to make terms with the precepts: how little or how many; how slowly or how soon. And to consider them as opportunities for contacting positive impulses already within ourselves, rather than treat them dutifully as burdensome obligations. They're guidelines for conscious conduct. Trainings in mindfulness. Blueprints for happiness. They reflect our own innate capacities for keeping our appointment with life.

The Least You Need to Know

- In tandem with meditation and wisdom, the precepts are an essential aspect of the Buddha's way. Precepts are ethical guidelines for conscious conduct along the Path. They aren't restrictions but rather a structure for living in harmony and peace, equanimity and joy.

- To not harm implies reverence for life, all forms of life. To not steal implies generosity and trustworthiness. To not lie implies deep listening and loving speech.

- Sexual restraint implies respect, intimacy, trust, and responsibility in relationships.

- Abstinence from alcohol implies sobriety as well as freedom from addictions, as well as mindful consumption, both physical and mental.

- The precepts relate to your own experiences. Listen to how they resonate within your life.

- Choose precepts with which you feel comfortable. Practicing just one precept fully will eventually lead to all the others.

Take Karma, Make Dharma: Key Concepts

In This Chapter

- ◆ Karma: moral cause and effect
- ◆ Interconnectedness, the web of life
- ◆ Impermanence, a cause for celebration
- ◆ Non-separateness: selflessness
- ◆ Nirvana: freedom
- ◆ Emptiness (infinite openness), and suchness

Now comes the capper to our tour of the Dharma: key concepts underlying and growing out of the fundamental teachings you've just learned.
Now that you have a sense of the steering wheel so as to steer clear of the
path of Old Man Sorrow, here's what you might call a combination diagram of stuff under the hood and a map of the general lay of the land.
(Part Three is like a driver's training tour of the most popular watering
holes, and the last part of the book—the whole last half—tours everyday
points of interest along the Way.)

You'll find the Buddha wasn't irrational or vague at all. He didn't preach some kind of misty woo-woo. Rather, the Dharma is totally on the dime, realistic, and impeccably accurate as a system of thought as well as amazingly perfect as a program for enlightened living. It's also multidimensional, with infinite interpretations and applications. So get ready to see the world in new ways. New worlds. And remember: These aren't ideas taken from a jar on a shelf—they're realities you can test for yourself in your own lived world. So don't feel you have to digest this all in a day. There's enough here for a lifetime. (Which—who knows?—may be a bit longer than an eternity.)

One Thing Leads to Another: Karma

The key concepts of Buddhism are all fairly simple, yet subtly overlap and combine to create a beautifully intricate, effective system or whole (Dharma). Let's return to karma as a good point of departure. It will link us in to two more key teachings, interbeing and impermanence. The latter will in turn key us in to the Three Dharma Seals, and then something that's also no thing, and just so. We'll cap it all off with some meditations.

As we've noticed, karma's as simple as pie. Whatever you think or say or do or feel has its effect. Period. We're responsible for what happens to us. Of course some things are inevitably beyond our control. But our lives aren't predetermined; just the opposite. We hold in our own hands the power to change.

We've noted how thoughts affect karma, when we discussed thought in terms of the Eightfold Path. Even if I don't act on a thought, bad intentions and guilty consciences certainly influence action, and affect others, as do good intentions and pure consciences. If you look at someone who's generous, kind, wise, I think you'll see someone who attracts good friends. Or look at someone who's angry all the time, bickering, loud, abrasive, and you'll see how angry feelings and thoughts and words and deeds create a person people avoid. Karma co-creates our world, as it were.

It's ultra scientific. And all-encompassing, once you start to think about it. That is, karma is so inherent in everything we do, and think, and feel, and say, all the time— creating ripples that will, in turn, create further ripples—that we must imagine the threads on the web of karma as more precise and complex than any supercomputer might envision. The mere rub of our sleeve on a stranger's in passing is accounted for.

We can sense this complexity through four categories of karma:

1. Common and personal
2. Primary and secondary
3. Fixed and mutable
4. Simultaneous

Personal karma is the typical idea of karma. Imagine, say, I've volunteered to be a soldier and then kill or maim innocent people in a war, no matter how just or unjust the cause. That's my own personal karma. *Common* karma is collective, such as shared by a family or citizens of a nation. Say I was opposed to an unjust war but enjoyed the economic benefits it brought my country. That's my common karma.

Then there's *primary* and *secondary* karma. To use a gardening analogy, primary karma is like a seed. Secondary karma covers conditions, such as sun, soil, moisture, fertilizer, and singing to the plants. Conditions are quite important. If I choose not to water seeds that are ripe for sprouting, I can alter their course by affecting their conditions.

Karma can be *mutable*. If I cultivate virtue and do good deeds, this might help reduce my karmic debts from previous bad deeds, as from an unpremeditated act of passion, or an unthinking whim. *Fixed* karma results from acts engaging body, speech, and mind, as in premeditated murder; fixed results are also such things as the species and family I'm born into.

And karma can be *simultaneous*. Fantastic as it might seem at first hearing, effect can be cause, and cause can be effect. When I plant an apple from a seed, I normally think of the apple as the result of the seed, the cause. Yet my apple (result) will produce seeds (cause). Similarly, Siddhartha was a person (cause) who became the Buddha (result) who then influenced other people (causes).

There are yet other categories of karma, but you get the idea. The web of karma is vast and deep, and its science (the Dharma) is very thoroughgoing. Going onward, let's look next at that web, which is called *interbeing*. It looks something like this ...

This Depends on That: Interbeing

Permit me to introduce this next concept through my own first personal experience of it. When I was a boy, it came as a vision. I was in the first grade when it happened. Our teacher was giving us "busy work" before the lunch bell, asking us to raise our right hand, then our left hand, and so on. Instead, I followed the sound of a different drum.

I looked out the window. Across the street, a crew was hammering at a wood frame that would one day be a two-story house. The weather this particular day was one for which Los Angeles is famous. (H. Allen Smith quipped that California is a fine place to live, if you happen to be an orange. Well, it was that kind of a day.) Warm, crisp, tawny light drenched the landscape. Listening to the rhythm of the hammers, and looking at the sun pouring down through the tree-lined street, my mind suddenly went on a riff.

It all came to me in an instant. Narratively, it went something like this. A house was going up … out of wood … as from the trees lining this very street. Trees … are nourished by sunshine, just like today's … which also helped make the cereal which the workers had eaten that morning for breakfast before coming to work at the site. I could see the foreman had blueprints, made of paper, which was, in turn, made of wood … the blueprints drafted by some man, who'd eaten cereal … *all* nourished by the sun: the man, his ideas, the blueprints, the wood, the building. (*Hammer, hammer.*) Wow, see the pattern to it all!? (*Hammer, hammer, hammer.*) Chlorophyll, sun energy, human energy, blueprints … and … since there were blueprints, a pattern, and patterns within and to patterns … then there must be some grand pattern to all the patterns: a master blueprint!

Aha! Seeing that with my own two eyes was an awakening. An illumination. Like seeing the face of God. (Or at least touching the veil.) I think everyone's had this recognition, sometime or other … seeing one's self as part of the stream of life … sensing from whence it comes, and where it's going.

It's largely a feeling as of being part of something greater. A wave aware, even if for just a glimpse, that it's part of something called "ocean." We don't always think of such things … like the 84 separate steps that food takes to get from a farm to our fork … or the split-second relays of modems and satellites to conduct a foreign currency transaction. Still, many of us recycle daily. And we speak of the wings of a butterfly in a rainforest in the Amazon as affecting the weather in our own backyard. As part of the Web of Life.

This way of seeing partakes of the continual interactions we've glimpsed in simultaneous karma. A flower will wither, to become mulch for future flowers. The drifting cloud will dissolve only to become radiant, a rainbow, *ahh!*, and the rain … nourishing trees, that might become a page in a book … with an important message for you. Life is happening everywhere, all at once, right now.

Anyway, I kept my vision tucked away, like a gold nugget at the bottom of my pocket, and when I was older, and learned about Buddhism, I discovered the exact description for what I'd seen. Thich Nhat Hanh calls it interbeing. (Have you heard the word?) Look deeply and you can see the cloud in the texture of this page, whose rain nourished the tree you can also see. In this page is the cloud and the sun, the rain and the tree. They inter-are.

> **Hear and Now**
>
> "I have been a leader in battle … I have been a sword in the hand … I have been a bridge that crossed sixty rivers … I was bewitched into sea foam … I've been a star … I've been a light … I've been a tree … I've been a word in a book …"
>
> —Taliesin (tenth century, Wales)

Different Mind-Sets, Different Worldviews

The Buddha once taught by just holding up a flower. (Imagine if he'd done that as a guest lecturer at some ivy league university.) But when we stop our hurried, isolated way of perceiving and bring mindful awareness to a flower, we can *see* a messenger from the whole cosmos, equipped with everything there is: the *water* cycle ... *fire* sparking its seed and the *sun* nourishing leaves ... exhaling fresh *oxygen* ... and *earth* grounding its growth. A flower buddha, teaching dharma. And so pretty!

> **This Is**
>
> The Avatamsaka Sutra illuminates the concept of **Indra's Net.** The Hindu deity Indra had a net created (perhaps to entertain his daughter). This net is of infinite size (perhaps our cosmos is but a part of it). At each node on the net, there's a jewel. To look closely at just one jewel is to see within its surface reflected all the other jewels of the infinite net. And in each jewel reflected within this one jewel is also reflected all the other jewels, *ad infinitum.*

One school of Buddhist philosophy deals in depth with the unimpeded interpenetration of all things. It's called *Hua Yen* (Chinese, "hwah yehn"; Japanese, *Kegon*), the Flower Garland School, based on the largest sutra in Buddhism, the Avatamsaka, Its motto might be "One in all, all in one": expressing mutual identity (unity) and mutual intercausality (universal interdependence). A drop of water contains all oceans, and a single instant all moments of time.

And at the same time there's a oneness to all things, being all of a piece. Trappist monk Thomas Merton said, "There is in all visible things ... a hidden wholeness." It's not hidden from us by God, but by our inability to see beyond our self; hidden by our identification with our "skin encapsulated egos" as author Alan Watts used to say. We and the universe are inseparably one. We inter-are.

Don't Sweat the Terminology

As with karma, the Buddha and his disciples observed and expressed the interconnected processes of the universe with rigorous curiosity and thorough-going, scientific skill. Indian culture excels at such thought, and Sanskrit can be very precise. So don't be put off when you read Buddhist tech-talk elsewhere. ("Tech-talk, which makes complete idiots of us all.") It's coming around to being translated into our contemporary idiom.

One gnarly-sounding Buddhist phrase is "codependent arising." It refers to interconnectedness, like the instant there's yin, there's yang, too. Everything's interrelated. Thich Nhat Hanh calls it *"interbeing."* (Have you heard the word?) It's already being taught in some public schools and should wind up in the dictionary.

He points out that when we see that sun and cloud are present in this page, interbeing's the word for that state of affairs, that condition. It's the general situation for any one thing's interdependency with another (this page depends on a tree which depends on the earth and a rain cloud and the sun). Page and tree and earth and cloud and sun inter-are. In my boyhood vision, I *saw* interbeing, and God was the only word I knew. Dr. Martin Luther King Jr., very impressed by interbeing, phrased it eloquently: "We are all caught up in an inescapable network of mutuality."

Now interbeing unlocks some interesting doors. Consider karma and interbeing, for instance. Karma is to interbeing as cooking is to food. If karma interlinks us all, interbeing's the web of all those links—and more. Interbeing not only helps us better understand karma, but also guides us still further into The Way Things Really Are. Interbeing helps us to appreciate the endless workings of change, and to grasp the ultimately boundless, transparent nature of identity. First, let's look at ever-changingness. (*Question:* Do you know what the Buddhist nun got at the beauty parlor? *Answer:* An impermanent!)

The Stamp of Reality: The Three Dharma Seals

Now we come to an item on our Reference Page called The Three Marks of Existence: impermanence, nonself, and nirvana. They're also called the three seals of dharma because they're always present in all the teachings.

It Was That, Now It's This: Impermanence

Along with the Four Signs which Siddhartha saw when he went beyond his palace walls, he saw other clues. One early morn, for instance, he'd seen garden leaves all covered with gorgeous, clear, little gems, radiant in the dawning sun. But when he came back to admire them in the afternoon, the magic gems were all gone. His faithful servant explained that it was dew, and that it's natural for all things to pass away like dew. It's a mark of all existence.

I pause in my writing to see if this is true in my own life, right now. Well, the cherry trees have been blossoming, and here in Chinatown, I, like my neighbors, have a couple of branches at home, in a large vase in my living room. Of all plants, they say, the cherry and the plum teach us about the floating, fragrant fragility of life. Ineffable perfume. And I'll keep them here for a day or two after the flowers start to lose their freshness, when there are just a few pink clumps where not long ago there were dozens. For me, that's part of their teaching, too.

All beings share the same nature, and so we all have the same potential for suffering and the same potential for enlightenment. The bended knee and praying hands of a fly about to be swatted are no different than mine. Like Siddhartha, we're all enchanted by the workings of change, and disillusioned when we face the realization that all things pass away, eventually.

Hear and Now

"Everyone knows that change is inevitable. From the second law of thermodynamics to Darwinian evolution, from Buddha's insistence that nothing is permanent and all suffering results from our delusions of permanence to the third chapter of Ecclesiastes ('To everything there is a season …'), change is part of life, of existence, of the common wisdom. But I don't believe we're dealing with all that means. We haven't even begun to deal with it."

—Octavia Butler, *Parable of the Sower*

The Noble Truths teach us how to see through the suffering that impermanence seems to cause us. The Buddha said if you really understand *duhkha*, then you'll have understood all four of his Noble Truths at once: *duhkha*'s existence, its cause and nature of arising, its cessation, and the means of being free from it harming you. We've defined it as suffering. A slightly more abstract definition is *impermanence*.

A Greek philosopher once said you can't step into the same river twice (You really can't step into the same river even once). The Second Noble Truth warns against trying to push the river, or hold on to it. To do so sets up the wheels of duhkha spinning at our heels. Change is essential to life, and so adapting to change is essential to survival.

Physician-poet Dr. William Carlos Williams reminds us, "What does not change is the will to change." Chögyam Trungpa Rinpoche affirms, "Impermanence is indestructible." Thich Nhat Hanh goes a step further by rejoicing: "Long live impermanence!" Why? Without impermanence, a flower wouldn't blossom. Waves wouldn't break upon the rocks. This week's issue of *Star* wouldn't be replaced by next week's all-new sensational never-before-revealed sizzle. Our hearts wouldn't beat. Our lungs wouldn't pump. We'd be like statues. Now that's scary!

Likewise, we pursue goals we think are permanent and will bring us lasting happiness, until we find out they, too, are impermanent, as all things are. So seeking happiness in things that are, like ourselves, also impermanent is like trying to put out a fire with kerosene, *kerblam!*, a perpetual house on fire. But when we accept the simple fact of things as they are, in the wonderful present moment, let go and go with the flow, *Ahh!* suffering goes, too. Simple.

Hear and Now

Three Haiku by Basho

falling the camellia spilt rain

the spring day not long enough
for the lark to sing its full

a roadside hibiscus …
my horse ate it

In our topsy-turvy dewdrop fast-changing world, maybe we're too close to impermanence to really see it. Maybe we're like that caterpillar who looked up when a big butterfly fluttered by, and nudged a caterpillar nearby and whispered, "You'll never get *me* up in one of those things." But the Way of the Buddha enables us to look clearly at impermanence. Cope with it. Conquer the problems we have with its inescapability. And rejoice in its inevitability.

It's Neither This nor That: Selflessness

The next mark of existence flows naturally from impermanence. In our fear of all things passing, we hang on to desires, which have no end, and become greedy to have it all. Until we face the universal reality of impermanence, we build a sandcastle called self (complete with moats, and little feathers and pieces of driftwood stuck in the top) which we pretend is permanent. But who are we, really? Are you the same person you were yesterday? Every seven years, every cell but your bones will have changed. So this next recognition is simply that just as nothing has any lasting, permanent identity, nor does anything have any *separate* identity or self. Ourselves included. We're all part of a one-ness, in which we inter-are. Where do you (or anything else) leave off, and the rest of the world begin?

Hear and Now

"What is this story that many of us tell ourselves and hold on to almost all the time? It goes something like this—I'm here and you are over there, my life is separate from yours, the objects of my awareness are external to me. This story is almost instinctive. Once it arises, it is almost impossible not to grasp it as real. Attaching to it as real is the origin of our suffering. With this story we are well equipped with anxiety but not well equipped to face it, so we embark on a career of trying to avoid anxiety and blaming it on others instead."

—Reb Anderson

Take my pencil, for instance (wait a sec, lemme finish this sentence; okay, now, take my pencil). Does it have any separate identity, really? The person who made it gave it a name: #2 Maspero pencil. When we look deeply, we see it isn't composed of anything that we can call "pencil" but is rather a composite of various nonpencil elements, all interbeing to concoct #2 Maspero. Its graphite lead comes from Sri Lanka (Ceylon), its wood from a cedar forest in Northern California, its label from carbon black, its lacquer from a castor bean product, dyed yellow … the metal ring at the end is made of brass, itself copper and zinc … and, the crowning touch, the eraser (which effaces itself as it corrects my mistakes) is rapeseed oil, from the Dutch East Indies, mixed with sulfur chloride and Italian pumice, bound together with rubber and pigmented with cadmium sulfide. Think, too, where each of *those* elements came from, in turn, and how *they* came together, and under what conditions: where the ropes came from, the workmen's coffee, and so on.

Of course its label says it's a pencil, but what *is* identity? Where is there any permanent, separate identity? Nowhere, says the Buddha, and says a pencil. (As my manuscript grows, my pencil vanishes.) Show me identity. If I take off the eraser, is it still a pencil? If I remove the coating? If I remove the lead? At what point does identity begin and end? My pencil is nonseparate from its elements. The same is true of a car, a flower, a human being, and our thoughts and desires. All contingent and conditional. Intertwined. If this, then that. Now the pencil's inherent, equal nonpencilness is an illustration of something that becomes actually experiential in meditation. Your average, daily stream of consciousness, your inner monologue, is like the interdependent elements of a pencil, none having any lasting or separate identity.

Consider, again, the life of the Buddha. His enlightenment began when he left fortress walls of a palace called self-indulgence, self-absorption. Then, seeing his self-denial was just another attachment to self, he discovered the Middle Way. And this differed from the spirituality of his day. He'd already tried freeing "inner self" from "the bondage of the flesh" and reuniting it with "the OverSelf," but discovered, hey, the body isn't necessarily the slave-driver. The real culprit is … building a fortress around an illusion, called self. Freed from that illusion, it then didn't matter whether you sought to recognize godhood within a more superconscious state. The path is to be free of self, and then see.

So we call this *nonself*. Where the established spirituality of the Buddha's day said *atman* (personal identity) is *Brahman* (ultimate identity), the Buddha said "There is no self" (Sanskrit: *anatman*, like "nonself"). *Selflessness*, if you will.

Clinging to and identifying with the concept of a lasting, separate self is the root of suffering. But don't worry. This self you're so familiar with doesn't quit its day job and vanish overnight. Buddhists still have driver's licenses. And what is this self, anyway, for which you might be afraid, if you think you'd lose it? (A question for meditation.) It's another form of interbeing, or impermanence. Selflessness is almost spatial; impermanence, temporal. Once you were a child and could only imagine adulthood. (Where is that child now?) A beginner at Buddhist practice (like the rest of us), you're only imagining enlightenment. Better to commence by saying "I don't know, let's see" than try to attain what you're only imagining; rather than perpetuate self-illusion. (You'll find there's nothing to attain: By merely being, you're already part of the ocean, you just didn't realize it. And that ocean is nirvana, as we'll see next.)

Hear and Now

"The more a human being feels himself a self, tries to intensify this self and reach a never attainable perfection, the more drastically he steps out of the center of being, which is no longer now his own center, and the further he removes himself from it."
—Eugen Herrigel

"Selflessness is not a case of something that existed in the past becoming nonexistent. Rather this sort of 'self' is something that never did exist. What is needed is to identify as nonexistent something that always was nonexistent."
—The Dalai Lama

You're IT: Nirvana *Now*

No self, no problem. *Freedom.* The third mark of all existence, beyond space and time, is nirvana: the peace that passeth understanding. The ultimate recognition that self and universe aren't separate. At one with the all.

This is both freedom *from* and freedom *for.* Freedom from ignorance and fear, isolation and suffering; and freedom for peace and love, compassion and wisdom. True happiness. Oneness. There's no self that has to attain this boundless ocean of freedom, called nirvana, any more than a wave has to attain wateriness. We already *are* it. It's our true home.

We're an ocean that manifests as a wave that then imagines itself as separate and permanent. (Ha ha ha: *Ker-splash!*) When life's no longer filtered through the lens of self, and the dualism of self/not-self falls away, there's no "I" that attains this enlightenment. There's unfiltered, direct awareness of what limitlessly is. (And all without a second phone line!)

> **Hear and Now**
>
> "Nirvana is everywhere. It dwells in no particular place. It is in the mind. It can only be found in the present moment.... It is empty and void of concept. Nothing can comprise nirvana. Nirvana is beyond cause and effect. Nirvana is the highest happiness. It is absolute peace. Peace in the world depends on conditions, but peace in nirvana is unchanging .... Suffering leads the way to nirvana. When we truly understand nirvana, we become free."
>
> —Maha Ghosananda

Here are a few more landmarks along the trackless path:

♦ The word "nirvana" refers to extinction of fire. To avoid comparing ancient Hindu physics to today's, it could be called "release" (release from needless suffering).

♦ A common metaphor for nirvana is "the Other Shore," and skillful means are like a raft. (But the raft is not the shore; a finger pointing at the moon is not the moon.)

♦ Nirvana originally meant the extinction of suffering. It's now used it to mean total enlightenment. It sounds more like a noun than enlightenment, like a state. But enlightenment is a process, not a product.

We've come more than a long way now. From karma and interbeing, to the three seals. What else is there to say? Well, *nothing*, really ...

It Is and It Isn't: Emptiness (Infinite Openness)

Beyond self, we can see the Middle Way in a new light. Between the palace of self, with its pageants of drama, and the forest of self-denial, on the brink of annihilation—there is a middle path. Between existence and nonexistence. Life and death.

Indeed, our final Buddhist teaching draws on and affects all we've learned so far. As a symbol or logo for it, consider a rainbow. It's a result of environmental karma, is completely impermanent, and its elements inter-are. With sun and no rain, no rainbow. Rain but no sun, no rainbow. But put them all together, and ... *Ahh!* Or, if you happen to be a night person, there's moon-in-the-water. On a clear full-moon night, it's rippling, dancing, doing somersaults in a pond, a teacup, or even a dewdrop.

Now rainbows and the moon-in-a-dewdrop are splendid metaphors for what Buddhists call "*sunyata*" (void; emptiness). Empty of any durable, solid, separate existence of their own, they represent *emptiness*. Don't be put off by the lingo. "Empty," in Buddhism, is shorthand for "empty-of-any-independent-permanent-tangible-existence."

Emptiness is not exactly *nothing*. Like impermanence, emptiness is actually a positive idea, only 1) *verbally* expressed in the negative, plus 2) requiring explanation as to what emptiness is empty *of* (lasting, substantial, independent existence). As a realm of limitless possibility, there's all the more reason for words not to get in its way. If "no boundary" seems better than "empty," try that. Boundless. Blank essence. Without limit, infinite oneness. Openness. Transparent. Spacious. Fertile void.

Because everything's contingent—continuously interacting, interreacting, interrelated with everything else—if just one thing had its own separate, air-tight, lasting identity, 100 percent pure of any outside ingredients or conditioning, forever and ever, then … nothing would ever come to be.

Just as we can say "Long live impermanence!" so, too, can we give thanks to emptiness. Impermanence allows events to keep happening. Emptiness permits being to inter-be, and create existence. The spokes of a wheel depend upon and revolve around the emptiness at the hub. A potter sculpts a bowl by centering it around emptiness. Things wouldn't exist without this fertile void. (Think of it as a cosmic cornucopia.) Right now, there's this book and everything-that-is-not-this-book. That everything-else, from the edge of this book to the furthest stretches of the universe, is the fertile void of emptiness out of which this book came and whence it eventually returns. Buddhist scholar Edward Conze once said, "Emptiness is not a theory, but a ladder that reaches out into the infinite. A ladder is not there to be discussed, but to be climbed." And, like a ladder, it is not only practical but unfolds successive stages of meaning.

Misconception #19: Buddhism's gotten a bad rap, I think, because of all the Sanskrit terminology phrased in the negative. Nonpermanence. Nonattachment. Nonself. *Duhkha* is often misconstrued to mean that Buddhism's pessimistic and believes in eternal suffering. That's like mistaking a closed door for the wall that enables it to be. Nirvana, likewise, is actually very here-and-now, not hither-and-yon. Absence of suffering reveals fundamental goodness. So, too, emptiness isn't nihilism ("nothing matters"). If a bank error added some zeroes to your account, would that be nothing? And none of this denies individual uniqueness by one hair, as we'll see next.

Emptiness, Unique and Full: Suchness

Imagine, what might the flip side or twin of Buddhist emptiness be? Not "separate identity," because sunyata shows how there ain't no such animal. "Somethingness" would be closer. What really fits emptiness like yang to its yin would be "suchness" (Sanskrit *tathata;* also translated as is-ness. Thus-ness).

We've all experienced suchness. Just think of a precise moment that was … well, indescribable. "You had to be there," is all you can say. The way the cat jumped off the refrigerator onto the kitchen counter and got a paw stuck in the empty jam jar. Or that moment in early winter when you feel a hush and new chill in the air and, then, suddenly, there are raindrops. Consider, too, a new, unopened ball of twine, fresh out of the box.

Like a nonstop Ferris wheel, the fertile void is continually giving birth to unrepeatable interpenetration of impermanences (say that eight times fast), each time just "this way": balls of twine, kitty-cat dances, clouds about to rain. White chickens beside a red wheelbarrow. Each is empty of separate, solo, lasting identity so each is *just so*, like the patterns of a mobile. The swirl of cream poured in a cup of coffee. The sound of wind in trees.

> **Along the Path**
>
> so much depends
> upon
> a red wheel
> barrow
> glazed with rain
> water
> beside the white
> chickens
> —William Carlos Williams

This Is

Scholar Christmas Humphreys defines **tathata** (suchness), equivalent to Buddha nature, as "… the ultimate and unconditioned nature of all things…. It cannot be called the One as distinct from the Many, for it is not distinct from anything. Nothing can be denied or affirmed concerning it, for these are modes of expression which exclude and thereby create opposition. It can only be understood by realizing that one can neither find it by searching nor lose it by trying to separate oneself from it. Yet it has to be found."

I've said emptiness and suchness dance with each other like the interplay of yin and yang. There's a Buddhist motto close to this: *"Form is emptiness; emptiness is form."* Form is matter, and also phenomena, the way matter takes unique form, suchness. Think of form as a *wave*, exquisite as it swells, curls, rises to its majestic height and then spills down, and merges. Think of emptiness as the *ocean*, limitless, vital, the womb of life, with no fixed center. Waves = ocean; ocean = waves. The vast ocean of pure being; and (quoting American poet Charles Reznikoff) its "ceaseless weaving of the uneven waters." Or as Einstein put it, $E = mc^2$; energy becomes matter, matter becomes energy.

No Thing: Even Emptiness Is Empty

Besides suchness, some landmarks of our experience of elusive but essential sunyata are:

- Spaciousness
- Cycles
- Combinations

- Consecutiveness
- Illusions
- Relativity

Focusing awareness on breathing, and nothing else, we become aware of blank *space* that's neither in-breath nor out-breath. As we free ourselves from the "traffic jam of discursive thought," as Chögyam Trungpa Rinpoche puts it, thoughts continue to flicker, but we become conscious, too, of the space in between them, the spaciousness in which they take place. And experience things as they are; open, transparent, bright, all there ever is. Instead of living in a cubicle called self, it's like living large, on the whole block. It's a great relief, but not the same thing as being spaced out. Many have described sunyata as our true home, like finally coming home.

> **Along the Path**
>
> Varying approaches to the Buddha's way illuminate emptiness. Zennists drink from a handcrafted tea cup (instance of suchness, kin to emptiness). There are ancient Tibetan bowls made of human skulls (reminder of impermanence, kin to emptiness). Theravada compares things to empty vessels. Mahayana says there are no vessels, really.

We've already seen a *cycle* in simultaneous karma. Effect can become cause, a seed becoming a flower that bears new seeds, and neither having any permanent, individual essence. Examples of *combinations* are the composite pencil, the rainbow, and the moon in water. Or consider the calligraphy for "wisdom," and for "listen" in the previous chapter, or the calligraphy a little further on here, things in combination express something else that is really intangible. The ultimate meaning (sunyata) exists in between the things. In between the words.

Consecutiveness is like a movie, a compilation of short strips of film, themselves made up of consecutive frames. We think a movie's real, but is it? It is and it isn't. Breathing is consecutive, too. In between an in-breath and out-breath, there's sunyata.

Big Misconception #32: People are mistaken who think Buddhists say "Everything is an *illusion*." Rather, everything is *like* an illusion. Our lives are empty of any permanent, tangible, separate identity, the way dreams interweave in our consciousness just before falling asleep, and just before waking up. Who am I, who am I really? "Gary Gach" is a label. I'm not an illusion, but I don't identify with my I.D. cards and Internet passwords and, ah yes, that reminder of the relative amid the transcendental, my bills. Like a pencil, or the rainbow, "Gary Gach" is a series of moments, states, events, cycles—a composite, and all composite things decompose. (That's what happens to musicians when they die, you know—they decompose. Ba-dum!) Irish poet W. B. Yeats expressed the illusion of self (sunyata) when he sighed, "Ah, body swayed to music, ah, brightening glance, / how can we know the dancer from the dance?"

Relativity was described by the Buddha in advance of Einstein's Theory of Relativity ($E = mc^2$). But thanks to Dr. Einstein we're accustomed to thinking in Buddha's terms. When we say, "One man's meat is another man's poison," that's relativity and it's also an example of sunyata. Another example is words. Words vary according to context. A nun's habit isn't the same as an alcoholic's. As Groucho Marx says, "Time flies like an arrow, fruit flies like a banana." The word "emptiness" itself depends on context, and so is itself empty (of any lasting, unique, single meaning), which brings us to one last aspect worth noting …

… *nothing.* (Or, better, no-thing … not anything … since the idea of nothing conjures up a vacuum, whereas no-thing is just blank. Like a movie screen. Or a blank piece of paper.) Emptiness itself is empty, meaning don't get attached to any concept of it. Even saying it's ineffable or indescribable already puts a label on it. You can't pin it down. The ultimate is uncategorizable. Even the Buddha is empty: not a concept, not a thing. Better to remain open. Personally, I find that emptiness or sunyata is a reminder that I *don't know.* A reminder to keep watching. Mindfully observing. Being attentive.

So I'll say nothing more about that which can't be said, except to recount that when some priests and monks from Westminster Abbey were visiting a Japanese Zen temple for the first time, they paused at a large, framed piece of beautiful calligraphy of the word "no-thing" and asked what that was. Rather than explain the whole nine yards, as you've seen here, the Zen guide just said, "God," and they moved on.

The Chinese pictogram to the left shows a clearing, as made by a natural forest fire. To the right, the fire is burning. Together, they present: no thing (wu, Chinese; mu, Japanese).

Calligraphy: Chungliang Al Huang

Living It: Meditations in a Floating World

We've reviewed eight of the Buddha's concepts: karma; interbeing; impermanence; non-self (selflessness); nirvana; emptiness (openness); and suchness. They're key concepts, as in keys that can open doors. If you only understand the Buddha's teachings intellectually and don't practice them, then Buddhism's just books and websites. (A carpentry manual's not a guide to living in a house.) Here are a few hints for actively seeing karma, interbeing, impermanence, selflessness, emptiness, and suchness, in your daily life. Like the Buddha, going beyond the castle walls of defined reality, be open for signs of what you haven't seen before.

Devote a few days to noticing *karma*, yours and others. Notice who seems to attract material things; observe whether they seem truly happy. Observe this potential in yourself. When you notice anger, in yourself and others, see how it creates more anger or confusion. When you notice calm, see how it attracts more calm.

Devote a few days to noticing examples of *interbeing*. Think of how things came to be here. How many ingredients and steps went into making each thing you encounter, then look at that thing up close in a new light, the light of its interbeing.

Devote a few days to noticing *impermanence*. Notice how impermanent is just one breath, and how complete. Notice seasonal changes. Do beginnings in your life seem easier than endings? If you sense attachment or surging feelings, make a note of those, too.

Devote a few days to observing how you define your *self*. What are your limits? Set aside some quiet time to look at your hand. As you look, try to remember how your hand looked when you were little. Then see if you can see your parents' hand within the patterns of your hand … the shape of the pads of your fingers, the fingerprints, the pattern of pores on the back of your hand. When you're done, put your two palms together and notice your breath.

Devote a few days to noticing examples of *sunyata* and *suchness*. Take a blank piece of paper. Pin it up where you can look at it for a few days. Notice its texture, color, how it catches light and casts a shadow (its suchness), and how you could write anything on it (its sunyata). Also see in it the tree it came from, and the rain and cloud that nourished it (its *interbeing*). Feel the interrelations of all these things so they're real for you, not philosophical concepts.

Just as we need a mirror to see our face, so can we use the heavens to see our mind. Weather permitting, go out and look up at a clear sky from a comfortable position as high up as can be. Notice variations in light and color, and how far the sky extends. Imagine to yourself, "I am this." Let your mind slowly grow as blank, bright, and vast as the sky you're looking into. If thoughts come, think of them as passing birds, and let them pass uninterrupted. When you're ready to end the meditation, notice how the sky seems both endless and without any particular location anywhere. Then stay with the presence of "big sky mind" (sunyata) for a few minutes and let your "busy daily routine mind" (samsara) find its way back on its own. Notice if it's clearer. Calmer.

Devote a few days to considering *no-thing*. Notice how automatically you label and categorize things. Look at things as if you've never seen them before. Practice admitting "I don't know" to yourself and others.

Think of song lyrics that illustrate any of these concepts. "I Got Plenty of Nothing" by the Gershwin brothers and DuBoce Hayward, for example (nothing's plenty for me), or "Tomorrow Never Knows" by The Beatles; songs of suchness, like "The Way You Look Tonight," and "My Favorite Things," and romantic farewell songs about impermanence. Celebrate. Sing these songs to yourself or with others. Make up new lyrics.

Devote a few days to just thinking about the Buddha and all he taught. Consider your mind as part of Buddha's mind. All human beings are all related, with common ancestors; concentrate on him as your relative. Thinking of his name, consider that you're invoking his presence in your life. See if this makes you feel happier, if your surroundings seem more pleasant.

Set aside a space in your thoughts for mental notes or observations. Check into it from time to time. See what works well, and what doesn't.

Once begun, all of these practices can be ongoing—and life-changing. So enjoy!

The Least You Need to Know

- Karma doesn't mean predestination. We have control over our words and deeds, thoughts and feelings, which cause reciprocal effects.

- All things are interdependent, interacting, interreacting, and interpenetrating. This can be summed up as "interbeing."

- Things change. Impermanence is a primary cause of sorrow, but without it life wouldn't be possible and so it's also a cause for happiness.

- Sunyata (void) means emptiness *of* any permanent, tangible, separate self. Nonrecognition of this fact creates suffering and illusion (samsara) but, like impermanence, it's positive, enabling things to come into being, each thing just so (suchness). It points to the boundless, open, transparent nature of all things, including the self.

- We are included along with the things having no permanent, solid, separate identity. Self is as much a product of transient, contingent conditions as a pencil or a rainbow.

- Nirvana is the nature of What Is. We don't need to attain it. We are it. It is the liberation from needless suffering the Buddha taught. Thank you, Buddha.

Part 3

Sangha: Joining the Path

Sangha means putting the Dharma into practice. The proof that's in the pudding. Fortunately, it's not like trying to learn to swim by diving into the middle of the ocean. Sangha, the community of practice, keeps you afloat. You're always in the company of best friends here. So if at first you don't succeed, keep on practicing.

(Some say that if the Buddha were alive today, he'd still be practicing … maybe that quiet person way up in front and off to one side …)

After meditation basics, we'll spotlight four major traditional schools of Buddhism as practiced in the West. But don't sweat the -isms. It's how you practice that's the important -ism. (Maybe they should have called it Youism ….)

Chapter 9

How's Your Practice?: Getting Set

In This Chapter

- ◆ Finding time
- ◆ Making space
- ◆ Stocking up on gear
- ◆ Practicing together
- ◆ Maintenance tips
- ◆ Reminder: The path is the goal

Most of what's been covered thus far may make perfect sense to you, headwise and heartwise. If so, the only missing ingredient is to make it real for yourself. A contemporary word for this is how you put it all into *"practice."* Integrating and actualizing the Dharma (the way things really are) into your daily life. Indeed, many who are making the sacred real for themselves today speak in terms of a practice. And if you're not sure what "sacred" means, practice will tell. Practice always clarifies whatever doesn't yet quite "click."

Calling Buddha's way "a practice" may seem a bit of a misnomer. The word usually implies repeating something to be performed or enacted in the future, like athletics or music. Yes, it is consistent and persistent. But there's no future destination. No, practice here's all about the present. True, you're already present. But you're missing it when assessing the past or anticipating the future. Like the sign says at a casino in Las Vegas, "You Must Be Present to Win."

Spiritual practice is about being present to your life, and so leading a genuine life. Life is a present, the greatest there is. Here's an introduction to appreciating life the Buddhist way. Here the path itself is the destination: going forth, finding, and staying on your path.

The path is called the Middle Way: the Eightfold Path of action, wisdom, and meditation. In this chapter and the next, we'll zero in on the meditative art, integral to the whole.

> ### Leaves from the Bodhi Tree
>
> Sharon Salzberg had been following the Way of the Buddha for 14 years when she became a student of U Pandita. She'd practice six days a week and, when she'd describe her meditation experiences to him, he'd just say, "Well, in the beginning it can be like that." No matter what, he'd say the same thing. After weeks of this, it finally dawned on her that he was saying it's good to be a beginner, not burdened by expectations or preconceptions based on past experiences. When she understood this, he stopped saying that and went on to something else.

Getting Started: Beginner's Mind

I'll let you in on a big, open secret. Maybe you've seen various books with titles like *Buddhism for Beginners*. Well, guess what!? Buddhists *are* beginners. It's a common habit of the wisdom paths, actually. Socrates was declared wise because he knew that he did not know. Fourteenth-century Christian mystic Meister Eckhart called it "learned ignorance." The Dalai Lama calls himself a humble monk. In Zen, it's sometimes called a "don't-know mind"; or *mu*, no-thing. Zen Master Shunryu Suzuki Roshi introduced the concept in the West as "beginner's mind." Beginners' minds are willing to scale the highest peak, or to settle for peanut butter and jelly sandwiches.

The words "expert," "professional," and "specialist" have a commanding ring of authority to them. But they also have a reputation at stake, and so grow timid, learning to like wearing blinders, and to repeat their specialty like a one-trick pony. The word *amateur*, on the other hand, has a slightly disparaging ring today but listening to its Latin root (*amare*, to love) reminds us of its original meaning: having a fondness for everything. As Suzuki Roshi put it so well, "If your mind is empty, it is always ready for anything; it is open to everything. *In the beginner's mind there are many possibilities; in the expert's mind there are few.*"

You'll find examples of beginner's mind in daily speech, such as someone saying "You never know!" or "Who knows!?" or "I don't know, I'm new here." In my own life, pounding the pavement looking for day jobs taught me how no prior experience can be a plus. You're not set in your ways; you're not going to say, "But that's not the way we did it where I used to work." Similarly, beginner's mind doesn't have any preconceptions of what nirvana should look like. Beginner's mind trusts itself to know when it gets there.

Leaves from the Bodhi Tree

A learned professor knocked on the door of the local Zen temple. He had a thousand questions. The resident teacher bowed and invited him in to sit down on a mat and share a pot of freshly picked tea. The tea steeped, and when it was ready, the host poured it into his learned guest's cup first. He poured and he poured and he poured, until the professor shouted, "What?! Stop!! It's overflowing! There's no more room!" The host put the teapot down and replied, "Exactly. Like this cup, you're full of your opinions and preconceptions. How can I show you Zen unless you first empty your cup?"

Have you seen the bumper strip?: "Minds, Like Parachutes, Must Be Open to Function." Here are three more examples of beginner's mind in everyday life: 1) Many people have experienced beginner's luck in sports or games, such as with a perfect first golf swing, or an initial lucky bet. 2) Being on vacation and playing tourist, everything's new. And 3), one reason I think we enjoy spending time with children is they have all of life ahead of them. They're absolute beginners.

All these examples reflect how the mind given us at birth, our beginner's mind, is still there beneath all the labels and decals and passwords over it, still impeccable, bright, fond of everything. Returning to that mind is like coming home … reclaiming our buddha nature … the boundless clarity of the mind at rest … our *mu*, our not-knowing … no-thing … and all the freedom that affords.

Start with where you are. And keep at it.

There's No Time Like the Right Time, and the Right Time Is: Now

You've come this far. Why not put this book down for just a minute to enjoy a moment of meditation? *Try this.* Here's all you'll do: 1) Check that you're comfortable and seated solidly. 2) Close your eyes. 3) Notice your breath. 4) Don't change anything. 5) Just take a mental snapshot of yourself at this point in time. Okay? Now, try it.

That mental snapshot is a benchmark as you progress along your own way. Keep it in your mental wallet and take it out and look at it from time to time. And remember, stopping and taking time for your practice is essentially as easy as *that*.

The Time It Takes Is the Time You Make

Five or ten minutes will just get your feet wet. It usually takes at least 20 minutes to begin to taste the depth and clarity of the practice. Scientists have recently agreed that it takes about this long for our primitive fight-or-flight hard-wiring to dim down and allow more evolved awareness to arise. Once you get a taste, you might want to find some minimum that's comfortable. I'd suggest 20 minutes, with the possibility of extending that later if you wish.

Once you have a sense of it for yourself, you won't have to be dependent on a clock. This is a time for stepping back from any push-pull of calendar, clock, and your schedule, so glancing at your clock the entire time runs counter to the whole point. Enjoy the beautiful awareness of now, which is timeless.

And once you've tasted meditation, you'll appreciate even more the ever-present value of a one-breath meditation, with which we began.

Favored times are morning and evening: morning, first thing, and evening either an hour or so before or after dinner, or before going to bed. Meditating right after a meal can be distracting as your blood sugar changes and digestion sees peak traffic.

Varying your daily practice period, you'll see how times of day feel different. In my own practice, I can feel how at 5 in the morning the first rays of the sun are striking my part of the planet, whereas at 5 in the evening I can feel the sun making way for noble nighttime. Spring equinox likewise feels different than autumn equinox.

More important than when and for how long is doing it regularly. It's a foundation. See if you can practice once if not twice a day, six days a week. Making it part of your ordinary life, for one thing, helps eliminate the idea of getting anywhere and instead opens up your familiarity with the range and phases of your mind. Buddha mind isn't off just out of reach; rather, it's available in your everyday mind, so don't be a stranger. In fact, you might think of meditation as if you're reconnecting with the best friend you have in the world, with whom you haven't spent enough time. As you get closer, you'll want to spend some quality time every day.

A Retreat Doesn't Always Mean a Step Backward

During the muddy, three-month rainy season in India, the Buddha used to retreat with his disciples to the shelter of one of their monasteries and practice together until the monsoons stopped howling. Thus began a tradition practiced in Buddhist life ever since. These days, it's not uncommon to pack up and head for a retreat. It might be a work-related productivity booster, a get-together of a special interest group, or a religious retreat. Not a strange practice.

The three-month retreat is still observed in the Insight Meditation communities following Theravada tradition. Zen also has a retreat called a *sesshin* (meaning "touching / receiving / conveying / collecting the mind"), which lasts anywhere from a day to a week. Everything is strictly meditation, whether it's listening to a talk or eating lunch, sitting or walking (as discussed in the next chapter).

But you don't have to sign up to enjoy a one-day retreat in your own home. *Try this:* a day of mindfulness. Set aside a full day. Clean house and do any necessary shopping the day before. Unplug the phone. Use words sparingly. From the time you wake up to the time you go to sleep, you'll go slow, go light, and notice your breathing, vowing to be mindful of whatever you're doing. Practice sitting and walking meditation at various times of the day. One day can inspire and inform practice throughout the week. This tradition is core to the Abrahamic traditions: Sunday, the Christian Sabbath; Saturday, the Jewish *shabbos*; Friday, the Muslim *jumma*.

Any retreat is an excellent opportunity for solidifying, clarifying, and deepening your practice, and encouraging you to fit what you find there into daily life. Which brings up the question of finding time.

Dharma Has All the Time in the World for You

Question: Without looking at your watch, right now, what time is it? (*Answer:* It's now.) It might take some getting used to the fact that time is eternally present. The Chinese have an adage expressing it quite well: "Life unfolds on a great sheet called Time, and once finished it is gone forever."

Time's like a river, everywhere at once: at the waterfall and at the docks, in the mountains, and flowing out to sea; always present tense. As always, the Middle Way pertains: nothing extreme. Stillness is inherent in activity, and vice-versa. Yet our society glorifies doing over being. The Buddha, on the other hand, found the highest attainment in the mind at rest. And in terms of nirvana, there is no time. No past, no future.

Nevertheless, I've gotten mail from a few who think they only have five minutes a day for meditation. Well, it's a question of priorities, of course. But if you think you only have five minutes a day for something that can be of incalculable value for your whole life, then maybe it's not for you, or else maybe you better look at your life. For busy beavers who think they don't *have* time, let me respectfully relay my dear teacher Lew Welch's pronouncement: "That's not a valid excuse. Time is really all we have. If we decide it's necessary, there's time for it." The Buddha tells us no one owns our mind but we ourselves. The same is true for time.

This reminds me of the haiku by Shou: "Birds sit and sing among the flowers, laughing at human beings who have no time to sing."

Buddha's in the House

Practice in community, sangha, isn't confined to the weekly or monthly meeting place. This morning, just before dawn, I practiced with the eucalyptus tree out back and the finches dwelling thereabouts. There's a sangha of living beings wherever you are. So now it's time to talk about place.

Setting Aside Some Breathing Room

Like a comfortable sofa, everyone can use the literal space in their lives where meditation can take place. Breathing room.

It needn't be a room all its own, just a place where you won't be disturbed. It could be an area just large enough to lay a mat upon the floor. Preferably near an open window, so the air's fresh. Shaded, so bright light won't distract you. And relatively quiet. Nothing more elaborate than that. If it's all you have, you could fold your blanket and sit on it on your bed.

 Hear and Now

Standing outside my pointed-roof hut,
Who'd guess how spacious it is inside?
A galaxy of worlds is there,
With room to spare for a zafu.
—Shih-wu (1272–1352)

Just knowing I have that space where I can go gladdens my heart and calms my mind. I take refuge there, renew my vows, and meditate. So, every now and again, I celebrate my growing buddhahood and place a flower, from the park near my house, in a simple glass of water, beside my mat, near the window. A little living buddha, sharing the light and air with me and my practice, and I with it.

Altars: The Buddha Within and Without

For growing buddhas who've found a breathing room and time zone for regularly nourishing and inviting their essential buddha nature, this is cause for celebration, no? By celebrating, we're not necessarily getting attached to these facts, but making them come alive for us through personal ritual. It's for this reason the statuette of the Buddha I have in my home is small. (If you haven't noticed yet, when you bow at something, it bows back. So my small Buddha gives me a small bow in return, every day; more than that I might have trouble with.)

You might nurture your own buddhahood, your growing link with the historical Buddha and his teachings, with an altar … a sign of respect … a re-presentation of the Buddha's wisdom and compassion … a mirror of your own heart and mind. It could be an image or statue, on a windowsill or shelf. You might add a flower, a candle, incense.

Bowing to a statue of the Buddha isn't idol worship. Vietnamese Buddhist monk Thich Tanh Thien explains, "You stand in front of Buddha, not to a statue, but to buddha inside yourself. It's important to know that, otherwise you're bowing to a piece of wood or metal. When you look inward to the Buddha nature, you feel peace in your heart. You give thanks to Buddha because without his teachings, you would not have found this way of understanding and loving."

Some personal altars can have precise symbolic details, depending on the practice and the practitioner; others, free-form. Some home shrines include cherished seekers and enlightened leaders. Some include pictures of relatives and teachers and close friends, a place where a practitioner goes to share personal news with them. For many, an altar's a way of deepening the meaning of home, and making the divine personal.

Portable altars have been an early fixture of Buddhist devotion, and the practice continues in Pure Land, Tibetan, and Nichiren Buddhism.

> ### Along the Path
>
> Seen against a Judeo-Christian background, an altar can smack of graven images, idolatry, paganism, (*avoda zara* in Hebrew). Yet within Buddhism itself there's a parallel, almost identical warning: "If you see a Buddha along the road, kill him." Don't bind yourself to an image or concept. As Quakers say, seek the living light within yourself.

> **Hear and Now** _____
>
> "… a butsudan … is a beautiful little cabinet. Inside you put things that represent the necessities of life: little candles for light, incense for smell, water, fruit, and so on. And you hang your gohonzon in there, too—a scripture, rolled up on a scroll. The butsudan looks like a little altar; but the idea is not that you're *worshipping* this piece of paper or anything. These things allow you to focus, to be in the right frame of mind to receive, and they are a form of respect."
>
> —Tina Turner

The meaning of an altar or shrine grows over time. A devotional image or artifact is like that snapshot of a loved one that someone keeps in their wallet or on their desk. To us, it's just another face, but to the one who knows that person and looks at the picture at various times of the day, the image is a doorway to love.

Remember, "Thou art *that*."

Stocking Up on Gear: Clean Socks, and What Else?

During his ascetic stint, the Buddha slept out in the open, naked. Had he attained Enlightenment that way, this section might have been devoted to information on bug bites and poisonous plants. Anyway, you should feel comfortable when you meditate. No need for tight watches or collars, glasses or belts that constrict circulation, or starchy or scratchy clothes. Just as the best clothes for meditation don't make you aware of your body, preferred apparel colors in some temples are blacks or grays, so as not to distract anyone. Tibetan Buddhists, on the other hand, favor bright colors, generating the glow of inner warmth.

Some people sit with a blanket over their knees because circulation slows down during meditation, and it's important not to catch cold. Clean socks? Many temples ask that shoes be removed when sitting in the main hall.

In seated meditation, posture often calls for elevating your fanny slightly higher than your knees and feet. A rolled-up blanket can do. A more formal amenity would be a pillow. There's one designed for sitting meditation called *zafu*, in Japanese. A mat placed under it is called *zabuton* in Japanese. Even in non-Japanese practices, zafus and zabutons are familiar fixtures.

Bells are a wonderful meditation tool. Listening to and just staying with the sound waves of a bell can clear the mind, its sweet voice reminding us to return to the fullness of the present moment. Meditation sessions often begin with a bell. A higher-sounding bell signals the end, time to str-r-r-retch! Some people carry two small brass cymbals in their pocket or purse, called a *tsingsha*, a portable bell of mindfulness.

The Sanskrit name for a Buddhist string of beads literally means rosary (*mala*, a garland, rose). They could be as small as a bracelet, or as large as a necklace with 108 beads, reflecting the traditional classification of the 108 varieties of ignorance to which minds are prone to (in Buddhism, there's a numbered list for everything). Beads can be used to count recitations of a mantra or of the Buddha's name, or to keep attention focused on the breath: moved through the fingers, bead by bead, one for each breath (such as out-and-in as one bead). Quieting the mind, in order to pay attention. A string of beads can also be just relaxing and fun to play with.

Some people time their meditation to the length of one stick of good incense. (Bad incense, on the other hand, smelling like sweet perfume, might only give you a headache.) There's Japanese, Tibetan, powder, rope incense, and so on. Sandalwood was used by Buddha's disciples to help them concentrate during heat waves. When the Buddhist monks from India took to the Silk Route, they brought along their incense. Like the fragrance of the Dharma, suffusing its ineffable fragrance everywhere, incense burns away impurities and refreshes body and mind. I find good incense can stimulate a feeling of alertness and calm, like a cup of fresh green tea.

And nothing warms the heart like a candle. Lama Anagarika Govinda observes how its gentle light is "a means of recalling and being mindful of the light of enlightenment that has shone within every one of us without any recognizable beginning, even though darkened by the self-built walls of the ego, which it is necessary to tear down." These can all be skillful means, but only if not taken as ends in themselves. Dharma isn't a thing, like a stick of incense, but rather what you make of its fragrance. Don't mistake all the various lamps along the way for the real journey.

Joining in Community of Practice: Friends Along the Path

A practice is, by definition, something you do. It's one thing to do it solo, yet another when in community. There's a limit as to how much you can learn on your own. Nothing can replace practice with others. Likewise, this book has many meditations for you to practice. But they all go only as far as a book can offer. Having a teacher and friends show you will open up their full dimensions.

True, it all depends on you. So you can certainly try and see if you can reach enlightenment solo. You might find it like trying to teach cats to dance. But even if you think you can, then how would you know you're not just building yourself up … trying another way of making a sandcastle at the water's edge … a lonely enlightenment of self-delusion?

As Zen priest and scholar Michael Wenger explains, "for the enormity of all that transforming yourself to Buddha is about, you realize that you can use all the help you can get." I'd add that if you don't yet grasp that enormity, a sangha helps you realize it.

True, the Buddha attained enlightenment sitting beneath a tree, after seven years, but had a head start, being a prodigy with a kingly training in all things, including meditation. And, on the night in question, the Buddha called all of creation as his witness, the sangha of all beings. For nearly 50 years thereafter, he practiced in the company of his friends along the path, and the tradition continues, expressed in a way appropriate to right now.

As Much or as Little as You Like: The Choices Are Yours

You don't have to go for ordination, that is, to be a monk or nun. Nor do you need to begin the practice by taking refuge in any sangha. Maybe Buddhist practice will enrich an already grounded religious practice, in which case you already have the sangha of your fellow congregants. But for the Buddhist practice, you still need a teacher. There's a range of options.

Picking and Choosing Wisely

As we've noted, Western Buddhist practice spans an unprecedented range of traditions and hybrids; certainly more than different kinds of Christianity. What'll yours be? Zen Pure Land? ... Native American Tibetan? ... Taoist Zen Islam? There's no One-Size-Fits-All practice. As R. H. Blyth, scholar of Buddhism and haiku, once said, "For every person there's a religion. And for every religion there's a person." Amen. This holds true for the Buddha's way, as well. It's said there are 84,000 Dharma doors (entrances to the Way) because there are at least 84,000 different basic kinds of suffering. (Here, too, there's probably a numbered list of them all in some monastery somewhere.) But remember: The Dharma has but one taste, the taste of liberation.

Sometimes the path comes with the teacher, as when you like a particular teacher and so will naturally learn of her or his lineage. Or you may start with a sense of what lineage you'd like, and then find an appropriate teacher.

Just as we've seen how interfaith spirituality can be nourishing, so can intra-faith: being conversant with different species of Buddhism. It's good to visit sanghas of other lineages from time to time. Different sanghas give you a fresh perspective; new teachers may have a healing or message that seems just for you.

Leaves from the Bodhi Tree

The master of a monastery interviewed a new monk. "Who'd you study with before?" he asked. After the monk answered "So-and-So," the master asked what he'd learned. "Well, I'd asked him what's the meaning of Buddhism, and he said, 'The Fire God comes for fire.'" The master said, "Good answer! I guess you didn't understand it." The monk replied, "But I did understand! If the Fire God asks for fire, that would be like my asking about Buddhism, because I'm really a buddha already." The master shook his head, and said, "I knew it. You missed the point completely." "Well, how do you handle it?" The master said, "You ask me." So the monk asked him, "What's the meaning of Buddhism?" "The Fire God comes for fire," replied the master, and the monk got it.

Don't Sweat the Isms

The more experience you have of the variety of the Buddha's way, the more you'll appreciate *your* way. As you move through Buddhaland, don't be shy. Listen to and learn from Pure Land, Insight Meditation, Tibetan, and Zen ... Hinayana, Mahayana, Vajrayana ... even Swami Beyondananda.

Understanding the essentials is always a good critical tool ("criticism" coming from Greek *kroinos*, to choose). Major paths of practice are spotlighted in the following chapters. But they're only doors. The true Way is underneath your feet.

When the Student Is Ready, the Master Appears

American author Erma Bombeck once said something very appropriate here: Never go to a doctor whose houseplants have died. That is, you could really like a teacher, but look around and look within. If, deep down, you don't feel comfortable, then they're not right for you. Don't worry. Another will turn up.

Just like you, each teacher's a unique human being. Some might have thick black lines around themselves, clearly marking off their lineage. Others might be eclectic. And just as each teacher's different, so will each student take what they need, differently. A good teacher optimizes the conditions for your own practice. How you respond and what you make of it all goes to make up the wonderful mystery of you.

> ### Along the Path
>
> Each practice emphasizes its teacher-student relationship differently. In Tibetan practice, the teacher (*guru*) must be worthy of unconditional trust, and the relationship will often be lifelong. In Korea, teachers (*sunim*) rotate, so monks eventually study under four teachers.

> **This Is**
>
> In Thailand, a Buddhist teacher is called *ajahn* (from the Sanksrit *acharya*, "*teacher*"). Theravada teachers are considered a *kalyana mitra* (*spiritual friend*) and act as mentors. In Japanese Zen, a teacher's called *roshi* (Japanese for "old master") and in Korean it's *sunim* (soo-neem). Here, as in Tibetan practice, a student works closely, one-on-one, in addition to guidance from monastic or lay meditation teachers. A Tibetan teacher is a *guru*, *lama* and *rinpoche* (RIHN-poe-shay) being two kinds; a *geshe* (geh-shee) is a scholar.

Often you can feel a special affinity, right off. Besides your deep-down gut feeling, here are a few objective road signs to check out in choosing a teacher:

♦ Does the teacher communicate in a way you can readily understand? Or do you have to mentally translate a great deal of foreign-sounding information?

♦ Is the teacher cold? Do they smile? Light's important, but so is warmth, compassion as well as wisdom.

♦ Do the teacher and the sangha seem harmonious and happy? Do they teach or emphasize the precepts?

♦ Check credentials. What was this teacher's relationship to their teacher? What do you hear from others you know? Avoid gossip, but listen to wise counsel and experience.

♦ Has a cult evolved around the teacher? Do other students copy his or her dress or speech patterns?

♦ Do they make lofty claims or promise easy enlightenment? Are they authoritarian about their power? Do they use threats, or fear?

♦ Remember, too, that teachers are only human and have quirks and foibles.

Go as a Sangha

The quote is from the Buddha. What he's saying is: When you step out onto a path, you can go alone, or with the whole universe. When challenged by Mara he touched the earth, calling all living things as witness. We can do this, too, when we practice. Listening to the sound of the wind through the trees, we can hear the voice of the Buddha teaching the Dharma. In the sunlight on a hill we can see the body of the Buddha teaching the Dharma.

With whom shall you joyfully join in with? Of all the e-mail queries I'm so happy to receive, the most common question has been, "Where can I find a group to practice with?" For those with Net access, I posted a page on this book's website (Dharma Door, http://awakening.to/sangha.html) with links to online directories plus a book or two. The backs of *Inquiring Mind, Shambhala Sun,* and *Tricycle* magazines have good directories.

Two tips for beginners. 1) To practice sitting quietly in stillness in community, see if any Quaker groups meet in your area (perhaps called "Religious Society of Friends" in the phone book). Make a visit, and see. 2) To become comfortable about posture, see if there's any Zen sangha that meets in your area, and find out when they offer an introduction for beginners. They usually take great care to go through posture in detail, which is valuable training. (We'll review sitting in stillness and posture in the next chapter.)

Most sanghas meet regularly, such as once a week or month. Sangha reinforces good habits of practice and, like potatoes bumping around together boiling in a pot, rounds out rough spots. You may well have experienced similar human communion. Authors and actors, for example, in front of an audience feel a "living link," an impalpable group mind. And there's a noticeable difference between getting up in front of a dozen and a thousand people. Consciousness is aware of other consciousness. This awareness is magnified in sangha. We're all part of one big living thing.

Sangha's buoyant as an ocean. My practice is upheld by the sangha as a boat upon water, as I uphold it by my practice. Sangha's also a community resource center. Sangha members are there for each other. Sangha is refuge. It's true security. And healing. A dear member of my root sangha once told us, following meditation one rainy afternoon, of his terminal cancer. He'd tried and given up on the painkillers. "*This,*" he said, "is the only thing that helps."

Viewless View and Effortless Effort

We've reviewed what a practice calls for. Before proceeding to basic meditation, I'd like to pass along one more very general tip (like beginner's mind, with which we began), for you to tuck away in your pocket and use whenever need arises. It dots the "i" in our *attitude*, and crosses a "t" in our *effort*.

Road Sign: Perfect View Begins Here

Why meditate? *Exercise:* Take a sheet of paper, and write these two words at the top. Then give it some perfect thought. Look below the surface. Ask yourself, "What are my inmost urgencies? My highest aspirations? My deepest wish? What would be nice side benefits as well?" You might frame your answers as verbs or adjectives, rather than nouns. For example, from a list written by a poet named Suvanna: "… to practice noticing … to understand simple things … to face inevitable difficulties … to make a conscious choice … to welcome my feelings … to learn without words … to unlock my heart …"

What you write will be like the mental snapshot you took at the beginning of this chapter. Review it from time to time. You might well find the reasons you take up practice to be different from why you were drawn to it in the first place. And you might stay with it for yet another reason.

Hear and Now

"Simply practice meditation in order to live a better life, or even just to live a good life, whatever meaning that holds for you. Or, meditate as a means of learning how not to be afraid—of death, or of all the insignificant concerns that paralyze your innate ability to live fully. Meditate to activate creativity. Meditate to recognize the value of the truly good things in life: friendship, honor, respect, compassion, and love."

—Ajahn Sumano Bhikkhu

It's good to have a sense of where you are and where you want to go. To get there, the best view is no viewpoint, empty of all views. Enlightenment *is* the ultimate goal. But it can't be reached, only found, not through grasping, only by letting go. A process of sweeping away instead of building up. Meditation reveals the delusions that have crusted over our true nature, and shows us how to gently scrub, polish, and appreciate its innate radiance. Yes, meditation could clear your thinking, sharpen your concentration, empower your intuition, deepen your compassion, elevate your wisdom, and might make you psychic and improve your tennis score. But you might think of these more as possible bonuses, rather than goals.

Striving after enlightenment is a setup for a fall. It's a vicious cycle, building up self and so only limiting our view. The true nature of mind is transparent, boundless. So when limited, illusory self, blinded by opinions and views, seeks selflessness by saying, "*I want* (grasping) to *calm myself* (believing there's a tangible, separate, lasting self to calm, and that it can be switched on and off)," that only reinforces the illusory self that perpetuates suffering. It's like trying to lift yourself up while sitting on a chair. (Don't go there.)

Let the Middle Way guide you, as well as your sangha. That is, don't use meditation to build up your sense of self. ("I can sit full lotus, nyah-nyah.") Nor try to annihilate your self through meditation. ("Out, out, damned spot!") Start with where you are. Work with what you have. Be compassionate toward others and yourself. Make friends with the universe and yourself. Take time. And don't worry about having to start all over again. Why do you think they call it "practice"!?

Effort Can Be Effortless

The Path has checks and balances. Examining and constantly re-examining one's view, one's attitude, one's intentions, is balanced by Proper Effort (persistence, continuity, and attention). Pay attention, for example, to linguistic traps that can reveal underlying confusions. For instance, a person might say "I want to calm my mind." Question: Where is your mind? It's like asking to bring back a pot of gold at the end of a rainbow—the more you search, the further it gets. You'll find that *trying* to calm your mind down often makes your mind only more restless, like a wild horse at the sight of a harness. (The next chapter is about how the mind gets calm.) Instead, you'll find that effort can be effortless.

We've also seen that effort means persistence, to be done regularly. And it's continuous, not only every day but *everyday*, as in all the time. (The next chapter shows how breathing meditation is always available to us.) True, meditation's but a part of the Eightfold Path, yet isn't separable from the whole. Conscious conduct is also a meditation; wisdom, ditto. *Practice* is continual. Whether sitting on a cushion or in a car. It's all practice. (You know what the man coming out of the subway said to the lost boy holding a violin case going in who asked him, "How can I get to Carnegie Hall?"—"Practice, practice!")

The Least You Need to Know

- Practice means finding and staying on your spiritual path. It's not like music you practice to perform at some later date, but, rather, an act to put you in touch with the present moment. It's more like musical scales, which musicians practice daily, no matter their level of achievement.

- The best approach is to take a beginner's mind, a "don't-know" mind, with no preconceptions or judgments. Always.

- Everyone can find a place for practice at home. It's more important to practice daily than sporadically for great lengths of time.

- Altars are an option. If you bow to an image of the Buddha, it's to acknowledge, pay respects to, and nurture the buddha within you. Beads, a bell, and incense are also optional for meditation.

- You might find a teacher through interest in a certain school, or vice-versa. When choosing a teacher, do some homework and listen to your heart.

- Understand that meditation isn't a means to an end, it is the means *and* the end.

Meditation: Base Camp

In This Chapter

- ◆ Posture and stretches
- ◆ Conscious breathing
- ◆ Relaxed body, quiet mind
- ◆ Walking meditation
- ◆ Common obstacles and how to get around them

Has this happened to you? You're in a religious congregation and it's come time for silent meditation. You put your hands together. Everyone closes their eyes, bowing their heads. Five seconds later, *zip!* it's over. (And not very silent if an organist doodled soft chords in the background.) It's like a small footprint of what was once a larger practice; a vestige, or clue. While established, mainstream religious practices are very rich in their ethical systems and wisdom traditions, the meditation component has diminished. And so the turn toward Eastern spirituality for meditation. Truth is where you find it.

I liken meditation to base camp, since we live in a meditation-deficient world. True, wisdom can be your base, or conscious conduct, each equally important. But once you conceive wisdom and conduct and meditation as inseparable, you'll see everything as an opportunity for meditation. With every breath.

Pure meditation is a mindful oasis where you can be still and renew your vision and vows while on your sacred pilgrimage called life. This chapter and the next will survey meditation fundamental within Buddhism as well as other traditions. Welcome to Base Camp! We'll start at Square One …

Be a Buddha and Sit Like a Buddha: Posture

Archeologists in the Indus Valley have dug up small figurines in the posture of yogic meditation dating back at least five millennia. That's a long time to be sitting. Sure, the sculptor might've been commemorating a sit-down strike or something. We don't know for sure; they didn't come with descriptive booklets. But just looking at them you sense a reverence. It seems as if the very posture of sitting cross-legged can mean so much.

In the full lotus, the classic meditation position, each leg's on the opposite thigh. In a half lotus, only one foot rests on the opposite thigh, the other rests on the floor or on the calf, and often with a pillow to support that knee. And in the Burmese position, both feet are folded in front of your body, not crossed over each other, both knees on the floor.

Have you tried it? Seated, cross-legged, your body gets the message that you aren't going anywhere. So all the little alarm bells hard-wired into our physiology, always on the lookout for dangers in the environment, dim down and cease. Your hands aren't manipulating any tools. There's nothing to say. Nothing to do, but sit and breathe, in the here and in the now. Now something else can come to the fore: the sheer simplicity of living! Peace can be as simple and solid as that.

Knees slightly apart, you can meditate while kneeling. You can sit on your heels, or a small bench, or your zafu on end. If you sit in a chair, see if you can not rely on the back of your chair for support. Rely on yourself.

Ears over Shoulders: Basic Posture

The basics have remained the same for millennia. If you can, you sit on a cushion on the floor, but a chair works, too. (I've heard someone tell of having a strong initial taste of enlightenment while sitting in a high-school auditorium chair.) Your contact with the ground should feel like a stable tripod, of knees and sit-space. Feel yourself sink down into this contact, like a mountain upon the earth. Let your tailbone make contact with the ground, and your anus tilt up, along with your hips.

Based on this tripod, you can feel like a pyramid, really upright, with your head on top. Your back needs to be straight so breath and energy can flow freely. Imagine there's a small ring at the top of your head, where your hair meets your scalp, and a hook comes down from the sky, engages that ring, and gently lifts you *up*, as far as your waist. Everything above your waist stretches straight upward. Your lower back naturally curves in and your upper back naturally curves out (shoulders, back). Your spine's erect and stretched, not hunched or scrunched.

Sit in a way that embodies dignity. Everybody knows that feeling and how to embody it. Rediscover it. Reclaim it. You can practice throughout the day. Think "sky hook"; think "dignity.")

Your shoulders are back so your chest can comfortably expand. Your ears are over shoulders. Your shoulders are over your hips. Your nose is aligned with your navel. Your eyes are horizontal with the ground, but you tuck your chin in, which lowers your head just a fraction. (You don't want to squish the back of your brain, nor your larynx.) You might imagine your head supports the sky.

Your hands can rest on your knees, palms down or up. (More on hands in a second.) Now, test your position. Sway front and back, then left and right. Get centered.

Hear and Now

"The state of mind that exists when you sit in the right posture is, itself, enlightenment. If you cannot be satisfied with the state of mind you have in zazen, it means your mind is still wandering about. Our body and mind should not be wobbling or wandering about. In this posture there is no need to talk about the right state of mind. You already have it. This is the conclusion of Buddhism."

—Shunryu Suzuki Roshi

Giving Body Language a Hand: Mudras

As the motionless posture of our legs and feet sends a message to our brain (that we're not going anywhere), so, too, does the placement of our hands hold meaning. An etiquette book, for example, may tell you not to put your little finger out at a 45-degree angle when you hold your fork, so as not to appear "backstairs refined." For Buddha, the two-fingered V-sign seems universal, akin to thumbs-up. In a grammar book of "body language," gestures would take up a chapter at least. All the Buddha's gestures (*mudras*) have meaning (not requiring verbal literacy), such as his earth-touching mudra. Fingers outstretched except tip of thumb and index finger meeting in a circle is the mudra of teaching.

This Is

Fingers aligned, palms join together for a **bow** (*namaskar/namastey*, Hindu; *wai*, Thai; and *gassho*, Japanese). Besides a bow, Buddhist hand gestures are called **mudras** (Sanskrit for "sign," or "seal"). Tibetan Buddhists particularly cultivate this art. By imitating certain gestures outwardly, we can cultivate the inner state associated with them. (Means become ends; the path becomes the goal.)

Two basic gestures practitioners use are in bowing and in meditation. Bowing is a meditation, in and of itself, and can be done just by joining palms, a universal gesture of spirit. There's a famous etching by Albrecht Dürer of two hands praying, as if by themselves. In the East, putting palms and fingers together is a gesture of spiritual greeting, instead of shaking hands. In India and Thailand, you put your palms together at your chest and raise them to your forehead, often followed by a bow, still in that position—eyes and joined hands going outward and down to a spot on the ground equidistant between the greeter and the greeted. A bow can also be a quarter-inch. However done, bow or no bow, "palms-joined" says "The buddha within me salutes the buddha within you" (*no dualism*). "Have a nice day."

The cosmic meditation mudra.

When seated, you can place your palms on your knees. One standard pose of great power is often called the *cosmic mudra*. Place the back of your right hand on top of your left palm. Adjust how close or far apart your hands are so your thumbs make contact ever so lightly, at about the height of your navel. From the front, the space between your hands resembles an egg (hold it without dropping it). Behind it is a point below your navel called *dan tien* in Chinese, *hara* in Japanese, considered your true center—physically in posture, and spiritually as central repository of life-force, also known as *prana* and *chi*. When you've got the gesture, you might hear the universe give you silent applause; forget about it, that's just extra.

Getting Down to Earth: Prostration

This is a good time to mention *prostration*. Muslims do it six times a day. In Buddhism, it starts with hands together, above your head. Then lower them to 1) the crown of your head, 2) your mouth or neck, and 3) the center of your chest (your spiritual heart). A half prostration takes kneeling, and touching the earth with hands and forehead. In full prostration, hands then slide forward, until completely lying down. Sometimes people then raise their palms slightly, while keeping heads down, before smoothly reversing the process to a standing position.

Prostrations are common in Chinese, Korean, and Japanese temples. Going for refuge takes three prostrations, reciting "I take refuge in the Buddha," "I take refuge in the Dharma," "I take refuge in the Sangha," one for each prostration. Here we see prostration + recitation + visualized image integrating body, speech, and mind.

Doing No Thing: How Relaxing!

Sitting in meditation, if nothing else, can be very relaxing. In our "go-there, do-this" world, this can take some getting used to. You know the saying?: "Don't just sit there, do something!" Well, Buddhists like to rephrase it: "Don't do something, just sit there!" When we're always in motion, doing things, our minds can get scattered, losing one-pointed concentration, and so never really do any one thing all the way through.

Sitting can be just that one thing. You're not trying to get anywhere. So let be. In the next chapter, you'll learn a Buddhist "body scan" technique for deep relaxation, but let's get a head start. (We'll start at the head.) Here's one exercise for you to try. You'll just let each of your muscles relax, group by group, head to toes. Start at the top. Relax your scalp; relax your face; relax the sides of your neck; relax the back of your neck; relax your shoulders. And so on. And notice your breath.

What about the eyes? Seeing is really a very intricate, complex process. Closing the eyes is a common way to begin to relax. It frees us from all that information: the rectilinear borders partitioning space, and which includes seeming domination by objects, and the primitive back-brain alert-system, on the look-out on the environment. Eyes-closed directs sight inward instead. Eyes closed, we feel rounder and more boundless. Pitfalls to eyes-closed are possibly hallucinating or falling asleep. Once relaxed, you might reopen your eyes, relaxed, still half-closed maybe. If you're facing a wall, pick some spot at eye-level. When concentration wanders, return to the spot. An alternative spot is a space about three inches from your nose. Or a spot on the floor about a yard away. When in sangha, maybe a spot on the back of the person in front of you.

Now, did you know?—there are about 300 muscles in your face alone. Letting them all relax takes a little time. As you do so, why not smile!? Exercising just one of those 300 muscles can actually make you feel happier. (Go ahead and try it, right now!) You need only lift one corner of your mouth, slightly, like Mona Lisa; or the Buddha. Breathe. And feel the smile. Thich Nhat Hanh has coined a nifty phrase for this: "mouth yoga." He remarks, "Why wait until you are completely transformed, completely awakened? You can start being a part-time Buddha right now!"

You might ask, "What do I do with my tongue?" Answer: Rest tongue on roof of mouth. Tip to inside upper lip. (*Mmmmm.*)

What if I Froze Like This?: Warm-Up Stretches

Oscar Wilde once prayed, "Spare me *physical* pain!" We're only human, so we're bound to feel discomfort. Sitting regularly for as little as a half-hour can be demanding of neck and knees, for example, two anatomic features that haven't changed a heck of a lot since we redistributed our weight from four legs to two. And when withheld energy starts flowing during meditation, it's wise to be bodily grounded. (I'm not suggesting that blue sparks will start flying out of the top of your head—yikes!) Physical pains often fall away on their own, just by being aware of the ebb and flow of distractions and any waves of our mindstream, without judgment, and letting them pass. But you're not inviting pain. So warm-ups are a sound investment in a healthy, happy practice.

Please check out *The Complete Idiot's Guide to Yoga* for information on such poses as the Bound Angle, the Butterfly, the Cat, the Cobbler, the Cobra, the Cradle, the Downward-Facing Dog, the Hero, the Locust, the Lunge, the Supported Bridge, and the Triangle. See *The Complete Idiot's Guide to Tai Chi and QiGong* for tai chi warm-up exercises, all of which make excellent stretches for meditation. There are also Tibetan Buddhist exercises called *Kum-Nye* you might want to explore, too.

Yoga instruction in such poses as the downward-facing dog (left) and butterfly (right) help keep the pain demons away from meditation sessions, and make you feel more human afterward.

Why Not Breathe: You're Alive!

It's amazing, but we forget we breathe all the time. Yet no matter the spiritual tradition, breath's an essential ingredient. What could be more impermanent and insubstantial, yet vital and universal? In the biblical creation story, human beings were fashioned out of red clay and infused with the divine breath of life. It's interesting that the word used in the New Testament for spirit literally means *breath*. Thus, in John 20:22, "Receive thou the Holy Spirit," the original is literally "Receive holy breath."

This Is

The Sanskrit word for breath, *prana*, also means universal energy, life-force. The origin of a Chinese word for this energy, *chi* (pronounced *chee*, also spelled *qi*), is steam, vapor. The word *spirit* comes from Latin, *spiritus*, *spirare*, meaning breath; to breathe. (Inspiration means breathing in.) Old Testament Hebrew and Greek words for spirit, *ruach* and *pneuma*, mean breath but also wind (merging within and without). And Hebrew and Arabic *nefes* means soul as well as breath.

I don't know if Jesus taught his disciples conscious breathing, but it's an interesting notion. (Consider Acts 2:4, for example: "And they were all filled with the Holy Spirit"—filled with holy breath; perhaps also filled with the awareness of the holiness of breath?) Christians who practice Buddhist conscious breathing sometimes call it "resting in the Spirit." Meditating on breath brought Siddhartha to Grand Enlightenment. And so he specifically addressed conscious breathing. Buddhism may be the only wisdom tradition with a complete manual on mindful breathing (called the Sutra on Full Awareness of Breathing).

Breathing's universal and ever-present. All living things breathe, all the time, *consciously* or not. It's integral to our state of *being*. So it's a perfect, ever-present vehicle for the practice of being conscious.

Meditation can be just one breath long ... an impromptu mini-meditation ... a pause that releases. One conscious breath. Breathing in, just being aware you're breathing in. Breathing out, just being aware you're breathing out. One-breath meditation can be an initiation into being consciously attentive. And when you've spent 30 minutes or more devoted just to conscious breathing, it forms a base camp which you can access with just a few conscious breaths.

So here follows a couple pages with some techniques to assist one-pointed mindful breathing meditation. Read and see if just one might sound especially interesting. Trying them all right now might be overkill. We'll explore just three such mindfulness techniques that may accompany conscious breathing:

◆ Body awareness

◆ Counting breaths

◆ Mantras and gathas

Hear and Now

"This is universal. You sit and observe your breath. You can't say this is Hindu breath or Christian breath or Muslim breath. Knowing how to live peacefully or harmoniously—you don't call this religion or spirituality. It is nonsectarian."

—Charles Johnson

Note: This isn't yoga. That is, you aren't trying to control your breath, nor make it any different than it already is. Your job is to just watch it. It may seem like a paradox: controlling the breath to control the mind, without controlling anything, just observing. But that's the name of the game. If you try to control the mind, it becomes even harder to tame, like a wild horse.

And these are only tools. The raft is not the shore. Your meditation's not about nose or tummy (not to mention the parameningeal epigastrum). Basic meditation is about letting body, mind, and breath get reacquainted, and seeing how these old friends work well together.

Having a Gut Feeling That the Nose Knows

Two areas of your *body* can help center your mind on your breathing—and then help your breathing center your mind. You can focus one-pointed awareness on either your *nostrils* or your *navel*.

Mouth closed, your breath comes and goes through your nostrils. Sitting still for a moment, right now, consciously rediscover that simple fact. When you're ready, put this book aside and see. Notice if one or both nostrils are open. Moreover, direct your attention to the very *tips* of your nostrils. Letting your breath just fall away, feel how hot it feels—a warm and fuzzy pleasure, perhaps. Breathing in, feel how cool breath can be—maybe even how fragrant.

Alternatively, you can focus concentration on your navel. Maybe you've heard Stereotype #164 of Eastern meditation as being "navel-gazing." Actually, it's not the navel, but an area called *hara* or *dan tien* that you focus on. About the size of a dime, it's three or four fingers down from your navel. If our nostrils are the doorway, then this might be thought of as the palace basement, the storehouse, the secret treasury. Just practicing conscious breathing on this acupressure point for 20 minutes can bring calm focus and a deeper, fuller connection with life.

Focusing on belly breathing may run counter to the way you've been brought up. I know I was taught to keep my abdomen hard, military-style. "Hold it in," the expression went, and, since body and mind are one, this applied to emotions as well; aren't they often called "gut feelings"? So it's not uncommon to see people trying to breathe deeply by expanding their chest rather than their bellies. When frightened, babies breathe in their chests, as if scared of contacting something overwhelming in their belly. Some people often carry this trait over into adulthood as a basic policy toward life. ("Uh-oh, this might make me breathe deeply: Houston, we have a problem.") Notice how far down your body moves with your own breath. Don't try to change or judge it. Just observe.

Breathing out, our belly naturally contracts, as the bellows of our lungs compresses, expelling stale air. Breathing in, our belly naturally expands. Concentrating on your lower tummy instead of your nose, be aware of this: how your belly fills when you inhale, and falls when you exhale. As you do so, feel a natural *softening* of any hardness in your belly, breath by breath. Breathe *into* any tightness in your belly. *Exhale* any tension this might release. (*Ahh!*)

After a few sessions of conscious belly breathing, you might find your breathing fills your belly more than before, automatically. If so, just notice it. If not, no sweat. Breath eventually deepens and slows and calms of its own. Belly awareness can assist the process. This is the Buddha's way—providing the nourishment for our seeds of awareness to blossom into a lotus.

Making Each Breath Count

Counting's another way to focus awareness on breath, and keep your mind from wandering. Try this: *Calmly let your breath fall away in exhalation and say to yourself "one,"* *then breathe in that "one." Breathe out again, and begin "two."* (Or breathe *in* on one, and count the exhale.) Don't think of anything else but your breath. Just your breathing in, your breathing out, and a very quick, light count. And nothing else. At "four" return to "one" again. If your mind wanders, as it does, begin all over again, at "one."

Here are some tips about counting. If you can't make it all the way to four, you're not an idiot (!) Buddhist friends of mine, even after decades of practice, are still at four. And if you can make it to four, you're a junior Buddha. Try ten. But remember, you're not trying to reach a goal—it's only practice.

You don't have to feel like a dummy to return to such simplicity as 1-2-3-4; these are basics of life. Buddhism's an opportunity for starting over. Back to basics. Beginner's mind.

And remember, too, to keep your attention on your breathing, not the count. And when you're ready, let go of these training wheels and just be conscious of your breathing, in and of itself. Simple as 1-2-3. Peace is every breath.

Consider conscious breathing as your base—from which to set forth, and explore, and to which you can come home. It's that center or *centering* you might hear about in spiritual circles. A *grounding* in something as indestructible as earth. Invest in regular practice to maintain this base camp. Build upon it by adding five minutes to your practice until you're comfortable just sitting, *enjoying your breathing,* for 45 minutes or so.

Words to Meditate by: *Mantras* and *Gathas*

Besides body awareness and counting, two more options for focusing awareness on breathing and quieting the mind are verbal:

♦ Mantra

♦ Gatha

Mantra is another Sanskrit word to have made its way into everyday speech. A mantra ("mohn-trah") can be like a word or phrase repeated to aid our memory. Thus, when we repeat the Buddha's name, we're remembering him. It can also symbolize and communicate a certain energy or deity, dissolving our clinging to negative habit energy by substituting positive habit energy.

One mantra for conscious breathing meditation is mentally saying "IN" while breathing in, and "OUT" while breathing out. Concentrating on each word focuses the mind on breathing. In. Out. One single word for one single breath. Some people mentally recite "in-in-in" and "out-out-out," emphasizing the whole flow of each breath. *Tip:* It's okay if you find yourself breathing out a bit longer than you're breathing in.

A Buddhist *gatha* ("gah-thah") is a verse from a sutra or an individual's expression of spiritual insight. Some can be recited mentally—you might think of them as prayers, but not exactly so because they aren't expressed to any supreme deity beyond our own mind. For example, here's a stanza in the Sutra on Full Awareness of Breathing:

> Breathing in, I know that I am breathing in.
> Breathing out, I know that I am breathing out.

Using that gatha as a conscious breathing tool, say the first line to yourself when breathing in, the second when breathing out. It's very suitable for a 20- to 30-minute meditation. You might find that during meditation you've made a mental shorthand of it to just the words "in" and "out." Just keep your mindfulness on the breathing, not the words.

Thich Nhat Hanh has written this lovely gatha, which I highly recommend for conscious breathing:

> Breathing in, I calm my body.
> Breathing out, I smile.
> Breathing in, I'm aware of the present moment.
> Breathing out, I'm aware it's a wonderful moment.

Think the first line to yourself, breathing in; the second, exhaling; the third, inhaling; the last, exhaling. Then return to the beginning. After you get the hang, you can use a kind of mental shorthand:

[In] think *"Calm"*
[Out] think *"Smile"*
[In] think *"Present moment"*
[Out] think *"Wonderful moment"*

Slow, Deep, Calm Release: Peace Is Every Breath

The preceding help spotlight breathing with a mindful ray of awareness. At first, you might not have even been aware you were breathing. Half the time, who is?! Gradually, you'll become more familiar with breath and its landscape. Don't try to change your breathing. This isn't yoga. If a breath's long, just notice that fact. If another breath's short, just notice that.

Become aware, too, of the beginning, the middle, and the end of each in-breath and out-breath. Also be attentive to how breath begins: after an out-breath. Without your willing it, a new breath will appear. All by itself. ("Ta-Da!") Notice, too, how breath flows. Is it powerful or soft; shallow or deep? And if there's a space in between breaths, notice that, too. Train yourself to notice each of these qualities. Emily Dickinson once called herself an "inebriate of air," but connoisseur of air will do just fine.

And breath helps spotlight awareness. As you learn to become more and more immersed in awareness of your breathing, one very interesting thing you'll eventually notice is that not only your breathing—but also your body, and your emotions, and your mind—will calm. Slowing down. Deepening.

You might experience a feeling of at-oneness … a sense of release … and pleasure. A new kind of pleasure, maybe. If so, go with it. You deserve it. You've earned it. By simply being.

Meditation can bring not only peace but also great joy. (See for yourself why the Buddha's smiling.) True peace.

Breath is a tremendous tool for unifying body and mind as one. Putting it a different way, Suzuki Roshi gives a marvelous teaching when he calls breathing a *hinge*. We breathe in, he says, and air comes into the inner world; exhale, air goes to the outer world. Inner world / outer world—both endless. Actually, there's but one world, the whole world. Breath passes through us like someone going through a swinging door. "When your mind is pure and calm enough to follow this movement," Suzuki continues, "there is nothing: no 'I,' no world, no mind nor body; just a swinging door."

Hear and Now

"'I am breathing in and making my whole body calm and at peace.' It is like drinking a cool glass of lemonade on a hot day and feeling your body become cool inside. When you breathe in, the air enters your body and calms all the cells of your body. At the same time each 'cell' of your mind also becomes more peaceful. The three are one, and each one is all three. This is the key to meditation. Breathing brings the sweet joy of meditation to you. You become joyful, fresh, and tolerant, and everyone around you will benefit."

—Thich Nhat Hanh

Turning Off the Radio: Quieting the Mind

"Turning off the radio" is Robert Aitken Roshi's phrase, and I love it. Don't you just immediately know what he means!? Of course, in the decades since he coined it, it's become only more apt. That is, we've become a soundtracked culture, with music to study by, cassettes to drive by, CDs to walk by, cell phone conversations you wish you hadn't overheard, and less and less opportunity for us to have big ears for the utterly unique and even amazing all-natural sounds all around, within and without. And the empty silence with which they're interwoven. Preprogrammed, artificial stimuli usually don't quiet the mind but pre-empt it, with somebody else's agenda and doings. Quieting the mind is very basic. It's a shushing of the mind's verbal activity the way an audience quiets down when a concert or movie is about to begin.

Our built-in mental radio talk-show roof-brain chatter fades off into the background, if we just let it. The drunken monkey stops twirling the dial, if no longer fed. Does it ever go entirely off? Misconception #97 is that Buddhist meditation is about becoming a blank. (*Click!:* "OFF.") No, and (#98) you don't just drift off and away, somewhere else. Rather, like an audience as the curtains part, we stop, look, listen … and hear. Here!

Our base camp of meditation makes available the solidity and clarity we need to be aware of and let go of our incessant inner monologues and dialogues. Listening instead of reacting, we can see how our mind creates an illusory sense of life and self. So we don't change the world; we change our minds, and we notice our world has changed, too.

Leaves from the Bodhi Tree

Contemporary Cambodian Buddhist patriarch Maha Ghosananda tells of a young monk who studied diligently, every day. But he grew upset that he couldn't learn everything, and soon couldn't sleep or eat. Finally, he came to the Buddha and asked to leave the order. "Please," he said, "there are many teachings and I can't master them all. I'm not fit to be a monk." The Buddha told him, "Don't worry. To be free you must master only one thing." The monk begged, "Please teach me. If you give me just one practice, I will do it wholeheartedly, and I'm sure I can succeed." So the Buddha told him, "Master the mind. When you've mastered the mind, you'll know everything."

Being aware of our breathing, we become aware of our mind. Here are three tips for optimal *mind-watching*, which we'll explore next:

◆ Just notice what you notice, without comment.

◆ Appreciate sounds as well as silence.

◆ Be mindful and compassionate toward yourself.

Notice What You Notice

Quieting your mind is like calming your breath. You're not trying to make anything happen. Your job's just to breathe and observe. Observe your breath, and all its qualities. And if thoughts come, observe them, too—but don't invite them to sit down with you for tea. Unattended, they'll go off on their own merry way. ("All conditioned things have their arising, and their passing away.")

Be like a mirror, or mountain lake, that reflects whatever passes before it. Tibetan Buddhists suggest just watching your thoughts the way an old person on a park bench watches children at play, without paying attention to which kids are yours or not. Your thoughts aren't necessarily you. By your not identifying with them, they dwindle away.

Note Sounds (*Plink!*) as Well as Silence ( )

The concept of silencing the mind is a kind of stereotype. Meditation's not a sensory deprivation tank, though in a real sensory deprivation tank you'll still hear your heart, and your nervous system. So don't be surprised to find meditation accompanied by the gentle drums of your pulse, the lilting flute of your breath, and the hummmmm of body-mind. They're just part of the furnishings, along for the ride.

Treat your senses the same as your thoughts. You might hear the jagged yawp of a bird, the corkscrewing siren of a passing fire truck, the rumble of a window shaken by the wind. Just hear what you hear. Without reacting. Passing cars might be more soothing than you'd expect, more like ocean waves. Let go of your prejudices and preconceptions, and listen. And notice how sounds overlap in curious, unrepeatable rhythms! All they mean is that you're here, and now. Let whatever comes to your senses during meditation awaken you to that fact. And continue to enjoy your breathing.

> **Leaves from the Bodhi Tree** _____
>
> *Sound meditation.* Sit where you won't be disturbed. Close your eyes. Relax. Take a few, slow, full conscious breaths. Listen to whatever sounds come to your ears. Be only ears. Big ears. Let sounds grow more vivid. Don't label, other than all being "The Sound of the Universe," or "Life." As if it's all music, a special symphony, the most contemporary ever, and you've been given the best seat in the house. When done, take some time to reacquaint yourself with your surroundings. And listen for encores.

Be Mindful and Compassionate Toward Yourself

Meditation can have its ups and downs. Remember to smile. Why not treat your mind as a mother would her own child? Have compassion for yourself. Smile at your habitual schemes and scenarios. By just letting them be, and being compassionately aware of them, you can let them go. Remember, there wouldn't be doors without walls, so don't bang your head on them! Be kind to yourself.

This also applies for dealing with other people's baggage. As you learn compassion for your own baggage, you'll have it for others'. Compassion for all beings includes yourself. If you can't be kind to yourself, who else can you be kind to?

Meditation in Action: Mindful Walking

"Slowly, slowly, step by step, each step is a meditation, each step is a prayer." That's Maha Ghosananda's saying, and I love it, perhaps because I love walking meditation and so I know what he means. It's often used as an opportunity to stretch after sitting. (In Zen, it's usually done for 5 minutes in between stretches of sitting; Theravadins also enjoy it in between sittings, for more like 20 minutes.) Just in and of itself, it can be a marvelous and very powerful practice.

Indoors or outdoors, find some place where you can walk without obstruction or interruption. A backyard will do, a quiet street, a big emptyish room, or a long, clear hallway. Your hands can be at your side. Or you can form a cosmic mudra (which is what I do). Some people join their palms in a gassho. Others make a fist and cover it with the other hand and hold them both to their navel or hara. Still others join their hands behind their back, like a bird with folded wings.

Check your posture (base camp). Let that sky hook pull your upper body up, and let your lower body just hang naturally. Your feet are apart about the width of your hips, and maybe bare, terrain permitting. Center yourself in your breathing for a moment. Then begin. Step forward with your left foot as you inhale. Exhale as you step forward with your right foot. One breath per step (yup! *that* slow). And when you come to a corner or the end of your allotted space, you just make a turn, 180 degrees or 90 degrees—two steps will do the trick—without breaking the pace.

Your assignment's to be aware of your breath *and* your motion, allowing them to coordinate comfortably, and see, too, how your mind interplays as you do so. At first, let the pace be slowwwww. Thich Nhat Hanh has a few fine suggestions for you to get the hang. Visualize you're a king or queen, making a decree with each step. Or visualize yourself a lion or lioness, walking so slowly. Or visualize a flower blossoming from every step.

Along the Path

It's thought that when primates first stood, that freed their forelimbs (wow! a whole new world). So brains expanded to meet that challenge. (Note which followed which.) Thus dawned the human species, the only species comfortable on two legs. In the mere act of walking, of being bipedal, we can reclaim an ancient wisdom hidden just beneath the whirl-a-gig surface of our ever faster-paced world. Walking literally creates the world, *our* world. Step by step.

It is said that, after Enlightenment, the Buddha's next meditation was walking, getting up and taking mindful steps around the bodhi tree, grateful for its having sheltered him during his long night. Having experienced total transformation, he put it into action.

I know for me, each step becomes a pilgrimage … a going forth and stepping out, into the unknown, embracing the entire universe, and recognizing oneness with it, realizing it … feeling the earth coming up, meeting my foot … kissing the earth from my soles to my toes, grateful for that literal solid support for my being, otherwise taken for granted … and finding tranquility, peace, and joy … the feeling of having arrived … the only destination there ever is: the present moment, our true home. Plus, it's a really nice body massage! But that's just my attempt to verbalize my own experience of it. Everyone will have their own. Try it, and see.

Once you've tried 20 minutes, notice if there's anything different about how you feel. Once you've gotten the hang, congratulations! You've established a new branch of your base camp. Then, next time, you can quicken your steps midway through, counting "in" for three steps, and "out" for three, say. You might say "in, in, in" as you step left-right-left, and "out, out, out," with the next three. Or you can try the four-line gatha (in the preceding section, herein), one line for each breath. And you might discover your own gatha for walking meditation. As Dharma teacher and gardener Wendy Johnson was practicing walking meditation one day, she found herself mentally saying to herself "Walking on the green earth" (*breathing in*), "each step is peace" (*breathing out*). (She says the words came up to her through the soles of her feet.) Try it out.

Hear and Now

"People say that walking on water is a miracle, but to me, walking peacefully on the Earth is the real miracle. The Earth is a miracle. Each step is a miracle. Taking steps on our beautiful planet can bring real happiness."

—Thich Nhat Hanh

Some tips for walking in mindfulness:

♦ Coordinate your breathing and your walking, and stay with just that. (This is subtler than trying to walk and chew gum at the same time—but not necessarily easier.)

♦ Bearing witness, shed all preconceptions. You're bearing witness to the universe, and your integral part thereof.

♦ Like all meditation, walking meditation is like dancing—you're not trying to reach any particular spot. There's no destination; you've already arrived: in the here and in the now.

♦ Notice what you notice, but don't get attached. Kiss the joy as it flies. (The orange-green iridescence on the wings of flies buzzing around some dung on the mosaic of the ground is no less perfect than dawn sunlight tingeing cloud tips with gentle gongs of peach incense.) Practice equanimity.

♦ If you're distracted, look at the ground a yard or so ahead, or the back of the person ahead of you in a group.

♦ Remember to practice mouth yoga.

♦ By taking just one peaceful step, you're affirming that peace in the world is possible. Don't just imagine it. Be it.

First-Aid Kit for Beginners' Problems

Your teacher and sangha are the best medicine for hindrances you may encounter along the Path. Meanwhile, here are a few remedies from an unofficial manual of Standard Operating Procedure (S.O.P.):

♦ Mind-wandering is natural. Don't beat yourself up over it. Just start over again. And again.

♦ Sometimes people feel a little dizzy when meditating. In that case, intervene for a moment and add a few extra beats to your exhalation. Exhaling more than you inhale rids the body of excess CO_2. Then you can resume. (You might have been forcing.) Allow your breath, don't force it.

♦ If you're going around in circles, try this: Take a slow deep breath, filling your lungs then your belly. Then slowly let it all out, belly then lungs. Repeat twice more. Now return to your practice.

- If you can't find 40 minutes a day, try 30. Even 20. (If you can't find five, re-examine your life!) Establish a comfort zone, then extend the perimeter. Practice regularly.

- Don't look for results. Subtle and gradual changes are just as good as dramatic and sudden. If a friend should remark you seem calmer or happier lately, you're on the right track.

- Being kindly to yourself, you'll find yourself seeing more connection with others.

- You can't step into the same river twice. Don't expect today's meditation to be like yesterday's.

And all the little tips and tricks in the world are just that. Counting to 4 or 10, mantra or beads. They can be very useful. Cherish them when you use them, but don't grow attached to them. They're like the finger that points to the moon, but isn't the moon itself. A raft is not the shore. Once you find you've reached the other shore, you don't go walking around wearing your raft on your head like a hat; you leave it behind, move on, and come back to it when you need.

So now don't do something—just sit!

The Least You Need to Know

- Meditation's like that center referred to when people speak of being centered. A grounding. Integral to wisdom and conscious conduct, it's a key to continual practice.

- Posture matters. The body isn't something to be escaped.

- Breath is a natural interface between body and mind, always available to us to work with. Conscious or mindful breathing means being aware of your breathing. Nothing else.

- You're not trying to control your breath, or your mind. Just be aware. Stopping and just being aware can calm your breath—and your mind.

- Quieting the mind doesn't mean turning into a stone statue. Trying to banish thoughts and control your mind only creates more thoughts and restless mind. Simple awareness can clear mental clutter and sharpen your mind.

- More than mere stretching, walking meditation is a powerful practice.

- Take a friendly attitude toward your mind. Everyone encounters difficulties. Learn from others' wisdom about common hurdles in meditation.

Look Within, and Know: Insight Meditation

In This Chapter

- ◆ Stopping and seeing—tranquility and insight

- ◆ Mental noting: hallmark of emotional intelligence

- ◆ The body scan: total tune-up

- ◆ Element meditation: our connection with the universe

- ◆ Impermanence meditation: insight into transformation

- ◆ Loving kindness (*metta*): basis for compassion, joy, and equanimity

When's the last time you experienced an *"Aha!"*? An *aha!* could be finding your keys and realizing why you hadn't been able to remember where they were; *aha!* You might be at a park and, suddenly, watching the behavior of some dogs, *aha!* you realize the answer to a puzzle that's been on your mind at work; *aha!* We all experience *aha!*'s. And, like realizing that by putting two building blocks next to each other you can put a third on top of them, *aha!* the accumulation of many little *aha!*'s lead to bigger *aha*'s: Awareness can lead to insight which can lead to wisdom. *Ahhh!!*

In Hebrew, there's a word for this aha!-experience: *"Shazam!"* A bolt out of the blue that lands precisely between the brows. It can also come from within. And gently. Insight/outlook; within/without—don't worry about seeming dualities. Learn the power of deep seeing. Look past walls and masks to Buddha's unerring teacher, your own living heart.

This is at the heart of the heart of Theravada Buddhist practice, also known as Vipassana (Insight Meditation). Surveying it, I think you'll see why its teachings continue to flourish.

Stopping and Seeing Deeply: Tranquil Concentration and Insight

Now that you know how to establish your own Buddhist base camp, you've already grasped parts of the twin concepts of *samatha* (stopping) and *vipassana* (insight). Basic meditation, as outlined in the previous chapter, balances, calms, and sharpens the mind. In Sanskrit, it's called *samatha* ("sah-mah-tah"), meaning stopping, calming, and also concentration. Stopping whatever you think you're doing and checking in with what's really going on. ("Call home.") Samatha chills you out from jangling distractions and peripheral static, inside and out, and lets you relax into one-pointed concentration in the here and now.

Stopping is a very good practice, anytime. It's not unusual to feel buffeted around like a pinball, from pillar to post. Today's ever-faster pace makes it seem harder to be simply present, but it's easy. When you see or hear something such as a bird or a child awakening your heart, consider it life calling you, a chance to practice stopping, on the fly. Stop, sense your breath, check in with the Here and Now. (Bowing is optional; an extra.)

We've seen how meditation in the Eightfold Path leads directly to wisdom. Now, with stopping (samatha) as our base of meditation, we'll see its flip side or twin, called *insight*. In Sanskrit, insight's called *vipassana* (meaning penetrative vision). Stopping lets our mind be calm, clear, sharp, and free; from such a place, insight penetrates to the essential nature of things, perceiving reality directly, through our own experience. What's reality? As we've learned from the Three Marks of Existence, all phenomena and all things are: 1) Impermanent; 2) Interdependent and thus empty of any separate self; and 3) Beyond duality, free, nirvana (the flip side of the duhkha pervading all things).

When we establish mindfulness within ourselves, we see things as they are, and from this place we can examine the truth of the Buddha's teachings for ourselves, and gain insight.

Using our own experience as a laboratory, with mindfulness we can look deeply at the Four Noble Truths. The life of the Buddha reminds us of his method of using his own life to understand the meaning of life. After he stopped his ascetic practices, his senses became more focused in the present. With mindfulness, he was able to concentrate on each aspect of every moment, which led to insight into the Three Marks and the Four Noble Truths. Having discovered that the human mind shapes our world and how we respond to it, he used his own mind as a key to fathom the nature of mind itself.

So we, too, can stop, develop our meditative powers of concentration, and look deeply at our life. To break a destructive habit, for example, we can examine karma with calm clarity, contemplating the root of our daily actions and their results. As noted Burmese vipassana teacher S. N. Goenka says, "The whole process is one of total realization, the process of self-realization, truth pertaining to oneself, by oneself, within oneself."

> **Leaves from the Bodhi Tree**
>
> The central vipassana sutra is the Satipatthana or Four Foundations of Mindfulness. Mindfulness is established in body and mind: 1) body and 2) feelings, 3) consciousness and 4) the objects and content of consciousness. The Three Dharma Seals apply to each.

For examples of samatha and vipassana and their relationship drawn from daily life, we might consider the delineations made by the early, popular Chinese Buddhist commentary *The Completion of Truth* (*Chengshilun*, or *Satyasiddhi Shastra*). It says that if samatha is like a calm meadow, then vipassana is like planting seeds there. With samatha, you can get a grip on weeds; with vipassana, you can cut them away, from the roots. And if samatha is like soaking beans in water, vipassana is like cooking them.

Stopping and Looking Deeply

	Samatha	Vipassana
Meaning:	cessation & tranquility	contemplation & insight
Similar to:	concentration & meditation	wisdom
Example:	washing	polishing
Example:	gripping	cutting

The Buddha's words on this are unmistakable. Come and see for yourself. There are hundreds of vipassana meditations. The rest of this chapter's devoted to five: mental noting, the body scan, element meditation, impermanence meditation, and *metta*. I think you'll find that they all reflect the Buddha's scientific outlook. Exploring these methods, you'll see for yourself.

> **This Is**
>
> *Vipassana* represents but one of hundreds of resources available in Theravada that embrace the entire Pali canon of sutras and commentaries. Relatively free of metaphor or ceremony, with informal teacher-student relations, and translated into Western idiom, often with eclectic borrowings, it's become the most popular Theravadin "import" in the West.

Noting the Itch, Without Scratching

Start with where you are. Your life this very moment is ample opportunity. With samatha as base camp of one-pointed concentration and tranquility, you can use vipassana for gaining insight and waking up to the nature of reality.

Here's a practice based on a technique popularized by beloved Burmese teacher Mahasi Sayadaw (1904–1982). He taught a process of *noting*, useful for both samatha and vipassana. We've already touched on it briefly, in the previous chapter: "noticing what we notice" as a means of quieting the mind. Let's review that and see how it can provide insight, as well.

Basic meditation, stopping and sitting, gives a chance for old drunken-monkey mind to sober up. Given the chance, our mind is capable of calm, clarity, and insight, once we step aside and let it be. *Trying to* can only make it more unruly. Once we just let go of our dramatic parade of trials and tribulations, we weather the storm and arrive in the here and in the now. The only place we ever really are. Our mind in this state, in its original nature, is likened to a still forest lake; surrounded by animals of appetite, off in the bushes. It mirrors whatever passes before it. If someone were to toss a small stone into such a lake, we'd see it fall all the way to the bottom.

Staying with your breath, incorporate noting its details. Make quiet mental notes of your breathing and as you do so allow yourself to go into greater and greater detail, while staying in a tranquil, meditative state. Be aware of and note, for example, the phases of your breath: "air fragrant at nostrils ... air filling nostrils ... belly expanding ..." and so on, experiencing breath as it is, insubstantial, limitless, and free; or however it seems to you. See if noting opens up conscious breathing so you can concentrate on it even more, and see if that makes you feel even calmer and more lucid.

And when your mind wanders, just make a mental note of it. Just say to yourself, "mind wandering, mind wandering." (Or note "ripples, ripples" of the forest lake.)

And return with your next breath to the present. If your mind doesn't wander, then fine. Just enjoy your breathing.

After 15–20 minutes of enjoying your mind's original state of calm, its true nature, then comes vipassana. If your mind wanders now, note it, watch the wandering fade away on its own from having been noted, then look deeply for a moment into how this particular trait of mind reveals an aspect of the teachings, such as the Three Marks or the Four Noble Truths. Use whatever you note as openings for inquiry into your true identity and relation to What Is.

Tips for Noting

Here are some tips from along the vipassana trail.

Mind-wandering can be tricky to track. At first, you might not even have been aware of your mind at all. Just as you might not have noticed you're not always living in the now. Then, once you start noting, your mind-wanderings might seem to go on and on before you stop to note them. In that case, you might note, "mind wandering, mind wandering; eight minutes" (guesstimate), or "mind wandering, on and on," and return to the present.

Don't get embroiled in a running commentary, like a sports announcer. That is, don't comment on your noting, much less comment on commentaries, like a pair of mirrors reflecting each other endlessly. Once it happens, you'll see what I mean. So instead of saying to yourself, "I'm now remembering the last time I noted my mind wandered like this, and feel as ashamed of myself now as I did then," just note "remembering, remembering." And move on. No need to narrate a whole chain of associations, which can never be reconstructed anyway.

Suspend judgments. Nothing's wrong. No blame.

Stillness is a state of letting be. As is. The little dances of monkey-mind are chitterings of "I like" and "I dislike," and the more neutral "okay." You might be surprised to discover how much mental activity's dedicated to this dance of thumbs up, thumbs down, and shrugs—and what a relief not to dance to its tune anymore!

Three basic generic mental Post-it labels for passing thoughts and sensations are:

- "... attraction, attraction ..."
- "... aversion, aversion ..."
- "... neutral, neutral ..."

Mental notes can be expressed as verbs. And see if you can phrase your notes without putting "I" into them; not "I am aware my fingers are tingling," but "fingers tingling." As you progress in your practice, you might abbreviate even further to just "tingling." (Some practitioners repeat the note, like a friendly, gentle bell, such as "tingling, tingling," as I've been doing.)

You'll also be surprised to discover just how powerful noting can be. It's as if each note contains a drop of a secret-formula cleansing agent that melts dirt and grime, and polishes pristine, shining buddha nature. Use it thus with a light touch.

As with basic meditation, noting's a gentle process. Go with the flow. Don't force the river. Don't be someone who staples posters to lampposts with your noting. Just tap the moment gently with your mental Post-it tag, and move on. The idea's to note but not react. Pause, observe, and proceed.

Insights gained from noting are your own realizations of the Three Dharma Seals: the impermanence of your thoughts and feelings, the lack of any lasting, separate self-identity, and how the door of suffering can swing open to nirvana.

And let go of noting, and enjoy pure awareness.

Internalizing the Practice

With practice, you can engage in noting meditation all the time, 24/7, not just on your meditation cushion. In walking meditation, for example, note your movements as a continuous series of separate sensations. Be comfortable, go real slowwww, maybe one in-breath per step / one out-breath per step, and note: "left heel reaching out," "left heel touching down," "ball of left foot touching down," "right ankle rotating upward," "toes of left foot touching down," "right knee bending," "left foot and ground in full contact," "right heel lifting up" … and so on. Directly perceiving walking, can you see how impermanent it is, and without any separate identity? Where is your walk but in each step? And if feelings accompany any phase, such as fear of falling or gratitude for solidity, note them. And if they reoccur, direct your mindfulness there and inquire if anything is associated with them.

Case in point: Last night, taking my evening walk over Russian Hill, I was experiencing an exceptionally intense nausea and stomachache. And I caught myself saying to myself, "Aargh! I'm in pain! Ouch! I can't make it go away! Can't concentrate! I'm not going to make it! Doomed!" and so on. I was practically ready to cry for my mommy, when I realized I hadn't noted any of it yet. So I shut up, got out of my own way, noted the sensation, "belly aching, belly aching." And *bing!* the feeling collapsed like a house of cards and vanished the way a TV image does when the TV's shut off. In its place returned awareness of my stomach rising and falling with my breathing the beautiful early spring night air, and I was able to concentrate on each footstep again. As I walked, I inquired a little and felt that my tummy ache was an accumulation of stress I hadn't faced (couldn't stomach), and I was literally belly-aching about it, rather than facing and accepting it, seeing how it was an illusion I was clinging to, and moving on.

So it's important to *note* feelings that come up, as well as to experience them. Buddhism doesn't ask that we ignore the fear or anger or anxiety of our emotional realms, but rather suggests that if they're experienced mindfully, they're no longer such threats. They no longer run us. For instance, imagine you're showing up for a basketball game and you hear somebody shout, "Hey, everyone: Pee Wee's here!" If that person sees you react, then he knows he has you. He has only to shout "Pee Wee" to make you lose your focus and miss a shot. But if you feel the irk, note its root at your self-image, and evaluate how reacting would result negatively on your game, then you're not letting your feelings run you. Now you're being *emotionally intelligent*.

Noting is a tool for transformation, furnishing an essential distance and process for smiling at unwanted habit energy and letting it go. Calmly noting, you can get a hand-hold on habits and traits and illusions of ego, break them down, and let them crumble away as you relax into freedom. The little Post-its of noting are like brackets placed around some thing, [like this], which enable it be dislodged, observed, examined, understood, and let go. No need to throw anything away. Throwing is too forceful, creating further karma to deal with. And noting provides an opportunity to see what works for you, and lets you water those seeds for the future.

(*Question:* How many vipassana meditators does it take to screw in a light bulb? *Answer:* Two—one to do it, and one to note it.)

The Chinese word for mindfulness. "Now," above; "mind/heart," underneath. Mindfulness brings our mind back to the present moment. Just one breath can bring body and mind together as one, in the now. (A block version of the word, on the left, cursive in the middle, and an even more flowing version on the right.)

Calligraphy: Kazuaki Tanahashi

Material Meditations: The Wisdom of the Body

Common Misconception #7,462: "Meditation is all mental." *Au contraire!* Rather, Buddhism's an opportunity to integrate word and deed and heart; body, spirit, and mind.

Here follow two meditations centered in the body's innate wisdom, and its wide amplitude of sensations full of emotional and spiritual resonance: 1) the Body Scan and 2) Element Meditation. These are then followed by two more kinds of meditation, on impermanence and on *metta* (like friendliness or love). They're intended as a kind of shorthand for your consideration, with an open invitation, if you like them, for you to be guided through them by a teacher.

The Body Scan: A Clean Sweep

First time out, start slowly. Give yourself 45 minutes to an hour for this meditation popularized by S. N. Goenka. Once you get it, and practice it a few times, you'll start to find a pattern. Once familiar with the pattern, you can do it in a few breaths.

It's done lying down, on your back. Your arms are at your sides, your legs uncrossed. Take a few mindful breaths, then begin by directing your attention to the toes of your left foot. Continue conscious breathing and see if there are any sensations there. Imagine your in-breaths are contacting this focal point of your body, and your out-breaths are exhaling any tensions. As tension and emotions are released, note them doing so. Note, too, how your sense of yourself changes with them.

After remaining with your awareness of your toes for one or two minutes, move on to the sole of your left foot. Stay with your breathing, and concentrate on your sole for a minute or two. Continue working your way up until you've scanned your left foot. Then scan your right foot the same way. Along the way, see if there are differences.

Hear and Now

"Your body can sink into the bed, mat, floor, or ground until your muscles stop making the slightest effort to hold you together. This is a profound letting go at the level of your muscles and the motor neurons which govern them. The mind quickly follows if you give it permission to stay open and wakeful.... It's the whole body that breathes, the whole body that is alive. In bringing mindfulness to the body as a whole, you can reclaim your entire body as the focus of your being and your vitality, and remind yourself that 'you,' whoever you are, are not just a resident of your head."

—Jon Kabat-Zinn, from his best-selling book with the wonderful title: *Wherever You Go, There You Are*

Following your feet, move up to your ankles, calves, knees, thighs, hips, and so on. Remain longer with any areas of tension or pain and sites of any medical conditions. Take more time when you scan your head. If you feel any tension in your jaw, note it, and let it release. The same is true for your chin, back of your neck, lips, tongue, palate, nostrils, cheeks, eyelids, eyes, eyebrows, forehead, temples, and entire scalp.

Finally, concentrate on the tip of your head, where your hair meets your scalp. As you do so, you might feel your entire skeleton. After a minute or two, move your attention beyond the tip of your head, to a point a few inches beyond your head. From that spot, let the focus of your awareness vanish into space.

Do you feel different than when you started? And did you note particular areas as reservoirs of tension or emotion? Common speech reflects this awareness when we say someone's carrying the world on their shoulders, or say life can be a pain in the neck, and so on. Four key emotional reservoirs are hips, navel, chest, and throat. Aligning our lower back to make contact with the ground thrusts our hips out, sometimes releasing withheld anger. The hara center below the navel can have a warm, strong, centering emotional influence. The center of our chest is our spiritual and emotional heart, reservoir of dark, tight sorrows as well as bright, expansive love. And, as messenger of our verbal feelings, the throat might feel tight or full, like tears or song. Noting enables us to be aware of the tight ropes and grasping knots within our body that keep us from flowing freely. It can also help us examine what we're holding on to. Or think we're holding on to, since what's clutched often proves to be not present in the here and now, buried in our body like heirlooms in attic trunks. Clinging; trishna. The scan is a good way to smooth out knots we've tied ourselves into.

This awareness is also very useful when in the thick of a seemingly dangerous emotional situation. First, we can defuse any sense of danger by noting it. Rather than saying to ourselves, "Oh no, end of the world, this is it," first we note the alarm. "Feeling angry," "feeling defensive," or whatever. Then we note where the feeling "lives" in our body. Noting "constricted chest," or "lightheaded," the sensation can dissipate. And the blockage can yield insight.

Meditation's not about becoming an emotional zombie. Rather, it's an opportunity to 1) root out unwanted feelings and habits, 2) water the seeds of good habits and feelings, and 3) establish and maintain the ability to have awareness of choices, and choose *wisely*, rather than feel overwhelmed, or react unthinkingly. We'll conclude with more on emotions. Meanwhile, here's one more bodily exercise that unites you with the universe. Welcome home.

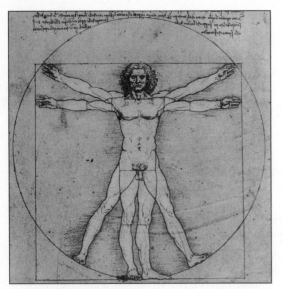 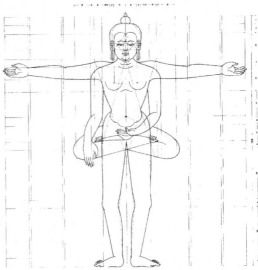

It's perfectly rational to stop and meditate. Our words "reason" and "rational" (of a sound mind) come from ratio, relation. "Meditation," similarly, comes from a root for measure. Both figures above measure the universe in human scale (macrocosm and microcosm), each differently. Da Vinci's person on the left reaches outward to encompass the circle (infinity, eternity); the meditator, on the right, drawing inward, becomes a kind of circle.

Hear and Now

"When the surf echoes and crashes out to the horizon, its whorls repeat in similar ratios inside our flesh.... We are extremely complicated, but our blood and hormones are fundamentally seawater and volcanic ash, congealed and refined. Our skin shares its chemistry with the maple leaf and moth wing. The currents our bodies regulate share a molecular flow with raw sun. Nerves and flashes of lightning are related events woven into nature at different levels."

Where's Self?: It's Elementary

Meditation on the elements enables you to experience firsthand how what you're accustomed to calling "me" is conditional and limited, and to experience a more un-limited, unconditional reality of being. If you will, a transformation from mere exis-tence to interbeing. It's a guided meditation first taught to me by meditation teacher and author Wes Nisker.

Practicing basic meditation, consider your contact with the earth as you sit. Sink into that space. Native Americans proclaim, "The earth is all we have." Feel that vital, solid connection. You might try and escape it but you can never fall off the earth. So where does the earth end and you begin? Consider how you carry the earth's minerals in your metabolism, its very clay in your bones. Stay with that awareness as you breathe a while more. Next consider water. We're 75 percent liquid. Our liquidity is our major transportation system, making everything cohere. Feel yourself as a kind of bag of water. Now consider how the salinity of our metabolism's precisely that of the sea. Feel how the sea runs through your veins and lymph, all over. We're affected by phases of the moon, just as the tides are.

Consider your blood, sweat, and tears (sounds like the name of a rock band!), urine, mucus, bile, and the fluid in your joints, connect it to rain and rivers. Consider this water the very place from which life first emerged, and stay with that gooshy awareness. Then our meditation turns towards air. Consider how air covers the planet, filling all spaces, everywhere. As you breathe in, notice how you don't have to will it; your lungs do it naturally, expanding and contracting with the universe. Feel that air-rhythm of which we're all a part. As you breathe in, consider you're inhaling the out-breath of trees; exhaling the in-breath of the grasses. No in or out, really—just one continuous motion. Feel that motion in yourself, and be one with spacious, boundless air consciousness. And just as the air you breathe isn't yours, so, too, consider the fire that fuels your metabolism. Along with chlorophyll, we literally eat the sun, and keep warm through our own internal campfire. Consider how that fire maintains a steady 98.6 degrees of warmth, keeping your metabolism homeostatic, and growing. Stay with that glowing warmth. This is you. All of this.

> **Hear and Now**
>
> "In meditation we can actively cultivate a sense of our coemergence with the elements and atmosphere, cellular life and sunlight, plants and animals, sentience—the whole evolutionary shebang. I have found that a deep calm and clarity and a sense of belonging can arise when people experience themselves in this way—as perfectly natural."
>
> —Wes Nisker, *The Big Bang, the Buddha, and the Baby Boom*

A vipassana instructor can take you farther along on this tour, but meanwhile I hope I've sparked a bit of humble appreciation for the interbeing of your mortal frame and the immortal elements. We are as they are. From these things we have come, we are, and to them we shall always return.

Here Today, Gone Tomorrow: Impermanence Meditation

The Buddha said, "Of all footprints in the jungle, that of the elephant is the greatest. Of all awarenesses, that of death is supreme." So Buddhists have traditionally visited graveyards as a meditation on impermanence. What more potent way to see through the illusion of a permanent lasting self?

One section of the *Four Establishments of Mindfulness* takes the practitioner on a guided meditation imagining his or her own death, becoming a corpse, bones whitening in the sun, turning to dust. In a museum once, I saw an elegant Tibetan goblet fashioned out of a human skull, to remind the user of the impermanence of life.

This might be a bit much for a culture that would rather sweep death under the carpet. As Woody Allen expresses it, "I'm not afraid of death. It's just that I don't want to be there when it happens." More on constructive, mindful awareness of dying is found in our final chapter.

For starters, I recommend just letting life teach impermanence. Its impermanence is a mirror in which to encounter our own impermanence, and liberate ourselves from the fear that comes from ignorance. I'm mindful of *change* in my daily life through the change of the seasons, and the changes in my life and those around me. When I see the first leaf of autumn let go of its tree and gently float down, it teaches me the meaning of trust. As simple as that. And the first, new leaves are always a surprise. Kids go off to school, start families, have kids of their own. When I see the noble way my elderly family members and neighbors carry themselves, I thank them for preparing the way for me. And living in California, I witness mudslides, power outages, raging fire storms, and so many earthquakes that real estate agents joke about offering beachfront property in Arizona. Insight shows us the suffering entailed in clinging, hanging on, particularly to our notion of self, past which we can see for ourselves the wisdom of insecurity, and the compassion of selflessness.

Medicine for a Healthy Heart: Loving Kindness (*Metta*)

How's your heart? When we say someone has a good heart, we don't just mean blood pressure. Qualities associated with good-heartedness are openness, empathy, generosity, loving kindness, compassion, and even wisdom—ideals all Buddhists work toward. This next meditation is all about massaging the heart. If you find too much dullness in your world—or depression, anxiety, fear, or anger—this might be of interest.

Sublime States: The Four Brahmaviharas

The Buddha taught people regardless of their caste or creed. It is said that when a man came to him who worshipped Brahman (God), and asked the Buddha, "How can I remain sure I'll be with Brahman after I die?" the Buddha answered in a way this man could understand. He taught a simple practice called *Brahmavihara*, which can be translated as "divine dwelling" or "heavenly abiding." Sublime state. Since Brahman is love, this kind of meditation opens the heart. Thus the Buddha spoke to the man, and us, not of a hereafter but to the kingdom of the divine dwelling in our own hearts. The abode of the sacred that's right here on earth. Immeasurable.

There are four such sublime states, or energies, which we ourselves can generate: love, compassion, joy, and equanimity. Living with them, in them, our hearts grow as immeasurable as life. As wide as the world. There's an endless supply of these energies. Before we explore just the first, it's interesting to note how Buddhist wisdom recognizes these states as close to but different from less skillful energies. That is, each of the four states has a "far enemy," the clear opposite of the quality. And each has a "near enemy," somewhere in between the two. The *near enemy* is like a toxic mimic, a deceptive substitute we settle for instead of the real thing. A near enemy reinforces our sense of self and separation and so can slide us into the *far enemy*. For example, sentimentality inherently implies clinging; pity implies feeling superior, or fear.

The Four Immeasurables (Brahmaviharas)

Virtue	Near Enemy	Far Enemy
Friendliness/love	Sentimentality/selfishness	Ill-will/hatred
Compassion	Pity/grief	Contempt/cruelty
Appreciative joy	Glum boredom/cynicism	Envy/jealousy
Equanimity	Apathy/indifference	Resentment/greed/aversion

Metta (Pali) translates as loving kindness, a friendly attitude. Compassion (Sanskrit, *karuna*), is the ability to feel *with* someone instead of *for* someone. It's thus a bit more active than metta. Appreciative joy (*mudita*) is the spontaneous response of gladness at good fortune or success, of one's self or others. (The media gossip industry, hanging on the careers of stars, is mock mudita.) And equanimity (*upekkha*) is nonattachment, even-mindedness, based on the insight into the way things really are, and is considered the closest of the four to enlightenment. The synonym for equanimity in Hindi is *tatastha*, meaning one who sits on the bank of a river, watching the waters flow.

Things Go Betta with Metta

To begin metta meditation, locate within yourself your own feelings of loving kindness or just friendliness toward yourself. Of course, first, stop and sit. Check in at base camp. Resting in tranquility, focus your mindfulness on your feelings about your personal health, happiness, and general well-being. Maybe you feel pretty good about yourself but feel vulnerable or even fragile about certain issues, such as illness or insecurity.

Next, see if you can fit all these feelings, positive and negative, into a feeling with which you're already familiar and which resonates with the notion of unconditional love, loving kindness, or just an attitude of friendliness and goodwill. (I use the word "friendliness" because friendship isn't as loaded a word as love.) Whatever you call it, the idea's not to try to reach for some new feeling off some imaginary shelf but rather use your personal experience. It's okay to draw from examples you remember in other people, and even animals. Pets exhibit friendliness and unconditional love, too, as do little children and even plants. This feeling we're spotlighting is a natural force, within you and all around you. This energy's called *metta*.

Metta opens your heart: to yourself, to those around you, even those you hate, and to the whole world. Begin by opening your heart toward yourself. If you can't be kind to yourself, who can you be kind to? So begin by thinking kindly of yourself. As you do so, say to yourself, "May I be well," and visualize yourself as being well. Send yourself a gift of metta. Then move on to wishing "May I be happy," and picture a happy you. Then, wishing "May I be peaceful," envision yourself at peace. It's as if you're harnessing this natural metta force, beaming it onto yourself, and visualizing the result. Rather than beaming pure, clear-light metta, you're varying the metta, as if using a different hue each time—wellness, happiness, peace. But it's all metta.

Hear and Now

"Just as a mother guards her child with her life, her only child, just so should you too cultivate boundless heart toward all beings. Let thoughts of loving kindness for all the world radiate boundlessly, into the sky and into the earth, all around, unobstructed, free from any hatred or ill-will. Standing or walking, sitting or lying down, as long as one is awake, one should develop this mindfulness: this is called divine abiding here."
—The Buddha

After you've opened up your heart to 1) yourself, the meditation opens out to your sending metta to:

2. Teachers	6. Neutral people
3. Parents	7. Enemies
4. Relatives	8. All beings
5. Friends	

If it's important, add a category, such as sangha or workmates. Similarly, you can rephrase your aspects of metta, depending on what meets your needs and what you're most comfortable with. For example, some people use these four phrases: "May I be free of dangers; free of mental suffering; free of physical suffering; and be well and happy." (*Note:* Each time you send metta, you include the whole phrase "May my friends be free of dangers. May my friends be free of mental suffering. May my friends ..." and so on. I've shortened it here for reasons of space.)

The format of a whole meditation might go like this:

> May I be well. May I be happy. May I be at peace.
> May my teachers be well ... happy ... at peace.
> May my parents be well ... happy ... at peace.
> May my relatives be well ... happy ... at peace.
> May my friends be well ... happy ... at peace.
> May neutral people be well ... happy ... at peace.
> May my enemies be well ... happy ... at peace.
> May all beings be well ... happy ... at peace.

Tips for Practice

Having been blessed to be taught metta meditation by Sharon Salzberg, I can attest that a teacher can not only help you slide into the tranquil stillness of basic meditation but also guide you through the various phases of metta. Practicing with a group of people, you feel metta in the air. And when facing a difficult phase, it helps to know you're not alone. Meanwhile, until you find a vipassana sangha near you, here are a few tips:

♦ You're not showering your loving kindness on the people in your mind's eye, or wringing their necks with it. Rather, with the same quick, light touch of noting, you gently tap them with the thought, then move on.

♦ Before sending metta to a new group of people, picture them very well in your mind's eye. When you pick "neutral people," think of people in your life for whom you have no particular emotions, no charge, one way or another. It's important to really make contact; otherwise, you might tend to rush to people with whom you're having difficult relations, enemies. Rushing in wouldn't be skillful; it would only reinforce the separateness you feel between you and the other person(s).

♦ One way to approach sending metta to your enemies is to see it as being the same as sending metta to your own inner enemies. That is, sending metta to yourself, you're embracing your problems and shadows as well as your accomplishments and lights.

◆ Metta isn't confined to a meditation cushion, but something to also be carried out in word and deed, as we write and speak, and in our daily actions. (Some American Buddhists, for example, sign their letters, "Much metta.")

Make friends with yourself. Expand your compassion for others. We're all in this sandbox for saints together. May *you* be well, happy, and at peace!

Hear and Now

"If we hold on to our humility, if we let go of our egos and stop clinging to whatever it is we're clinging to, we'll find the wonderful surprise that behind all that gunk is a natural kindness, a love for everyone and everything that we never thought we had. And if we let ourselves act from that place, we'll discover a kindness without limits and an unutterable peace."

—Geri Larkin

Stop: In the Name of Love

Now you've gotten a taste for mindfulness and insight. There may be practice centers near you. Remember, focused meditations may be like base camp but the real challenge remains: to incorporate the teachings in daily life. Moment to moment. For example, next time you see a stop sign, welcome it as a reminder to return to the present moment. Feel bone and blood and breath. Just getting into a car can be a meditation. Stop. Remind yourself that when you put your foot on the gas, the car will go faster, but *you* need not go faster. Robert Aitken sees the occasion of kids fighting in the car as an opportunity "to show how the car doesn't move unless all of its parts are engaged." It's all practice. All occasion for mindfulness, and insight.

The Least You Need to Know

◆ Vipassana meditation (also known as insight meditation) is the most popular form of Theravada in the West. It might be called scientific in that its insights are obtained and tested through personal observation.

◆ Insight meditation teaches how to observe our experience from a place of tranquility, enabling understanding, letting go, and experiencing life intimately, genuinely, and fully. It enables us to realize for ourselves non-separateness, impermanence, and liberation from suffering (nirvana), using our own lived world as our example.

◆ Vipassana combines stopping and seeing, using mindful awareness to look deeply into the nature of What Is.

◆ Of hundreds of vipassana techniques, five popular meditations are: noting, the body scan, the elements, impermanence, and metta.

◆ Vipassana applies to body, heart, and mind, and isn't limited to meditation sessions, but is a continuous meditation, integral to all our daily life. (Start with breath ....)

Chapter 12

See? Words Cannot Express: Zen

In This Chapter

- ◆ Zen = meditation

- ◆ Lineage: three patriarchs

- ◆ For the sake of all: the Bodhisattva Vow

- ◆ Using words to go beyond words: koan and mondo

What can I tell you about Zen you don't already know? You *are* it. Zen isn't a way of life. It's life itself. We don't *do* Zen, We join with the universe being itself.

But, wait: all the books, all the tapes, all the websites, all the catalogues about Zen—none have revealed the Ultimate Zen Truth, ever, until now—which, in a *Complete Idiot's Guide* first, I'm going to tell you right here. And it is this:

(And you can quote me. Verbatim.)

So now that I've told you what you already knew (no?), what else is there to say?

Hear and Now _____

"When Buddhism first came to China it was most natural for the Chinese to speak about it in terms of Taoist philosophy, because they both share a view of life as a flowing process in which the mind and consciousness of man is inextricably involved. It is not as if there is a fixed screen of consciousness over which our experience flows and leaves a record. It is that the field of consciousness itself is part of the flowing process, and therefore the mind of man is not a separate entity observing the process from outside, but is integrally involved with it ... The practice of Zen is to experience the overall [flowing] pattern directly, and to know one's self as the essence of the pattern."
—Alan Watts, *What Is Zen?*

Look, Where's Buddha?

Question: Where's Buddha? Zen answers, "Asking where Buddha is, is like hiding loot in your pocket and then declaring yourself innocent."

To repeat a question we've asked before: "Why be a Buddhist when you can be a buddha?" Now, you might consider yourself only a part-time buddha, and that's perfectly alright, too, holding down two jobs at once. Amazing. Or you might insist you don't know, but are as perfect at being an unenlightened buddha as a full-fledged buddha. What can I say?!

The human is present within nature as part of an unbroken continuum. (See the fishing boats?) So, too, is the embededness of each of us within essential buddha nature.

Mu Chi (1210–1280), Southern Sung Dynasty. Evening Glow on a Fishing Village *(detail). Nezu Art Museum.*

Now, if you're a buddha, then please read this chapter and check up on what people are saying about you these days. If you're not a buddha (yet), I hope you're still serene and calm amid all the trials and tribulations of not being a buddha (such as being a buddha and saying you're not). If so, your awakening mind is ever ready to spring into 100 percent total response when life's next emergency falls on your dear sweet head (_ker-plunk!_). But if you're not serenely ready and readily serene, then this chapter will fill in the blank, _____, to fill you in on your buddhahood, Mr. or Miss or Mrs. Buddha.

A Few Drops of Zen

Even before you begin any further, I'd like you to stop. (We explored stopping in the previous chapter, so that shouldn't sound as funny as it well might otherwise.)

Zen Is Meditation Right Here, Right Now

Here's an invitation for you to awaken your mind. First I'll explain how. Then note your place, and close this book.

Take a moment. Notice your breathing, as it is, without making any verbal note. Notice, then let your circle of attention widen outward, a larger circle of gazing at other objects around you, beyond your face, beyond your hands. Be aware of textures and colors and shapes, without necessarily considering what they represent. Don't think about anything. Widen your attention further, aware of these myriad things all present, interbeing together in this moment. Let go of verbalizing and conceptualizing. Let your mind quiet down. Just enjoy being where you are.

Now let your gaze flit where it will, with equanimity, and without dwelling on any one thing. Your attention's clear but not attached to any thing. If you like, now, close your eyes. Let your mind continue to flow, awake, without dwelling anywhere, without fastening it on anything in particular. No thoughts. Continue with that. Then, when you're ready, gently let go of your meditation. (But continue to enjoy being, and being where you are, a bit more!) Can you go about the rest of your day with the same attitude? As choiceless awareness. Perpetual meditation. Everything you do is Zen.

Zen Is Emptiness in Action, as Natural as Pie

Welcome to the _Zen_ zone. The base camp of meditation _is_ the destination here. No intellectualization about it. No dualism and no nondualism. Zen is emptiness in action. _Question:_ How many Zen Buddhists does it take to screw in a light bulb? _Answer:_ None. (A light bulb's empty of separate identity, as is everything, and everyone. No light bulb, no Buddhist, no separation. So how is there no difference between a Zen Buddhist and a light bulb? Tap them, they both sound hollow yet are full of light.) Sometimes you have to admit that logic can only go so far, and to get right at the real nitty-gritty the best sense can be non-sense. Hey, you gotta admit—when there's no problem, there's no solution.

This Is

Zen literally means meditation. All activities are embraced as meditation. It's a wise, nonintellectual, and direct approach to Buddha's way, clearing away concepts so you can see buddha nature, and your buddha nature, for yourself. *Za* means "sitting," so *zazen* means sitting meditation. A more precise definition of zazen would be *shikantaza* (*shikan*, nothing but ... *ta*, precisely ... *za*, sitting); just sitting and nothing else. One of the most durable forms of Buddhism in Asia, its influence has extended to architecture, martial arts, gardening, tea, haiku, motorcycle maintenance, you name it.

You might look at it this way: Whereas various other paths focus on subject matter (content), such as impermanence or loving kindness, or use a variety of tools—such as noting, or recitation, or mantras and visualizations and prostrations—Zen steps out off a thousand-foot pole with hands free. No content, no subject. No tools, no objects. (No hands.) Not even a "no" (itself a concept, a word, a two-edged blade, cutting everything in two, and setting up shop with price-stickers on everything, scales, and a cash register at the door). Zen enters the stream without a splash, and is one with the water, going with the flow. Sure, counting breaths are okay for launching forth, to ease one's way in—but in Zen, even the counting, the "one," the "two," become meditation—as is letting go of counting. And just sitting. And getting up again.

Just Do It!

Sit just to sit, *shikantaza* (shih-can-tah-zah). You don't assume meditation posture in order to attain enlightenment. Rather, the posture is the enlightenment. (You don't sit like a Buddha to be a Buddha, you are a Buddha.) That is, assume an enlightened posture to realize (and enjoy) that you're already enlightened. (So even if you're a part-time buddha, you can sit in the boss's chair right now—it's empty.)

The more I say, the more I might intellectualize it for you. Thus, I've invited you to meditate, yourself, at the beginning of this chapter. Now what might make that impromptu meditation a bit more Zen might be improving your posture just a little, ("shoulders back, chin in, stretch the backbone") so you can breathe freer ... letting your thoughts clear a little more ... exploring opportunities to practice meditation throughout the day … inviting you to see into your mind … encouraging you to realize your own mind as Buddha mind … identifying your practice with the universe all around. As profound as that, and as ordinary.

To give you more of a feel, we'll take a look at three Zen ancestors, Kasyapa, Bodhidharma, and Hui Neng, founders of the tradition. (Other important historical figures include Chinul, who helped shape Zen in Korea, and Dogen, who brought Zen to Japan from China. Actually there's quite an illustrious line-up in the Zen Hall of Fame.) Plus, we'll explore another important figure we've already touched on, known as the bodhisattva. Then we'll take a look at Zen's famous way with words. And we'll wind up … continuing to begin.

Lineage: Direct from the Buddha to You, with Love

Do you have any family rituals? Spiritual practices do. Unbroken continuity is important in transmitting a coherent body of doctrine and discipline. Generation unto generation. New voices ask, "How much can we vary tradition?" (Adaptation being important, too.) Others wonder, "How do I know this is the real deal?" Tradition and change are questions that can be explored in terms of the direct lineage-holders, the teachers.

A vipassana teacher acts as your friend on the Path: more your mentor than master. To earn accredited lineage as a vipassana teacher, there's a review process by a senior patriarch, but it's not necessary to study under him (or her) for long periods of time; a number of teachers can recommend a student for advancement. In Zen, more emphasis is placed on a student's intimate guidance by a teacher. Otherwise a person might become self-conceited and think Zen is just wacky riddles, and ultimately lose the Way completely. Here are three links in the Zen lineage chain, from the Buddha to here.

The First Zen Patriarch: Kasyapa's Smile

The Buddha and disciples were on retreat, on Vulture Peak. Everybody gathered for the day's Dharma talk. The Buddha sat on the peak, in peace and at harmony with everybody and everything, and said nothing. Then—more silence. After three or four minutes, some recent visitors wondered to themselves if the Buddha was feeling well. Still more silence. Then, unexpectedly, he held up a flower, for all to see. Silence. Then a profound smile became clearly visible on the lips of a star student named Kasyapa. The Buddha looked at him, and could see that he got it. Smiling, he put the flower down.

Well, it was a golden Zen moment. The Buddha then announced that he'd transmitted Dharma to Kasapya. Naturally, many people there wondered what'd just happened.

What did the Buddha teach and what did Kasyapa understand? The inescapable impermanence of reality? The flower's interdependence with the whole universe? Huh?! What!?

(Only the Buddha and Kasyapa knew, being of One Mind.) And the Buddha continued, with a short explanation that bears four fierce characteristics, almost a Pledge of Allegiance of Zen:

◆ Special transmission outside orthodox teaching

◆ Not depending on words

◆ Direct pointing at mind

◆ Seeing your true nature, become Buddha

The First Chinese Zen Patriarch: Bodhidharma

We flash ahead now to the phenomenal transmission of the Dharma from India to China. One of the first major carriers, of historical record, was a prince who went by the name of Bodhidharma. Being from India, he's often portrayed in Chinese, Korean, and Japanese paintings as looking rather foreign (to the painter), with formidable beard (rare for East Asians). And round, somewhat bulging eyes (also rare, where eyelids are narrower and often have an extra fold). But legends had sprung up around him already, like the one where, in order to keep from nodding off while meditating, he'd shaved off his eyelids, and where they fell, the first tea bushes grew.

Now the emperor of China at the time had become quite interested in Buddhism. When he'd heard this Bodhidharma had braved the three-year Spice Route trek to get here, he invited him to his court. CNN wasn't there, but the meeting reportedly went like this ...

Emperor Wu: "I've had temples and monasteries built in my realm, and commissioned translations of Buddhist scriptures. Tell me, what virtues have I accumulated for myself thereby?"

Bodhidharma: "None whatsoever."

Emperor Wu [a little flustered]: "Well, then—please tell me, sir, what's the basis of holiness?"

Bodhidharma: "There is no holiness, only emptiness."

Emperor Wu [now quite perplexed]: "Then—then who'm I talking to right now?"

Bodhidharma: "I don't know." [So saying, he stood up and walked out.]

Along the Path

Bodhidharma's famous "I don't know" to the Emperor is characteristic of Zen, which urges us to think no-thought. To not know. To have a don't-know mind. One word for it combines mind (*shin*) below the character for no-thingness (*mu*). Mushin isn't mindless, heartless (you know, an idiot) but, rather, means getting out of one's own way. Having no conception, much less preconception. Not living in one's head. Experiencing life in full participation.

He crossed the Yangtze River (separating north and south China), on, of all things, a single blade of grass (what a guy) and settled in at a temple in a northern province called Shaolin (*shao* pronounced like *now*), where he sat facing a wall for nine years. No, he didn't stare at a wall out of frustration because he didn't speak Chinese! Hardly. He was practicing and teaching … Zen.

Bodhidharma is often depicted scowling, eyes glowering at the top of his balding head. Here's my favorite: six brush strokes, plus some extra brush-wipes for his mat. But if you think it could be just anyone seen from behind, look again. That fierce determination, that "no bull," commanding presence could only be …

Daishin Gito, Wall-Gazing Daruma. *Ink on paper. 25" × 10¼" New Orleans Museum of Art: Gift of an Anonymous Donor (79.220).*

One more Bodhidharma story: The legend was that Bodhidharma would only accept a student when the snows ran red. No takers, until one winter this guy named Hui K'o ("hwee koh") cuts off his own arm and brings it to Bodhidharma as a token of his sincerity. (Don't ever think Zen is trivial!)

Bodhidharma accepts Hui K'o as his student and says, "Okay, what do you want me teach you?" Hui K'o asks "Well, I have no peace of mind. How do I pacify my mind?" Bodhidharma looks at him and says, "Bring me your mind, and I'll pacify it." So Hui K'o bows, leaves, thinks it over, comes back, bows, and replies, "Where *is* my mind? I can't *find* my mind anywhere!" "There," Bodhidharma announces, "I've pacified your mind." In that instant, Hui K'o becomes enlightened.

What a story. And so now Bodhidharma had found someone to whom he could entrust his hard-earned sword of wisdom: a one-armed man.

The Illiterate Sixth Patriarch: Hui Neng

Now, Kasyapa and Bodhidharma were both noblemen from the Indian subcontinent. But the seminal patriarch of what would become the distinctly East Asian practice we know today as Zen was a man named Hui Neng ("hwee nong"). And the funny part of it is: He was illiterate! Who would've thunk it? (Maybe he was just faking it, playing dumb out of humility. Who knows!)

We go next to China five centuries after Bodhidharma, and Buddhism's finally taken hold here. Meanwhile, Hui Neng just gathers and sells firewood for a living. Delivering wood one day, he overhears someone reciting the Diamond Sutra (a popular scripture on emptiness and wisdom requiring sublime meditation more than lofty erudition). Well, it may be news to him, but when he hears the phrase, "Awaken your mind without fixing it anywhere," *Shazam!* he becomes enlightened, right there on the spot. This is really curious: no counting breaths, no mantra, no noting of the watcher and the watched, no six years of training, no nothing! Blam, right out of the box, alikazam shazam, he produces awakened mind out of nowhere. He attains *kensho* (a.k.a. satori), Oneness. Awakening to the immediacy of sunyata. His beginner's mind *is* infinite Buddha mind.

So what does he do? He hikes over a thousand miles to the Zen monastery, knocks on the door, and asks to join the sangha. The head of the monastery, its roshi—and current Zen Patriarch (Number Five, now)—opens the door, and greets Hui Neng with some derision: "Ha! An illiterate from south China!" Hui Neng replies, "Literate/illiterate, north/south, dualities don't concern the Buddha's way." "Smart guy," the roshi figures, so he admits Hui Neng into the sangha, and gives him menial duties, pounding rice in a shed way in back.

Meanwhile, the roshi had been fixing to retire. The official rules were that the vacancy would be open for competition, by writing a gatha, to demonstrate intuitive understanding. Everyone knew that Shen Xiu ("shen syew") was the shoo-in, so no one else tried. But Hui Neng asked someone to read to him the gatha Shen Xiu had posted on the wall, a quatrain about our body being the Bodhi Tree and the mind being a mirror we must constantly polish. *Ha!*, Hui Neng dictated his own gatha, rephrasing Shen Xiu's nice idea but without any duality whatsoever, and posted that: no tree, no mirror, only infinity, hence nowhere for dust to alight.

> **Leaves from the Bodhi Tree** _____
>
> Hui Neng was out for a walk when he came upon two monks quarrelling beneath a flagpole.
>
> "The flag is moving," one monk said.
>
> "No, the wind is moving," argued the other.
>
> So it went, as amongst two little kids, "flag," "wind," "flag," "wind," until Hui Neng stepped in.
>
> "Your mind is moving," he said, and walked away, leaving them both stunned.

Well, that night, the old roshi appeared in Hui Neng's little monastic cell, and bowed to him. He said, "I know you wrote that second gatha and I can plainly see you clearly possess radiant Buddha mind and appoint you my Dharma heir. Now this is sure to cause a great ruckus when Shen Xiu finds out you're the Sixth Patriarch, and not he," the roshi says, handing Hui Neng his ceremonial Patriarch's bowl and robe, "so here—take these, go out the back gate before everyone wakes up, lay low for a while somewhere, then teach Dharma a good ways away from here." He recites the Diamond Sutra to Hui Neng. Hui Neng understands it perfectly, departs and goes underground, living with hunters. Twenty years later, he starts his own monastery on the other side of the Yangtze, near the big port city of Canton (Guangzhou)—but that's another story.

Illiterate or not, Hui Neng not only upheld and taught the Dharma, but consolidated the Zen Movement and shaped it into a resilient practice capable of weathering political upheavals and becoming a unifying force throughout East Asia. And, based on his own enlightenment, his teachings could be understood by an illiterate peasant. In fact, an ink brush portrait shows him wildly tearing up a bunch of sutras. (Show me your mind: Is it in a book?)

You may now wish to close this book, walk away, and consider that last image. Come back whenever you wish. If at all.

Now Why Not You?

Zen's gateless gate is wide-open. Come on in. Every session begins and ends with the same rituals. Even if you don't know the drill, it's easy to clue in. Everyone takes off their shoes before entering the meditation room, called a *zendo*. You sit a stretch. Then you walk; then sit some more. Next, often, someone shares their understanding, giving a little Dharma talk. Tea and cookies afterward, optional.

> **Leaves from the Bodhi Tree** _____
>
> If you take refuge in a Zen sangha, you're often given a woodblock *lineage tree*. (It's not a universal practice.) At the top of the scroll is a circle representing the Buddha. Below him, there's Kasyapa. Like a family tree, the genealogy branches out and down, until you get to your own roshi. Below your roshi, there's a circle, representing you. And, sometimes, in the margin, there's a red line, extending directly from the Buddha to you.

You can just show up, no introductions necessary, as often as you like. If you finally decide to seek refuge there, then you'll have a one-on-one interview with the roshi who'll ask you, "Why have you come to study?" Be honest. "I don't know" can be just as valid an answer as "To attain enlightenment." You might find your roshi answering, "Me, too." But if your inmost urgency sounds like self-improvement, or some other way of getting off to a bad start, the roshi might go over your intentions with you (right view/right thought) and clarify the practice. After formal initiation into a sangha, you visit the roshi for periodic chats, called *dokusan*, or *sanzen* ("going to Zen"). And you can attend meditation retreats, called *sesshin*, usually up to one week long.

Universal Participation: The Bodhisattva Vow

The previous chapter offered Theravada approaches to reaching nirvana. But there's an emphasis of initial motive that historically distinguished Mahayanans, including Zennists, from traditional Theravadins: Mahayanans take the *Bodhisattva Vow*. As printed in our Reference Page, it is:

- Beings are numberless; I vow to awaken them.

- Delusions are inexhaustible; I vow to end them.

- Dharma gates are boundless; I vow to enter them.

- Buddha's way is unsurpassable; I vow to become it.

A bodhisattva has an aspiration for nirvana, enlightenment, an awakened heart (Sanskrit, *bodhi-citta*), not for his or her self alone but for the welfare of all. This is not to say Theravadins don't recognize Oneness with all, nor are any less compassionate or do fewer good deeds in the world. It's just a matter of emphasis of initial motive: for all beings, from the very outset. And from this emerges traditions of reverence not found in Theravada scripture, but which Theravadins often practice in their own way anyway.

This Is

A *bodhisattva* is one whose being or essence (*sattva*) is enlightened (*bodhi*) with the wisdom of direct perception of reality and the compassion such awareness engenders. He or she renounces all rewards for personal deeds, dedicated to the ultimate enlightenment of humanity, all beings, everything. An archetypal bodhisattva is Avalokiteshvara (*Kwan-yin* or *Guan Yin,* in Chinese, in feminine form; *Kwannon,* Japanese; and, in Tibetan, *Chenrezig,* as male, and *Tara,* as female), embodying compassion; another is Manjushri, embodying wisdom.

The Buddha himself took a bodhisattva vow when he answered Mara's question, "Who are you to say you're enlightened?" by touching the earth, invoking all beings. He continued that bodhisattva path when he left the Bodhi Tree and taught for the rest of his life.

You may hear hairsplitting over a few doctrinal fine points, but I wouldn't worry. We'll explore the more important ramifications in some depth in the next chapter, when we discuss bodhisattvas who become transcendental Buddhas, making their presence felt from within nirvana.

A giant step in your own practice could be taking refuge in the Bodhisattva Vow. The Vow connects your practice with all bodhisattvas. On one level, that's all our ancestors, including your grandparents, and parents, who cared for you above themselves, as well as such singular human figures as St. Francis of Assisi. On another level, that's all the energies embodied by the bodhisattva archetypes, primordial energies often called deities. (Remember, in the Buddha's time, thoughts were deities. In Sanskrit, Brahma gave the Buddha the flower to hold up to Kasyapa, for example. Mara the tempter is another example. And throughout east Asia, gods are a fixture of everyday life, from the kitchen god to the ancestral deities.) You might think of them as aspects of the Buddha's enlightenment.

And the Vow connects your practice with all living beings; since all things possess Buddha nature, with all *beings*. A tree, a rock, a cloud are beings. When I sat zazen this morning, I didn't do so alone. I did so with all beings, vowed for enlightenment, together. The first thing, the one thing needful. This awakening isn't of a solitary soul, but rather one that finds its place within community, finding meaning in connection.

Moreover, there's a seeming paradox (a word whose original Greek meaning is "beyond thinking"). How can anyone honestly vow to help *all* beings? The sheer idea's overwhelming. Mind-boggling. But that's partly the point. The practice is just that all-encompassing; like swallowing the entire sea in one gulp. And yet a sparrow does precisely that when squawking the news of spring's arrival. Plants do just that, unfurling a flower to the universe. So why not us, too? As Michael Wenger points out about the Vow, "You don't take it because it's doable. You take it to make it so."

Kuan Yin here contemplates the moon and its reflection in the water (which is more real?), meditating in an informal pose of sheer grace and royal ease, with an awakened heart and a smile of pure compassion.

The Water and Moon Guanyin Bodhisattva. *Eleventh to twelfth century, China. Polychromed wood. 95" × 65" (241.3 cm). The Nelson-Atkins Museum of Art, Kansas City, Missouri. (Purchase: Nelson Trust; 34–10.)*

Photo: Robert Newcombe

Without a Trace Along an Untrod Trail

What's the particular taste of Zen? Like the taste of clear mountain water to a dusty traveler, and like the Dharma itself, it's no-taste, ever-present within everything; uncategorizable, yet …

- ◆ Not one, not two
- ◆ Complete
- ◆ Immediate
- ◆ Authentic

- ◆ Everyday
- ◆ Selfless
- ◆ Dedicated
- ◆ Intuitive, spontaneous, and humorous

Aware of the interpenetration of all things within each moment, a Zen practitioner can be enlightened by anything. Enlightened by all things, your being *with* things as they are also means being *one* with all things. The relative and the timeless worlds overlap, so neither *duality* nor *nonduality* are given more primary weight than the other: only the present moment, in which they both dwell intertwined, is all, all we ever have. This is what Michael Wenger calls Buddhist math. It takes yin and yang to know nondualism. We need them both. And we draw a circle around the symbol, also, to represent the void, out of which it comes. Emptiness.

If Zen had a symbol it might be this. A circle ("enso," Japanese) universally implies completeness; all. A Zen circle can also imply zero, sunyata, absolute, true reality, enlightenment, no beginning/ no end in all phenomena, no symbol, the spread of Dharma as a turning wheel, harmony, and womb. All in one stroke.

Calligraphy: Kazuaki Tanahashi

Bowing, for instance, there's no separation between you, your act of bowing, and what you're bowing to. Not one, not two. And there's no preconception about what the next moment might be like, because there *is* no other moment than now. Sitting, you're completely sitting, nothing else. Eating a grape, you're completely eating a grape, and nothing else. And everything is *complete*, as it is, an adequate instance of Buddha nature. Everything and everybody have all they need for enlightenment, in the present moment.

And it's always *immediate*. If a practitioner dons a robe, or bows, or quotes a sutra, it's not because of history but as an act of enlightened understanding in this very moment. There's nothing beyond or behind it. So it's fully *authentic*. The person is fully present in whatever he or she does. From the toes to the scalp. Intimate with life, their own life is *genuine*.

A lived activity, Zen's in the *doing*. Zen sitting isn't passive but a total commitment. It's as much an occasion for my complete immediate expression of my understanding of the Dharma, a total enactment of Buddha's way, as is tying my shoelaces (an interesting analogy since the Buddha wore sandals).

Zen isn't about waiting for nirvana to get it right. Nirvana is now or never. Every aspect of the *everyday* is an opportunity to practice. Since we become enlightened in this life, not another, our ordinary mind is Buddha mind. Everyday life is the scene of enlightened activity, not somewhere else.

Traditionally, even higher members of a Zen monastic order also perform everyday chores, like doing the dishes. (A bookkeeper might be asked to work in the garden or something else they don't know, lest they identify too much with their number-crunching habit-self.) Making everything part of practice cracks and wears down the tough shell of self. If Zennists often have short hair, it's because they're *selfless*, not investing time in a fashion statement about self-image. Zen isn't self-expression but expression of awakening mind, wherever that occurs.

Zen takes *dedication*, effort, like wearing shoes until the soles become thin. Shunryu Suzuki Roshi once told everyone present, "Each one of you is perfect the way you are. And you all could use a little bit of improvement." He stressed that when you engage in an activity, that you stand behind the activity, with the confidence that you are completely there, that you are the activity itself. Maintaining this attitude fulfills your experience and backs up your day-by-day *effort* to just sit. Great trust is placed in your own *intuition*. Deep-down, you know. This is true in Theravada as well, but with perhaps even more emphasis.

Put all these together, and you're likely to bump into *spontaneous* Zen happenings, such as the improvised, quick circle; rather than a detailed, devotional icon. (Both are selfless.) Quick thinking, such as averting a spill, or catching a ball, where's self? Zen *humor* is a popular manifestation of this special love of spontaneity, as well as its compassionate heart. Indeed, Zen itself, like enlightenment, is like a joke, in that no one can explain a joke to you, you either get it or you don't. Zen hasn't cornered the market on wry, hard-boiled, crazy wisdom, but it sure has its fair share.

Expressing the Inexpressible Without Words

The last landmark along our tour of Zen is the *koan* (say *koe ahn*) and *mondo*, Zen's hallmark contribution to the annals of crazy wisdom. If Zen's typified by a minimum of techniques, we could say the two most important are just sitting (shikantaza), and koan/mondo. In the West, many Zen sanghas practice both.

I *Swear* This Is True: "I Am a Liar" (*Koans*)

The above two statements are completely contradictory. Huh!?

Let's flash back to Hui Neng. Soon after Hui Neng had been appointed Sixth Patriarch and gone underground, an ex-soldier sniffed him out, ready to force him to return the robes and bowl. But once in Hui Neng's presence, he said, instead, "Master, teach me the Way beyond good and evil." Hui Neng replied, "Don't get hung up on good and evil. Instead, seek your original face, your face before your parents were born." Through this challenge the ex-soldier broke through the veils of rational thought, intuited his original nature, his Buddha nature, beyond labels of good and evil, and attained enlightenment.

This Is

The Japanese word **koan** means public notice or legal precedent. Just as a lawyer might refer to *Brown* v. *Board of Education* regarding segregation, so can each koan be referred to when illuminating a particular principle—such as Buddha holding a flower up and Kasyapa smiling, a teaching without words. Life's holding out a flower to us, but do we see it? Like that particular story, all koans are a direct pointing at mind. Never to be explained, only realized. There is no answer as in a solution to a math puzzle, but rather a response for each person to discover within themselves.

"Show me your original face, before your father and mother were born," is a primary koan. At first glance, it might seem like a riddle. But even a nonsensical riddle has a rational answer. Koans aren't rational. They use words to go beyond words ... to short-circuit or bypass habitual thought patterns ... hard-wired into both language and our brainpan ... requiring something else, deeper within us, like intuition ... a shock, almost, to enable us to perceive reality nonconceptually ... to perceive reality directly. When that happens, to respond fully, genuinely, there is an "answer." It's not an answer in a book, as in a math problem, but rather an answer within each practitioner.

Hear and Now

"What's true meditation? It's to make it all—coughing, swallowing, gestures, motion, stillness, words, action, good and evil, success and shame, win and lose, right and wrong—into one single koan."

—Zen master Hakuin (1686–1769), who devised the famous koan: "What is the sound of one hand?"

—A koan by Hakuin

For example, a Zen monk once held up a bamboo stick before some other monks and said, "If you call this a stick, you fall into the trap of words, but if you don't call it a stick, you contradict facts. So what do you call it?" (*Answer:* A monk went up to him, took the stick, broke it over one knee, threw the pieces into the room, and sat down. And so it was resolved—at least, for that question at that time, in those circumstances, by that monk.)

"What!?" you might say. "What's the point?" Well, a koan's another way of asking "Who am I, really!?" This is actually one generic koan: "Who am I?" Another one is "What is this?" You might try either one and see for yourself. Next time you settle into tranquility meditation, ask yourself "What is this?" Listen to your answer and challenge its incompleteness. This is tranquility? But what is tranquility? Ask again, further. Tranquility is less stress? But that's a negative definition, what *is* it? As answers (this, that) and feelings (reverence, frustration) arise, look deeply into their roots, too, and ask further. Don't become attached to any answer. Stay with the question, "*What ... is ... this?*" Stay with it through your day. Your week. Life-long. That's your koan.

You might consider a koan as another tool for focusing awareness. Unlike counting your breaths or fingering beads, koan contemplation addresses awareness itself ... zeroing in on logic, conceptualization, thought ... inviting *doubt* as part of the process ... like the inevitable dragon in your path, in this case logic, words ... so to get around it requires not only one-pointed concentration but audacious fearlessness. But even that's not enough. There it is—

—not just something for while you're perched on a cushion. You take your koan home with you. Wake up with it in the morning. Look at it in the mirror. Brush your teeth with it. Have breakfast with it. Take it to work. Until you can't live with it—and can't live without it. And when you've finally mastered your koan, congratulations: You're ready for all the others.

Leaves from the Bodhi Tree

Maybe koans seem remote or exotic. If so, consider the one-line zingers of Samuel Goldwyn and Yogi Berra. Goldwyn was the "G" in MGM, an irascible movie mogul who drove Hollywood people crazy by barking such unarguable, twisted statements at them as, "A verbal agreement isn't worth the paper it's printed on!" A koan might ask, "Show me that paper." (Would you shake hands with me on that one? It's a done deal! Now let's do lunch.) Yogi Berra, when not playing baseball with the New York Yankees, came up with such gems as, "When you come to a fork in the road, take it." "No one goes there anymore—it's too crowded." "It's déjà vu all over again." And, "It ain't over until it's over." Next time you're asked the time, remember how Berra replied: "You mean now?"

In Asia, over the centuries, about 400 Zen koans have been amassed and indexed out of about 1,700 in all. Each deals with particular phases of the Way. Primary ones, such as the sound of one hand, are designed to help tip the practitioner over the edge of fabricated self into immediate, boundless reality. Following this first breakthrough, there are more koans, to gauge how far the first breakthrough went, or assist further breakthroughs. Lest you go off in this state of enlightenment only to get tangled up farther along down the road. Koans can be grouped into categories:

- Initial insight into the true nature of things

- Differentiating within the realm of nondifferentiation

- Understanding the lives and teachings of forerunners, beyond the literal words

◆ Resolving difficulties, such as about any seeming dualisms between the transcendent, absolute dimension and the historical, relative dimension

◆ Five more sets of koans, as a graduate course of testing

If you're prepared to take on koan practice, your teacher will work with you, asking you during dokusan, "How's your koan?" You can pick the koan you'd like to work on or be assigned one by your roshi. With koans, a roshi can guide a student through the Zen landscape of unimpeded interpenetration without limit, so you can appreciate all the roses along the Way.

Who's on First?: *Mondo*

Another Zen example of testing attainment, and really playing with it, is question-and-answer style of dialogue called *mondo*. When Bodhidharma had that wild conversation with Emperor Wu, that was mondo. When Hui K'o asked him to pacify his mind, and he asked Hui K'o to show him his mind: mondo. Hui Neng and the monks arguing about the flag and the wind: mondo yet again.

Watch what you say. Here's another example. One Zen monk said to the other, "Hey, that fish's flopped out of that net! How will it live?" The other monk answered, "When you've gotten out of the net, I'll tell you."

It takes two to tango like this: You can't surprise yourself! Some call this kind of exchange "dharma combat." It can be like two jazz soloists, exchanging riffs, or a vaudeville routine ("Who's on first?" "Who's on second—I-Don't-Know's on first."). You could say that a koan is a *special case* of mondo (remember, koan literally means "case"). The Buddha's holding up a flower was the koan and Kasyapa's smile made it a mondo.

Even if you don't take up formal koan practice, you can recognize the source of koans and mondo in your daily life. Forks along your own path to take, straight ahead. The whole world's a koan, by virtue of including everything that is the case—just requiring a certain twist to make into Buddhist teaching, as well. And, like the Way, real koan practice becomes all your life long.

> **Hear and Now**
>
> King Milinda said to learned monk Nagasena, "I'm going to ask you a question. Can you answer it?"
> Nagasena replied, "Please, ask your question."
> The King: "I've already asked."
> Nagasena: "I've already answered."
> The King: "What did you answer?"
> Nagasena: "What did you ask?"
> The King: "I asked nothing."
> Nagasena: "I answered nothing."
>
> —Milindapañha

By way of a non-conclusion let me tell you what a Zen priest once told me, sharing the Stairmaster next to me, working out. No one gives our gym's Stairmasters as much of a workout as he, as if they're so many toothpicks. Yet he's invariably reading a book as he does so. So I once asked him, "Roshi, Zen is a path beyond words. So how come there are so many Zen books?" He smiled. "Because Zen is nonintellectual," he replied, "and that isn't easy."

The Least You Need to Know

- Other schools teach meditation. Some ingredients that combine to make up the special Zen flavor are: immediacy, completeness, "not one/not two" (neither dualism nor nondualism are primary), authenticity, everydayness, selflessness, dedication, intuition, spontaneity, and humor (sometimes to the point of crazy wisdom).

- Like other branches of Mahayana, Zen emphasizes the Bodhisattva Vow. A bodhisattva's awakening is, from the initial motive, linked to the awakening of all beings. Bodhisattvas include embodiments of archetypal energies, such as compassion (Avalokiteshvara) and wisdom (Manjusri), as well as living personages (our ancestors).

- Zen is typified by a minimum of means. Its practice might be typified in just sitting, koans maybe, and ...

True Devotion: Pure Land

In This Chapter

- ◆ The story of Pure Land
- ◆ How it works
- ◆ Essential elements
- ◆ Comparisons and contrasts
- ◆ Other schools

We come now to the most universal Buddhist practice of China, Vietnam, and Japan, and very popular in Korea—so widely practiced as to make it probably the largest of all schools of Buddhism on the planet. It's not only largest, but also simplest.

And, until now, it's been the least-known Dharma path in the West. It has flourished for over a century now, making it our oldest Buddhist tradition here. Continuing to thrive and grow, it's finally receiving the attention it deserves.

There's a sixth-century Chinese saying: "A ray of light into a room that's remained dark for a thousand years dissolves a thousand years of darkness." Here's a glimmer.

The Story of Pure Land

To preface our story, we recall that the Buddha had said the seeds of enlightenment are present within everyone. Yet originally the Middle Way seemed unavailable to many; reserved for monastics or the wealthy few, those with sufficient understanding and the freedom from cares to cultivate it. But what if you hadn't been privileged to have met the Buddha? What about servants of the wealthy, say, who might have seen the Buddha but didn't have an entire day to themselves, much less three months? Oneness in sunyata is fine, but not with hungry mouths to feed. Well, the seeds of practice for common people were present from the very beginning, and Mahayana practitioners watered and nurtured them. Eventually, these Mahayana paths reached out to the common people, which was very good news.

For example, in the time of the Buddha there was a meditational practice of remembering him. Anyone could practice it. Surely, just remembering him would bring calm and clarity, keen awareness and open-heartedness. Later on, a similar path arose in India, about a century before Christ, and was developed further by such Indian luminaries as Nagarjuna and Vasubandhu between the second and fifth centuries. Known as the Pure Land path, its story goes like this.

> **Hear and Now**
>
> "There shall be no distinction, no regard to male or female, good or bad, exalted or lowly; none shall fail to be in his land of purity after having called, with complete faith, on Amida."
>
> —Honen Shonin (1133–1212)

It is said that once there was the son of a king who discovered the suffering that's the human condition of us all. So compassionate was this being that when he saw anyone suffer, he suffered too. And he resolved to bring everyone to a place beyond suffering. So he devoted himself to the Way, and eventually became the most excellent student, known to the Sangha as Dharmakara ("Storehouse of Dharma"), for his ability to live the teachings to the fullest. Finally, at last, he came one breath away from crossing over completely to the other shore, nirvana. (Now, if you remember what we've said about Mahayana, you might guess what occurred next.) On the spot, he made 48 vows, including the vow to forsake becoming a buddha if all beings could not do so, too. (Even a wretch like me.) Thus he became a bodhisattva. And what a bodhisattva!

In the Land of the Buddha: Say His Name, and You'll Be Free

But how could ordinary people like you or me ever make good on this vow, if they'd never seen him, or lived in another country, or another time? Simple. Anyone could reach him, anytime anywhere, by sincerely reciting his name, since he and his name are one. And his new name as a buddha (as we'll see in a moment) includes all beings. They'll be joined with him, in a field created by his enlightenment, called *Sukhavati* (Sanskrit, "Blissful Realm"), where he now dwells, yonder (or maybe here, too, but we just haven't realized it yet).

That is, so pure was his enlightenment that it created this realm capable of purifying all to arrive there. From that place, all the Buddha's teachings will be as easy for you as opening a fist. Or a lotus! And his name, now that Dharmakara's transformed into a deity, is *Amitayus*, eternal life, also *Amitabha*, infinite light. Amitabha's enough to get you through the door. Amitabha Buddha's our guy.

This Is

Rebirth in the Pure Land is hosted by the compassionate vows of Amitabha Buddha, a supreme emblem of cosmic compassion. *Pure lands* (also known as *buddha fields*) are outside realms of desire (our impure world), form (realms of lesser deities), and formlessness (realms of higher deities), as well as samsara (never-ending wheel of deaths and rebirths), but some are present *within* samsara. In the Amitabha Buddha's pure land, we study the Bodhisattva Path without hindrance. Depending on interpretation, we can be reborn there after death, or be reborn in the purity of our own mind, our own buddha nature.

Reciting his name is sometimes called remembrance. The word "mindfulness" in Sanskrit, *smirti*, means remembrance: remembering to be in the present moment; remembering our true home; remembering our limitless buddha nature. When we recite Buddha's name, we're remembering him. Hearing just the name of Buddha is the same as hearing his voice. His name embodies his awakening, so invoking that name makes manifest his enlightening awareness. In which there's no separation between "speaker" and "hearer."

This Is

In Chinese, Amitabha Buddha is invoked Namo Ami-to-fo ("Na Mwo Ah Mi Two Fwo"). This *recitation* is called *nien fo* ("contemplation" or "remembering"). In Japanese, it's Namu Amida Butsu; the recitation is called *nembutsu*. In Vietnamese: Nammo Adida Phat. *Namo* or *namu* is like a form of homage, like saying "In the Name of the Father." It invokes the one upon which we rely, in whom we take refuge.

Hear and Now

"When reciting the Buddha's name, you should gather your thoughts together. Recitation originates in the mind and is channeled through the mouth, each phrase, each word, clearly enunciated. You should also listen clearly, impressing the words in your mind. Manjushri taught: 'Hearing within, hearing one's Nature—one's Nature becomes the Supreme Mind.'"

—Patriarch Yin Kuang (1861–1940)

Since our minds can conceive of Buddha through a word, then our minds must indeed partake of the Buddha's mind. Through the Buddha's name, we can touch within ourselves our own buddha nature, which is one with all things. So when saying the name, the word, listen deeply, and hear its meaning resonate: *Buddha.*

Venerable Heng Sure explains:

> "Buddhas have realized the virtuous qualities, or essential goodness, of the Awakened Nature that we humans share with all beings. When somebody brings to fruition the virtue of their nature, they "wake up," and become a Buddha. By reciting the Buddha's name, we invoke the power of that virtue already latent inside us."

Nothing could be simpler. Sincerely and single-mindedly recite Amitabha Buddha's name, and, thanks to his compassionate vow to awaken all human beings who do so, you'll be reborn in his pure land. No questions asked. It needn't imply anything otherworldly, either. You could be reborn into the pure land of your own mind, your very own innate buddha nature. As J. C. Cleary comments in his book *Pure Land, Pure Mind,* "In reciting the buddha-name you use your own mind to be mindful of your own true self ..."

Transferring Merit: Instant Karma?

So how is Amitabha able to make good on his vows? Well, it's due to something in Buddhism called *merit.* To appreciate merit, let's consider karma once more; the universal law of moral cause and effect. In early times, it was thought of like an ethical bank account. Everything we do generates debits and credits that link us to other beings. You help me out, I owe you. The settling of accounts takes place after reincarnation (a reason reincarnation's even an issue at all). Unless we could completely clear our karma once and for all, reincarnation might continue indefinitely (samsara).

This brings up the question of motive. Back in the early days, people did good deeds in order to earn merit for a better rebirth next time. Easier to study the Way as a wealthy human in the next life than, say, a chicken. For some people, earning merit only built up selfish ego, greedy for merit, under cover of good motive. (Thus the king asked Bodhidharma: "I've done so many good deeds, aren't I pure?! Haven't I accumulated much merit!?" To which Bodhidharma scoffed, "None whatsoever," hearing only a big show of ego.) Now, with the bodhisattva vow, we direct the merit of our good karma toward the enlightenment of all beings.

Now we can peek at how *transference of merit* works. (If only a mortgage were this simple.) As you'll recall, Amitabha had been called Storehouse of Merit before he entered the realm of celestial buddhas and bodhisattvas. So what happened to all his accumulated merit when he finally attained enlightenment? To use a contemporary analogy, you might say he invested it, to create a fund, for everyone.

Along the Path

"The world of things is really nothing more than a kind of reflex of people's deeds. An environment can exist only as long as there are persons whose karma compels them to perceive it. In the same spirit, one now claims that the merit of a Bodhisattva may be great enough to create a Pure Land not only for himself but also for others to whom he transfers it."

—Edward Conze

In other words, his karmic merit had been so vast as to not only enable him to create his own realm (for himself and for all who wished to join him), but he also still had a limitless surplus of karmic merit which he could *transfer* to anyone who'd asked. His immense good karma overshadows any weaker one. It's as if there were a rain cloud hanging overhead, but a strong wind blows it away. Amazing, but then any bank, to continue our original analogy, links up with all the other banks in the world, in one huge banking system. So being one with Buddha means also being one with Buddha's infinite store of karmic merit.

Amitabha has two great bodhisattva disciples keeping him company in his pure land: Great Strength and Avalokiteshvara. Here is one of 33 different ways of depicting Avalokiteshvara. It is said that when she beheld the suffering of the world, her head burst from the pain. Amitabha put the pieces back together as nine new heads. The thousand arms are a result of her vow to help all beings.

From Tibetan Mandalas *[International Academy of Indian Culture].*

Courtesy of Dr. Lokesh Chandra

Hear and Now

"On a single atom, there are as many Buddhas as there are atoms in the world, sitting in the midst of an ocean of his disciples. Likewise, the entire sphere is filled with an infinite cloud of Buddhas .... On each atom, there are as many pure lands as the number of atoms of the worlds. In each pure land, there are infinite Buddhas sitting in the midst of the disciples of the Buddhas. May I see them and perform enlightened activities with them."

—Gandavyuha Sutra

But transference of merit is so marvelous as to take us to the brink of the inconceivable. Consider, for example, being one with the Buddha. What if the Buddha weren't just one but one of many, yet still one with all those Buddhas? Even the Theravada Pali canon states that Shakyamuni Buddha was but one of myriads of enlightened beings, all Buddhas, to have lived amongst us and taught the Dharma throughout time, everywhere. And each of these Buddhas is accompanied by bodhisattvas, whose enlightened buddhahood is dedicated for the sake of all beings. And some of these bodhisattvas have themselves now become deities and are teaching the Dharma in realms of their own creation, in parallel dimensions: pure lands, buddha lands, marvelous buddhaverses.

We'll explore deities further in this chapter and the next. For now, we can bring our current speculation back home by reconsidering karma. One way of explaining karma is that, in effect, we help create our own reality. And, if we sincerely open our heart-minds, we can tune in to Amitabha Buddha's karma as well. With his enlightened karma comes the reality he's now living: his pure land. It's inconceivable, yet there it is. To really bring it home, we'll consider next the thread running through it all: compassion.

The Primal Vow Is Universal Compassion

The compassionate essence of transferring merit helped universalize the Buddhist path. (Actually, you and I are enjoying its benefits right now because this is why movable type was invented: so people could generate and dedicate karmic merit in spreading the Dharma.) The Buddha's enlightenment represents a new way of sharing our common life, and dedication of merit is one logical outcome. When we directly pray for someone, this is, in effect, our aim: to transfer merit. So it's only natural that people would want to call upon Kuan Yin or Amitabha to transfer a little merit. Since Buddhism is about oneness rather than isolation, a key factor here is that the petitioner's perspective shares that of the bodhisattvas: for the sake of all.

Hear and Now

"We surround all men and all forms of life with Infinite Love and Compassion. Particularly do we send forth loving thoughts to those in suffering and sorrow; to all those in doubt and ignorance; to all who are striving to attain Truth, and to those whose feet are standing close to the great change men call death, we send forth oceans of wisdom, mercy, and love."

—Jodo Shin-shu benediction

We saw in the previous chapter how the Bodhisattva Vows play an integral part in Zen, and now look further into this approach. A clever interpretation might see a bodhisattva as being a special case of selfish altruism. Say I became enlightened (a big IF, indeed) and holed away off in the wilderness to enjoy my bliss. What would prevent some crazy person, say, from coming in and killing me, and spoiling my meditation? But if everyone in the world were enlightened, too, then of course I'd stand to benefit. Thus there could be a selfish motive for altruism, it all comes back to you. But Pure Land isn't "clever" like that. Rather, it's purely, simply, passionately *devotional*, like the *bhakti* branch of yoga, linking the practitioner to the sacred through faith and devotional love. Pure Land fuses that devotion with its recognition of the Buddha's *boundless compassion* and gives it a base of wisdom, with its philosophy of creative emptiness. This aims to realize the wish of all life: for each being to be free.

Three Keys: Faith, Vows, and Practice

The Pure Land path asks at most three things of us: faith, vows, and practice. We must have faith: in ourselves; in the benefits of a pure life; in the existence of the Pure Land. We must make vows: to enter the Pure Land, and to follow the Bodhisattva Path. And we must practice, worship, and follow our devotion, by cultivating and following the teachings, and cherishing their virtue.

So if we have faith in Amitabha's vow, then in following the Pure Land path we come to a bodhisattva outlook ourselves, as we become one with Amitabha Buddha. As reciting his name and hearing his name become one, we are drawn to that vow as by a magnet, vowing to save all beings. More than a matter of a possible miracle or two, the recognition of the boundlessness of the bodhisattva's compassion embraces and eventually transforms a person's entire being. And everything on earth, and beyond. With one simple, seemingly sideways step, the Pure Land path crosses a barrier steeper than the Himalayas: the eighteen inches between our head and our heart.

As such, it's really utterly nondualist. It might not seem so if you're a stranger to the landscape, or the nomenclature. If so, perhaps you might still be accepting its nondualism intellectuality, without appreciating how this wisdom really feels. So let's say it just involves a different way of seeing and being with Buddhism that takes some familiarity. To get more familiar, let's look next at the most remarkable development along the Pure Land path.

Saint Shinran

Twelve centuries later, after numerous developments, the Pure Land path underwent its supreme formulation, by Shinran Shonen (1173–1262). So deeply did his reinterpretations resound that they were now celebrated as the path of the *true essence* of Pure Land teaching, hence the name of his school, Jodo *Shin*-shu (*True* Pure Land School). Of all his contributions, it was his interpretation of the Vow we need to look at. Of course, it wasn't necessarily an interpretation, since he was only bringing to the foreground something that had been there in the background all along.

What Shinran says of the Vow is truly radical. The idea had been that faith in the Vow would bring a person to the Pure Land. But, Shinran argued, that's as if the Pure Land (or enlightenment, or buddha nature) were a reward, rather than a fait accompli. It's our common heritage, like the sun in the morning and the moon at night. Why? Because we're all already enlightened (remember?), we just aren't always aware of it (especially while leading workaday lives and in a world such as ours is today). Amitabha has not only already guaranteed our ticket to his pure land, but we arrive without traveling. A done deal. So recitation of his name need be done only in gratitude. Like saying "Thank you." Recitation with any expectation would only continue our delusion of self. Once we realize our true identity as no different than Buddha's, and that it has always been thus, there's nothing else to realize, except gratitude, and seeing how illusion has kept us from awareness, and perhaps relieving the needless suffering of others who still haven't awoken.

We've already seen this in the trap of *trying* to quiet the mind, rather than letting it be. And it's emphasized in holding Perfect View and Thought, in the Eightfold Path. Entering Buddhism with an attitude that it's like some kind of self-help or do-good movement is booby trapped from the get-go. That's like trying to grab a bar of soap with wet fingers. The harder you try, the farther away the goal slips. An English-language dictionary has pages of definitions all beginning with the suffix "self-," and so it's no wonder how self-centered Westerners are in need of a more balanced view.

Shin's realism and wisdom is truly from the heart. We can hear this in the way Jodo Shin-shu expresses enlightenment. Of course it speaks of it in terms of the enlightenment of Amitabha (*Amida*), with his Vow at the center of his story. But as for us mere mortals, it speaks of a transformation within our own everyday lives. Not some pie-in-the-sky State of Enlightenment for us to hanker and hunger after. But a transformation which, interestingly, begins with an awakened sense of our own limitations. A fiercely honest awareness each of us comes to of our shortcomings ... failure, even (a verboten word to most Americans) ... that each of us might have tried to clamber up a 10,000-foot pole to grab a slice for ourselves of some of that tantalizing enlightenment pie up at the top ... and even felt some kind of spiritual pride at how much progress we were making on our way up and up ... only to slide back down, realizing ultimately how much we were only patting ourselves on our back, self-congratulatory; really fooling only ourselves. What fools we mortals be!

Then comes the sideways step. Here we'd been like worms inside a dark stick of bamboo climbing up and ever up, when all the time we can just bore a hole, *zip!*, right where we are, and climb out. Horizontal liberation!, we're already enlightened as we are. Shin asks us to look at ourselves in the plain light of day, just as we are, and be grateful. And try to live up to that self-realized truth through study of the Middle Way, listening deeply to our teacher's Dharma talks, and learning in community with our sangha. Indeed, the pure land of Amida resembles very much the monastic Sangha, only in Shin we hold down jobs and raise families.

If we want to learn more about Zen or Insight Meditation, or whatever, that's fine, too. Dharma doors are endless, and a bodhisattva vows to enter them all. But just so long as it isn't *practice:* self-effort. Indeed, Shin is so simple you can't even speak of a practice. You say the name of Amida Buddha, Namo Amida Butsu, out of gratitude for his Vow. Instead of practicing anything, just be joyful for What Is.

> **Hear and Now**
>
> "We realize true gratitude when we are awakened to the fact that the foolish being who fails in being compassionate is the very object of Buddha's compassion."
> —Rev. Ken Tanaka

Other Power

Shinran's quintessential phrase to express this radical interpretation we've just seen is *tariki*, "other-power." Traditional Pure Land practices include visualization of the Pure Land and of Amitabha (Amida), recitation of his name (the more, the better), and reading the three sutras that pertain to the path: The Amitabha Sutra (*Smaller Sukhavati-vyuha*), Infinite Life Sutra (*Larger Sukhavati-vyuha*), and Meditation Sutra

(*Amitayur-dhyana*), detailing the Pure Land for contemplation. But Shinran said this is all self-power (*jiriki*), only perpetuating the delusion of separation. Useless. We already are enlightened, and only need to surrender to that fact. Surrender to tariki, surrender to other-power.

To many Westerners, the other-power of Shin might seem too much like a religious tradition they already know and want to get away from, and I don't just mean uncomfortable pews. Misunderstandings here are easy to make, and I hope to dispel them. The Pure Land isn't superstition, nor is it dualism, nor is it identical to Jesus Christ (although some early Christians came into contact with the Pure Land School). That is, our life goal isn't as superhuman as to become one with the original creator of the universe, but rather to *be* the buddha we are. (Saying "I'm enlightened," is as ridiculous as saying "I am God.") And other-power may sound way too easy, but it ain't necessarily so. You've heard it's easier to give than to receive. Well, that means giving requires self-power; receiving, other-power. Thus, other-power's really more challenging than you might first think.

Recitation becomes a mirror in which we can see our self-centeredness as well as our buddha nature. I might recite nembutsu and feel good about myself for doing so but this is still foolish self-satisfaction; what Prof. Takamaro Shigaraki calls "no better than an ornamental or armamental accessory to our life."

Hear and Now

"The true nembutsu totally jolts and upturns *myself*, mercilessly exposing my present reality before me and causing great pains to my inner self. While the nembutsu was my own choice in my earnest efforts toward Buddhahood, at the same time it begins to severely criticize and negate what I am…. Then the nembutsu transcends myself to become the nembutsu of non-effort, and the nembutsu itself begins to say the nembutsu … no longer the nembutsu I say, but that which is only heard, coming from some place beyond myself…. In the true nembutsu, therefore, I choose to call the Buddha's Name, and yet at the very same time, the Buddha is calling me."

—Professor Takamaro Shigaraki

Surrendering to nondualism means allowing ourselves to receive the compassion of all the Buddhas, which happens to appear to our limited form of perception as acting on us externally: as "other-power." Actually, however, Amida transfers not only his merits, his incredibly wholesome karma surplus canceling out our personal self-destructive karma. He's also transferring to us his enlightenment: his nondualist, infinite mind, which is one with the Compassion of All the Buddhas. It's that simple, but maybe you wish a nudge of more clarification …

Self and Other: No Dualism

Two simple proverbs show how self- and other-power are really only seemingly dualist, to our limited perspective. The Vow is like the almost universal saying, "The Kingdom of God is within you." Actually, the divine is everywhere, it's one, but we're limited human beings and so need to understand from our perspective: within us. Shinran anticipated the charge of dualism, stipulating the goal was "to be free from any form of calculations." Elsewhere: "What is called other-power is the same as saying there's no discrimination of This or That."

You've heard the saying, "The Lord helps those who help themselves." Well, there's a lesser-known, Basque saying: "God is a good worker but he loves to be helped." (Even God likes other-power!)

The Story of Deities: Room for Interpretation

We'll discuss deities in some detail in the next chapter. Having already encountered here the notion that the historical Buddha was but one of countless tens of thousands of Buddhas, it's good to pause to discuss deities a little further here. We've seen how the Buddha sidestepped the question of God and of heavenly afterlife (because they didn't further the matter of why we suffer and how we can free ourselves from suffering). Yet it is said he taught the Four Brahmaviharas, heavenly abodes, to a Hindu wishing to remain united with God in heaven. (All roads lead to Om.) So if you believe in God, or not, either way is fine according to the Middle Path, so long as it's not extremism. Yet now we see Mahayana talking about gods: adepts becoming bodhisattvas becoming deities living in alternate, parallel universes (buddhaverses). What to make of all this?

Many Westerners tend to have more difficulty with the concept of deities than Easterners do. And so I've emphasized aspects about which Easterners might not even think twice, such as history. But in the Buddha's time, deities were commonplace. A thought coming to someone was described as a deity visiting them. Mara, the Tempter, could be seen as a projection of the Buddha's own mind. (A more complete survey of deities can be found at our website, Dharma Door, http://awakening.to, at awakening.to/deities.html.)

Deities in Buddhism are open for interpretation. Some adherents worship them as actual cosmic entities. Another interpretation is that they're manifestations of supreme enlightenment, putting a human face on formless qualities, to feel greater kinship with them—conceptual entities representing qualities they wish to instill within themselves, or as being already within themselves which they wish to open up to. It's up to each sangha, each teacher, and, ultimately, each practitioner.

When you visit a Pure Land sangha, you'll find members who think of the Vow in terms of deathbed assurance of rebirth in nirvana, and others who're open to deconstructing the Vow as myth, sacred story. Story is a time-tested means of pointing to truths which must be felt, not analyzed. A way of using words to sidestep their inherent dualist tendency. No this, no that.

Notice how we started the story of Pure Land, "Once upon a time ... there was the son of a king ..." Some contemporary interpreters see the Pure Land sutras as the Buddha telling a story about his own enlightenment, using the coinage of deities, popular in his day. Overall, a tendency for story, and deities, is typical in Mahayana tradition, as, for example, regarding Buddha's own story. The Theravada paths tend to hold to the teachings as truth whether or not he actually ever lived, or was one of thousands of other Buddhas or not. After all, the mathematics of Euclid works whether or Euclid really lived or not. Mahayana paths, on the other hand, revere the Buddha so as to hold his very life story itself to be a teaching. Of course, what you wish to make of stories is up to you. After all, Amitabha Buddha made his vow for *you*.

The Pure Land Is Wide, with Room for Varied Emphases

Some Adherents Emphasize	Some Adherents Emphasize
Pure Land as afterlife, only reachable after death.	Pure Land not apart from this world; found in essential purity of mind.
Historical Amitabha, with arms to hold us, ears to hear us.	Amitabha as formless power of universe removing delusions of ego; infinite Buddha nature.
"Other-power," outside assistance, granting favors.	"Self-reliance," use as manifestation of mind.

> **Hear and Now**
>
> "If you want to go to the pure land,
> then purify your mind.
> When your mind is pure,
> then whatever you see will be pure,
> and wherever you go
> you will find the buddha realm."
> —Vimalakirtinirdesa Sutra

So do people who believe in God necessarily conceive of a man with a long white beard with a crown seated on a throne? Fine, if it helps conceptualize the nonconceptual. This is like the story, in the previous chapter, of the Christian monks touring the Zen temple. When asked, the monk says the Japanese word for emptiness stands for God. (And indeed, when understood, it does come closest to the Western notion of God.) But the word *God*, too, is merely a label, only pointing to God. Similarly, the idea of the Kingdom of God seems fairly universal. Some see it as only attainable after a lifetime of austere deferral while others see it as present all around us. (Others as a Queendom; others as a Republic.) Certainly the descriptions of the Pure Land rival biblical poetry in splendor and detail, worth reading as travelogue alone. Whether it's one's own mind or one's sangha, an earthly realm or a celestial one, is up to you.

There are as many religions as people. So just as Buddhism isn't a one-lane path, neither is Pure Land. Therefore, next, let's examine the Pure Land schools in relation to some other schools along the Way.

A Simple, Universal Method, Alone or in Combination

Where other Buddhist paths might seem like those of an ant climbing the alps, Pure Land resembles a boat sailing downstream, *with* the wind. A log rolling downhill. The Pure Land schools live up to the name of their collective branch, Mahayana (Great Vehicle), in welcoming rich and poor, man and woman, monks and nuns, young and old, saints and sinners. It's easy to see how Pure Land became the most popular form of Buddhism in east Asia. Its wise faith is like an ocean, buoying up everybody. It can provide deathbed reassurance of a blessed afterlife, and it can be a general, moment-to-moment panacea throughout life. No arcane metaphysics to study. You don't have to shop around for a teacher, roshi, or guru. Go straight to Amitabha, who's vowed to save everyone, even the lowest of the low, and who accepts you just as you are.

Hear and Now

"This medicine is the 'Calling upon the Name of Amida,' and is wrapped up in the six syllables Na Mu A Mi Da Butsu.... For this medicine no money or special wisdom is needed. All one has to do is recite the words with your mouth.... Here indeed is a pivot of fundamental power."

"Do I hear you say, 'Too easy'? 'Such wares are intended only to deceive old men and women.' Many doubt their efficacy and ask of the wise if there is not some other way more suited for clever people. And Sakyamuni pointed straight back at the heart of man and said that within one's heart there is to be found the true Buddha nature."

—Hakuin Zenji (1689–1769), Zen master, founder of koan school

It's a universal method, and so it can also dovetail nicely with other schools. Pure Land's commonly associated with most other schools of Chinese Buddhism. A mutual practice of Pure Land with Zen (*Nien-fo Ch'an*, in Chinese) provides a fail-safe, for example. If you don't crack the koan part, recitation will still earn you a seat in the

Pure Land anyway. Moreover, the two can cross-fertilize each other well. Where Zen ropes off thought entirely by using the koan as the poison of words to wipe out the poison of our egocentric, dualist verbal responses to the world, Pure Land uses conceptualization to fight conceptualization. (Recitation also entails deep listening as well as deep aspiration or deep gratitude.)

In Zen, the object of concentration is one's own innate buddha nature; in Pure Land, it's Amitabha Buddha. Zen places faith in Buddha, bodhisattvas, and teachers; Pure Land, in Amitabha, his vow, and his pure land. The turning point in Zen koan study is the raising of "Great Doubt"; in Pure Land, the turning point's the experience of "Serene Trust."

Comparing/contrasting is a dualist tendency, of course, but we might employ it a bit further for purposes of seeing how Ch'an/Zen and Pure Land can complement each other. In the light of Pure Land, Zen's aspiration for enlightenment can be seen to emphasize direct realization of formlessness (sunyata), interbeing, which further deepens one's initial compassionate vow. In the light of Zen, Pure Land can be seen to emphasize realization of oneness with Boundless Compassion, which assists in opening the eye of wisdom. (A zennist might ask, "Or is it the other way around?" A purelander might reply, "Call on Amitabha, and see.")

Pure Land in Daily Life

Pure Land is so simple, I hope I haven't detracted from its utter simplicity by attempting to explain what, after all, is marvelously inconceivable, ultimately a matter of faith. Wrapping up our tour, let's look at Pure Land in terms of our own everyday life. First, to bring it all back home, to the only place where the Dharma ever is, which is life, let's see how it might feel to you.

Meditation: Take a little time out sometime to get comfortable, relax, and consider the pure land. First, ask yourself if you've ever thought about heaven, and remember what your images were. Next try to imagine yourself actually living in a heavenly realm, and ask yourself what it might look like. Be the architect of your farthest dreams. Ask yourself what you would do there. What other people would do. When you feel like you've come to some general working model, rest in its light.

Then, ask yourself one more thing: What if there already were a heaven just as you'd imagined it, waiting for you, except your imagination of it is only the faintest shadow of its true splendor!? Rest in that thought for a while.

Lastly, now, as you return to your everyday surroundings, see if you can realize your vision through your actions, words, and thoughts in this very life.

Hear and Now

"Heaven. Now there's a thought. Nothing has ever been able, ultimately, to convince me we live anywhere else. And that heaven, more a verb than a noun, more a condition than a place, is all about leading with the heart in whatever broken or ragged state it's in, stumbling forward in faith until, from time to time, we miraculously find our way. Our way to forgiveness, our way to letting go, our way to understanding, compassion and peace."

—Alice Walker

Giving Chants a Chance: Recitation

In east Asia, monastics typically recite the Amitabha Sutra and the Buddha's name every day. Some monks take as their personal practice the recitation of the Buddha's name up to 10,000 times a day, or more. Here in the West, laypeople get together (on Sundays, usually) to study Dharma and recite together (plus enjoy community activities), perhaps with monastics.

Recitation is a wonderful congregational practice, as well as a personal one, and Chinese and Japanese temples are very convivial. If you're a newcomer, you'll be most welcome; many sanghas are already very diverse. If it's a Chinese-based sangha, "Namo Amitofo" is a common greeting, whether they're practicing Zen (Ch'an) that month or reciting the Amitabha Sutra. They often furnish sutra recitation booklets transliterating Chinese for English-speakers. If you get lost, the person next to you will usually notice and kindly point in your book to where everyone is. Whatever they're reciting, it's a wonderful practice to join in the chant. A serpentine melody emerges while every syllable is pronounced, taking on a life of its own. Whatever the temple, a good tip for chanting in a group is to be neither too soft nor too loud, just blend in. At Shin service, they listen deeply to a Dharma talk, then chant nembutsu. And then people hang out together, often over some home-cooked vegetarian food. (I love those persimmon ginger cookies!)

At home, you might start and end a day with a few minutes of recitation. Get quiet. Center down. Try this gatha: "Namo Amitabha Buddha of Infinite Light." (*Namo* [in-breath]; *Amitabha* [out-breath]. *Buddha* [in-breath]; *Light* [out-breath].) You can use a mala to count, in groups of ten. (Count: in + out = one breath.) As with basic meditation, don't alter your breath. You might face west, or an image of Amitabha. Over time, you might notice the arising of meditative awareness and one-pointed concentration. And you might feel aware of a mindful, nondiscriminating, spacious state of light and peace. You might be entering the state of mind where you'll realize the Pure Land in this world.

As with mindfulness meditation, you can recite while washing the dishes or driving a car. You can recite aloud or silently. While doing something repetitive, or doing nothing. Before and after sleep, and even during. Scientists now concur with Buddhists that in one split second the mind conceives of literally thousands of thought formations. For most of us, they're mostly irrelevant fragments—"… blue, a new car, yesterday, on sale now …" and so on. How good to direct our clinging habit energy away from the constant wheel of illusory roof-brain chatter, and redirect it toward our aspiration for awakening, with the majestic, virtuous name of the Buddha, the primal vow of Amitabha.

A period of recitation during samadhi or Zen meditation can dissolve the barrier between subject and object as effectively as koan practice or just sitting. That is, the mind that's the *subject* reciting the name, and the awakening Buddha that's the *object* of invocation, are really one. Reciting the Buddha's name can thus be its own kind of koan, and continuous state of meditation. In Pure Land, this is often called "real mark" Buddha Recitation, because it goes beyond marks, or any attachment to distinguishing characteristics.

Exercise: Recite "Namo Amitabha Buddha." Or "Om Amitabha." Or just "A-Mi-Ta-Bha." Or even "Bud-dha."

Try this: Meditating on the name of the Buddha, notice the space in between the two syllables, *bu dha:* the spacious, nameless, formless, perfect blank of infinite possibility. (Koan: "What is that!?")

Or try this: During seated meditation, think "budh" on your in-breath and "dha" on your out-breath. Then when you feel yourself seeing clearly and deeply, ask yourself, "Who's reciting the Buddha's name?" You might find your own mind and the Buddha and all sentient beings are one. No separation.

Further Pure Land Paths

There are other approaches to Pure Land. *Contemplation by thought* visualizes the 32 distinguishing marks of Amitabha, as set forth in the Meditation Sutra. He's inconceivably vast. It is said that there's a white hair in between his eyebrows, which alone is five times longer than the tallest mountain in mythology, Mount Sumeru, which is about a million miles above sea-level. So don't sell yourself short. Think big. Think, for example, of Amitabha's purple eyes, deep and clear as the four great seas. Expand your mind. Think of the light streaming from his body, in a nimbus of 48 rays, one for each of his vows (set forth in the larger Pure Land sutra, Infinite Life Sutra).

Another approach is to recite Amitabha's name while facing an image of him, on a home or portable altar, or even a wallet-size picture. In *contemplation by image*, you might concentrate on that white hair between his brows. You might see it emit a ray of light, traveling to the ends of the universe of Dharma. (Amitabha, you'll recall, means infinite light.) Within his light are limitless buddhas and bodhisattvas, teaching and practicing the Dharma. In this light, you might smell heavenly perfume (such as the nectar of compassion) wafting from the Pure Land. Listening, you might hear its celestial music in the wind through the trees.

For the follower of Jodo Shin-shu, for whom practice smacks of self-power, a mindfulness in everyday life comes about here, too, in that mirror of which I spoke. For example, I'm already gratefully awakened by the primal vow, but *ow!* I bump my head. So I stop and consider where my attention was directed (three places at once?). This can begin a path of inquiry, through the Buddhist teachings, on up through to the meaning of infinite light and eternal life, immeasurable wisdom and compassion. In gratitude, I might then recite nembutsu.

Other Schools

Pure Land is simple: nothing esoteric. But for inquiring minds interested in advanced studies, a related sutra is read in Pure Land, called the Avatamsaka. The longest book in Buddhism, it's a complete theoretical system, of mind-boggling proportions and implications, and with supremely inspiring poetry.

Last, but not least, a common misconception about Pure Land is: "where people chant for a BMW." Well, chanting for material benefits is not uncommon in east Asia, mostly at the village level, but is a very provisional approach to Buddhism. Moreover, it's a misinterpretation about practice found within some of the Lotus Sutra schools, not Pure Land.

The Lotus Sutra Schools include *Nichiren Shu*, *Nichiren Shoshu*, and a modern outgrowth, *Soka Gakkai International* (*SGI*), plus others both traditional and newly conceived. For them, the Lotus Sutra is the ne plus ultra, and they invoke it by reciting the words *Namu Myoho Renge Kyo* ("Devotion to the Wonderful Dharma of the Lotus Flower Teachings"), known as the *odaimoku* (equivalent to *nienfo* and *nembutsu*). The Lotus Sutra Schools follow the lineage of Nichiren, a thirteenth-century Japanese Buddhist priest and reformer, and so are sometimes called Nichiren Buddhism. Tangentially, it's interesting that in Nichiren's commentaries on the Lotus Sutra, at one point he sees himself as a character in the sutra … because we'll see a somewhat similar meditative stance in the next chapter, as well.

The Least You Need to Know

◆ Pure Land is the largest and simplest school of Buddhism, and one of the most devotional. It's predominantly east Asian, and temples in the West (some being the oldest in North America) have been largely ethnic but are now becoming mixed.

◆ Amitabha Buddha dwells in a pure land, to which he will bring anyone who sincerely calls upon him. This bodhisattva vow on his part is reciprocal on the part of his followers, who likewise dedicate their practice for the sake of all beings.

◆ There is no one school of Pure Land. Interpretations vary from traditional to progressive.

◆ Japanese schools of practice include Jodo Shu and Jodo Shin-shu. The latter is marvelously simple, considering practice as further manifestations of ego, and instead stresses gratitude.

◆ In Chinese, recitation of Amitabha Buddha's name is Namo Amitofo (called *nienfo*); in Japanese, it is Namu Amida Butsu (called *nembutsu*).

Chapter 14

Diamond Way: Tibetan Buddhism

In This Chapter

- Shifts in emphasis
- Tantra
- Step-by-step meditation
- Empowerment (initiation)
- Body, speech, and mind as one
- Ritual and symbol

Tibetan Buddhism is the last school of practice to reach Western shores. That's curiously appropriate because it's the repository of the final teachings of the Buddha. Whether you find it's for you, it's a Dharma door and so no less worth entering and looking around. And it puts everything we've learned so far in yet another light, equally radiant.

Long veiled by Western stereotypes of Shangri-la and "lost horizons," Tibetans are really very down-to-earth, warm human beings. They're also rightfully proud of their own Buddhist brand, called Vajrayana. Like the summit of Mt. Everest, there are differing approaches to choose from: four main schools (Nyingma, Sakya, Kagyu, and Geluk).

Some speak of three major schools: Theravada, Mahayana, and Vajrayana. Another possibility is to speak of Vajrayana as Mahayana—with a tantric twist. Decide for yourself.

Tibetan Buddhism in 500 Words or Less

Differences in Buddhist traditions are primarily cultural, and with variation in emphases. All roads lead to Om. As a point of departure here, consider the lightning bolt, the most awe-inspiring phenomenon in all of nature. (How do you spell the sound of thunder? *Shazam!?*) Ancient India placed lightning in the hands of the king of the gods, Indra (whose interpenetrating, luminous jewel net we often refer to). Then Tibet later appropriated and adapted it as their symbol of the teachings of the Buddha. Awesome. Elemental. Supreme mastery over the universe. And from the get-go, we can say that, as with Pure Land, Tibetan Buddhism is rich with story, myth, and sacred symbol to thread us past where words leave off.

This small ritual scepter, called a vajra *in Sanskrit (Tibetan,* dorje), *is a weapon against ignorance. It represents* upaya *(skillful means, method, or art; also the masculine principle). It might be hand-held by a deity, who might also hold a ritual bell in the other hand, representing* prajna *(perfect wisdom, or emptiness; the feminine principle). (Next time you're browsing a bookstore, you might note it's also the logo for Shambhala, leading publisher of Buddhist books in the West.)*

From The Encyclopedia of Tibetan Buddhist Symbols and Motifs *by Robert Beer © 1999 by Robert Beer. Reprinted by arrangement with Shambhala Publications, Inc., Boston, www.shambhala.com.*

This Is

Tibetan Buddhism is also called **Vajrayana** (or, equally, **Tantrayana**). *Vajra* means "diamond." Vajrayana means the Diamond Path: indestructible as a diamond; multifaceted; having crystal clarity; supreme of its kind. It merges Theravada and Mahayana elements with a Buddhist adaptation of an ancient Hindu yoga (*tantra*), also is related to pre-Buddhist Tibetan *Bon*. It's arguably the most complex branch of Buddhism, and the most complete.

As mentioned in our historical survey, Buddhism rode north from India to Tibet, in about the eighth century, during its last phase in its country of origin. As such, these teachings can be seen as a kind of retrospect plus further developments and with subsequent local modification. So Vajrayana is based on Mahayana yet also includes Theravada. Thus there's stopping and insight meditations, but with additional unique versions, such as concentrating on particular bodily regions to achieve tranquility, and by so doing insight can arise of itself. Ancient Hindu views of karma and reincarnation (or rebirth) re-emerge here in a view that Zen master and poet Gary Snyder once aptly typified as "interbirth." Indeed, we all give birth to each other, continually. All beings are as precious as our mother (or grandmother). And so we have a compassionate bond with all beings. The Four Brahmaviharas (Immeasurable Minds) are practiced, opening the heart to the fullest dimensions of love, and from the perspective of the bodhisattva, for the sake of all beings.

Along with the bodhisattva motivation for enlightenment, there's an emphasis on enabling the practitioner to realize his or her own mind as Buddha mind through personally retracing the terrain the Buddha crossed through. So we can see on a simple level how Tibetan Buddhism shares the analytic approach of Theravada, original Buddhism. And emphasis on meditation, of Zen. Plus it's a devotional path, as in Pure Land, with oodles more ritual (skillful means). Here we can introduce the primary element of different emphasis, called tantra, suffusing the approach from the very first to last. Along with the basic ideas of Buddhism and many of the meditations we've reviewed plus quite a few more, the practitioner also relates to the various deities associated with the Buddha, through *deity yoga*, with the ultimate goal of recognizing his or her mind as Buddha mind.

We've prepared the ground for deities, in understanding Amitabha's transformation from a devoted student to a bodhisattva who then became a transcendental buddha. Now we widen the curtain, as it were, to glimpse Tibetan Buddhism's cosmic parade of bodhisattvas, transcendental buddhas, celestial clowns and fire-eaters, fierce lions and tigers, multiple light shows, and infinite pageantry. Even with a humanist approach to deities, demystifying them would never detract from the distinct realities they each represent. Scholar Georg Feurstein calls them "practical energetic presences," and notes how there's no clear boundary between their being "intelligent energy, personified symbol, and … divine background." If you prefer a convenient handle, you might think of them as aspects of the Buddha's enlightenment, thus aspects of the same ultimate reality of which we all partake, and aspire to be aware of. As we'll see, the deities are called upon through prayer, visualization, mantra recitation, gesture—body, spirit, and mind.

But deities are efficacious only through initiation from a teacher in the lineage, somewhat like a television's being only a box unless plugged into a socket conveying an electric current. The teacher provides that current, a direct connection to Buddha juice, as it were. And without that teacher's guidance, they say you might get a jolt that could stand your hair on end. ("Don't try this at home alone.") Transmission of the tantric teachings formally begins during a special ritual of initiation (called an *empowerment*), following the lamrim preparation yogas. At this time, you're given your own deity to visualize, including the meaning of the deity's hand-gesture (*mudra*) and the deity's *mantra*. But transmission can also take place in ordinary conversation, or by a mere gesture. (*Thwonk!*)

Lastly, the end result is blissful, luminous awareness of the here and now, sometimes called *Dzogchen* (a.k.a. *Ati Yoga*) or *Mahamudra*, depending on the Tibetan school. It might sound like the satori arrived at through Zen, but it's arrived at through a different travel itinerary than via the Zen zone. So: Vajrayana recapitulates everything we've already studied, but with a tantric twist, from the very beginning. And that's our executive summary. Next we'll open that out, to open our heart-mind even more, to the most recent addition to our own Buddhist shores.

Vajrayana Is Mahayana with a Tantric Twist

With Tibetan Buddhism we come back full-circle to India, land of the Buddha's birth, where tantra was born. Tibet received Buddhism direct from India, unlike the other Mahayana branches which filtered through China first. Tantra can be found throughout Indian traditions. The story goes that the Buddha—having used skillful means to modulate his teachings so as to reach the many different kinds of people he encountered— toward the end of his life introduced a final system, incorporating tantra. The resulting Tantric Buddhism, or Vajrayana, was passed northward to Tibet, Mongolia, and Siberia, and east to Japan (practiced as *Shingon*).

Tantra's defined as "weaving" as well as "continuum," and "system." Basically, tantra recognizes the *continuity* of sunyata at all levels. Also, this path further *continues* Theravada and Mahayana practices with the *thread* of tantra running through them all. Tantra recognizes the interdependent, inter*woven* nature of reality (interbeing), and so is a *weaving* of truths both outer and inner, self and other, personal and cosmic, yoking them and the practitioner together (yoga), and threading beyond to ultimate, complete, *innate* enlightenment.

So we can draw from other schools we've seen to understand it a little better. For example, there's a similarity to Vipassana, where obstacles to our meditation can become levers into insight. And we've glimpsed from a Pure Land perspective how infinite buddha nature pervades every atom of the universe. So now we can appreciate tantra telling us, "Since everything has potential buddha nature, it's thus all suitable for practice. It's all *stuff* … all sacred … use it!" One example maybe you've seen: Tibetan prayer flags. These bright red, yellow, green, and white squares of cloth with Buddhist prayers printed on them are strung out where the winds can spread their merit. That's tantric. Another example would be difficult emotions. Rather than suppress or disassociate from them (which would be the mistake of asceticism), tantra recognizes they, too, contain buddha energy, capable of purifying their own destructive tendencies. That's tantric, too.

Thus, each practitioner (called a yogi, or siddha) is treated as both a unique individual and as part of an infinitely interpenetrating matrix of all being. The primal energies eternally shaping the cosmos also mold each individual. Its gradual *system* of stages (which we'll see next) threads each practitioner through the Buddha's own evolution—from Theravada self-disciplined awareness to Mahayana compassionate awareness, to totally enlightened awareness—in a process appropriate to his or her individual temperament.

Along the Path

Texts unique to Vajrayana are called *tantras,* as distinct from *sutras;* yet both words have similar meanings (to sew and to weave). And our word *text,* from Latin, also means a weaving. Some mystics *read* the world as their text. Tantra interweaves an individual's personal life with the Buddha's way. And it's a yoga (a word akin to religion), yoking together the sacred and the mundane, wisdom with compassion.

Lamrim: Step-by-Step Stages Along the Path

Since the eleventh century, Tibet has maintained manuals, called *lamrim,* mapping the spiritual path step-by-step. At the core is a now-familiar premise: The seeds of enlightenment are present within all beings. A basic meditation is how being human is the best opportunity to realize this truth, yet with it also comes foibles. Another meditation is how another human is indispensable to unlocking the teachings for you, your guru. You could learn all the stages in a few months, but they could take five years to practice well.

Consider, for example, *tonglen*, the meditation of exchanging self for others. Here you are to take in the sadness and suffering of others and give them back your own happiness and capacity for nirvana. You might visualize someone's problem (anger, poor self-esteem, greed, and so on) as a black smoke. Then inhale it into your heart-mind.

This Is _____

Lamrim means "stages of the path." This includes meditations on: the preciousness of human life, death and impermanence, samsara, taking refuge, karma, equanimity, remembering kindnesses of others, disadvantages of self-cherishing, advantages of cherishing others, exchanging self with others (*tonglen*), developing *bodhicitta* (the compassionate aspiration to attain enlightenment for the sake of all beings), tranquility, and identifying with sunyata rather than ego.

Once it's settled there, exhale the innate bliss of your pure heart-mind, visualized as radiant white light, upon them and the whole universe. Now that visualization has become a popular practice in the West, many people often associate light with inhalation and toxins with exhalation, but the reversal here's instructive. Setting the pain of others before yours is a positive force, dissolving the personal ego, and generating bodhicitta, transforming yourself as you help others.

And learning to identify with sunyata, no-thing-ness, blank essence of infinite possibility, means that none of the meditations, before or after initiation, are to be attached to. All the rituals of Tibetan Buddhism are always wed to this deep wisdom. Next, let's spend a little time with the lamrim topic of relying on a spiritual guide (learning from someone already on the path).

Connecting with a Teacher

Who was the Buddha's teacher? (Who's asking!) Do *you* think you can be as fully realized as the Buddha, without a teacher? It's a question the Buddha faced when Mara the Tempter smirked, "And who are you to think you're the Enlightened One?" (A certain subtle, sacred pride is justifiable in the path, but presumption and hubris can be ruinous.) To really find out, we connect directly with ultimate buddha-mind through the lineage of teachers from the Buddha (the original teacher) on up to the present. In Vajrayana, your teacher (guru, *rinpoche*, *lama*, mentor, preceptor) becomes the living embodiment of the Buddha, taking *you* through the Buddha's own path. Tantra can be challenging, and will affect different people differently. So you need your teacher's wisdom and compassion to personally make it through.

This Is _____

A Tibetan teacher can have many names, besides mentor, preceptor, and spiritual friend. **Rinpoche** (*rin-poh-shay*, "greatly precious") is akin to the Japanese *roshi*. And *Geshe* (pronounced *geshey*) is like a Ph.D. A **lama** has completed three-year training and usually gone on to head a monastery. Certain heads of monasteries, believed to be individuals intentionally reincarnated, are designated *Tulku*. Sometimes Tibetan Buddhism is mistakenly called Lamaism, somewhat akin to calling Catholicism "Popeism" (except there is no pope). And a llama's like a small, woolly camel, with two "l"s. (Sorry, there's no lllama.)

This relationship's often sparked by an amazing sense of affinity ("when the student's ready, the teacher appears"). Besides Vajrayana instruction, a guru can advise in personal matters and family affairs. A guru can be more important than a parent, because while your parents raise you in one lifetime, your guru takes you through all your lives and brings you up in the most profound way. Utter devotion is requisite since he or she represents your own Buddha mind and inner teacher, as well as the Buddha's teachings. And besides that selfless perspective, it also makes sense from a selfish point of view: Vajrayana teachers, having been there, will know where you're at in what's new terrain to you, and know how to guide you through.

Our rule of thumb is to spend up to three years before making a commitment to a particular Buddhist teacher, no matter the tradition. In Tibet, however, a practitioner might take up to 12 years. Westerners, and perhaps Americans particularly, take heed. This isn't like impulse buying; point and click. Another interesting comparison that Sogyal Rinpoche once pointed out is that Americans want to hear why they should do something *before* they go and do it, while Tibetans go ahead and do something, then their teacher would tell them why they did it.

Hear and Now _____

"Buddhists ... call the mentor 'spiritual teacher,' and 'spiritual friend,' as a close friend, not an absolute authority. This emphasizes how you have to free yourself, develop your own enlightenment. No one else can do it for you. But in Tantra the sort of transference relations to the teacher is very important. You spend twelve years to investigate such a central figure. You don't jump into receiving teachings from the first teacher. Not initiatory teaching."

—Robert Thurman

Empowerment: Initiation into Tantra

A lamrim book contains practices that have remained unchanged for more than a millennium, but it's not a do-it-yourself manual. Buddhism's not in a book; the map is not the territory. Practical application's necessary, which requires guidance. If tried out from a book, it wouldn't be the same. This is somewhat similar to people enjoying a sweat lodge purification ceremony without grounding in the path of indigenous spirituality of which it's but a part. We need to expand upon and clarify this critical point: grounding in a method through preliminary preparation (*ngondro*, pronounced nundro*) and *initiation* (*Abhisheka*, Sankrit; "consecrating, anointing"), personal *empowerment*.

The mantra *Ah*, for example, can symbolize the entire Heart Sutra and Diamond Sutra. But to understand and practice that requires initiation by a teacher. It's often called *secret*. This seems quite opposite from Pure Land, say, with no bar to entry. But even that requires proper care: sincerity, faith, and joy, as well as good grounding in the basic teachings of the Buddha.

> **Hear and Now**
>
> "Now I will tell you something about the Secret School. It's not that mantras are secret. The Secret School is the efficacious response which comes from *your* recitation of mantras; I can't know your response. I recite mantras and have my efficacious response, and you do not know of it. This is 'no mutual knowing.' The ability and power are unfathomable and unknown, and are therefore called the Secret School. It's not the mantras themselves, but the power of mantras that is secret. This is the meaning of the Secret School."
>
> —Venerable Tripitaka Master Hsüan Hua

Actually, these secrets aren't the kind of cloak-and-dagger mysteries as they might sound. Having worked for years as a secretary, I'm proud to say the word *secretary* means "one who keeps the secrets." And just so has the Tibetan lineage faithfully preserved these precious teachings. Make no mistake, Vajrayana isn't a members-only secret society. Rather, it unlocks mysteries only to those adequately trained. A good way to explain this is by comparing it to a radio. I invariably wonder if my brain might be influenced by all the radio and TV waves that pass through my noggin ("More when we come back … and now *this!*"). Actually, I know they're there, because I know that with a TV set I can tune in. But my brain doesn't necessarily unscramble the signals. And this is what secret teachings are like. Not having a set is equivalent to not having been initiated; something's there but it doesn't quite register.

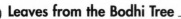

Leaves from the Bodhi Tree

A visitor came upon a small crowd of Tibetan Buddhist monks. Their attention was riveted upon a single priest sitting on a platform. He joined them, watching this priest. When the ceremony of watching was over, he asked one of the monks what had happened. The monk told him that the priest had demonstrated the power of levitation. "But I didn't see him levitate," the visitor told the monk. "Oh," the monk said, smiling. "Then obviously you didn't receive initiation for the ceremony beforehand."

It's like Lao-tzu saying, "Those who know, don't speak; and those who speak, don't know," then going on to write 5,000 words. The words obviously aren't secret, they're only road signs. And it's like the Buddha holding up a flower, and Kasyapa smiling; except that legendary transmission was mind-to-mind, and Vajrayana transmission works on mind, speech, and body, as we'll see next.

To continue the analogy to Zen, a curious occurrence concerning koan practice is relevant here. About a century ago, a book was published in Japan with a "cheat sheet" of answers to a couple hundred koans—answers that had been passed down teacher-to-teacher secretly for two centuries. Scandalous, but it was like trying to draw legs onto a snake. The koans are meant to be practiced, not read about. They're not math problems. The right answer isn't in a book, but in each practitioner. Just as I can't eat dinner for you, I can never know how you answer your koan, I can only know how I answered mine. So a guru isn't giving you an abstract truth but something crafted for you personally. The secret isn't in any particular mantra, it's in your own response to their power.

Body, Speech, and Mind as One: Some Essential Tantric Practices

As you've noticed by now, Buddhist logic is fond of groupings and subgroups. The Fourth Noble Truth is the Eightfold Path. In Vipassana, the Three Marks of Existence are examined within each of the Four Establishments of Mindfulness. Since things overlap, this gets very rigorous as one examines, say, the nature of impermanence, non-self, and suffering/nirvana of the body within the body, the body within the feelings, the body within consciousness, and the body as an object of consciousness. This rigorous analysis is also in evidence in tantra, where, for instance, a practice can have an *outer, inner,* and *secret* dimension. (Don't ask about the secret secret: that's marked "Top Secret." We're just opening up the middle and bottom secret files.)

Hear and Now

"The fault that I always found in Western philosophic logic is that it doesn't have an ultimate courage in questioning whether the self exists. It starts with that assumption. Now if you take this logic to its absolute extreme fearlessly and question that, then you have a pure logic, and you can start building castles that have meaning on that basis, which is what the Tibetans have done. It's questioning the very basis of all reality, all existence, and the self itself. All phenomena."

—Richard Gere

Vajrayana also breaks practice into *body*, *speech*, and *mind* (and by so doing integrates all three)—for example, through prostration and *mudra, mantra recitation*, and *mental visualization*, as we'll explore in this half of our survey. But we've seen examples already, worth recalling. We've noted how the *ritual* of taking refuge can engage body (prostration), speech (recitation of a mantra or refuge prayer), and mind (concentration on a deity).

Similarly, we've observed visualization in the previous chapter (a trait of Amitabha or of his pure land), and recitation (of his name); just add prayer beads to count recitations while visualizing and you're integrating body, speech, and mind. Now that's really cooking!

The Path Is the Body

The Buddha broke with the asceticism of his culture, but asceticism is deeply embedded in world civilization. If you listen deeply to Western religion, you often hear the human body denigrated as a vessel of filth because sin (the Fall) is linked to the human body. In general, tantra displays great acceptance of physicality and all its potentials and powers, together with the fullest program for their development and transformation. We've already mentioned Tibetan physical yogic exercises, Kum-Nye, in Chapter 10. Vajrayana also makes extended use of prostrations, such as 100 per day; 100,000 times is another common set. (At a more advanced level, this set might then be done in sets of 108, the number, say, of ways we're ignorant of the Dharma; the number of beads on a mala.) Many rituals must be practiced 100,000 times before they're considered to fully take hold. (*Question:* How many Vajrayanists does it take to screw in a light bulb? *Answer:* One, but they do it 100,000 times.)

Other bodily engagements found in Vajrayana include meditation on six primary energy centers, called *chakras*, also found in yoga. (Ever-simple, Zen focuses on just one, below the navel). Plus there are *channels*, *winds*, and *tigles* to be explored, bodily pathways and means of internal circulation of concentrations of subtle energy (similar to *prana* in Hindu yoga, and *chi*, as in chi kung and tai chi, in Taoist yoga). Emotions also travel here and can get tangled up. Once these energies are recognized, liberated, and flow freely, they too can be transformed into buddha energy.

Mudras (ritualized hand gestures) are a good example of a skillful means of integrating mental with physical. Emulating a particular gesture of a buddha or bodhisattva deity further imparts their energy to us, physically (much in the way that smiling, or mouth yoga, awakens the feeling of happiness).

Say the Word: Speech Vibrations Can Set Great Things in Motion

In our Square One study of meditation, we introduced mantras or recitation as a means of stabilizing the mind, and more recently we've seen it as capable of calling upon the universe's primal energies of enlightenment through the compassionate vow of Amitabha. Tibetan practice has a treasury of mantras, requiring initiation.

One etymology of the word *mantra* combines the Sanskrit root *man* ("to think") with the suffix *tra* ("tool"), to mean "a tool for thinking." It could also be read as *man*, from *manas* ("mind") and *tra* from *tranam* ("protect"), meaning "mind-protector."

Mantras can be as short as one syllable. And some are believed to have intrinsic power, in and of themselves, setting up a resonant powerful vibrational field, such as "Om" (pronounced *Ohhhhwwwwmmmmmm*). Hindus consider *Om* the primeval sound (or vibrational frequency) of the universe; in Vajrayana, *Om* might manifest the Buddha's many bodies, for example. The syllable *Ah* manifests the Buddha's speech, source of all sound. *Hung* manifests the mind of the Buddha. (It's also spelled Hum, but pronounced, to our ears, a tad like a funk singer grunting "hunh!") Reciting this three-syllable mantra with one-pointed concentration bestows the blessings of the body, speech, and mind of all the buddhas.

Thus, after settling into tranquility meditation, a practitioner might meditate for fifteen minutes on the mantra *Om Ah Hung*. (Eventually, five minutes would be sufficient.) Recite Om to yourself while breathing in. In between breaths, concentrate on the center of your chest (your spiritual heart), recite Ah. And on the out-breath, recite Hung.

Seeing with Your Mind's Eye: Mandalas and Deities

Some advanced physicists have speculated that the universe is made out of photons (quanta of electromagnetic radiation). So when we visualize something, such as a peaceful beach, even though the image we conjure up in our mind's eye might seem purely subjective, it actually participates within the universe's interconnected net of light (Indra's web, again). Potent stuff. Actually, of all our five senses, our brain invests most of its sensory activity dealing with visual information. Thus, people often close their eyes to meditate, to quiet the brain. Thus, too, we speak about knowing in terms of sight, and wisdom as light. ("You see?")

Along the Path

Images came before words. We think in images. Visualization is an ancient practice. It takes place in the intuitive, artistic, nonlinear, holistic side of our human brain (the right side, whereas the left is verbal, linear, analytic, critical). Images are stored in the cerebral cortex, which influences the autonomic nervous system, and, in turn, the pituitary endocrine system, and so on down to every cell and atom of our body.

Visualization's an everyday phenomenon of which we're seldom aware, yet with vast, untapped potentials. Think of the name of any movie star, and you're also visualizing them; meaning, we think through visualization. Or think of your best friend out with someone else, and you're visualizing; feeling through visualization. And when you catch sight of someone you know on the street, and it turns out to be somebody else, that's visualization, coloring the way we interact with the world. Tibetan Buddhism asserts that we're not only continuously visualizing the world without being aware of it but also using our preconceptions and views as a filter, interpreting as we do so. So visualization can enable us to bypass our habitual, automatic critical consciousness (which looks but does not see), in order to access our innate, alert, boundless awareness, which really sees.

Now we'll see how Tibetan practice interlinks visualization with body and mind. A major tantric practice is deity yoga. A guru initiates a practitioner in the image and qualities of a particular deity, chosen to match the yogi's personal temperament or need. A deity is enthroned in his or her particular pure land, called a mandala. There's wisdom in their circularity; close your eyes, for instance, and ask yourself if your mind is square (or try it with your eyes open, for that matter).

This Is

A *mandala* is a circular form that can represent the world of phenomena, as well as realms of consciousness and pure lands of bodhisattvas and deities. Mandalas can be made up of heaps of rice or sand, or painted on scrolls (called *tangkas*). They can be three-dimensional yarn sculpture, or even the design of temples, such as Borobudur in Java and Samye in Tibet.

A drawing of a mandala is like a two-dimensional blueprint for a three-dimensional visualization. A deity in the center is pictured at the pinnacle of a pagoda-like pyramid shape, with narrowing ascending levels. Eventually, a mandala can be visualized eyes-open as well as eyes-closed. It can just appear, of its own. And it's considered as existing within and without the yogi. Mandalas range from simple to complex, a common layout having four quadrants.

A beginner might visualize a deity in a mandala, and petition it for assistance. Practitioners might further imagine themselves touring or circumambulating its pure lands. In advanced practice, they imagine themselves as no longer separate from the deity in the center or nucleus, becoming one with it. Nothing to ever become attached to, after creation and meditation mandalas are visualized as dissolving into emptiness.

Here is an image of a deity for visualization. Manjushri embodies the wisdom (prajna) of all Buddhas. He is holding the flaming sword of nondual wisdom in his right hand, symbolic of cutting off ignorance. This wisdom is not the kind of knowledge one gains from books or lectures, but wisdom born from insight into the nondual nature of reality, or emptiness. Usually Manjushri is holding a book in his left hand (the Prajnaparamita Sutra on emptiness) or a flower upon which the book rests. In this particular form of Manjushri, created by the artist for a special sadhana (tantric meditation) for students of Trungpa Rinpoche, he holds a vase containing the nectar of immortality, symbolizing the undying nature of nondual wisdom.

Drawing: Sanje Elliot

Tip: When you see Vajrayana deities that look like monstrous demonic ogres, they're called "wrathful" deities, whose role is to destroy ignorance. They might look nasty, but visualizing and relating to them, they're found to be actually protective and exhilarating.

The central deity of this mandala is Jananadakini, a goddess with three heads and six arms. She is surrounded by eight goddess assistants. A guardian sits by each of the four gates.

From Tibetan Mandalas *(International Academy of Indian Culture)*

Courtesy of Dr. Lokesh Chandra

As another example of integrating body, speech, and mind, we can extend the Om Ah Hung mantra to our mind's eye. In Vajrayana, the written word for each syllable has its own visual symbolism. So you'd visualize a diamond-colored Om at the crown of your head, that your body might be merged with Buddha's enlightened body; a ruby-colored Ah at your throat, merging with his enlightened speech; and a sapphire Hung at your heart (center of your chest), merging with his enlightened mind (heart). Additionally, you can meditate on Om as the Sangha, Ah as the Dharma, and Hung as the Buddha. Now you can begin to appreciate why the great Tibetan teacher Naropa said, "My mind is the perfect Buddha, my speech is the perfect teaching, my body is the perfect spiritual community."

We might also note how integrating body-speech-mind can have an extra little tantric twist to it, working with what is, rather than trying to avoid or transcend. Practicing a trio of skillful means can transform idle mind-wandering into constructive mind-wandering. For instance, if your mind wanders off while reciting a mantra, let it wander: It can alight onto visualization, and if it gets tired of that, you can do more prostrations—each shift of focus allowing the very tendency of the mind to wander to propel your practice, transforming butterfly mind into innate buddha mind.

Skillful Means of Ritual and Symbol

Before concluding our survey of Vajrayana, we might consider again its deployment of a wide span of *skillful means*, and its symbolic approach, to round out our understanding of tantra.

> **This Is**
>
> *Upaya kausalya* is Sanskrit for **skillful means,** device, method, art. It includes any number of excellent expedients to facilitate enlightenment, such as visualization, prostrations, bowing, miracle, mantra, koan, plain speech, the *thwack!* of a stick, insight, etc. They're traditionally compared to a raft, with nirvana as the other shore, to be set aside once nirvana's attained. They not only lead to enlightenment (of self), they are enlightenment (compassionate service to others).

Now that we have a better understanding of tantra, let's return once more to our premise, that Vajrayana gives Mahayana a tantric twist. Consider taking refuge, as a primary example. Along with the Triple Gem (Buddha, Dharma, Sangha), Tibetan Buddhists take refuge in a very personal way, called the *refuge tree*. At its crown, you visualize your guru, as a manifestation of the Buddha. And you visualize your guru there with all the gurus of your guru's lineage, and their sanghas, back to original Buddha. That's for a start. Along with that you might visualize all the deities and bodhisattvas, and their guardian deities, and their teachings, and sanghas. And so on, down to your family, friends, worst enemies, and animals—all looking at you—and vow your going for refuge will help all of them. This is accompanied with appropriate prayer and prostrations.

A typical ritual for meditation, such as one that involves visualization, prostration, and a mantra such as Om-Ah-Hung, might start with a candle or some incense at one's altar, and bowing or prostrating, going for refuge. It might end with another bow, putting out the candle, and dedicating any merit possibly earned by the practice toward the benefit of all beings. Mantra practice could continue during daily activities, perhaps reinforced with prayer beads or even spinning a prayer wheel.

From that, you could say that tantra emphasizes more ritual than other schools, though Zen practice can get pretty ritualistic, too. And this isn't necessarily a bad thing. Ritual in general connects a person or group with knowledge, an idea, belief, or power. People of every spiritual tradition give thanks for food. Furthermore, as we become aware, we notice how much of our behavior is habit energy, personal ritual but done unconsciously. Of all Buddhist paths, Vajrayana has most actively engaged a wide variety of tightly integrated rituals to clear away the obstruction of our automatic, knee-jerk, ingrained responses so that our Buddha nature can fully arise.

Tantra uses our own habit energy to transform itself. You could say it teaches us a very good habit: not doing anything out of habit. The tantric approach to mindfulness in daily life is thus often symbolic. Quoting the *Sutra of Great Approximation*, Bokar Rinpoche suggests that, when opening a door, we can wish, "May the door of profound reality open." Walking, we might wish, "May I progress on the path of Awakening." In a car, we might wish, "May I ride the horse of diligence." Upon arrival, we might wish, "May I arrive at the city of Nirvana."

These are similar to mindfulness gathas we've already seen in Theravada and Zen, though with a slightly greater emphasis on symbol. Tibetan Buddhism is rich with symbolic images, symbolic phrases, and symbolic stories that require a teacher to interpret. This overall tendency is good company with such other language strategies as the koan, the "language of the birds" of Western alchemy, and The Song of Songs. An insight is found in the roots of the word *symbol:* from Greek, literally to pull or draw together, similar to yoga as yoking, or tantra as weaving, as opposed to diabolic, tearing apart. There's an element of sympathetic "magic," even (sympathetic meaning "fellow feeling"): realizing kinship with the primordial innate wisdom within all things. The magic of a beautiful dawn. The spell within a seashell.

The End of the Road

Now you have a better understanding of Tibetan Buddhism, though I may not have even scratched the surface. This is why it's called the Diamond Path. Only a diamond can penetrate another diamond. (Only mind can know mind.) I'll just add a road sign pointing toward the end of the road. If you follow through and are empowered in tantra by a teacher, he or she will reveal for you a glimpse of the goal, so you'll have something to work for. Scholar Bernard Guenther likens the process to a heat-seeking missile. Once it locks onto its target, they're one; although the fusion's off in the future, the contact begins here and now.

The Vajrayana teachings called Mahamudra and Dzochen culminate in what might outwardly seem like basic tranquility meditation or zazen's "just sitting." But they're arrived at following rigorous tantric training. In the end, it matters not if you find out that the secret was that there was no secret (I'm not telling, because I don't know!). Be thankful you found out, once and for all—and send the rest of us a postcard, from the summit of Mt. Everest. (Postcards without correct zip code will be returned to sender.) Have a good journey!

The endless knot (Sanskrit, shrivatsa; Tibetan, dpal be'u) harmoniously weaves motion and rest, simplicity and profundity. Symbolic of interdependence, interpenetration, interbeing, tantra— it has no beginning, no middle, no end. Like the Buddha's wisdom and compassion, it's infinite.

With Tibetan Buddhism we complete our tour of the four major schools of practice in the West. But, really, the Buddha taught one truth differently, depending on the capacity of his listeners. Note, he didn't teach different things to different people. The rain of Dharma falls equally. Big trees soak up more, while saplings are happy with a sprinkle. (And each time the rain penetrates a little further than before.) This core varies from one school to another, just as people do, but at its heart is one. One taste. No divisions, no institutions, no fixed location. There's only Dharma. One Dharma. Hinayana, Mahayana, Vajrayana—all are Dharma-yana. The Way of the Way.

There's a saying that the Dharma is excellent in the beginning, excellent in the middle, and excellent in the end. This is reminiscent of what Saint Catherine said about heaven—everything between here and heaven … is heaven. On that note, let me close with these lines from Tilopa's *Song of Mahamudra:*

> "At first a yogi feels like the mind is tumbling like a waterfall; in midcourse, like the Ganges, it flows on, slow and gentle; in the end, it is like a vast ocean, where the lights of Child and Mother merge into one."

The Least You Need to Know

♦ The most recent major traditional school of Buddhism to awaken the West, Tibetan Buddhism (Varjrayana) claims the most evolved teachings of the Buddha, and the most complete; vast, yet step-by-step; intellectually rigorous, yet devotional.

♦ Migrating from India to Tibet, Vajrayana is the only Mahayana school that didn't pass through China first. Vajrayana could be seen as Mahayana Buddhism with a tantric twist. Tantra represents a late development within Buddhist practice in India.

◆ Tantra requires initiation, and invests great importance upon the teacher-student relationship.

◆ Tantric ritual engages body, speech, and mind, through such means as prostration and *mudra*, recitation of *mantra* and prayer, and visualization of *mandalas* and deities.

Part 4

Buddhism in Action: Applications in Everyday Life

Congratulations! You now have a map … have seen how to drive … and know the basic rules of the road. (Applying your foot to the gas pedal, you know the vehicle will go faster … but your mind needn't go faster.)

In this second half, we'll put the pedal to the metal. So where shall you go today? There's nowhere the Way doesn't make major inroads. Take your pick. Touch one deeply and you touch all the others.

See how ordinary encounters illuminate Buddhism in action for you … and how Buddhism illuminates ordinary encounters … and how the interaction illuminates your own path. May these occasions brighten your way like festive lights. And may your journey always be safe, pleasurable, and fulfilling.

Chapter 15

Bringing It All Back Home: Mutual Relations

In This Chapter

◆ The Buddha's family life

◆ Relationships as mutuality

◆ On love, and other difficulties

◆ Marriage and parenting

◆ Education and lifelong learning

◆ Living our dying

Moving on from an outline of living Buddhism to Buddhist life, we start through seeing Buddhist life as all about relationships, with emphasis on *inter*-relationships, and the compassionate wisdom born of such understanding. I know a dear person who's ordained as a Zen priest, and shares a diary with friends. One thing striking in them is seeing how interpersonal relations never go away. Whether we're in a monastery or in the world at large, we're all part of the enormous journey of life on this planet. Our simple feelings for trees and sky, clouds and sun, might arouse our sense of our mutual interbeing with the universe. Our human-to-human relationships are a similar kind of field wherein we realize our common humanity and kinship with all life, over and over.

We're always in relationships. Do we see suffering in them? Can we see through to the cause? Will seeing the cause open a way through? Our everyday relations can show us how they're intertwined with our ultimate relationship: our original nature, our limitless and luminous True Self. Our lives as life itself.

The Buddha and his Asian followers found monastic life the predominant ideal. Westerners, in the majority, opt for the householder's life. Either way, our everyday relations are a wonderful opportunity for spiritual realization. Here's a short survey of various phases of being one family.

The Way of Relation: Interrelation

Realizing our interdependence, we attain *greater intimacy with life*. And so we ask ourselves, "Am I in right relation?" We're all in some kind of relation (if you don't think so, try missing a couple of payments on your credit card). Furthermore, the Buddha rejected rank, a stance which didn't exactly jive with the culture of his day and remains a challenge today. No superior, no inferior. No equal, either. Rather, all is *mutuality*. It doesn't mean everything's the same. Each relationship is unique. I'm sure you can relate to this.

The Buddha's Own Family: Back to the Shakya

Let's begin by returning to the life of the Buddha. He transformed the spiritual path of his time from one of extreme renunciation to one embracing all aspects of human life regardless of race, sex, or social status. Sitting beneath the bodhi tree, he'd truly realized, "I and the universe are one." Self is interdependent with the universe; or, to put it another way, there is no self but in relation. The selflessness of interbeing, as True Self.

So how did this play out with his own family? He'd vowed to return once he attained his goal, and so he did come back to the Shakya Kingdom. Only, instead of heading straight home, he went, as everywhere else, as a mendicant, on foot, going from door to door. When his father heard about this, he nearly blew his stack, disgraced to hear of his own son, a prince, descended from a clan of warriors, begging for alms. He went and found his son, but, in confronting him, the Buddha's explanation of the Way of life he'd found was so righteously correct and illuminating that the king experienced awakening right there in the street. The Buddha taught his father the Way, and the king ultimately attained enlightenment, within his own palace walls. He also accepted his stepmother into his order.

Still, maybe you wouldn't want your daughter marrying this kind of guy. Certainly this wasn't exactly the happily-ever-after kind of outcome most parents dream of. Yet it is said, too, that his wife, Yasodhara, perhaps ready to bawl him out for playing deadbeat dad and hitting the road, knelt when they were reunited. She could clearly see he was now supremely enlightened. With divine love, he asked forgiveness. If he hadn't been fair to her, he said, he'd been true to all sentient beings, and asked her to cross the sea of suffering with them. So she, too, renounced royal life to study the Dharma. And their seven-year-old son followed him as he left, asking for his inheritance, and became the Sangha's youngest monk. The Buddha's cousin Ananda also followed, becoming his closest attendant for the rest of his life.

Exercise: With a simple meditation, we can realize how our own family ties reflect our interconnection, our lack of separate self. Sit and, when settled, put your hands out in front of you in a comfortable manner, palms down. Look at your hands. Notice the shape of your fingers and knuckles, the patterns of your veins and skin. See how you feel about your hand. Generate and send loving kindness to yourself, looking at your hand. Now see your mother in those shapes and textures, and see how you feel about her. Send her loving kindness. Now see your father in your hand, and see how you feel about him. Send him loving kindness. Turn your hands over, join palms, and thank them for this meditation. Gassho.

If Emily Post Met the Buddha: Treating All Beings as Created Mutual

Hindus of the Buddha's time worshipped facing in different directions to honor sun and moon, mountains and rivers, and the tall trees. The Buddha adapted the practice to create a cube of six surfaces, for people to remember (be mindful of) life's major relationships: Father and mother, in the east; students and teachers, in the south; husband, wife, and children, in the west; friends and kin, in the north; colleagues, employees, and workers, below; spiritual teachers, monks, nuns, and saints, above. These all interface, as we say today, to form the matrix and network of human affairs. And all these relationships, the Buddha explained, are of reciprocal power sharing. A mutual support system (sangha).

For example, consider relations between a community and its temple or church. The secular population provides economic support to the monastery or priests who transmit sacred ideas and ideals. The monastery or priests, in turn, provide the local community with not only spiritual support but such material services as education (such as Sunday school)—and, in the Buddha's day, lodging and medical care, and in our own time, charitable services. (Did you know?, the world's third-largest bone marrow registry is maintained by a Buddhist charity, Chu Tzi, as one of its numerous worldwide services.) So from this one plane of relationship, we can see how the other relationships are already implicated. Each connects to all the others. And all on a win-win basis, to use contemporary lingo. But, before we proceed to our own lives, let's pause to imagine how such egalitarianism might have conflicted with such cultural climates as the hierarchical societies of Brahmanic India … or Confucian China.

Cultural Relatives

Generally, Westerners define themselves as independent ("I'm a go-getter, my job title is …,"), while Easterns tend to think in terms of interdependency ("I work at the same company where my mother did.") As individuals, we each typically represent a diverse web of intertwined networks known as *civil society*, which might include participation in affinity groups, sports, and clubs, as well as unions or trade associations, political affiliations, religious associations, cultural programs, and so on.

For contrast, consider Confucianism, still dominant in China and much of east Asia. In Confucius' ethical universe, relations are mapped in concentric rings. At its core are husband and wife, then parents and children, older and younger siblings, companions and friends, and, finally, political leaders and the public—each relationship mirroring the others (for example, the ruler on the throne being like the father in the house, and vice versa).

This reflects the Eastern cultural tendency to think of others before self, and value harmonizing with the group. In the West, individuality is more the primary unit. So in the East, the family takes care of each other throughout their lives; in the West, we speak of our "nuclear family," a nest we leave and come back to periodically. Now, what might it be like to think of our relationships in terms of interdependencies?

Happily Ever After? How About "Happily Ever Here"? (Love)

We came into life through a father and mother, so we, too, naturally seek a mate. Yet Buddhism might seem bereft of romantic love, compared to such legendary couples as Krishna and Radha, Abelard and Heloise, Muhammad and Khadijah, Majnun and Layla, and Solomon and Sheba. Yet the world's first novel, *The Tale of Genji*—an epic of intertwining tales of love and romance, as well as friendship and family—was written by a Buddhist, Lady Murasaki Shikibu.

Recently, I saw some cute ideas for Buddhist Valentine's greetings by Suvarnaprabha, passed around the Internet: "I can never extinguish my thirst for you." "I love you neither more nor less than I love all beings." And "Let's you and me interpenetrate

Reality." Indeed, what's called romantic love can really be another setup for disappointment. ("Dear Abby: How can I go on living?") As Coleman Barks points out, "Western love … is identifying with an idea that can't quite be consummated. It's *Romeo and Juliet*." It's an assortment of chocolate-flavored duhkha in a pretty, red, valentine-shaped box. (Not that I'm knocking chocolate, but it sure can be an addictive rush.) How many people fling themselves on another person, only to stagger back, later, licking wounds from a wild but wobbly relationship that finally crashed and burned, yet still hoping to find "that certain someone" who'll relieve them of "all this agony"? It's the same old story: the suffering caused by viewing self as separate and permanent, and that an "other" will end (rather than reinforce) that delusion.

Buddhism enables you to know and love yourself. Your primordial self; without division. Being fully at home in the present, adequately complete. Security can be found … in the insecurity of impermanence. Then you might selflessly identify your undivided self as part of a living family extending in all directions in time as well as space. The family of life. So, in that kind of sense, Buddhism's an excellent training ground for loving and being loved.

Buddhist practice provides wise support for the work required to maintain an intimate relationship over time. For instance, it readily accommodates the demand for "giving someone space." Space as well as silence are positive, not negative. And emotional intelligence crops up in this chapter, again. Surveying a trying emotional landscape through mindful meditation won't necessarily result in any greater "solution" than being able to come back and calmly and clearly say, "Here are the emotions that the situation arouses in me" (rather than trying to issue commands: "Don't do such-and-such!"). Knowing you're working toward a common *direction*, you can be *direct* with each other and state, "When you do *that*, it makes me feel like *this*."

See if you can be a mindfulness bell keeping your beloved in the present moment. When you see your beloved's mind wander, why not invite them back to the present by saying, "Is it just me or is it getting colder?" Or "Doesn't the air taste fresh?" This isn't necessarily to push them away, but instead invites them to join you at the base camp of the marvelous present moment, whence all roads depend.

Along the Path

There are no dictates in Buddhist ethics about homosexuality. The Fifth Precept would apply here, too. Being aware of the consequences of sensuality and sexuality. Not causing another or ourselves pain through breaking the bonds of trust. Gender (not the same as sex), like self, can be seen to be a construct, of no permanent, independent, substantial identity.

Love puts the third precept into focus, deep listening and loving speech. Listen to what your beloved says and also to what your beloved is not saying. When you sense your beloved is hurt, why not say, "When you hurt, it hurts me, too"? When you sense your beloved is happy, why not say, "Your joy makes me glad, too"? (Wouldn't you like them to say this to you, in similar situations?)

If two beings come together, aware they're spiritually complete in themselves, then living together they'll find how their souls can be quite different, yet learn to recognize themselves in each other. It's an everyday cosmic dance of yin and yang ("not one, not two") complementing and balancing each other. Relationship becomes a sangha. "Whenever two people gather in my name," the Buddha said, "I'll be there."

Would You Promise to Be Mindful of the Present Moment with Your Beloved? (Marriage)

A marriage or committed relationship can be a two-person sangha. A splendid occasion for practice: the practice of love. Two people, interbeing. The intimacy of realizing we're all interconnected, through the interaction of just this one person with just this one person, accepted as all people. Now that's a pretty good vow.

But marriage isn't a specifically Buddhist ritual, per se, rather an event for which each sangha might have its own liturgy. A Buddhist can perform a legally binding ceremony, but he or she isn't acting as a divine intermediary ("… by the power vested in me …"). In such wedding vows, a bride and groom affirm their vows of refuge in the Triple Gem and the Precepts; additional vows might affirm the continuity of life and the importance of understanding and mutual respect. More than vowing to honor and cherish each other, which they already do, they're vowing rather to honor and cherish their committed relationship and their practice. So the emphasis isn't so much on how marvelous it is for two particular people to be coming together, but rather that they're both walking the same marvelous path together.

Mutuality of bride and groom permits either to divorce if need be and also remarry, all without stigma. They're not necessarily breaking any Buddhist vows, which they still hold sacred, still holding unconditional love for each other and staying on the path. When two practices each support each other, two can build well. If one is and the other isn't Buddhist, the dance is just as interesting. ("Hi, honey, I'm home! Guess what? I just spent seven days looking into my mind!")

> **Leaves from the Bodhi Tree**
>
> Here's a tale in which a wife's no less wise than a husband. A Tibetan arrow smith named Saraha asked his wife to make him some radishes. He then meditated for 12 years nonstop. When he arose, he asked his wife, "Where are my radishes?" His wife replied, "You think I'd keep them?" He huffed and said he'd go off to the mountains to meditate. She responded: "A solitary body doesn't mean solitude. The best solitude is when the mind is far from names and concepts. You've been meditating for 12 years, yet you still haven't gotten rid of the idea of radishes. What good will it do to go to the mountains?" He realized she was right, and so abandoned names and concepts and ultimately attained enlightenment.

Nobody Does It Better

Love invariably summons the fifth precept, the importance of having an ethical basis for dealing with sexuality. But, as Suzuki Roshi once pointed out, the minute you say "sex," everything is sex. (Considering how many days he spent sitting before a blank wall, I'm willing to take him at his word.) Contemporary life offers up as many options for escaping the prison of a separate self as there are light bulbs in Las Vegas, with sex at the top of the come-ons. Sex sells. Of course, it's natural. Sex shapes the blueprint for how we get here and perpetuate ourselves. That's a powerful energy to tap into. So sexuality can be awakening, but also samsara, sweet illusion. The Buddha knew, hardly a virgin himself. He'd not only fathered a child, but dallied daily with his harem of 500 concubines before he went forth.

Humans seem the only species who engage in sex not only for its *regenerative* aspects (producing children), but for its generative aspects. It can generate not only pleasure, in and of itself, but also intensely shared feeling capable of transporting one out of one's self. Thus it can be sacramental, but also a potential threat to the whole house of cards called ego, set up as a separate self. In the latter case, ego sometimes pulls back and reasserts itself, resulting in sexual power politics of dominance and submission; at its worst, sexual abuse. In Buddhist sexual relations, it still takes two to tango, and welcomes the dance of yin and yang.

> **Along the Path**
>
> The Western concept of *sexuality* might be summed up by Plato's analogy of a sphere that seeks wholeness after division: the union of two incomplete halves. In Buddhist sexuality, two wholes can come together and experience something larger. Tibetan Buddhists say that orgasm is a glimpse of sunyata. Asian terms for sexuality imply natural processes, such as *"cloud-rain,"* evoking the union of heaven and earth.

This exquisite, nearly life-size Mongolian Vajrayana bronze is a purely symbolic representation of the tantric union of polarities called yab yum *(Tibetan, "father/mother"; Sanskrit,* maithuna*). Dissolving selfhood, the couple enjoy attentive, mutually appreciative, enlightened contemplation.*

Zanzabazar (1635–1723), Sitasamvara with His Consort *(White Samvara; Mongolian, Caghan Demcig). Late seventeenth century. Gilt bronze. H: 21½" (54.5 cm). Diam.: 13¼" (33.8 cm). Chojin-Lama Temple Museum.*

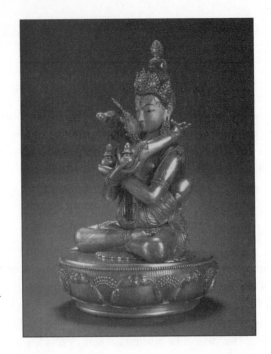

Extremism can also manifest in imagining Vajrayana as bursting with spiritually condoned eroticism. This is to confuse Buddhist tantra with tantric sex therapists. In Vajrayana, images of deities paired with their consorts in sexual embrace (called *yab yum*, literally "father and mother") are symbolic. The male represents compassion through skillful means (upaya); the woman, wisdom (prajna). To be understood only in the deepest, most sacramental sense, such allegorical imagery is a bit akin to *The Song of Solomon* and Christian mystics who seek union with Christ the Bridegroom, ecstatic communion. It should be borne in mind that the Vajrayana practitioner visualizes and identifies with both deities, thus unifying the energies they each represent, as well as identifying with the emptiness at their inmost core.

Awareness of the impermanence at the heart of life can have its own eroticism. Thai meditation master Ajahn Chah (1917–1992) once confessed that when he'd walk in the forest in his early years as a monk, every sensation gave him an erection. And, viewing everything as sacred, eccentric Zen master Ikkyu (1394–1481) wore his monastic robes to the brothel.

No matter the school of Buddhism, the path calls forth an openness to relations beyond costume or mask. The capacity for naked awareness, if you will. And, with commitment, the literal nakedness of two human beings can be a sublime occasion for experiencing and expressing love, a sacred trust, sought and found in the everyday bliss of reciprocal relationship.

Mama Buddha, Papa Buddha, and Baby Buddha (Parenting)

A baby's not automatically born Buddhist, per se, even if he or she looks like a little Buddha, smiling serenely within all that juicy baby fat. It's up to parents to offer dharma seeds to their children and let them decide for themselves. Father, mother, and child all share buddha nature. Each can remind the other of their True Nature. Consider, for example, the testimony of Patricia Ikeda Nash:

> "We are all, fundamentally, made from our mother's bodies and their love. Each night before going to bed, my son sits on my lap and presses his ear against my chest, listening to who I am, remembering. I gaze into his face, listening to his breath, remembering the night after he was born. Quiet and wakeful, we looked at one another for a long time. I felt as though his newborn body were the gateway to an immense tunnel filled with a crystalline ladder spiraling backward in time, containing the genetic and karmic essence of all our ancestors, and extending back to the first life form. How it shone! At that moment I understood the rightness of human life continuing itself, and despite the darkness that surrounds us, our capacity 'to enjoy life, living in honesty and strength.' I was contained within my baby, and he within me, a resonant abode of many voices."

Parenting as Practice

The strict schedule of parenting is comparable to monastic discipline; parenting adds the test of a child's continuous stream of interruptions wearing down the ego. But a child can also be a role model. Little kids can live so intensely in the present that just witnessing them as we go by is like a bell of mindfulness, awakening us to the marvelous present moment. And watching your own bald little baby grow that first hair, cut teeth, and sprout up like a beanstalk is quite a lesson in accepting impermanence.

Kids are also masters at beginner's mind, questioning everything. Just think of their letters to God. ("Dear God: If you are in my heart, don't you get bloody?")

So, in their way, kids can be exacting little Zen masters, demanding a parent be fully present to whatever comes up, and testing parents' ability to deal with fear, anger, bodily needs, and the whole soap opera of life (tune in again tomorrow to *As the Wheel Turns*). When we're mindful of our feelings, we don't pass their charge along to our kids.

If a parent or child is riding out an emotional storm by going to the breathing room, ringing a bell of mindfulness, and just sitting quietly beside a flower, the whole family can hear the bell and practice stopping. In a word, as Thai teacher Sulak Sivaraksa affirms, "When even one member of the household meditates, the entire family benefits."

Family Sangha, and Dharma for Kids

Buddhism isn't based on a book, but on practice. Teaching by example, a child learns to value what a parent values. A child familiar with mindful sitting, for example, can sit by a parent who's meditating in the family breathing room, and practice just being together. Dharma family practices include visiting a hospice, going on nature walks, singing and recitation together, enjoying mindful meals, celebrating Earth Day, and hugs. You might also consider teaching kids yoga, so that the lotus position isn't so much of a stretch. The Dharma will come as needed.

There's no set way for teaching Buddhism to kids. ("Paints mandalas within the lines; meditates well with others.") Some public schools are adopting daily meditation for calmer classrooms. (And there's no place like Om.) Being a mindful parent means listening for when a child wants to be taught a particular lesson, attuned to when they need to enter into the parents' practice, and able to frame it for their child's particular level. Everyday life situations can be teaching opportunities. For instance, children can be taught to care for others by the example of how they play with their own possessions.

> ### Along the Path
>
> A classic body of Buddhist literature for children is found in the *547 Jataka tales* ("birth stories"), originally written in Pali. Some were adapted from folktales of the Buddha's time. They tell of the Buddha and his followers' past lives and so generally illustrate various workings of karma. They also have specific themes such as the spirit of forgiveness, the importance of correct faith, the value of charity, and so on.

Maybe I'm prejudiced, but books are also useful. A number of Buddhist books for children are now available, in part because Western-boomer Buddhist publishers have been becoming parents. Along with the life of the Buddha, and his basic teachings, the precepts can be a core curriculum as a child becomes a young adult. Guidelines for conscious conduct can show kids how they must define for themselves their Do's and Don'ts, how that will define who they are, and how that can't ever be taken away from them—a major step in the transition from child to adult, as we'll explore in our next section, but first let's ask: What's your E.Q.?

What's Your "E.Q."?: Emotional Intelligence

We touched on *emotional intelligence* in our chapter on Insight Meditation, and it's invaluable for parents and children. One individual who grew up in a Buddhist household remembers that he never heard his father say, "Don't push your brother!" but rather, "Think about your state of mind when you push your brother." And that stuck with him, gently initiating him into mindfulness. Like the red, yellow, and green lights at a traffic intersection, a three-step strategy for emotional intelligence includes being able to 1) be aware of problematic emotions rather than being run by them, 2) to evaluate what to do about them and the situation in which they arise, and 3) testing out insights through action.

Hear and Now

"When we teach our children, we focus on technical skills, on computers, on math, on content, on intellectualism, which are divorced from the human heart. In fact it is the paradox that our skill in working with emotion is a far greater determinant of our success, let alone our personal happiness. That of course is the paradox of modern education. We have focused on the wrong things."

—Daniel Goleman

When Daniel Goleman wrote *Emotional Intelligence* in 1995, he could track down fewer than a half-dozen school programs in America teaching the ability to manage feelings and relationships. Five years later, there are hundreds of such programs (sometimes called SEL, Social and Emotional Learning) in tens of thousands of schools. New research has revealed that the centers of the brain regulating emotions continue to grow into adolescence, rather than stopping after the first years of life as previously thought. In fact, they're the last parts of the brain to fully mature. So, for example, 10-year-old girls who've had difficulty differentiating between feelings of anxiety, anger, boredom, and hunger might risk developing severe eating disorders when they're 12 and 13. Paying attention to self-awareness and adapting to social relations over the full course of a child's school years not only promotes emotional and social maturity but has also been proven to help prevent depression, addiction, violence, and suicide.

Welcome to the Club: Rites of Passage

Every path has its *rites of passage*. Initiation into the tribe. Our society as a whole may not do as great a job of it as our ancestors did. As Bo Lozoff, director of the Human

Kindness Foundation, succinctly puts it, "Life is deep but the national lifestyle is not." Yet an adolescent can find his or her place in spiritual community by confirmation or bar/bas mitzvah. Buddhist culture also has rites of passage, as the West is discovering.

Our ancestors were very wise in creating rites of passage, initiating a new generation into the community and its customs. They understood an adolescent male is full of testosterone, which can be very dangerous. Without such rites, young men might wreak violence on the community itself, as seen today in youth gangs and youth violence. Commercial teen "girl culture" is another example of a superficial substitute for maturity with possibly dangerous consequences.

In Tibet, children are given a herd of yaks to tend, to acknowledge their growing independence. In southeast Asian countries such as Thailand and Myanmar, a young man becomes a Buddhist monk for at least three months, usually after high school. He may return to the monastery at any point in his life. It is thus shared culture of the community at large.

Western Buddhist schools have much they can learn about Buddhist parenting, rites of passage, and education from Pure Land temples in operation here for six or so generations now. Predominantly white sanghas began incorporating day care into the practice about twenty years ago, and family days and rites of passage ceremonies have now evolved. In Boulder, the Tibetan Buddhist Shambhala Center, for example, has a rite of passage for which children prepare themselves by studying such Buddhist arts as archery, flower arrangement, and poetry. During the actual ceremony, children and parents bow to each other and exchange gifts representing childhood and maturity. They vow to be kind to themselves and to others.

Children are our future, and thus they're our teachers as much as we are theirs. This reciprocity, the model for all Buddhist relationships, is a key attribute of Buddhist education, as we see next.

Learning How to Learn: Buddhist Education

One honorary title of the Buddha is "Original Teacher." Indeed, he teaches us the ultimate purpose of our existence; as Aldous Huxley put it, "To know the ultimate Not-self, which transcends the other not-selves and the ego, but which is yet closer than breathing, nearer than hands and feet ..." And his pragmatic, noncoercive, nonauthoritarian approach to teaching is typified in his saying, "See for yourself." You're the learning lab, and ultimate authority.

From the beginning, the first Buddhist teachers were also students, and the model was lifelong learning, actually the world's first such program. During the three-month rainy season, Buddha's core followers would reconvene to share with each other what they'd learned and receive further training.

Nalanda became humanity's first college, and Buddhism has traditionally furnished an educational space in Eastern society. Buddhist temples in ancient China, for example, filled the void of any national educational system. Buddhist temples had complete sets of books, not just Buddhist but also Taoist, Confucian, and ancient Chinese. As monks were familiar with all the works, the temples acted also as libraries and translation centers, becoming full-fledged schools, scattered across the nation and beyond, along the Silk Route. As we've also noted, Buddhist centers have provided educational opportunities for Asian immigrants for more than a century in America. Buddhist Churches of America, for instance, began Sunday schools in 1913, and by their first 25 years had taught 7,000 students such concepts as the Golden Chain, through 56 temples. And more recently there have sprung up such colleges as Hsi Lai University, Institute of Buddhist Studies, Naropa Institute, and Soka University.

> " " **Hear and Now**
>
> "I am a link in Amida Buddha's *golden chain* of love that stretches around the world. In gratitude may I keep my link bright and strong. I will try to be kind and gentle to every living thing and protect all who are weaker than myself. I will try to think pure and beautiful thoughts, to say pure and beautiful words, and to do pure and beautiful deeds. May every link in Amida Buddha's golden chain of love be bright and strong and may we all attain perfect peace."
>
> —Buddhist Church of America, Sunday school

Buddhism has a nonverbal dimension, teaching through experience. Buddhist student-teacher relationships are seen in the guru-yogi relationship, and in the Zen doctrine of "direct transmission of mind." As master Sokei-an (1882–1945) explains it, "At the moment the disciple's student reaches the same understanding as that of the master, a fusion of minds takes place, and the understanding of the disciple becomes one with that of the master, or, in traditional words, the master 'transmits' his mind to the disciple." For this to happen, teacher needs student as much as student needs teacher. Contemporary educators are learning such Buddhist wisdom. Teachers are playing Guide on the Side, rather than Sage on the Stage. (I like to arrange classroom chairs where I teach in a circle.) And studies are finding students learn from hearing, but best from doing, seeing for themselves.

As with all relationships, all components have Buddha nature—the teacher, the student, and the teachings. That means whatever you've learned here, didn't you already know? (Your own School of Light Within diploma, however, won't arrive until its printer graduates kindergarten.) Wisdom isn't necessarily the accumulation of bits of knowledge but can also be the shedding of the veils of ignorance that keep us from our innate knowing. Next, we come to seemingly the final veil.

Hear and Now

"Listen. Giving birth is like starting a fire: the father's the flint, the mother's the stone, and the child's the spark. Then, once the spark touches the wick of a lamp, it will continue to exist through the secondary support of the lamp's fuel. When that's exhausted, it flickers out.... Since the parents too have no beginning, in the end they, too, will flicker out. Everything grows out of the void from which all forms derive. If you let go of the forms, then you reach what's called 'the original ground.' But since all sentient beings come from emptiness, even the term 'original ground' is only a temporary tag."

—Ikkyu (1394–1481)

Good Life: Good Death

Death. Whether we're married or single, it's a fact of *nature* that eventually our life will make way for more life. But *human nature* doesn't readily accept it. Whether it touches loved ones or ourselves, as nonattached as we might be, death like love can be difficult. We'll examine engaging with the death of others in our last chapter, so here we'll explore our own personal relationship. Here's our ultimately unknowable relationship, which Buddhists often call the Great Matter.

The Buddha said, "Just as the elephant's footprint is the biggest footprint on the jungle floor, death is the biggest teacher." Indeed, our relationship to death includes all other relationships. For example, sex pokes its head at us when we consider death. You probably wouldn't think of death as part of "the facts of life" (although people whisper about death and shield children from it as if it *were* sex). The fact is if it weren't for sex, we might not ever face the mystery of death. Consider, for a minute, that if we still reproduced by cell division, one cell dividing into two, two into four, and so on, instead of Harry meeting Sally and later bringing up baby Harry Jr., we'd have Billy becoming Bill *and* Lee. MaryLou would become Mary and Lou. And so on for everyone. (Imagine what weird family reunions all *that* would make.)

Now, if we look at death as part of life's transformative, sexual embrace, we see simply one thing becoming another. A caterpillar becomes a butterfly. (Does the caterpillar die?) An infant becomes a teenager. (Does the infant die?) A breadwinner becomes a retiree. A strong parent becomes a frail being, lying in a bed, sipping nourishment through an I.V. tube. Who dies?

This Is

Our culture distances us from *death* through vocabulary. A funeral *home* (where no one lives) is now a chapel. An undertaker (formerly a *mortician*) is now a funeral director. He doesn't sell *coffins* but caskets. A corpse is viewed in a slumber room and isn't *embalmed* but prepared. Cremated ashes are remains. A *funeral* is a memorial service, attended by relatives and friends, not *mourners*. And *filling up a grave* with earth (not *dirt*) is now referred to as closing the interment space.

As impermanence is inherent in all our relationships, we come now to the question: How can we face our own lives, and the death of others within our lives, if we don't face our own deaths? The Zen answer is, "Die before you die." Recognize buddha-mind, the Unborn. Then, when your time comes, you'll be attentive to the moment. Nobody said it's easy. There's no right way.

Ultimate nirvana awaits. Die before you die. Then, when your time comes, you can be present during your final moments, without going into a panic (such as, "Oh no! Did I leave the stove on!?"). If you get it right this time, this lifetime, then you can spend the rest of eternity doing absolutely *nothing* really well.

One of the West's first discoveries of Tibetan Buddhism was through the translation of what was called *The Tibetan Book of the Dead*, whose title is literally *Liberation Through Hearing in the In-Between State*. In addition to its ceremonies for death and a kind of travelogue of realms after death, it contains meditations that can be conducted within this life. Life is a continuous stream of moment-to-moment deaths and rebirths. We begin to see this when we notice various in-between states (*bardo*, Tibetan), such as in between breathing out and breathing in … falling asleep and waking up … in between thoughts … in   between   words …

Thinking about her own death, Buddhist teacher Geri Larkin decided she'd like all her friends to gather at her funeral to write poems about her, string them all together, and tie them up in a tree for the seasons to weather. How about you?

Take some time to visualize your own death. See what holds you back … what frightens you … what would make you most happy. Explore your feelings. Let the truth of death overcome your fear of death. Include your death in your life. Discuss your funeral with your loved ones, just as if you were talking about buying a house. Let the reminder of death motivate your efforts to live each moment.

Like they say, life isn't a dress rehearsal. This is it. No curtain calls, no encores. No forwarding address. Live the words of the epitaph you'd like to leave behind as your exit line. Then the stone slab will be merely extra.

The Least You Need to Know

- Buddhism isn't an escape from relations. Its approach to all relations is mutuality.

- Buddhism provides insight into the slippery slope of romance. When a couple share a commitment to Buddhist practice and to each other, sex can be a natural, sublime expression of love. Buddhism can provide a strong framework for marriage based on sincerity and trust.

- A family can be a sangha of parents and children.

- At its core, Buddhism is an educational system, fostering the first university, as well as lifelong learning.

- The final relationship is confronting your own death, integral to living a meaningful life.

Chapter 16

Food for the Heart: The Meal of Life

In This Chapter

- Food as metaphor
- You are how you eat
- Hungry ghosts
- Vegetarianism
- The way of tea

Somebody once scolded the ancient Greek philosopher Socrates for eating little, and he replied, "I only eat to live, whereas you live to eat." This links right in to what we've just learned about working and living.

When we treat our work as a mere job, we're missing out on its opportunity for practice. So, too, when we eat. Like our livelihood, food sustains us, and in the deepest sense. So we can just put on the old feedbag and chow down, never really connecting with the meaning of our eating; or we can be aware of food as nourishment for the heart. (As we've learned, our heart is our blood bearer … our spiritual center … our mind. All in one.)

Socrates may be right. Yet we can also see that eating and living are interdependent an eternal cycle. There's a Middle Way within the two. Our culture tends to emphasize the material over the spirit, price over value. A Martian visitor might sense this from our super-size french fries … our gummy bread you could use as an eraser. But to sense the spiritual side of food takes only stopping and … smelling the coffee. Life is a meal. And we have all the ingredients. Here follows some thought for food … food for the heart.

Food as Food for Thought

Quick: Do you know who invented bread? Such an incredible invention! And a wonderful *metaphor* for the Dharma, and all its juicy richness. How a human being becomes a Buddha is quite like how dough becomes bread. And the recipe, cherished and handed down, is like the teachings of the Buddha. So given the proper ingredients, attention, and care, it produces steaming hot bread, as fresh today as the first loaf ever baked. Its basics are really quite simple, yet different people like to vary the basic recipe, emphasizing different textures and tastes, like the way the Dharma has different modes we call schools. Whatever the school, cooking is a practice. And tasting the food we've made is like the peace we attain from the Way.

If we're mindful, cooking always tests our understanding. All good cooks know that no recipe is to be followed exactly. A recipe is not the meal. A raft is not the shore. And we might crave a taste that's in our minds, that this recipe just won't yield this particular time. But if we're Zen chefs we always know we have all the ingredients we need at hand, even if we don't always see them all at first. Satisfaction applies to us as eaters, as well. The first noble truth is about never being satisfied. And the second noble truth likened this to an unquenchable appetite, a ravenous hunger; mental or emotional, as well as physical. The fourth noble truth, the Path, shows us how food will never make us happy as long as we think of it in terms of some thing external to ourselves. So food is one of the most literal opportunities we have of practicing awareness of our interbeing with our ancestors and the entire universe. To lift an elbow, and enjoy.

In this chapter, we'll survey four big ways of being mindful of the full meaning of our meals. Then we'll dip our toe into food issues, such as obesity, and meat. And we'll conclude … with a simple cup of tea.

You Are How You Eat: Heart Nourishment

When I first heard the now-commonplace phrase, "You are what you eat," in the 1960s, it seemed as radical a concept as artist Allan Kaprow's "happenings" (spontaneous Zen environmental performance art). But then I was raised on frosted flakes and hamburgers. It's a very succinct illustration of Buddhist truth: Life is inter-dependent, interpenetration. Have you ever considered that every seven years your body completely regenerates all its cells (except bone, though even marrow is renewed)? So the "you" that you were seven years ago is no longer here except for your skeleton. And from where do you derive this new you? From the food on your table …

… which is, in turn, part of the life of the soil, the watershed, the clouds, the sun, the farmers and the truckers and the grocers … and on down. It's all there to be experienced at your table, an intimacy with life we too often let slip through our fingers, reading or watching TV as we eat. So it's how we eat, as well as what.

Any meal is, in and of itself, an invitation to see deeply into life and gain insight into our place in the universe. (*Wow!*) A childhood pal of mine is now a yoga instructor who's so busy she says the only time she has for meditation is when she sits down to eat. Fancy, a meal as meditation! Not just an affirmation of belief, that the material world is indeed no different than the divine, but to actually renew that faith, bite by bite. As the Bible says, "O taste and see!"

Here are four ways to enhance your mindful eating pleasure: 1) Give thanks. 2) Make meals a meditation. 3) Practice with family and sangha. 4) Expand your food awareness.

Thanksgiving's Every Day

We are *how* we eat. Every spiritual practice on this blue Earth blesses or gives *thanks* for food. Like saying Namu Amida Butsu, it can never be forced. Yet we always have occasion.

Actually, I find food tastes better if I stop to thank it. Try it, and see. I don't doubt that scientists will discover it is more nourishing. Cooks know that food tastes better when cooked with love. And that's true for how it's eaten. Food is love.

One traditional Buddhist meditation of thanks before eating is the *Five Contemplations*. The general outline of it goes like this:

- ◆ **Regarding your food, consider all its ingredients and all the moves they took to come from farm to fork.** Consider the roundness of your plate as representing the whole universe, and the food within as its messenger. Be compassionate for the suffering *and* joy that brought it to your plate, the farmers', the truckers', the grocers'. And be aware of those who have not.

- ◆ **Regard your meal and vow to be worthy of it.** Being worthy of your food means eating it mindfully. Eating a carrot, eat a carrot; don't chew unresolved tensions or anticipated pleasures or anything else but the carrot buddha nourishing your own buddhahood in the present moment.

◆ **Look at how much food there is and vow not to be greedy.** Eat in moderation. Recognize there's a point beyond satisfaction where eating becomes greed. Also practice equanimity. Don't identify your personal likes and dislikes. This means that even if you're a vegetarian, you might eat meat if it's offered.

◆ **Consider your food as good medicine.** Considering food as medicine means treating food as more than a comfort. Notice its *chi*, its life-force. Be mindful that food can help cause health or illness. Be mindful of what is and isn't healthy.

◆ **Vow to eat that you may realize the Way.** From considering food as a gift from the *whole universe*, to being a matter of *health*, it's only a hop to seeing food as *holy*. See your meals as an essential part of your journey of awakening.

As the aroma of your meal wafts in your nostrils and you contemplate it in these five ways, try joining your palms, in gassho, bowing to the food and all it contains. Like you, food has buddha nature, too: asparagus buddhas, broccoli buddhas, carrot buddhas …

Actually, it's nice to dedicate a blessing, prayer, invocation, or gatha before *and* after a meal. In Judaism, for example, we give thanks for the food before us, and afterward we give thanks for the food within us. An appropriate Buddhist after-meal prayer can be the Bodhisattva Vow. Another might be to generate and send metta. Here's a fine model Donald Altman includes in his book *Art of the Inner Meal* which you can modify however feels right for you:

> May all beings be free from pain, hunger, and suffering. May all beings live long and be healthy. May all beings receive physical nourishment, well-being, and spiritual awareness through food. May all beings experience loving kindness and serve others with compassion.

(More Buddhist thanks givings are posted online at: http://awakening.to/nourishment.html.)

Hear and Now

> The farmer hoes his rice
> in noonday glare;
> I see his sweat pour
> in huge drops down to the soil.
> Ah! for the meal on your table,
> are you aware
> that each small grain
> costs the farmer bitter toil?
>
> —Li Shen (T'ang dynasty)

Mindful Meals

As you now know, meditation doesn't begin or end on a cushion. Have you tried mindful noting during your daily life yet, as sketched in our chapter on "Insight Meditation"? Eating is good occasion for it. Or should I say "the process of eating"? Each mouthful can be a self-contained world, akin to the birth, growth, and flare-out of a galaxy. (Someone once asked Suzuki Roshi what nirvana was and he replied,

"Following each thing through to the end." Another time, he nibbled on some olive pits a student left in a bowl at a diner, because there was still olive meat left on them.)

Consider one bite. Imagine we're mindfully tuning in to bread, for example, noting: "eye looking at bread" ... "intention to eat bread" ... "hand breaking bread" ... "seeing texture and color and shape" ... "considering and visualizing ingredients and their origins" ... "smelling bread" ... "noticing salivation" ... "hand lifting bread to mouth" ... "opening the mouth" ... "lips taking bread" ... "lowering the arm" ... "tongue taking bread" ... "mouth feeling texture of bread" ... "front teeth chopping bread" ... "molars grinding bread" ... "flavor of bread" ... "bread softening with saliva" ... "bread releasing sweetness in mouth" ... "bread mostly liquid, with little crumbs" ... "bread all liquidy" ... "taste disappearing" ... "noticing impulse to swallow" ... And all the while—following breath(!) As with walking meditation, this might best be approached by beginners in slow motion.

Eating mindfully, let the flow of events come to an end. Then, do you lift your hand again, out of habit? Or do you *intend* to do each action before you do it? We can break those two down more. Do you follow through after each mouthful's swallowed, staying with the food and feeling it traveling down? Supposedly, there aren't taste buds past your throat, but my tummy has a range of subtle messages it can send, like "warm," "sour," and even shadings like "pepperminty." After that, do you remain alert to feelings? Do food sensations spark desires? Do desires create intentions in your mind? Does your mind act on intentions by causing bodily movements? Check them out. Take note. Be mindful.

Leaves from the Bodhi Tree

Jack Kornfield teaches a meditation in which participants mindfully note the process of eating one raisin: It takes about 10 minutes. Likewise, Thich Nhat Hanh suggests an orange as meditation: fully experiencing each slice slowly, rather than peeling while eating. And Zen chef and author Edward Espe Brown has led a meditation on eating one potato chip, one orange slice, and one Hydrox cookie, each, "attentively in silence." His students have discovered that one potato chip wasn't satisfying (maybe why people crave more). Everyone loved the orange. And about half the participants couldn't even finish the Hydrox cookie! (See for yourself.)

By tuning in to the whole chain of mini-events, desire-as-craving-as-self becomes transparent, seen as a kind of fictional device ("Wow, am *I* hungry!"), telling a story not present in the immediate situation (food as reward, as failure, as security, as identity, as guilt, as blame, as shame, and so on). In truth, there's only a series of present-moment events, none with any intrinsic identity, and none like any other.

Just as breathing naturally slows under the lens of mindfulness, so, too, does hunger dwindle away when eating mindfully. We discover we can make do with less. We're no longer feeding abstract desires. We're directly experiencing through the evidence of our own senses the miraculous reality of food. Each bite. And it's enough.

The last bite—the last morsel—the very last crumb—can be a whole meal in itself.

> ### Leaves from the Bodhi Tree
>
> The Buddha once told the parable of a man walking across a field who saw a big tiger. He ran, and the tiger chased him. He came to a cliff. He caught hold of the root of a wild vine and swung over the edge. The tiger sniffed at him from above. Trembling, the man looked down and saw another tiger, far below, waiting to eat him. Meanwhile, two mice, one black and one white, came and started to nibble at the vine that sustained him. Just then, the man saw a strawberry growing within reach. He plucked it. How sweet it tasted!

Lifting an Elbow Together

Eating mindfully *in company* magnifies the experience. But according to some reports, as many as a third of American families don't eat together. It's interesting that countries with more eating rituals, like eating together, have fewer eating disorders. And, difficult as it might seem at first, eating together in silence can be a way of sharing appreciation of being, and being together, in marvelous ways that words cannot express.

To keep you from wavering, here are five mindful tips:

◆ Don't read or watch TV while you eat. (There's a bonus health benefit here. Digestion activates one part of your brain; reading, another. You digest better when letting your body do its thing, rather than getting your neural network's wires crossed.) Just eat while you eat.

◆ Be mindful of your breathing and your body. Sit up straight, shoulders back, lower back curved, soles of your feet firmly upon the earth. (You might think of the extra few inches it might take to lift the food to your mouth as bridging the gap between your heart-center and your head-center.)

◆ Chew each mouthful through to the end. (Mixing food with saliva has a health benefit, as well, beginning the digestive process in your mouth, taking a load off other digestive organs.)

- Midway or three-quarters into your meal, stop. See if you're still mindful of your breathing, or whether you're escaping into the act of eating. Also see if you're still hungry, or if you're already satisfied. (You might be surprised.)

- What about the last spoonful? Enjoy it as fully as the entire meal. Or save it for compost, if you garden.

Even if it's your one meditation amid a busy schedule, betwixt life's bumpy roads, the oasis of a mindful meal can keep you on the path of peace.

> **Hear and Now**
>
> "The ritual of coming to the dinner table was once the very basis of community."
>
> —Alice Waters
>
> "Let the progress of the meal be slow, for dinner is the last business of the day; and let the guests conduct themselves like travelers due to reach their destination together."
>
> —Jean Anthelme Brillat-Savarin

Food Awareness

Expanding your food awareness is another recipe for mindful meals. You don't have to grow your own food, but you might be surprised to learn what's edible that grows wild. Or it just might mean making your own food more often. Or knowing more about nutrition. It means being conscious of good ingredients, fresh produce, and a balanced diet. For example, many Americans over-emphasize fat, salt, or sweets. If this is you, please realize it will take some time once you've weaned yourself off your habit before other foods begin to taste right, and you'll feel more whole again.

Maybe your extra dosage of fat, salt, or sweets comes from prepared foods, which typically use these substances. (Do you read labels carefully?) There's nothing like being able to make your own food. (But … is that Buddhist? Heck, yes.) Being self-reliant, seeing for yourself, getting to the source—these are all Buddhist virtues we tap into when we cook.

If you're worrying about pesticides in your foods or genetically modified crops, poverty, or the increasing lack of diversity of species (well, the list seems endless), I have a modest proposal: Bake bread. As Edward Espe Brown says in *The Tassajra Bread Book:* "Bread makes itself, by your kindness, with your help, with imagination streaming through you, with dough under hand, you are bread making itself, which is why bread making is so fulfilling and rewarding." Just the savor of the sweet, earthy fragrance of freshly baked bread might persuade you.

A second option I'd offer is also about grain: whole grains. Whether you bake or buy bread, try whole grain. If you make cereal, try oatmeal (Irish, or steelcut). For lunch or dinner, consider brown rice, millet, quinoa. But, more importantly, eat a balanced diet (such as grains, greens, and beans). Overall, I'm suggesting you might invest some time into researching nutrition, and ingredients, and prepare your own meals. Include patience, joy, intimacy, and learning from mistakes. (Sit for 20 minutes, and enjoy.)

Hear and Now

"I take leftover whey out to the chickens who slurp it up contentedly. It's full of nutrients that flow into the eggs, the composted chicken and cow manure go into the garden to flow into the vegetables.... Simple miracles. Satisfying work, like baking bread or building a shelf. Fresh, delicious food. Nutrient cycles close right at hand. Health for land and people. Sometimes I wonder with all our supposed progress, what we're rushing toward and what we're leaving behind."

—Donella Meadows, on home cheese-making on her farm

So take time to cook. And eat fresh. Patronize small farmers if you can, a vanishing breed now. (When's the last time you actually visualized a farmer's sunburned face and hands as you ate the food he grew?) Farmers can tell you exactly what they're selling, and many have a variety not found in stores. When's the last time you tried a Jonathan Spy apple, a Blenham apricot, or a Chandler strawberry? It was getting kind of critical with apples not too long ago, with only one red and one green on the shelves. At one time, there were 500 different kinds of apples in America. (Fortunately, there are seed savers still out there.)

Moreover, when you buy produce from a farmer's market, you're bypassing the whole process of shipping and freezing and storage that food goes through commercially. Fresh is best. Buying direct, you're taking home a fully realized buddha that needs nothing else but a little steaming or baking (don't overcook), plus hearty, mindful appreciation. If it's been in the refrigerator for two or three days, then you might need to fix it up a little, with a recipe.

Don't have a farmer's market near you? How about a community garden? No community garden? How about a backyard patch or unused empty lot? (Another possibility for a Buddhist entrepreneur.)

Do You Hunger and Thirst?: Food Issues

All living things hunger and thirst. So naturally our appetite for edible food and for evanescent happiness are intertwined. We see their mutuality in the Chinese word for harmony, peace: a seed of grain next to an open mouth. Similarly, the Catholic Eucharist unites the physical with the divine through the sacrament of consecrated bread and wine.

Yet food can also represent an antagonistic split. Even the Buddha had food issues, remember, pitting the material against the spiritual. He tried fasting his way to enlightenment, to probe and transcend the searing bonds of hunger hardwired into our physical makeup. Prior to that, he'd had his pick of the palace pantry. From these extremes of luxury and poverty, bingeing and craving, he discovered and taught a nondualist alternative, the Middle Way. Furthermore, he showed that our discontent, our suffering, is deeply rooted in our unrealistic *cravings*—not so much in our objects of desire (banquets, diet programs, self-image, and so on) but our attachment to them.

Meditation: Please revisit the picture and caption of the hungry ghost in Chapter 5. Then see if you can imagine your own hungry ghost. That is, if you're like me, you may harbor a hungry ghost (or two), and have been feeding it without much awareness. See if you can visualize yours. Can you give it a human face? (I don't give mine a name, just "That Old Hungry Ghost." But you can give yours a name, if you like.) As you go about your day, see if you and your hungry ghost can teach each other some Dharma.

Facing food and food issues means making peace with the wonderfulness and total adequacy of the present moment; as is. But looking around, it's ironic to note that in a land with a relatively high standard of living, America also has such a high number of people with food issues, overweight, starving themselves, suffering from ulcers, or otherwise hung up about food. See if you can visualize their hungry ghosts. And see the universal condition in theirs as well.

Leaves from the Bodhi Tree

In tantra, even eating disorders can lead to enlightenment. A master named Saraha chanced upon a glutton named Sarvabhaksa, writhing in pain because he couldn't find anything to eat. Saraha told him what a hungry ghost is, and the glutton asked how he could avoid such a fate. Saraha told him to visualize his belly as empty as the sky, all visible phenomena as his food and drink, and his appetite as a fire consuming it all. He did so until the light went out because he'd devoured the sun and the moon. Saraha then told him that everything he'd eaten was now nothing and to now meditate without food. Soon the sun and moon reappeared as he realized that appearance and emptiness are one.

Mindless Food

Having a mindful diet means also being aware of what other people eat as well as ourselves. If you only eat brown rice and tofu, try fast food; and vice-versa. While more and more people are becoming health conscious, lack of health consciousness is becoming a serious problem worth noting.

Fact: There is a rise in unhealthy substances mixing in with the food we eat and the water we drink, as well as the air we breathe. Pesticides, for example, have become a cornerstone of agribusiness (which is making the farmer and rancher practically defunct). (How many people drink bottled water to avoid, say, carcinogens?)

The third precept, mindful consumption, seems more apt now than ever. *Fact:* The second leading cause of mortality in America, after smoking, is … obesity. (Both matters of consumption.) *Fact:* The rate of obesity among American adults is twice as high today as in the early 1960s; for children, twice what it was in the late 1970s. About a quarter of the vegetables today's kids eat are either french fries or chips. *Fact:* As of this writing, Americans now spend more money on fast food than on higher education; that's more than on movies, books, magazines, videos, and recorded music combined, making fast food a hundred-billion-dollar industry. Connecting the dots, we see a proportionate relationship (as they say in algebra) between obesity and fast food. This correlation is becoming true in Europe and Asia, as well.

Meditation: Visit a fast-food diner. Order a coffee, if nothing else. (And if your friends have started to say you're becoming a bit fanatic about eating healthy, order a burger, with fries!) Sit down, and mindfully observe life around you without judgment. Bear witness. *Be* the entire scene. Counter clerks, manager, patrons, to-go, eat-there, the décor, the ambience. This is what all your ancestors and the entire universe have come to, yourself included, now, in this present moment. Note your feelings, without becoming attached to them, likes, dislikes, or neutral. Give yourself time, later that day or night, to reprocess what you experienced.

Meat, Chewing It Over

It's up to you. Chapter Seven touched on the ethics of meat. Three other factors come with the package, and then I'm off my vegetable crate. First, there are the health factors. Vegetarianism seems to reduce the risk of heart disease and cancer.

Second, there are the environmental factors (anticipating our last chapter, on engagement in the world). For starters, about half the world's grain today goes to feed cattle, which yield a proportionately poor rate of return in nourishment for such a big investment. Soy can produce 20 times more protein than can be raised on an acre of land used to feed beef cattle. And, third, it's always good to try a new discipline, just to see. Read up on how to make the gradual transition, and how to get your protein through a balanced diet. Then see how it *feels*. You might find your mind feeling a little calmer, more open … and happier. (End of lecture.) Like I say, it's up to you.

Mindful Food

For every recipe book, there's a diet book. Every yin element has its yang counterbalance. Americans spend $26 billion on vending machine food, and $33 billion on weight-loss programs, books, and tapes. Growing up in southern California, I remember roadside hotdog, hamburger, and taco stands that would be pioneer outposts of the fast-food industry; but, at the same time, this being Hollywood, eternally questing for the fountain of eternal youth, there were already one or two stores where you could buy mom-and-pop brand vitamins, herbal compounds, exotic juice drinks, proto-granola, gnarly fruit labeled "organic," and macrobiotics. (The book about the macrobiotic diet in those days used the word "Zen" as a marketing ploy.)

Today this is all called "health food" (a redundancy no less funny than the oxymoron of labeling needless gunk added to packaged food as "natural"), which is a growing trend. The Zen of baking and cooking has contributed to a national re-evaluation of our eating habits, in a major way. As of this writing, organic food has become a six-billion-dollar industry. (*Organic food* is raised and processed without pesticides, irradiation, or genetic engineering or modification.) In a nutshell, we're becoming more aware, more awake, to food as part of our overall health: body, spirit, and mind.

Now let's cap our survey of the art of food with a brief tour of one of its greatest masterpieces …

Take Tea and See: The Tea Ceremony

The American Revolution had its roots in tea. It had been the national drink of England, featured in a ceremony known as "tea time." In the New World, colonial New York drank as much as all of England, and on even into the early twentieth century; in 1933, the observation floor of the new Empire State Building was an art deco tea salon with more than a hundred choices. Yet most Americans today think of tea as, at best, a side-order beverage, usually served up in the form of a bag on a string, faintly resembling a mouse with a tail. But—is it Buddhist?

Well, as we'll see, tea can be a model for the whole Zen way of life. Imbibing tea has roots extending back at least a millennium. The first records are from eighth-century China, when a Buddhist named Lu Yu spent five years compiling the first book about tea. He was a great press agent for his subject, laying out the whole ritual for appreciating tea, including no fewer than 24 different implements for preparation and serving. Actually, in true Taoist spirit, the rules are meant to be absorbed and then forgotten, untouched by any formality, simple, relaxed, and spontaneous.

> **" " Hear and Now** _____
>
> "There are few hours in life more agreeable than the hour dedicated to the ceremony known as afternoon tea."
>
> —Henry James
>
> "If Christianity is wine and Islam coffee, Buddhism is most certainly tea."
>
> —Alan Watts
>
> "When tea is brewed with water drawn from unfathomable depths of the spirit, then we have truly realized the Way of Tea."
>
> —Toyotomi Hideyoshi

Tea came to Japan with Buddhism. When Japan learned about tea, two things happened. One, Japan liked following rules, and embraced the then-current Chinese affection for powdered green tea. And two, the tea ceremony became closely allied with Zen, which likewise had its formal rules. But both sets of rule books were, as in square dancing, designed to make the spirit accessible to all.

Now, the Japanese Zen Buddhists became so fond of tea they began repeating the legend that during Bodhidharma's nine-year stint of zazen, facing a wall at Shaolin Monastery, he grew angry at his own dozing off. So he tore off his eyelids and threw them to the ground, where they took root and sprouted up as tea bushes. Hence the eyelid-shaped leaves with invigorating properties.

> **" " Hear and Now** _____
>
> "The philosophy of tea … expresses conjointly with ethics and religion our whole point of view about man and nature. It is hygiene, for it enforces cleanliness; it is economics, for it shows comfort in simplicity rather than in the complex and costly; it is moral geometry, inasmuch as it defines our sense of proportion to the universe. It represents the true spirit of eastern democracy by making all its votaries aristocrats in taste."
>
> —Kakuzo Okakura (1863–1919), *The Book of Tea*

Since Zen and Pure Land practice were lay as well as monastic, they suffused all aspects of Japanese culture (as we'll see in the next two chapters as well). Of all Japanese arts, the tea ceremony is closest to being total, like musical theater or a High Mass, a pure land involving all the senses. Each element is worthy of study unto itself. Ideally, guests will first become acquainted at the host's exquisitely landscaped and groomed tea garden. The ceremony proper is traditionally held in a simple, 10-foot-square tea room. It resembles a Zen monk's cell—a style which, in fact, highly influenced

Japanese domestic architecture in general. The door's low, requiring a bow. The floor's made of textured straw matting (*tatami*); the small, irregularly shaped windows with paper panes admit a subdued light. At the entrance, in a small alcove, is the only decoration, a flower below a scroll of Zen calligraphy. One stick of incense purifies the air. The only music is of a bamboo water pipe dripping outside and the water boiling inside on a charcoal burner.

The utensils and their arrangement catch the eye, and handling them pleases the touch. The cups aren't perfect porcelain but, rather, Zen pottery—unglazed at the bottom, often with a drop of glaze running down the side as a Zen "controlled accident." The fresh tea is a fine green powder, whipped into a "froth of liquid jade," as one Chinese writer put it. When ready, the color's to be admired, the fragrance savored. Then taste and aftertaste are appreciated, slightly bitter, walking the middle way between sweet and sour.

Along the Path

"It was at once as if nothing at all had happened and as if the roof had flown off the building. But in reality nothing had happened. A very old deaf Zen man with bushy eyebrows had drunk a cup of tea, as though with the complete wakefulness of a child and yet as though at the same time declaring with utter finality: 'this is not important!'"

—Thomas Merton, on having tea with Zen scholar D. T. Suzuki

In America today, outposts for the Japanese tea ceremony dot the landscape, in Alabama and Georgia as well as New York and Los Angeles. Even more importantly, tea in all its many forms (over 500 varieties from China alone) is available online and at several teahouses around the country. (Some pointers are at our website, Dharma Door; check out http://awakening.to/nourishment.html.) But just knowing about tea can be inspiring, too. That is, it's applicable to all the arts, which are the topic of the next two chapters, as well as to the culinary arts, and so to your practice of the art of the Way. As a complex, highly codified ritual, it takes a lifetime to master; but the spirit is something you can practice at home, with friends, at work, or anywhere.

You are how you eat. Imagine if we ate our meals the way tea-people treat tea: in harmony and respect, with purity and tranquility. Plus a potent dash of joy.

Next, we'll continue on from the Way of tea to other popular arts that are opportunities for expression, understanding, and realization.

The Least You Need to Know

◆ Giving thanks to our food is a primary and universal spiritual practice. (It also makes food taste better.)

◆ A meal is a wonderful opportunity for active meditation.

◆ Food awareness includes understanding nutrition, buying fresh ingredients, and preparing your own meals.

◆ Even just a simple pot of tea can be a meditation and way of life, whose lessons all can enjoy.

Chapter 17

Working as if You Didn't Need the Money: Right Livelihood

In This Chapter

- ◆ The Middle Way at work
- ◆ Workplace as practice
- ◆ Right livelihood
- ◆ Measuring wealth
- ◆ Four mini case studies

Our exploration of relationships continues, with a look at work as an opportunity for practice. Our title draws from a quote by baseball legend Satchell Paige: "Work like you don't need the money. Love like you've never been hurt. Dance like nobody's watching." Of course, hearts inevitably get broken (the first noble truth). And the whole universe is always watching (interbeing). And money? Well, as we'll see, price isn't necessarily the same as value.

Raised in a palace, the Buddha knew all that money could buy, and that it would never ultimately satisfy. After years in a forest, with only the clothes on his back, he knew values apart from money. All the money in the world can't buy happiness, nor can having no money. The Middle Way finds a mean between the quest for the greatest good and the thirst for the greatest goods.

Work can call upon our practice of the Middle Way in interesting ways. If I can relate to the entire universe, and all my ancestors, through my interrelationship with another person, how about with work mates, at my job site, and through all the interactions rippling out in the course of a day? Certainly, Buddhism can bring us less stress, and more efficient ways of working, but it can also call into question whether our path of work is enabling us to live to our fullest, and show us how it can. It teaches us how to average out between the daily and the immeasurable cost of living.

Here are some interoffice memos. From the Desk of … the Dharma.

The Middle Way Between the Greatest Good and the Greatest Goods

In the Garden of Eden, our ancestors didn't have to work until the Fall, then it was punishment. And work's gotten a bad rap ever since. There may exist human societies without war, such as the Senoi, but none without work, and it wasn't always a curse. Ecologist Ernest Callenbach estimates that, for hundreds of thousands of years, ancient hunter-gatherers might have put in a 20-hour work week, at most. Only with the shift toward an agricultural basis of society did work become a burden, repetitive, with variable yields, necessitating armies to protect the surplus. With the rise of technology, the industrial revolution made humans into machines. Yet there is a spiritual dimension to work, which the Buddha addressed, during a time of rapid economic development and consolidation, and whose truth continues to be heard. It may be difficult to learn, but a teaching which more and more people are heeding in our own times of longer work hours, diminishing job security, and general lack of fulfillment through work. Hearing the Buddha's simple message and putting it to use can be a wonderful vocation, perhaps the greatest one of our career.

The spiritual nature of work is not dependent upon religion, but religion naturally colors our outlook toward work. The American work ethic, for example, is based in part on Calvinist theology, which says if you're not a worldly success then you're not destined for heaven. But success is no cause for slacking off, on the other hand, since you'll only know if you've been chosen for paradise after your life's all over.

On the other hand, I also remember another time trying to post a letter at noon my first day in Venice, Italy. All the doors seemed closed except of churches and cafes. So people dropped in to a cathedral and reminded themselves that their immortal soul is saved, then celebrated by hanging out over a cappuccino in the plaza with everybody else. Eventually, work resumed as usual. After all, doing nothing can get to be hard work.

In the renaissance of spirit now seeping through the West, Buddhism has much to offer as to work. Some people, of course, may suffer from the misconception of the Buddhist as a ne'er-do-well slacker. But Zen, for example, introduced the idea of monasteries being self-sufficient from the very beginning, in T'ang Dynasty China. No work, no eat. As Zen priest Norman Fischer puts it, "For Zen students there's no work time and leisure time; there's just lifetime, daytime and nighttime. Work is something deep and dignified—it's what we are born to do and what we feel most fulfilled in doing."

Leaves from the Bodhi Tree

In Tibetan lore, a plain cobbler named Camaripta begged a Buddhist monk to teach him the way of the Buddha. The monk suggested he transform himself as he changed leather into a shoe: identifying his attachments and conceptualizations (the roots of bondage) with the leather—placing it on the mold of friendliness and compassion (two immeasurables)—and piercing it with the awl of his guru's instructions (an instrument by which ordinary life is penetrated)—then, with the thread of equanimity, sewing together appearance and boundless reality with the needle of mindfulness—and, with the needle of compassion, clothing the beings of the world (in Buddha's body of the Dharma). Over time, the cobbler became a perfectly realized master (*siddhi*).

Let's look at mind and mindfulness at work. Then, after exploring right livelihood, we'll tour a gallery of some case studies.

Inter-Office Memo: "Less Stress!"

Here are some criteria to consider next time you evaluate yourself for internal job review. For starters, ask yourself who's your boss, really? Nobody owns your mind but you. Your desires and choices, your satisfactions and dissatisfactions, they're all products of mind. Notice how your day goes, and where duhkha arises and where it ceases. Some recent translations of duhkha use its contemporary workplace connotation: stress. There is a cause of stress, and a way to end it. See where are occasions for awakening of mind, opening of heart, and where do ignorance and fear, anger and greed still dwell?

Explore your space. Stake out your turf. Find breathing room. Where can you go to sit undisturbed? Where can you walk mindfully for ten minutes? And practice isn't confined to your breaks. When you hear a phone ring, stop, notice your breath, and return to your original nature. An altar by a desk is an optional reminder. Giving each task your undivided, mindful attention, you'll find your energy's reinvigorated, not exhausted. One-pointed concentration gets more done in a day than if you begin by dividing tasks into those things you like and those you don't. Of course, every job has its monotony. But that can be used as a very good tool for generating one-pointed concentration, and thence mindful awareness.

So much for things, but what about people? Emotional intelligence means handling difficult emotions, rather than have them handle you. Be mindful when you feel yourself caught in an uncomfortable emotion. Step aside for a moment, and allow yourself the space to let go of the negative charge and respond with clarity. Re-examine the difficult emotion next time you practice sitting. The Four Noble Truths apply to everyone, as well as you. We're all working for common goals, way down deep. Any workplace can be a mindfulness classroom in awareness, wisdom, and compassion. There's an emergency ward of a Northern California hospital where a few members practice mindfulness; above the ER door handles are a note with one word: Breathe.

It might be ideal if your work mates were on the same path. The publisher of one of my books, Parallax Press, is a sangha that publishes what they practice (and vice-versa). Everyone bows in and sits together in the morning, enjoying their breathing together. They share mindful meals and walking meditation breaks. It's like a monastery of monks and nuns except at the end of the day they each go home to their families. But Buddhism's a minority religion, of course, and "Buddhism" is rarely a criteria on a job description. Yet everyone can appreciate its benefits without having to all be on the path. It's wonderful just to keep up your own practice at work and watch the quality of your work rise, and others' consciousness as well. As in a family, when even one person meditates, everyone benefits. If asked, you don't have to call it anything exotic, and thus set up separation. Mindfulness and stress reduction are now part of the vocabulary. "Less stress" is universal.

The Practice: Right Livelihood

These days, it's not uncommon to change jobs during a lifetime. Even the Buddha held a number of jobs before he became the Buddha. But then that's because he was looking for something more than relative job satisfaction. He walked away from ruling an entire empire. Later, he turned down teaching positions offered by supreme yogis of his day. And he eventually stepped aside from his following amongst the forest ascetics. Was he a continual failure? No, his life became his work, and influenced the entire world.

Jobs come and go. If you think only in terms of having a *job*, then you may not yet have found *work*. A job's what puts bread on your table. Work's what you do because it focuses and fulfills your deep needs and highest values. It's a livelihood. This is not a remote idea. Today, there are *livelihood consultants*, for example, as well as *employment counselors*. They assist clients to evaluate their beliefs and life goals, manage their time and money skillfully, and move toward their personal purpose.

Work like you don't need the money. That saying comes from Satchell Paige, who also said, "I never had a job. I always played baseball." He'd discovered what Alan Watts called "the real secret of life—to be completely engaged with what you are doing in the here and now. And instead of calling it work, realize it is play." Right livelihood should be fun as well as fulfilling. The Buddhist Kingdom of Bhutan, for example, measures its progress according to its Gross National Happiness.

When the Buddha shone a light on livelihood, he ticked off basic job descriptions that harm others or harm the ecosystem. Such toxic environments, like anguish-filled jobs, do exist, like anguish itself (first noble truth). But the Buddha says don't go there. Karmic meltdown ahead. Today, in a sense, we're already there: already globally enmeshed with everybody else's karma. The question boils down to: "How do we go about our lives as mindfully as we can?"

Consider cops. Their job environment can be such a violent, intense pressure-cooker that their suicide rate is, alas, twice the national average. In September of 2003, Thich Nhat Hanh led a meditation retreat for law enforcement officials in Madison, Wisconsin. Afterward, he reported:

> Police officers learned to go home to themselves and release the tension in their body; release the fear, the despair in the mind; learn how to get in touch with the positive elements of life that are in them and around them for their nourishment and healing, so that they can better relate to their families, their colleagues, and so that they can serve better the people. They are called "peace officers," and they should be. They should have enough peace in themselves in order to do so.

So a key is not only what you do, but how you do it. Consider the high-stakes, high-stress dance that lawyers do, for another instance. Here dualism is the ruling premise: plaintiff vs. defendant. Right vs. wrong. And yet there's a growing number of lawyers finding that the practice of law and the practice of the Way don't have to be an adversarial relationship. Attorney Steven Schwartz, for example, has combined both practices for three decades now. It brings him to continually see if he's in right relation. When he represents a client, for instance, he looks at the sameness and the difference between him and them as a fundamental koan. "Seeing the sameness between me and the client inspires me," he says, "to use the difference impeccably. It ceases to be work, and becomes an opportunity."

Federal Trade Commission attorneys take a break on the Mall in Washington, D.C.

Photograph: © David Burnett/Contact Press Images

Price or Value: How Do You Measure Wealth?

The harmony of right livelihood can lead to great wealth. But how do you measure wealth? Defining it in terms of satisfying your desires, you'll find yourself returning to the Four Noble Truths. There's never enough. Desires are endless. The craving self is never satisfied. It measures itself against the world, setting itself apart. Indeed, typical measurements of wealth are usually dualist. Pleasure, pain; praise, blame; fame, shame; loss and gain, are all the same. The same old grind. Notice in your own outlook if you label work choices in terms of success/failure, boring/exciting, work/play, me/them, and so on. When you do, examine the self-image that accompanies them. Then look deeper and imagine what goals might satisfy your vision of life, based upon your unchanging True Self.

Hear and Now

"I remember how destitute I was when I first arrived in Taiwan, fleeing China during the tumultuous years of World War II.... Even though I did not possess many things, I felt most fortunate and content. When I went to the market before the break of dawn to buy vegetables for the day [for the monastery], the stars in the sky kept me company. Flowers and trees were there for me to enjoy. Roads were there for me to travel. I also had the opportunity to meet people from different walks of life. Though I possessed nothing, I had all the wealth the universe could offer me."

—Venerable Master Hsing Yun

Measuring wealth in terms of money can also be a set-up for frustration. Whether as a metal coin or a tinted etching, money is a tangible symbol of the illusion of a substantial self, permanent, and separate—the illusion at the root of the second noble truth. Money can symbolize craving, a seeming substance to plug up a bottomless pit, a vicious cycle of fishing for what won't really bring us true happiness, causing us much unnecessary woe. Furthermore, money is only a means, not an end. (You can't eat it, wear it, sleep in it, bathe in it.) So money can also symbolize the concepts at the core of liberation. Money is a freeze-frame snapshot of the infinite web of interdependence. And money is sunyata, blank essence. (In fact, a dollar no longer even represents a fixed amount in gold or silver, so its value is now really whatever people say it is, thus truly a construct of mind.) Its true emptiness of any ultimate, fixed value can be ignored and thus cause suffering. And it can alleviate suffering of self and others.

Dissolving the needy, skinflint, tabulating self in the light of insight and compassion, unconstricted selfhood is limitless. Sunyata, selflessness, can mean a fertile cornucopia of abundance at the heart of the universe, perpetually creating itself. And when the goal is for the benefit of all beings, the universe seems even more glad to help out. We'll see examples of such prosperity at the close of this chapter. But first let's consider three more criteria for wealth: sustainability, scale, and self-sufficiency.

"Small Is Beautiful": Economics from the Heart

The phrase "Small is beautiful" originated in the 1970s as the title of a book by E. F. Schumacher, rallying for *human scale*, *sustainability*, and *decentralization*, among other good things.

Sustainability can be defined by a motto enshrined in the Iroquois Confederacy: "In every deliberation, we must consider the impact of our decisions on the next seven generations." Today we speak of long-term planning over short-term gain. As Gandhi said, "There is enough in this world for everyone's need, but not enough for everyone's greed." What are the limits of growth? What is enough? There's nothing Buddhist about passing the cost of unlimited expansion on to generations further along. On the other hand, sustainability can generate secure profitability. It requires appreciating the interrelatedness of human needs.

Scale matters. Success needn't mean the biggest market share. Taiwan, for example, is a great economic success story built primarily of small businesses. We may not think about it, but half of America's businesses are small. Now, too, there's the home office, a workforce unit of one, or sometimes two, as couples find ways to work together. In terms of right livelihood, smaller scale can mean an individual spends less time contemplating karmic ramifications of actions that could result in exploitation of the environment and other people, providing more time instead to concentrate fully on what's really at hand to be done. This is sometimes a motivation for "down-shifting," for "voluntary simplicity," living lower on the food chain, realizing "the maximum of well-being with the minimum of consumption." Less fuss, less muss.

> **Hear and Now**
>
> "The Buddhist point of view takes the function of work to be at least threefold: to give a man a chance to utilize and develop his faculties; to enable him to overcome his ego-centeredness by joining with other people in a common task; and to bring forth the goods and services needed for a becoming existence."
>
> —E. F. Schumacher, *Small Is Beautiful*

Traditional business models use a hierarchical mode, maximum power filtering down from a centralized point. A *decentralized* model is more like a network of units creating power bottom-up, a whole greater than the sum of its parts. The components add value to each other's services, and the fluidity keeps it all adaptive to change. Another thing about such decentralized systems is that they tend to be self-organizing. Self-organization permits businesses to remain small yet build complex webs of interactions. This is also Buddhist in its respect for autonomy and the value of interaction, as well as spontaneous arising.

Dharma at Work: Zentrepreneurs and Tantrapreneurs

Two right livelihood options are being an entrepreneur and creating your own work. Or coming onboard an already-formed Buddhist enterprise. Here are four examples. They're striking examples of how Buddhism is finding its way in the West. The first two reflect the Zen work ethic.

At a Zen monastery, you'll find everyone working, those of highest rank often doing the most menial chores. Job skills often mean ego, so a former receptionist might be assigned to chop carrots, rather than work in the office. As we'll see, one of the outcomes of beginner's mind is a sense of playful aimlessness, embracing a serendipity that might be more fortuitous than any prearranged scheme. That's what happened after San Francisco Zen Center, America's first Zen monastery, established a second monastery on mountain property formerly run as a hot springs resort, in the idyllic forest wilds above Big Sur, California. It supported itself by renting out the guest houses in the summer. But so many guests wanted to take home a loaf of their home-baked bread that they followed their nose, rather than stick to any master plan, and started their own bakery in the city. That led, in turn, to a book of their recipes, *The Tassajara Bread Book* (1970), which became a shot heard round the world, sparking a national revival of homemade bread as well as of locally produced, organic grub. So in creating a business, they helped spark a national movement. Zen Center later opened a third monastery and grew more businesses organically, including a restaurant over-looking the San Francisco Bay called Greens, which has not only survived 20 years in a highly competitive gourmet arena, but also produced more influential cookbooks, such as *The Greens Cookbook*.

Our second example illustrates how a small enterprise can take wings and thrive when following the Way—blending a spiritual mission and a social mission in a business mission. On the East Coast, a Zen meditation group led by a former aerospace engineer, Bernard Tetsugen Glassman, borrowed $300,000 in 1982 to open a small storefront bakery called Greyston, in the poor neighborhood of Yonkers. It would provide economic support for the sangha, and in a socially engaged way by employing the unskilled and disadvantaged. Tassajara's bakery was an influence on their choice of a bakery but they concentrated on gourmet pastries, enabling the company to stay competitive but small. Niche marketing.

Maintaining an open, "don't-know" mind, Roshi Glassman *became* the bakery, and bore witness to the suffering therein (the first noble truth). People didn't show up for work, or didn't have the skills. So Roshi Glassman and his wife, Sensei Sandra Jishu Holmes, rolled up their sleeves further and moved to be closer to their employees. He better understood why batter had been wasted, because people lacked such basic skills as knowing how to measure properly. Workers sometimes didn't show up because they were addicted to alcohol or drugs. And he witnessed extended families living jammed together in tiny dwellings, like fish in a sardine can, or with no dwelling at all.

So, as the bakery grew, the goal expanded to integrate personal growth and community development. It reached out to bring the chronically unemployed into its thriving workforce: people getting out of prison, or coming out of substance abuse programs, or off welfare rolls, or out of homeless shelters. One future Greyston employee had been unemployed simply because she couldn't leave her kids alone in her drugs- and violence-infested neighborhood.

So Greyston began building a socially responsible mini-conglomerate which they call a mandala, a combination of for-profit business with nonprofit social services, interfaith programs, and alliances with the community. As of this writing, the bakery employs 55 people and generates $5 million in revenues, which fund the nonprofit activities for the needy in the community, whether or not they work for the bakery. (The bakery isn't run as a charity, because the goal is to give people on-the-job training in a real business.) The nonprofit work began with a bakery training program that included "basic life and work skills." Then came Greyston Family Inn, providing housing and support, day care for kids, and job training and placement services. After that, listening to the new tenants of the Inn, Glassman heard the need for after-school tutoring for children, and classes for the adults on parenting and money management, and responded to those needs. Later a support community was formed for those challenged by HIV/AIDS. None of this would have happened had the bakery followed a preset five-year plan, and stuck to it. Instead, they've organically grown a model for other socially conscious enterprises. Here, "self-sufficiency in community" is the motto: realizing one's full human potential in the context of community. People matter as much as money. "This," they explain, "is a path from dependence through relative independence to an active state of interdependence."

Our third Buddhist enterprise, Windhorse Trading, started as a merchant stall in a market in East London. The founder, Kulananda, is ordained in the Western Buddhist Order, and today still earns the same as the company's warehouse people. A little over two decades later, Windhorse carries 15,000 products from around the world, which they design, manufacture, or import. Of its $1.75 million in annual profits, from $15 million in sales, about $850,000 is donated to Buddhist charities around the world. The company's statement of ethics, on its website, begins:

> **Hear and Now**
>
> "Often people attempt to live their lives backwards: they try to *have* more things, or more money, in order to *do* more of what they want, so they will *be* happier. The way it actually works is the reverse. You must first *be* who you really are, then *do* what you need to, in order to *have* what you want."
>
> —Margaret Young

Well, we're a bunch of Buddhists & Buddhist ethics come from the belief that all things are interconnected; that might sound a bit spacey but in practice it means that we try to live and work in a kind and aware way, doing as little harm as possible. All 100 of us who work here want to work with other Buddhists and want to help make money to give away. Our profits support Buddhist activities all over the world. We all earn roughly the same and are committed to living a simple and sustainable lifestyle. We even share seven cars between us!

And our last case study starts with the Asian Classics Input Project. This nonprofit disseminates books of Buddhist thought, digitized and given away for free. In so doing, the project not only preserves vanishing cultural traditions, but employs people who come from the countries where these books were written, often as refugees. It thus trains them in new skills for supporting themselves while saving the great books of their heritage. At-risk refugee teens and the disabled get an extra incentive: For every dollar they earn, another four are donated to a food fund for their village. All this is but one aspect of the parent organization, the Asian Classics Institute, with many educational activities plus a Tibetan Buddhist monastery and nunnery, Diamond Abbey, New York.

At the heart of this diamond mine of merit has been Geshe Michael Roach. Geshe denotes he's a scholar of Vajrayana, the Diamond Way; appropriately enough, from 1981 to 1995 he's been Vice-President of Andin International, specializing in diamonds. He's run this company on Buddhist principles, to which he attributes its remarkable success. Begun with $50,000 in loans, it now turns over $125 million a year, employing about 500 people.

He notes five Buddhist tenets in his business approach (though for the first five years he never told anyone they were Buddhist, nor that he was a monk): tonglen (exchanging self with others; asking "what would help this person?"); lojong (mind training; turning a problem into an advantage); total honesty with everyone (good karma); creativity (all employees now go on one-month paid retreats twice a year); and the bodhisattva vow. This last, key factor means Geshe Roach, a monastic, never owned a penny, donating his salary, minus a living wage. He attributes his success to having a good attitude and being generous. Thus he says he'd constantly be getting it and giving it away, and the happier for it.

Hear and Now

"I love my work. It's very useful for a spiritual person to have a whole life around normal people. You get to understand the suffering that normal people go through—the stress that's involved in earning a living to feed your family. When I travel around as a big lama, no one criticizes me to my face. Everyone's always telling me what a wonderful person I am, and congratulating me on the things I do. But when I'm at work the boss screams at me. There's greed to deal with. There's the jealousy of my other vice-presidents to deal with. Your spiritual life gets challenged every few seconds. It's a laboratory for Buddhist practice which you don't get in a monastery."
—Geshe Michael Roach

See your work as an opportunity to practice mindfulness, whatever it is. And if you're considering changing your work path, follow your heart, and your ethics, and the money will follow. There's nothing to making money, if that's all you want to make. See if you can make a Way for yourself in the world.

The Least You Need to Know

- ◆ Work is a fact of life. As the Zen saying goes: "Before enlightenment you chop wood and carry water, after enlightenment you chop wood and carry water."

- ◆ Work is yet another opportunity to practice mindfulness. Mindfulness practices can be beneficial to your work.

- ◆ Be aware of people as well as products. In the human scale, size matters. Decentralization is another way to consider the work environment.

- ◆ Sometimes work can create situations calling for "on-the-spot" practice.

Chapter 18

Everybody's Doing It: Buddhism and Popular Culture

In This Chapter

- ◆ Flower power and garden gurus
- ◆ The inner athlete
- ◆ Buddhist soul music
- ◆ Buddha at the movies

Exploring Buddhism's myriad applications in everyday life, we arrive at art. What is art? What isn't! Everything we do (and don't do) has its art. But somewhere along the line, somebody sorted the arts into two heaps: "high" and "low"; or "fine" and "popular." (Sounds too like monastic and lay.) Unwritten, this boundary's as divisive as that seemingly clearer unwritten line between East and West. Study Dante, Shakespeare, or Goethe, you have walls of books available for study. But arts of haiku and tanka, tangka and sumi-e, shakuhachi and the Tibetan Dance of the Skeleton Lords have been relatively unknown in the West. Interestingly, their ultimate purpose is to go beyond words, putting us in direct contact with reality, in the here and now. No need for walls of books. (What else can we say?!)

Pick your art form. In Japanese culture, for example, Buddhism is everywhere. *"Do"* means way, in Japanese, and it applies to *chado* (tea way), *chikudo* (bamboo way), *kado* (flower way), and *kyudo* (archery way). And so we hear now, too, about the Way of Pooh and the Zen of changing diapers. Indeed, where's the museum of things that *aren't* art?! Where's the temple of things *not* to worship?! It's all meditation—which is an art.

Call them skillful means, uppaya. Vehicles of the Way. Opportunities for awakening mind and heart, and for expressing that awakening. In a Buddhist sense, then, all arts are popular arts, since anyone is capable of awakening heart and mind, awakening to nirvana, here and now. And the popularity of Buddhist arts in the West attests to its adaptability to our culture. Let's start in by getting our hands in the earth, then proceed to further physical cultures. Next we'll have a taste of Buddhist resonance in music and film. And this chapter spills over into the next. All about seeing the Way in our own backyard.

A Gift from a Flower to a Garden

Indeed, as I think back, I'm struck by how many of my first impressions of life came from nature. And I'm struck at how fortunate I was to have grown up near a garden, where my sister and I would commune with nature. When I was little, I wrote my first haiku about a neighbor's garden. And in the neighborhood in Los Angeles where I grew up, there was a Japanese movie theater where I spent some time. One thing that impressed me, in my many armchair travels to the countryside of Japan via film, was the way windows worked over there, as if most of an entire wall slid open. This way, the garden isn't only an extension of the house. The house is also a gift from the garden. I'd grown up seeing Modernist buildings merging inside and outside, such as those designed by Frank Lloyd Wright, who took cues from the East, where garden and grounds are an integral part of the design.

So I tell you, it's never too late to have a happy childhood. Just take up gardening, or flower arranging!

Flower Power: By the Flowers, of the Flowers, and for the Flowers

I learned some powerful dharma once on a Buddhist retreat in a forest of old-growth redwoods. After a mindful walk through this living cathedral, led by Zen gardener and Dharma teacher Wendy Johnson, we returned to the meditation hall and she passed around a large bowl of the topsoil we'd just trod. Talk about reverence for life! Here we were passing around billions of microorganisms, each one of us inhaling them like some rare perfume. Of such stuff are we made, yet how often do we have the occasion to gaze into its mirror?

Hear and Now

"We are intertwined. Some bacteria sip nitrogen from the living air and fix it on the roots of host plants in plump pink purses of protein, while other bacteria consolidate sulfur from stone and render it available to our classic roses. And all the while, throughout solid ground where well-intentioned gardeners prune and pontificate on the surface, mycelial threads of a vast fungal network spread and radiate out in widening circles, attaching to plant roots for nourishment while fending off disease in the garden."

—Wendy Johnson

You might not realize you're always interacting with the web of life. For example, there's the invisible carpet of microscopic beings along floors. Underneath chairs. A film of invisible life in every nook and cranny. (Imagine how we might look to them!) What better way to affirm and enjoy our kinship with all life, than by cultivating a pretty plant or two? Just tending a houseplant draws us into the cyclically unfolding dharma of the seasons, the sources of life, the earth. And such practices as using weeds and waste for mulch to nourish our flowers are good models for our own practice.

If you have a backyard, enjoy the blessings of sun and wind and water and the gift of good land. If you have a front yard, you share your gardening with others. And taking this into the larger world, you might get involved with a community garden movement. An empty lot can make many rows of fresh edibles, flavorful herbs, and bright flowers, plus community involvement. Let a little Earth into your life. Plant a seed and tend its holy mystery. Something comes up and flourishes. It's nice. Tend to this new life as if it were your own life. When your garden flowers, your work is being applauded by charming flower faces, simple buddhas happy to be alive.

Whether or not you raise them yourself, you can contemplate a flower in your breathing room and at your altar. A messenger of the entire cosmos, a complete Buddha unto itself, making radiance with just the few ingredients it's given. When I pass by flowers I've set out, I sometimes forget who put them there. Instead, I stop and admire them and wonder how I am any different.

Saying It with Flowers

I don't just stick flowers in a bowl willy-nilly, but seek an arrangement, as a living thing. Japanese master flower arrangements, however, might seem thin or skimpy compared to the more abundant still-life style preferred in the West. But with an un-prejudiced eye, Japanese flower arrangements look as if they were still growing, an extension of a garden. The style is somewhat abstract, to convey the essence of things. A pointing directly to mind, outside of words. A skillful means in which each person can recognize their own essential Buddha nature through direct communion.

Seven chrysanthemums (an autumn flower) in a bed of pebbles, their stems bent and shaped to appear as a single plant. The design is triangular: heaven, human, and earth. Heaven is the highest stalk. Intermediate and somewhat diagonal branches are the human realm. The earthly realm is at the base. (The triad also correlates with Buddha, Dharma, Sangha.) Next to it, a sketch of an imaginary arrangement shows the complexity and elegance potential in such a design. But neither photo nor drawing can ever convey the space making the art possible.

Chrysanthemum arrangement by Cynthis Lewis; drawing by Master Enkiduwasa Mori. (Collection of Beth Burstein.)

You can find Shinto and Confucian symbolism in Japanese flower arranging, but the Buddhism was there right from the start. When Prince Umayada brought Buddhism to Japan, he sent envoys to China to seek cultural and spiritual guidance. One of these envoys, named Ono-no Imoko, eventually retired, living as a hermit priest by a lake. He was devoted to arranging flowers for altars. One of the early Japanese masters of the art describes the process: "Flowers should be placed in the container as one throws pebbles into a garden pool. It is done quietly and deliberately, and then left alone. To make changes is the sign of a novice." Priests of newly built temples came to him for instruction. Thus was born the first known school of flower arrangement, called *ike-no-bo*, meaning "hermit by the lake," which gave birth to Japanese flower arranging, *ikebana*.

It's interesting to note how something originally designed as decoration for altars became a devotional art in itself. You might consider this in Pure Land terms, in which meditation on a bodhisattva's pure land becomes as powerful as meditating on the bodhisattva itself. And this is, in part, what happened in Japanese gardening.

Ooh, Ooh, Ooh! What Just Five Rocks Can Do

Sand as ground cover goes all the way back to the beginning of Japanese history, but gardens made of sand began around the eleventh century and came into their own around the sixteenth. For one thing, a pond made out of granite gravel or sand was less expensive to make and maintain than one of water. They're called *karé-san-sui*, meaning "dry mountain water," a kind of koan in itself. They became a common feature at the growing numbers of Buddhist temples as well as homes of the elite.

Like traditional Japanese rock gardens set amidst vegetation, karé-san-sui often imitate classical Chinese ink-brush landscapes. Flat-topped rocks looked like brush-stroke mountains, and raked gravel or sand imitated waterfalls, rivers, and ocean (usually blank space in canvases). Overall, they might represent a pure land, or the river of life, or the progress of a monk's practice. Five qualities common to these gardens: asymmetry, simplicity, austere sublimity (lofty dryness), subtle profundity (deep respect), freedom from attachment (nirvana), and tranquility.

Detail of rock garden in Zhuiho-in Temple, Japan.

Photograph: Frantisek Staud, www.phototravels.net

The acme and enigmatic sphinx of rock garden art is at the Temple of Ryoanji (Peaceful Dragon). Fifteen stones are set in five groups across a horizontal bed of gravel about the size of a tennis court, raked horizontally and in concentric circles around the stones. (An interesting phenomenon is that you can never see all the rocks at once. You can only see, at most, 14 at any one time. Turn slightly to take in the fifteenth, and one other rock drops out of sight.)

The only literally living thing evident is moss on the rocks. Some say the stones resemble mountain peaks jutting through clouds, or islands in the sea (like Japan herself), but the overall impression is more nonrepresentational, like the play of volume and mass in abstract art, an arrangement of stones almost random-seeming yet perfect, just so. Viewers are thrown back on themselves, inducing concentration which, as we know, can lead, in turn, to mindfulness. A common impression people come away with is an indescribable feeling of both presence and spaciousness. It thus embodies the Middle Way between strict rules and utter naturalness. Planned spontaneity, if you will. Which is to say, it's a powerful and unique fusion of both aesthetic and Buddhist doctrine: a monumental reflection of form being no different than emptiness, of emptiness being no different than form. (*Tip:* If you visit, go when they first open to avoid the crowds. People often come again and again.)

Physical Culture Is Culture

Culture isn't just high-brow stuff. Physical culture is also a culture—of growing popularity as attested to by all the joggers and baseball caps, plus 24-hour workout palaces dotting the landscape. Buddhism has key moves here, too, in martial arts (which are an art) and sports in general. So let's huddle!

Martial Arts Are an Art

Martial arts date back to pre-civilization. ("Hey, Joe, where ya going with that rock in your hand?!") But Shaolin Temple, in China, is a good candidate for Mother of All Martial Arts as we know them today. Located on Mount Sung, in Honan Province, legend has it that Bodhidharma settled here after his interview with the emperor, sitting zazen before a rock wall in a nearby cave. He learned that monks at the Temple were either falling asleep during meditation or were too restless to concentrate. He diagnosed they were out of shape, and devised exercises for them (being from India, this probably included yoga), which later became the basis of *kung fu*. Shaolin Grandmaster Wong Kiew Kit finds Shaolin kung fu contains all the techniques of the world's martial arts today: karate punches, *tae kwon do* kicks, judo throws, *aikido* locks, wrestling holds, Western boxing's jabs and hooks, Siamese boxing's elbow and knee strikes, and Malay *silate*'s twists and turns. Though Grandmaster Kit didn't include others, such as Brazilian *capoeira*, perhaps no less to the point, you could say the sun of Shaolin shines on all martial arts today for having combined physical culture with moral character development based on spiritual awareness.

> **This Is**
>
> **Kung fu** ("skill from effort") is a generic catch-all for the numerous forms of Chinese martial arts, with hundreds of styles and sub-styles. Some are soft, redirecting an opponent's momentum and energy; some are hard, meeting force with force. Some work internally on *chi* ("life force"), such as chi kung (a.k.a. qi gong, "energy work") and **tai chi,** with its slow, flowing movements; others are external and work on muscular energy.

Bodhidharma allegedly taught the martial arts to keep the Shaolin monks in shape to meditate, and to help them overcome that renowned enemy fear, child of ignorance. Now, since bandits periodically raided the Temple, monks excelling in kung fu were designated to defend the grounds. Some were later enlisted into service by the emperor to save the throne from usurpers. This helped lead to the multiplication of Buddhist temples across China, with official patronage. And at some monasteries were undoubtedly those who'd became monks to learn martial arts.

Flash forward. Martial arts didn't become widely visible in the West until the 1960s. Phrases like "Look within" crept into the vocabulary thanks to a TV series called *Kung Fu* (created by Bruce Lee but starring David Carradine). In 2001, the epic Taoist martial arts parable *Crouching Tiger, Hidden Dragon* won 4 out of the 10 Academy Awards for which it was nominated. And Eastern martial arts continue to enjoy a growing following in the West—except for the art of the sword, which, as we'll see next, was reserved for the warrior elite.

Way of the Warrior: Zen Swords and Arrows

Buddhism, as we've seen, varies with the person. Pure Land is the most democratic form. Japan's royal family, on the other hand, studied the Lotus Sutra. Shingon's esoterica appealed to the nobility. And, as we've seen, it was the samurai who first took to Zen in a big way. The warrior class had been on decline and when Zen came along the samurai loved the fearlessness, immediacy, irreverence, intuition, and strict discipline of Zen, supporting it generously, and devoting themselves to its rigors. And their military aristocracy was to remain in power for nearly seven centuries (until 1867).

The samurai shaved their heads like the Zen monks, donned Zen robes, practiced such Zen arts as flower-arranging and haiku, and learned Zen freedom-through-discipline: one-pointed concentration, dissolving the ego, remaining present to the moment. Indeed, for these soldiers who lived by their sword, swordsmanship became literally a

Hear and Now

"The mind must always be flowing. If it stops anywhere, the flow is interrupted and this is injurious to the well-being of the mind. In the case of the swordsman, it means death. When the swordsman stands against his opponent, he is not to think of the opponent, nor of himself, nor of his enemy's sword movements. He just stands there with his sword which, forgetful of all technique, is ready only to follow the dictates of the unconscious."

—Takuan Soho (1573–1645)

life-or-death test of Zen attainment. When a samurai holds a sword, it becomes one with his purified heart, his *mushin* (no-mind). Without fixing it anywhere, his attentive mind flows everywhere—for any move that comes to his mind, his opponent will make a countermove, and so he'd lose the higher ground of original nature.

One martial art the samurai practiced which is a heck of a lot safer, and more common, is archery (*kyudo*). (*Zen tip:* Don't learn archery to learn Zen. Keep your mind empty. You learn archery to learn archery. The Zen will arise along with it.) The Zen archer pulls back an arrow on an outsized bow, becomes the bull's eye, and the unwritten koan's answered … with a *thwack!*

Maximum Performance: Go, Sangha! BE the Ball!

Buddhism is a natural in any sports arena. Buddhism is a training that unites body and mind so as to perform at maximum potential. The Middle Way in sports, as in daily life, means a Buddhist can remain alert in tranquility, and calm amid danger. And with the Zen swordsman and archer, we've seen another aspect of no-mind: a mastery that merges with art, without any thought. When a classical pianist performs without a score, without even thinking of what note to play next, that's no-mind. For example, did you ever throw something into a wastebasket, without thinking, and have it sink right in, but then miss it a second time, because you thought about it too much? Buddhism helps foster and maintain that spontaneous, intuitive excellence.

This Is

Sports buffs often talk about players entering **the zone**, a mystical state of consciousness that seems neither physical nor mental … effortless amid tense exertion … as if playing in slow motion … perceptually sharp, keenly alert, with heightened concentration … almost as if being psychic. Such profound experiences, often commonplace to athletes, bear comparison to daydreaming, communion with nature, and spiritual contemplation.

Golf legend Tiger Woods has explained his fantastic success in terms of his upbringing. He's acknowledged his Thai Buddhist mother taught him to understand the power of the mind. When Tiger Woods tees off, he isn't thinking about how he's going to look on TV, or will he miss the ball and slice the turf, or any of that. His goal *is* winning, but, like enlightenment, if you strive for it, you lose it. So he's bringing all his training in one-pointed concentration to the moment in front of his nose. On the course, following his victory at the 2001 Masters tournament, he declared he was never thinking about its landmark significance (a winning streak including the four most prestigious tournaments of the era all in a row). "I was so attuned to each and every shot," he said, "that I focused so hard on just that one golf shot. I finally realized I had no more to play. That was it. I was done. It was such a weird feeling. Then I started thinking, I had just won the Masters. Then I started losing it a little bit."

Mindfulness applies no less to team sports. A coach who's understood this well is Phil Jackson. Raised in a Christian fundamentalist family and holding a degree in divinity, he was coach of the Chicago Bulls, during six NBA championships, including 70 wins in one season, before moving to Los Angeles to help the Lakers win a few more. Not too shabby. Like a good chef, Jackson doesn't reveal his secret recipe, but, along with Sioux lore, yoga, and love of God, he's had Vipassana instructor George Mumford train his teams, currently for about one week every month. Mumford initially shows them how the zone isn't a matter of self-will, but rather an outcome of self-awareness. Like anyone else, in order to overcome difficult emotions, such as fear, they learn to become aware, accept, and move on. By bringing awareness to their experience, they can understand and take responsibility for their own lives.

Jackson has taught teamwork to such multimillion-dollar superstar egos as Kobe Bryant, Michael Jordan, Shaquille O'Neal, Scotty Pippen, and Dennis Rodman. His emphasis on teamwork, with its selflessness and interconnectedness, shows on the court. Sangha in action. In the crunch of competition, a player can keep his cool and awaken to what's called for in each moment. Because of Jackson's trademark triangle defensive strategy, his players keep flowing. Win or lose, up or down, they cleave to the Middle Way, and grow as a team. The selflessness of the players enables their best to make a direct link to the audience's best. It's a joy to watch, even when the ball wobbles out of the rim instead of in.

> **Hear and Now**
>
> "Basketball is a complex dance that requires shifting from one objective to another at lightning speeds.... The secret is not thinking. That doesn't mean being stupid, it means quieting the endless jabbering of thoughts so that your body can do instinctively what it's been trained to do without the mind getting in the way."
> —Phil Jackson

Now, if you don't relate to competitive sports, consider swimming or Frisbee. The bottom line was laid out by Bodhidharma, back at Shaolin. Be it race-walking or sit-ups, tai chi or tae kwon do, keep in shape! Form (training) is the key to emptiness (unlimited potentiality). Notice how meditation improves your physical skill, and how physical culture improves your meditation. It's a slam-dunk double-bogey rare-orchid rock-solid wisdom-eye homerun!

Play It Again, Samadhi!—Musical Meditation

Music may be the oldest of human arts, requiring only a hand beating on a knee, or a solo voice. And it's perennially new, being created in the present moment; as jazzman Eric Dolphy once said, "When you hear music, it's gone, in the air, and you can never capture it again."

Music's a present-ation, making present. So it's Buddhist to the degree its performance attunes us to the freedom and fullness of the present moment; and its impermanence. And, as we've noted, there's something about the resonant quality of music that mirrors our own self-consciousness, itself a kind of echo, or extra little reverb on top of experience. The filigree of a little icing on the cake of life. Other living things have awareness, but we two-leggeds are aware that we're aware.

Mindfulness Exercise: Listening to any music, follow your breath, and note how the music moves it, taking us out of ourselves and bringing us back.

Broaden your horizons. If you've never listened to world music (sitar, African drums, flamenco, and so on), take a chance. New rhythms, harmonies, melodies, and scales seem strange at first, then eventually as familiar as an old friend from far away. Follow how a single note can slide, wander, and go *boing* in elastic, mind-bending ways. Let your body and soul become one big ear. Be one with the musicians and the music, feeling each note resonate in your heart. And with your hands in meditation, you offer silent applause every moment.

Each land has its own musical flavor. I find Korean music invigorating, for example, once you get accustomed to its wonky asymmetric zigzag, like a hummingbird or dragonfly. Vietnamese chanting, such as recorded by the monks and nuns of Plum Village, is, to me, one of the most soulful sounds on the planet. But the dharma has one taste. Like Willie Nelson once said, "It's all one song."

Giving Buddhism Its Chants

In and of itself, music is a mystery. Where did it come from? Who knows. We do it anyway, humming a little tune just because we like to hum. Maybe we're serenading the microorganisms. Joining the music of the spheres (not so silly a concept, now that we know that matter is a form of vibration). Vocalizing the deep rhythms of life that surge in each cell of our protoplasm and throughout the galaxies.

A vibrational field to our voice with a cosmic dimension is singing in unison. Whether it's the *Heart Sutra*, or the name of Amitabha Buddha or of the *Lotus Sutra*, chanting in community makes the practice even more powerful. And we become conscious of being a part of something greater than ourselves. There are numerous recordings of Buddhist chants, some even with standard tunes, such as the lovely one for chanting the name of Avalokiteshvara.

Now consider what happens when chanting has definite vibrational properties. If you haven't heard Tibetan *multiphonic* chanting before, check out a recording by the Gyuto Monks to get a sample of this unusual vibrational resonance. It's a truly tantric art of unification with universal energies. For one thing, the monks chant two octaves below C, a feat unrivalled in Western music. Such tones of low vibration travel farther and through more obstacles than high-frequency sound. Asian and African elephants communicate long-distance using this "silent thunder," and whales can communicate this way from Newfoundland to Puerto Rico (what might they be saying?). In such deep tones, you can hear overtones within a single note.

Plus, each monk can chant in three octaves *at once*. In effect, individuals are singing chords.

Poet and Sanskrit scholar Andrew Schelling has described it as "craggy guttural prayer, like the sound of stones crumbling down a mountain precipice … comforting to hear as your own mother's voice, but above that, almost on wings, a distinctly audible angel's tone, sublime as its originating note is terrifying."

Now, a mantra that has this kind of innate vibrational power is Om (pronounced *aum*). *Exercise:* You can center yourself by breathing in, and on the out-breath chanting "Aum." Close your eyes. Feel its one syllable form three waves: *ahhhh*, as your breath releases, *ooooouhh* expressing your calm and peace, and sealing it off with your lips, *mmmmmmm*. Then do it again, and see if it's slower, longer, calmer, or lower; then one last time. Over time, see if you can let the chant come from way back down deep in your throat and resonate in your belly. Follow it with your mind. Let your consciousness be with Om.

Blowing Your Mind the Buddhist Way

The oldest wind instrument on the planet may be the Australian didjeridu, a four- or five-foot trumpet of termite-hollowed wood, operating in the lower frequency range, with a continuous tradition dating back at least 30,000 years. Tibet has a similar-length horn made of copper, 10 feet long, said to represent the strength of the earth.

It's often played with shorter horns representing the delicacy of the heavens, bringing these two forces into balance in the mind of the listener.

As the didjeridu is native to indigenous Australian spirituality, and the long horn is unique to Tibetan Buddhism, so is the Japanese flute called the *shakuhachi* truly Zen. Made from the root of thick timber-strength bamboo, its sound is made by blowing perpendicularly across the end. Just as it takes time to learn how to sit Zen, or make one even, continuous line with Asian brush and paper, so with blowing one note on the shakuhachi: The hard-earned result expresses the player's distinct signature.

The sound is hauntingly like a voice and all its moods, but as with a rock garden, abstracted. It's evocative, as Debussy's impressionism for the piano can conjure fireworks, goldfish, dancing snowflakes, gardens in the rain, and so on. Listening to shakuhachi, I wonder where else have I heard the cry of distant deer, and the voices of cranes as their young ones leave the nest? And distant thunder echoing within precipitous peaks.

Rhythm isn't foot-stompingly obvious, but there's always a pulse or heart rhythm. There's a melodic line, but sometimes the notes seem placed at random, like rocks in a garden, or an act of nature. Each note's variable, the listener's mind slows down to pay due attention to each one, and, like good jazz, you're continually surprised to find where it's going next. Just like life.

Country 'n' Eastern, and Other Soundtracks

Certain Western compositions mirror Buddhist meditation. Bach is a great example of Zen, especially such solo pieces as his "Pasacaglia and Fugue in C minor" and "Chaconne." One of my favorite genres is country 'n' eastern, which is country 'n' western plus Eastern influences. The group The Flatlanders, for example, from Lubbock, Texas, is composed of angelic tenor Jimmy Dale Gilmore, ex-circus rouster Joe Ely, and, my flat-footed favorite, Butch Hancock, composer of such mindful ditties as "My Mind's Got a Mind of Its Own" and "Just a Wave, Not the Ocean."

To expand your horizons, I heartily recommend two more composer-musicians, who've both done double-duty with soundtracks: Kitaro and Philip Glass. Shelved under "New Age" somewhere in between Enya and Yanni (say those two names together fast, three times), Japanese composer-musician Kitaro ("Man of Many Joys") interweaves traditional Eastern instruments with electronic synthesizers in ever-unfolding soundscapes to heartily, mindfully hum along to.

On first listen, Philip Glass's music might sound like something's stuck. Actually, he weaves minimalist soundscapes out of very small, rhythmic, repeated fragments. The string quartets and violin concerti are very lyrical, plus he writes symphonies, operas, and film scores. He's compared musical composition and meditation like this: laying down a foundation, paying attention, putting in effort, and having the patience to repeat the same exercise over and over until you become the object of your attention. A similar but freer use of patterning is often evident in the music of Terry Riley ("In C" being the landmark), with Hindu yet eclectic Asian roots.

So listen, and you shall hear. Sing in the shower. Join a choir or a recitation sangha. Serenade the spheres. Stay tuned! Meanwhile, we turn next to the most totally resonant of art forms, one whose very nature mirrors consciousness …

> **Along the Path**
>
> Modern lyrics with Buddhist meanings, intended or otherwise, include: the Beastie Boys' "Bodhisattva Vow" and "The Update," Leonard Cohen's "Here It Is," and "Love Itself," Donovan's "The Evernow" and "The Way" (from *Sutras*), George and Ira Gershwin's "I've Got Plenty of Nothing," Robert Hunter and Jerry Garcia's "Eyes of the World," Joni Mitchell's "Both Sides Now," Malvina Reynolds's "Where Have All the Flowers Gone?" John Lennon's "Imagine" and "Tomorrow Never Knows," Natalie Merchant's "All I Want," Alanis Morissette's "All I Really Want" and "Thank U," REM's "Everybody Hurts," Patti Smith and Tom Shanrahan's "1959," and Van Morrison's "Enlightenment."

Mind Mirror: Buddha at the Movies

Looking back, the most popular art form the twentieth century bequeathed to posterity was … movies! Nothing goes around the world like a ticket to the movies. This holds for TV, too, also speaking the universal language of cinema but on a much reduced scale. As mystic movie maven and filmmaker Stephen Simon says, "Movies are the most electrifying communications medium ever devised and the natural conduit for inspiring ourselves to look into the eternal issues of who we are and why we are here." So, of course, this has its Buddhist lights, and we can break that down two ways: film itself as Buddhist, and Buddhist films.

Now Playing: Film as Buddhist

Whatever's playing, I always enjoy the hush that settles in when the lights dim before the show. The sheer act of gathering together with fellow villagers for some story-telling around a campfire (the flickering lights and shadows on a movie screen) has primal roots, deep within the sacred. And film can, in and of itself, provide an apt model for our mundane consciousness; conscious *of* something—but what? Illusion, quite often. Plato once described the unexamined life in terms akin to sitting in a theater never aware of the projection booth where the images come from; instead, we take what we're seeing for reality. So it is, the Buddha shows, with the projections of our own minds, which we take as the reality of our experience.

There's a visual metaphor in Buddha's motto: "Come and see!" Vipassana: clear seeing into the nature of things. Burmese vipassana master Sayadaw U Pandita notes that when we watch a movie, the process can be like insight meditation. Each has four phases: 1) appearance of object; 2) directing of attention; 3) close observation; and 4) understanding.

In insight meditation, 1) we focus attention on our belly, say, which leads to 2) appearance of rising and falling of the abdomen, followed by 3) noting the process and our feelings, then 4) discovering special characteristics and how they actually behave, not how we think they do.

Watching a movie, 1) we focus attention on the screen, which leads to 2) appearance of characters and scenes, followed by 3) making out what's happening by observing carefully, then 4) discovering the plot and appreciating the movie.

Cinema provides another metaphor: for reality's Eternal Now. I remember once sitting behind a five-year-old and an adult at a matinee, and every ten minutes or so the kid would ask the adult, "What's happening now?" and the adult would answer, "Now they're getting to know each other." Or "Now they're going to get married." Or "Now they're on their honeymoon." If you think about it, every moment in a movie is (like life) always about "now." Continuous present tense. (Even flashbacks.) And this Film Now can be elastic, instead of like clock time: 10 minutes compressed into 3, or 3 stretched out into 10 (very reminiscent of quite a few sitting meditations I've had). Indeed, the more familiar we become with the eternal nowness of time, the more we sense its elasticity.

Our minds are elastic in the same way. A good analogy is space. As with time, movies are always breaking the ancient Aristotelian Unity of Time and Place (everything unfolding in linear "real time," 1-2-3). A film opens space out like a jigsaw puzzle, constantly changing locations and points of views. So when we're engaged by film's space-without-particular-locality, we're also experiencing the limitless possibility of emptiness, and of our own mind. Felt everywhere but nowhere to be seen.

Fiction films are usually a neatly patterned karma tale. For an interesting meditation sometime, buy a ticket to a movie you otherwise don't care about and walk in on the middle (at a multiplex this is easy to do). Then stay for the beginning up until you walked in. You'll see how everything that happened in the second half was a result of the characters' actions in the first half. (You can also try this at home, fast-forwarding into the middle, starting from there, then returning to the beginning.) See karma, study dharma.

Here's another meditation. Watch actors in group scenes when they're not saying or doing anything, and see if they're compassionately making the other actors look good. Movies can nourish our compassion, as well. Typically, we hope it all turns out okay, and so identify beyond our selves (which is what compassion means, feeling with), identifying with the other characters. And without compassion, we'd be aware we're sitting in our chairs the entire time. And this is a secret part of the fun of watching movies: sitting there in our jeans and T-shirt, and at the same time being superstars, 33-feet tall, and sliding back and forth between the two realms. ("Great *kiss!* Please pass the popcorn.")

If we stop to think about this further, we see that when we're engrossed in a movie our ability to exchange our self with others' reveals the basic insubstantiality of self. It's conditional on the factors of the story. This is how a great actor such as Laurence Olivier could say, late in life, acting didn't teach him to "get in touch with himself" but, rather, it taught him how he'd no idea who he was, really, having realized his heart's potential for being so many different people. Drama teaches that, given the circumstances, we could change who we thought we were in a second. Like they say, there but for fortune go you or I.

This Is

Any permanent, substantial identity is a dramatic fiction. In ancient Greek theater, actors wore big masks called **persona,** the origin of our word *person.* In the Zen-influenced dance-theater called **Noh,** wooden masks even change expressions as the wearer shows them in different angles and shades of lighting.

Hear and Now

"… the metaphor of movie for life is an interesting one. The frames go by so quickly that we retain the illusion of continuity and are distracted from the light that shines steadily through each frame."
—Robert Aitken Roshi

"… If you want to enjoy the movie, you should know that it is the combination of film and light and white screen, and that the most important thing is to have a plain, white screen."
—Shunryu Suzuki Roshi, *Our Everyday Life Is Like a Movie*

But film can never duplicate what I see when I settle on my cushion and look into my own mind screen. This is particularly true in insight meditation, when visualization is personalized. And it's a key feature in Tibetan Buddhism, where visualization empowers us to realize our unity with sacred energies by identifying with pictorial images of deities embodying them—and then recognizing their intrinsic emptiness (returning back to the empty movie screen). And the cosmic implications of Pure Land devotions reveal realms that are inconceivable. Cinema's painting with light pales beside the recognition that we are bodies of light, interbeaming and intergleaming on the luminous mandala of Indra's infinite net of light.

Is *Gone with the Wind* About Impermanence?: Buddhist Films

There isn't an Oscar for Spiritual Cinema, at least not yet, but tens of millions of people enjoy it when they see it. Themes include the nature of reality and identity and time, mythic quests, and the power of love. Within this unofficial genre, there are Buddhist films a-plenty, as testified to by the International Buddhist Film Festival. Their first call for entries in 2003 pulled in 300 films, from around the planet.

My personal all-time favorite has a longish title, *Why Has Bodhidharma Left for the East?* a koan which is asking, in effect, "What is the meaning of Buddhism?" "Is it worthwhile?" A young man renounces city life and makes his way to a remote Korean mountain monastery. The first words we finally hear are, "There is no beginning, no middle, no end." It took producer-writer-director-editor Bae Young-kyun five years to put this intimate spiritual epic together, and it's deservedly made it to the top of many Top Ten lists since. The *2001* of Zen Cinema. G. G. says "Check it out."

Stillness pervades, yet flows on, in this frozen moment from Why Has Bodhidharma Left for the East? *The calligraphic composition is representative of the film's highly stylized, visually expressive manner of storytelling. In this scene, a monk is asking another whether he should stay or return to the world. Or are we seeing him really debating with himself? Of course, a picture says more than words can tell.*

Photo: Courtesy of Milestone Film & Video, New Jersey

Leaves from the Bodhi Tree

More films of Buddhist interest include *The Razor's Edge* (compare the 1946 and 1984 versions), *Afterlife* (1998), *Caravan* (a.k.a. *Himalaya*) (1999), *Jacob's Ladder* (adapted from *The Tibetan Book of the Dead*, 1990), *Beyond Rangoon* (1995), *Enlightenment Guaranteed* (2000), *Fearless* (1993), *Heaven and Earth* (1993), and *Samsara* (2003).

Documentaries include *The Jew in the Lotus* (1996); *Peace Is Every Step, The Saltmen of Tibet* (1998); *Chasing Buddha, Genghis Blues, Jews and Buddhism: Belief Amended, Faith Revealed* (1999); *Regret to Inform* (2000); *Rivers and Tides* (2001); *Words of My Perfect Teacher, Home Street Home* (2003); and Ellen Bruno's films about Tibetan, Burmese/Thai, and Cambodian women (*Satya, Sacrifice,* and *Samsara*).

There are dozens of Buddhist films from Japan. Kon Ichikawa's *The Burmese Harp* (1956) is a response to the search to find spiritual meaning after the destruction wrought by war. We see a Japanese soldier injured in Burma at the end of World War II. A Buddhist monk takes care of him, and he returns to his military unit in Buddhist robes. In the films of Yasujiro Ozu (*Early Summer*, *The End of Summer*, etc.), the Buddhism's implied rather than explicit. A character doesn't experience a climax so much as undergo a subtle change that enables him or her to appreciate the suchness of things. And we mustn't forget *Rashomon* (1950), in which a monk hears of one event told from different points of view.

Hollywood films can have unintended Buddhist themes, such as *It's a Wonderful Life*, in which we see what life would be like if one single person hadn't lived, revealing how each person affects everyone else. A film worth seeing more than once is *Groundhog Day* (1993), in which one man relives the same day 10,000 times until he gets it right. George Lucas refused to specify whether The Force referred to by Yoda in *Star Wars* stands for the Tao, the Holy Spirit, Buddha-mind, or something else, nor whether Luke Skywalker's journey represented the Buddha's. After all, the motto in Hollywood has been: "If you want to send a message, use Western Union." A more recent phenomena was the *Matrix* trilogy, with threads from several traditions. (Question, when does a luminous message outweigh violence served up piping hot?)

Recent films about Tibet, such as *Seven Years in Tibet* (1997), *Kundun* (1998), and *Windhorse* (1999), have come a long way from the Hollywood moonshine stereotypes of *Lost Horizon* (1937). Bernardo Bertolucci's *Little Buddha* (1993) crosscut the life of the Buddha (played by Keanu Reeves) with the fictional story of a contemporary boy in Seattle thought to be a reincarnated Tibetan lama. Plus, there are now such documentaries as *Anguish of Tibet* and *Wheel of Time* (2003). And, from nearby Bhutan, *The Cup* (2000) was the first film made by a Buddhist lama, Khyentse Norbu, who followed his debut with *Travellers & Magicians* (2003).

And there are films in which Buddhist elements pop up like weeds between cracks in concrete, such as in the 1993 biopic about Tina Turner, *What's Love Got To Do With It*. Just one line in a movie can be undeniably Buddhist, such as in *Monsters, Inc.*, when Mike says to Scully (about Boo), "Oh no!, now that you've given it a name, you'll become attached to it!"

For filmmakers, new technology is raising the bar to entry. It's relatively easy to shoot a video, edit it on a home computer, and put it up on a website. As the media octopus expands, I hope it's not idle speculation to anticipate the eventual reality of a Buddhist TV channel, as there is in Amsterdam as well as Korea. I want my B-TV! Meanwhile, I'll just wait … and sit on my cushion, set my mind screen up, and inquire into what's projected there. (Please pass the popcorn.)

The Least You Need to Know

- ◆ Everything can be an art and an occasion for conveying an awakened mind and heart.

- ◆ Gardening is a Buddhist activity. In fact, the first flower-arranging school was Buddhist.

- ◆ A variety of martial arts can all be traced to Buddhist origins. Athletes and sports stars, already familiar with "the zone," are finding Buddhism can add a winning ingredient to their training.

- ◆ Traditional schools of Buddhism have particular brands of music associated with meditation, such as shakuhachi and chanting. In the West, Buddhist influence can be heard in rock, country, and soundtracks.

- ◆ Film has analogies to Buddhist concepts, through such physical components as its projection and blank screen, and through its aesthetics, such as its eternal present tense. Besides film itself, there are also particular films with Buddhist insights.

New Ways of Seeing and Being: Buddhism and Fine Arts

In This Chapter

- ◆ What is sacred art?
- ◆ How to haiku
- ◆ Dharma painting
- ◆ Art as life, life as art

Continuing our tour of Buddhism and art, we'll amplify two concepts we'd introduced in surveying Buddhism in the West, in Part 1. First, seeing how our own culture reflects Buddhist ideas and ideals is a barometer for how Buddhism adapts to various cultures, in this case our own backyards.

As we explore Buddhism in our culture, we're also exploring here the idea of a continuing renaissance. Just as the revival of Greek and Latin in Italy in the fourteenth to sixteenth century contributed to one of Civilization's

Greatest Hits, called the Renaissance ("new birth"), so, too, might the West's relatively recent study of Sanskrit and Chinese be molding Renaissance II. Thus, some call our era the Pacific Century.

I know, the words "renaissance" and "culture" can sometimes conjure up all sorts of dreary, pretentious nonsense. Don't worry. Buddha's Museum of Art and the Great Buddhist Novel are all open for interpretation, 24/7 (24 hours a day, 7 days a week). Buddhist culture's way cool. Check it out!

But ... Is It Art? And ... Is It Buddhist?

A major theme of this chapter is borders. (No, not the bookstore.) Or lack of borders, to be more precise. There's really no border between art and life (often called a "frame"). And therefore not between art and Buddhism either (since dharma teachings are all about life; their meaning's not to be found outside of life). This border is akin to that between high and low culture, an illusory divide here, too, as we see from Shakespeare's plays, often full of enough action and romance to please the general public, while a few pointed remarks weren't lost on the elite patrons up in the balcony, and enough for everyone in between. Yet for years, people threw away woodcuts by the great Buddhist master Hokusai because they were made in mass production and sold for a pittance, often winding up as lining to pack boxes. (Is the price the value?)

Moving beyond borders, consider the similarity between spiritual practice and art. *Appreciation* of beauty and truth takes us out of our sense of a bounded, limited self. Sharpening our *perception* of reality awakens our hearts and minds to What Is, within and without. And making our *imagination* active is certainly an important spiritual dimension, though often overlooked. There's obviously no border between the sacred and art when we see religious paintings and sculpture, illustrations to sutras, and the sutras themselves. But Dharma also suffuses culture and its artifacts like an intangible fragrance or morning mist, rather than anything solid like the columns erected by King Ashoka. As philosopher Friedrich Nietzsche said, "Soundlessly, on doves' feet, they make their way amongst us—the ideas that change the face of the earth." This can lead to some interesting detective work.

Let's say we're walking through a museum of art, and our guide points out how a landscape painting has a low horizon line, emphasizing more sky, to give a feeling of spaciousness. Some of us beginning Buddhists might say to ourselves, "Aha! Sky represents emptiness, sunyata." But does this mean the painter was Buddhist? If not, can't the picture still be Buddhist anyway? Like the wide, blue sky, truth is everywhere. A quote by John Cage is relevant here: "We open our eyes and ears seeing life each day excellent as it is." Which begs the question, "Does art facilitate this realization?"

Consider Andrew Goldsworthy. His medium is the environment itself: ice, leaves, stones. As documented in the film *Rivers and Tides*, his creations include a large dome of driftwood, for the tides to play with and disassemble. Or gigantic snowballs, left to melt on London streets, revealing natural objects embedded inside. With a "don't-know" mind, he works by trial and error, his art often collapsing in his hands before nature even gets a chance to reclaim it.

Perishable sculpture. Art of the impermanent, using eternal elements of life.

Or consider artists Richard Long and Hamish Fulton, whose art consists of taking walks, communing with nature. As documentation, museums show photos of things done along their journeys. Are they Buddhist pilgrimages? Moreover—is it art?!

Hear and Now

"Zen students understand that the conclusion of Zen is daily life; but there is one more stage—that is Art."

—Sokei-an (a.k.a. Sasaki Soshin, 1892–1945)

First things first. Sleuthing the spiritual in art, let's take as fact that art's a formal expression of a feeling or idea. (Formal, as in "form no different than emptiness.") The skillful communication of a perception, conception, or understanding. (Skillful, as in skillful means.) And this fact has roots in sacred origins. Rewind back: 10 to 24 millennia ago. Our human ancestors painted animals on the walls of caves, expressing their awesome, transpersonal interrelationship with the universe.

Now flash forward through Western civilization, to the twelfth century. A continuity of such selfless artistic expression ends with the shift in emphasis upon the individual and self-expression (a legacy from the Renaissance). The greatest experiment in individuality would be America, founded upon Puritanism and Calvinism, which rejected pictures from the church, and spread that austerity to the rest of everyday life. After that blow to the head, the Technological Revolution dealt devotional art a massive body blow: standardization and mass media. The telegraph, for example, was dedicated to messages of commercial or military matters rather than anything like devotional poetry, which dwindled away like a faded blossom. Dit-dot-dot dash …

Catching up with the present, however, we find renewed interest in devotional poetry and art (Rumi and Georgia O'Keefe, for instance), and the beginnings in the West of adopting and adapting spiritual traditions of the East. Renaissance II draws away from self-expression and back to selfless expression. More specifically, we can see Eastern tradition in the revolutions of modern art: subjective impression as well as objective expression ("see for yourself"); movement away from isolation, permanence, the independent self, and fixed frames (the mind flows); and new emphasis on a decentered subject, and the environmental space around it. And even no subject, evidenced by such artists of pure light as Richard Irwin and James Turrell.

Now, for some working criteria to mindfully appreciate contemporary spiritual art, consider these three categories suggested by Asian art scholar Ananda K. Coomaraswamy:

1. Phenomenal (objective/outside world; "no ideas but in things")

2. Mental/Imaginative (subjective/inner world; "only the imagination is real")

3. Consciousness (spirit/mind; "everything is buddha")

The first is like the painting of grapes so lifelike a bird might peck at them. The second is like a semi-abstract painting, making us reach inside for its meaning. Combining the two, you might get the painting of two gigantic, floating, red lips, formed of clouds at sunset. Or something seemingly obvious, like the birds of Morris Graves.

The painter uses a bird to speak for himself, and so for us. In the top figure, the bird's attention is riveted on the snail shell. (Anybody home inside?) In the bottom figure, seeker and sought are close together, of similar substance and shape as well as size. Neither drawn from life nor symbolic, there's nothing beyond the bird, beyond the snail, beyond the beet. Just this, endless life, thus, just so.

Morris Graves, Bird and Snail, *sumi-e, 1950;* Bird and Beet, *pastel, 1979. Private collections.*

The spiritual in art is a mindful mirror of the origin, workings, and ultimate experience of our own consciousness. It shares our own quest for the meaning of life and supports us in our journey. Such art calls us to personally seek its resonance within ourselves.

This is different than shuffling through a museum with a guide spelling everything out. It calls upon our own spiritual participation to fulfill its meaning, as co-creators. There may be as many different versions of such art as it has viewers or readers, but it's timeless in the same way that a sight is impermanent but seeing is timeless. Or in the way we each respond to some masterpiece like the Sphinx, or the rock garden at Ryoan-ji: each differently, yet each the same.

Here follow further clues to finding *awakening* in art. Keep an eye out for them as you journey on the path, and ask yourself: Does this journey have any borders?

Words for the Wordless: Buddhist Literature

Words and the Wordless aren't mutually exclusive. Yes, Buddhism dissolves the dualism born of language, but doesn't set up another dualism in its place, such as of silence vs. speech. Words have their place, as skillful means, such as a mantra or a koan. And "Please pass the chopsticks."

For example, Zen is often considered "anti-words," with its emphasis on silent meditation or illogical koan. In traditional Zen, however, one commemorates a stage of awareness or enlightenment with a short poem. Once a student answers a koan, the teacher might follow up by asking, "Now what's a verse to express that?" And the student makes up a poem, or draws from the monastery's commonplace book of "Zen verses," an album of classical poetry and folk proverbs. After all, the student could have gotten lucky, so the poem acts as quality-control inspection. (A great collection and study in English of Zen verses is *Zen Sand.*) Let's take a brief look at some other cool picks from the library.

Some Picks for a Buddhist Reading Group

Sutras make excellent reading, beginning with those of your chosen school of practice, plus their commentaries. The longest, the Avatamsaka, is three volumes, and poetically soars. The Heart Sutra, on the other hand, is so short as to be printable in Chinese on a teacup, and so good that Buddhists read it over and over throughout their lifetimes. Zen's *Gateless Gate* and Tibet's *Lives of the Mahasiddhis* make for great summer or winter reading to curl up inside. Closer to home, Roshi Robert Aitken has written his own Zen tales, *Zen Master Raven*, showing influence of Native American storytelling, as well. And Michael Wenger has been writing his own koans, currently *33 Fingers*, and counting. Numerous online sutras, commentaries, and texts are available for free at this book's internet adjunct, Dharma Door, which also has an evolving bibliography of selected Buddhist titles (http://awakening.to/books.html).

What about fiction? A novel takes time, and Buddhism is anything but escapism. But *Tale of Genji*, the first novel, was written by a Buddhist. Some popular, earlier representations of Buddhism in fiction include Hermann Hesse's *Siddhartha*, and Rudyard Kipling's *Kim*. Acceptance of Buddhism as a household word was later furthered through novels by J. D. Salinger (his Glass family saga, such as *Seymour, An Introduction*) and Jack Kerouac (*Dharma Bums*). Also recommended: *The Gary Snyder Reader*. And American author Charles Johnson has been writing fine Buddhist novels: In *Oxherding Tales*, slavery is a vehicle for exploring Eastern philosophy; *Middle Passage* is a sea adventure involving a fictional Buddhist African tribe; and *Dreamer* is based on the last years of Martin Luther King, Jr.

There are Buddhist detective novels, such as *Bangkok 8*; *Sherlock Holmes: The Missing Years*; and *The Skull Mantra*. And Tsai Chich Chung's *Wisdom of Zen* and *Zen Speaks* render Dharma as cartoons. But the literary genre cutting across high and low, sacred and profane, is poetry: where words can be looked at as if under a microscope. (Plus a heroine, say, doesn't have to be transported from Scene A to Scene C with changes of weather, wardrobe, etc.) The Chinese word for *poetry* literally means "temple of words." After all, didn't Jesus, Mohammed, and the Buddha all speak in pure poetry? Not meant to be read the same way you would a cereal carton.

Along the Path

American poets with affinities for Buddhism include Antler, David Budbill, Thomas Centolella, Jim Cohn, Diane di Prima, Kevin Davies, Norman Fischer, Allen Ginsberg, John Giorno, Susan Griffin, Sam Hamill, Steve Hirsch, Jane Hirshfield, Garrett Hongo, Lawson Fusao Inada, Robert Kelly, Joanne Kyger, Russell Leong, Peter Levitt, Jackson Mac Low, Michael McClure, Laura Moriarty, Kenneth Rexroth, Al Robles, Albert Saijo, Steve Sanfield, Leslie Scalapino, Andrew Schelling, giovanni singleton, Gary Snyder, Charles Stein, Chase Twichell, Amy Uyematsu, Anne Waldman, Lew Welch, Philip Whalen, and David Whyte.

Shakespeare is rich with Buddhism. ("A rose by any other name would smell as sweet." and "So shalt thou feed on Death, that feeds on men, / and Death once dead, there's no more dying then.") And, with or without sheep, Wordsworth can be very Buddhist. ("To sit without emotion, hope or aim, / In the loved presence of my cottage-fire, / And listen to the flapping of the flame, / Or kettle whispering its faint undersong.")

But I'm just cribbing from a sturdy Buddhist literary guide by R. H. Blyth (1898–1964), called *Zen in English Literature and Oriental Classics*, which even ferrets out the Zen of *Don Quixote*.

Now, of all genres of poetry, my pick for Most Buddhist would be … haiku.

One-Breath Meditation: Haiku

If you don't know what haiku are yet, ask kids. Just as recycling came to national consciousness through kids (taught it at school and then bringing it back home), so, too, have haiku found fertile soil in kids, who live naturally close to the subtle, vivid, wild mind of haiku. It's no wonder millions of kids are being taught haiku in school.

> ### This Is
>
> The most popular traditional Japanese poetic form is *tanka*, five lines (5-7-5-7-7 syllables, respectively). It also formed the basis for group composition of long sequences of linked verse (*renga*). The opening of a renga, the first three-liner (5-7-5 syllables), later took on a literary life of its own and became known as **haiku**. A haiku is a breezy, delicate, miniature impressionist sketch in words. (*Example:* "Islands … shattered bits in the summer sea." —Basho)

Kids are invariably flashing on life around them like fireflies. Haiku is an expression of such life-flashes. Awareness buzzings. Half on the page, and leaving the other half for the reader to fill in. Here are a few:

- Plum blossoms here, there—it's good to go north, good to go south.
- In the dark forest, a berry drops. … Splash!
- The old dog looks dazzled by the song of the earthworms.
- Seconds before the next sneeze; waiting. What a funny face!

(And the authors, respectively, are Buson, Basho, Issa, and Anonymous.)

They're printed here as one-liners, though they're often done in three lines, like this one by James W. Hackett:

> A bitter morning:
> sparrows sitting together
> without any necks.

Haiku originated in Japan, where there are many precise rules for them, which the West has been trying to adopt and adapt (not unlike our relationship with Buddhism, really). Sometimes this can be like holding a plant next to a rock and just hoping it will transplant, until enough suitable conditions are present, as now they seem to be.

The biggest misconception persists that a haiku is anything written in three lines of five syllables, seven syllables, and five syllables, respectively. That's okay for getting started, like training wheels, but not always necessary. Many practitioners prefer three lines of two beats, three, and two, respectively. What's important is paring the words down to the bone. And that resonates with counting breaths in Buddhist meditation, 1 2 3 4, returning to the simplest things, again and again.

Here are five general haiku basics. 1) Like photographs, or mini home videos, they're about real, present-moment things. 2) They often give a sense of time (winter, noon, graduation day) and place (backyard, garage, secret waterfall). "Snowy hill," for example, indicates both time and place. 3) They usually don't refer to the speaker (third-person narration). Buddhist art isn't self-expression, much less exhibitionism. 4) Subjects are drawn from nature, or human nature.

And 5) they often present two related images, leaving the connection to be made by the reader, as in this one, by Bashô: *A flash of lightning … and the jagged screech of a heron, flying through the dark*—here evoking the unity of heaven flashing and a bird's call in the night. Like a bell, it calls us to stop and return to our true home in the present moment.

Similarly, a haiku often has a little space in the middle where it breathes, like in the middle of the line, "To be or not to be, that is the question," or as in *"alone even when I cough."* (After "not to be" and after "alone.")

How does all that translate into Buddhism? Well, they're like hinges of form and emptiness, suchness and transparence (tathata and sunyata). That incompleteness factor, we've seen, is an expression of sunyata, and here highlights how nothing's separate. The space forces the reader to take a leap, make a mental flip, and connect.

At the same time, they're precise instances of bearing witness to nature's wildness. They treat reality as is, in its utter suchness, just so—not to mention oneness, impermanence, interbeing, compassion, and karma. And their being in the present moment is what Buddhism's all about!

Haiku are one-breath meditation; just that long. And by omitting "I" from their vocabulary, they demand an active awareness of nonself. Plus, being short but not small, they're hymns to the bigness of mere being. *Ants float down a river on a twig, singing.* (That's by Issa, whose Pure Land faith led him to hear Dharma in even the lowliest. He wrote more than 1,000 haiku about snails, fleas, flies, mosquitoes, etc.) Once bitten by the haiku bug, you'll probably want to try your hand at writing them, too. Here's a Buddhist art everyone can *do*.

How to Haiku

You can write a haiku a day because at least one happens each day, if you stay open for it. One of the charms of haiku is that you don't have to even think about being a "writer" (just like you don't have to *be* "Buddhist"). Amateurs welcome! Haiku *are* beginner's mind.

Now, you can't go after haiku with an elephant gun or a butterfly net, any more than you can *try* to become enlightened. Haiku only require: 1) mindfulness, 2) a notepad, and 3) a pencil (with eraser because you might get a haiku right on the first try, but you should get used to editing also being part of the process).

Haiku can be about a flash of lightning if that's something you experience where you live. Or buds, or bugs. Your town, or your toe. That is, they're about your own ordinary life. This is an important point in Zen: Enlightenment isn't some pie in the sky. Everyday mind is Buddha mind. Chopping wood and cooking rice.

Just as haiku appear in between the words, so too will you see them in between whatever's going on around you. Haiku are a skillful means for enriching and developing contemplative practice; opportunities to read the world as a text illustrating Buddhist truths about your own life, and spontaneous bells of mindfulness returning you to the wonderful present moment.

Three final tips. 1) *Pay attention.* Notice what you notice. 2) *Bear witness.* Don't dramatize or judge. Take your subject's point of view. 3) *Keep it simple.* Be concrete, vivid.

Just so you know that haiku don't have to be masterpieces, like the ones already quoted, here are two of my typically so-so haiku, both written during my lunch break walk today:

from out of nowhere …
one vine of ivy, creeping
into hollow tree trunk

life in the city …
taking a walk just to see
if the car's still there

(You're welcome to use the opener of either if you want a little nudge to get you started.)

The Eye in the Heart of the Heart

"Show me your mind," Bodhidharma asked Hui Ko (and us). And, *aha!*, we realize it's invisible, imageless, boundless, without fixed location. So how can anyone *show* buddha mind to anyone else? And yet Buddhism reveals a canon of visual art equal to Rembrandt and da Vinci, as mind-opening as it is eye-opening.

Drawing Attention: Drawing the Buddha

In traditional Buddhist art, devotion and enlightenment shine through the national cultural aesthetics of each school and each country. The West has become familiar with east Asian examples, while Tibetan or Mongolian paintings, masks, and bronzes are only recently being seen in the West. The bronzes are sublimely refined and uncannily lifelike. (The yab-yum reproduced earlier and the Tara in our last chapter are actually life-size.)

And the pristine, Baroque paintings (*tangka*), such as the Manjushri we've seen, are exquisitely vibrant icons of compassion. Dualism is both evoked and dissolved through a balanced symmetry that embraces difference. Compare the image of the Russian Christ and the Tibetan Buddha side by side in our chapter on interfaith. Two sides of the same selfless coin, each fuses analytical accuracy with elegance of movement. Such freedom found within strict guidelines hearkens back to pre-Renaissance arts in the West, when cathedrals and icons were completely anonymous works of devotion.

There's a curious side to some Tibetan art. Museums of fine art now commission Tibetan monks to construct on their premises such painstakingly meticulous mandalas as the *Wheel of Time* (*Kalachakra*), out of colored sand. It's a bit ironic to the nature of museums as repositories of permanence, everything with its neat descriptive tag, that, in the end, the monks ceremoniously scatter their masterpieces to the elements, in affirmation of the interpenetration and impermanence of all things. No less impermanent are their renowned, intricate multicolored sculptures carved out of ... butter!

The Way of the Brush: Zen Eye-Openers

On another side of the hall, as it were, is the art of the Zen brush. Consider the tools: hand-ground ink on rough brush applied to highly sensitive, porous paper. When you see art students in a museum, copying a work in their sketchbook, they use pencil or pen but seldom brush. That is, they're copying lines and forms, but, as Zen brush master Kazuaki Tanahashi puts it, "When you copy an Oriental piece of art, you attempt to copy the process—the posture, the way of holding the brush, the order of strokes, the way of putting pressure on paper, the brush moving in air, the breathing, feeling, and thinking."

With a Zen brush, training and craft are essential, yet heart and spontaneity are also paramount. (As for any tea-master or samurai, golf pro or classical music virtuoso.) At the slightest. The Zen artist becomes one with her or his subject matter (be it a mountain, a river, or a mere circle), its essence poised on the tip of the brush. (Hesitate here and the ink dries up. Hesitate in action and the ink will blot and spread on the extremely fibrous paper.) With blank mind, facing a blank page, the artist takes the leap and *Aha!* a single word, a single image, a single circle can be an unpremeditated discovery. And the work doesn't need a signature: The entire work is signature, an expression of the artist's unique mastery of selflessness.

The calligraphic Eastern words in our book are also interesting in that they're often pictures. So *reading* involves *seeing* as a direct means of making meaning, rather than through deciphering letters representing abstract sounds, (Language made visible, words become art.) And a reverse angle holds. Viewing classical Chinese and Japanese brush art, our seeing becomes a reading of the artist's brush mind. (Consider, again, the portrait of Bodhidharma, in our chapter on Zen, as well as its *enso*, and landscape of the fishing village.)

 **Hear and Now**

"In the Oriental calligraphic tradition, you are not supposed to touch up or white out a trace of your brush. Every brush stroke must be decisive; there is no going back. It's just like life. If each moment is our entire life, how dare we kill time? If each stroke is our entire breath, how dare we correct it?"

—Kazuaki Tanahashi, *Brush Mind*

Following a 15-year hiatus from making art, a friend gave Kazuaki Tanahashi some handmade cotton paper. "One day," he recalls, "without any definite intention, I drew a straight horizontal line across the center of a piece of paper. At the moment the brush would have moved to another stroke, something stopped me from adding anything. I had a feeling that what I wanted to express was all there—in the single line and in the space above and below. So I put down the brush .... As a calligrapher, I seemed to be stuck at stroke one."

Untitled one-stroke painting. From Brush Mind, *Kazuaki Tanahashi (Parallax Press, 1990).*

Zen calligraphy gives sunyata's limitless openness a chance to take a dip in the waves of form. Part of its formal art is in placement, often de-centered. (Think of Hamlet's line, "By indirection find direction out.") To depict a famous mountain, a painter might show just a face looking off into the fog at the unseen mountain. (The expression says it all.) We're shown relations as well as things. In the painting a little further on here, for example, the persimmon that's not in a row calls attention to the poses of the other five. Or Bodhidharma: seen from behind. And he's the same as the wall he faces: utter blank. Which brings us to space.

The Zen painter often uses space to call forth awakened mind, or sunyata (the undifferentiated, fertile void). (How do you show someone the sheen of the full moon, or of the enlightened mind, the awakened heart?) So what the West calls negative space, in the East becomes positive. Look again at the landscape of the fishing village. On first glance, you might think it looks unfinished (as life is). The canvas is intentionally unpainted, conveying cloudless sky, and flowing river. And we can sense twilight mist in the paler grays, as boats and birds find homes for the night.

Michelangelo was asked, "How did you create David? He replied, "I took a block of marble and chipped away everything that wasn't David." Lao-tzu said a potter can't make a bowl from clay without empty space. (Thus, you must have space inside yourself, in order for things to take place.) As in rock gardens, haiku, and Zen itself, the space as well as the thing being pointed at must be intuited within your own heart. (This effect is much like radio drama, which relied on the listener's imagination to fill in details. A young kid once told Norman Corwin, a writer of radio drama, that he preferred radio to movies. Why? "The pictures," he said, "are better.")

Seeing spirit in art means bearing witness to essence as a mutual dialogue. Let your gaze unfold the way you'd listen to music. Imagine the landscape of the fishing village becoming an internal portrait, a mental soundscape. Awakening your mind without fixing it anywhere, the artist will guide your awareness to the infinite and eternal in the immediate present, the picture right before your eyes. Here the essence of the painter, the natural object, and the viewer become one mind.

Curiously, portrait can become landscape, and vice versa. Bodhidharma can resemble a mountain, monumental, a force of nature, appropriate to his towering place in Zen history. And an imaginary terrain, such as a river flowing through glowing hills, can depict an interior landscape, as well. Landscape becomes human in-scape, rendering the invisible landscape of the mind's lofty peaks and deep valleys, twists and turns. So a seemingly plain picture of swimming fish, or persimmons, can be taken on different levels: literal, figurative, and ultimate.

(Next question: might the art of the Zen brush hold true, too, for brushing ... your teeth?!)

 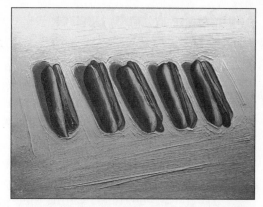

Two studies in suchness. Is-ness. On the left, a classic Chinese Zen brush painting of persimmons. Each with its own distinct, unique shape, texture, and sheen. Each a buddha ... placed just so. As fresh today as when painted. On the right, five hotdogs by a contemporary American painter. Each hotdog sits in its bun with its own personality. Each perfect thus. (The background in each: without horizon, empty.) And each persimmon and hotdog is so subtly interdependent, it's hard to choose just one.

Mu Ch'i, Six Persimmons *(1269). Ink on paper. 14" × 15". Daitokuji, Kyoto. Wayne Thiebaud,* Five Hot Dogs *(1961) Oil on canvas. 18" × 24". Private collection. Copyright Wayne Thiebaud/Licensed by VAGA, New York, New York.*

Art as Life: Life Is Art

When you meditate, you discover the source of all art within yourself. A fountain of images. The heart of creation. Art's presence in our landscape is a great reminder, encourager, teacher, sacred space (pure land). Thou Art That. Yet we needn't become attached to it. In the final analysis, what *isn't* art?

To end where we began in this chapter, Buddhism suggests it's not a matter of erasing boundaries between life and art, but rather observing them and recognizing boundaries are an illusion to begin with. For background, consider two key artists of the twentieth century, Pablo Picasso and Marcel Duchamp. Picasso, as we know, put two dots along the side of a nose, so the portrait faces front and sideways at the same time. In so doing, he takes the flat two-dimensional canvas and reproduces not only three dimensions but the fourth, time. Duchamp, on the other hand, went beyond paint entirely and concentrated on the mind behind the retina. In 1913 (about six years after Picasso began Cubism), he took a bicycle wheel, mounted it very nicely, and exhibited it as art. And why not? As Duchamp once said, "The only thing that is not art is inattention." And so we'll see next how Buddhism, *the art of attention*, questions any boundary between art and life.

Soundscape Without Horizon

Smack-dab in the middle of the twentieth century, an American composer named John Cage asked us all to consider life as art when he premiered his concert piece entitled *4'33"*, (pronounced "4 minutes, 33 seconds"). The pianist performing the work, David Tudor, sat down at the piano and played not one single note for precisely 4 minutes, 33 seconds. (Maybe you've heard this somewhere before?)

Actually, it's in three movements. And it can be played by any number and combination of instruments. Anyway, at its premiere, at the Maverick Concert Hall in Woodstock, New York, the back of the hall was open to the surrounding forest. During the first movement, you could hear the wind sighing through the trees. Light rain pattered on the roof during the second movement. And during the final movement, the audience whispered amongst itself, in counterpoint to the sound of other people exiting.

No two performances are alike. And once performed, it never ceases. Mind you, it's not some mere bagatelle just anyone can perform. I've seen an art student perform it very timidly, and it didn't quite work. But another time I saw a pianist in a tux perform it quite well, and still remember the high sound of a bus turning a corner as a girl's wooden heels tapped out a faint metronome on the street, outside, as a few people inside rustled in their seats like autumn leaves, and a generator hummed. The generator was the keeper: Who would have thought such an ugly-seeming sound could be art!? What overtones lurk unnoticed in its electronic hum! It took shedding my prejudices to hear it, as it is. And so I began to listen to my hearing itself, tuning in to the sheer act of attention.

Leaves from the Bodhi Tree

In 1946, John Cage learned Indian musical counterpoint from Gita Sarabhai, who told him that in her country the purpose of music is to quiet the mind. He later attended D. T. Suzuki's lectures on Buddhism at Columbia University for two years. The year before composing *4'33"* he visited Harvard's new soundproof chamber and was surprised to discover he heard his nervous system (high sound) and his blood flow (low). He realized the difference between silence and sound is awareness, or intention, and spent the rest of his life creating music without personal intention, in order to stimulate awareness.

Cage came to see music "not as communication from the artist to an audience, but rather as an activity of sounds in which the artist found a way to let the sounds be themselves." This could then "Open the minds of the people who made them, or listened to them, to other possibilities than they had previously considered .... To widen their experience; particularly to undermine the making of value judgments." In this way, he aligned the purpose of his art with meditation's goal of changing habitual mind-sets.

This is like the unintentionalness of haiku. That is, you don't go out of your house declaring, "Today, I'm going to write a haiku about dogs." That creates an unnecessary gap between writer and dogs, thought and reality, as two separate things. Haiku *happen*, like the sound of a berry falling in a stream. Or the sound of the refrigerator. The sight of the morning star. Or a bug.

And it's about time. Think of all the tragic lives spent chasing after some lofty ideal called Art, up on some pedestal in an airless museum. From the moment David Tudor first opened a piano to play *4'33"* and didn't press a single key, artists no longer had to create timeless objects of art: what a relief! Critics, grasping for labels, called this new approach "formless." But such art is shapely because mind and life are shapely.

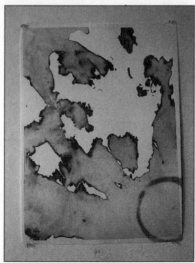

Printer Larry Hamlin with John Cage in the Crown Point Press studio, 1986. John Cage, Eninka 26, 1986. One in a series of 50 smoked paper monotypes with branding printed on gampi paper chine collé. Published by Crown Point Press. "Eninka" is Japanese for "circle, stamp, fire." These etchings were created by setting fire to newspapers, putting the fire out by running the press across them, laying a piece of special Japanese paper on top, and running that through the press. Then the paper was branded with an iron ring. (The circle echoes the Zen enso; see Chapter 12). Utterly non-representational, the work has a perfect naturalness of form, as of a pavement being painted by raindrops. Yet it was created under very controlled conditions: the number of newspapers, the duration of the fire, the placement of the ring, the strength of its mark (its temperature) were all predetermined by tossing coins— "imitating nature in her manner of operation," as Cage liked to say, quoting St. Thomas Aquinas.

Photographs: Kathan Brown and Colin McRae

> **Leaves from the Bodhi Tree**
>
> In 1961, visitors to an art gallery were led by Yoko Ono to each piece of hers on exhibition there. For each work, she'd give them instructions. For *Smoke Painting*, for instance, the viewer was asked to burn the canvas with a cigarette and watch the smoke; the piece was finished when the canvas had turned to ashes. Many of her works are instructions, whose printed form she considers visual art, "painting to be constructed in your head," such as her *Lighting Piece, 1955: Light a match and watch till it goes out.* (The flame is never the same twice. And who watches?)

No Borders to Erase

Life Art often bears a wry, wacky Zen humor. In a 1966 piece called *Postman's Choice,* for instance, artist Ben Vautier dropped a postcard in a mailbox. On one side, it was addressed to a friend, and to another friend on the other side, with stamps on both sides. The postman (life) thus became part of art. This was part of a movement called Fluxus (great name), with ideas often evoking koans, and whose antics often resembled "Zen vaudeville." Korean artist Nam June Paik, for another example, proposed having an adult seated in lotus posture on top of a baby carriage, pushed by another adult or several children through a shopping mall or some calm street. He called his instructions *Zen for Street.*

Around this time, Allan Kaprow founded a Zen environmental performance art called a *happening.* The word crept its way into common vocabulary, but does anyone remember his wondrous explanation at the time? "Not satisfied with the suggestion through paint of our other senses, we shall utilize the specific substances of sight, sound, movement, people, odors, touch. Objects of every sort are materials for the new art: paint, chairs, food, electric and neon lights, smoke, water, old socks, a dog, movies, a thousand other things which will be discovered …"

Amen. Sometimes we need artists to remind us of things Buddhist teachers only imply, such as the importance of *imagination,* and the *continual nature of practice* and its limitless *applicability throughout our everyday life.* Buddhism is an art. An art of awakening … into freedom.

The Least You Need to Know

♦ Buddhism returns us to long traditions of selfless, Western sacred art that diminished following the Renaissance.

♦ There are numerous examples of literature expressing Buddhism. If "poetry says it best," then haiku may be Buddhism's ideal literature.

♦ Haiku are as much a way of life as an art. There's no bar to entry. Anyone can see, write, and appreciate haiku.

♦ When Buddhists express their devotion and enlightenment through pictures, it shines through the national cultural aesthetics of each school. Appreciation of this devotion and enlightenment can be an act of meditation.

♦ Contemporary artists in the West are becoming influenced by Buddhism. One way Buddhist liberation is manifesting itself is in the blurring of the boundary between life and art.

Chapter 20

Within and Without: Buddhism and the Sciences

In This Chapter

- ◆ New science reappraising old worldviews
- ◆ Fuzziness, chaos, and complexity
- ◆ Holistic healing: body, spirit, and mind
- ◆ Buddhist psychology
- ◆ Mind/body and mind/mind interrelations

Art is ranked one of our highest human expressions, but takes the back seat when riding with science, which has become a kind of gold standard of truth in our day. Traditionally, art and science are set in opposition to each other. But that's dualistic thinking. Science and art are both constructs of mind, which is one with all things. Buddhism is proving to be a perfect place for the two to have dialogue. As we'll see, they have much to say to each other.

Buddhism's an art, to be discovered, practiced, and expressed by each person differently. So, too, is it a science. You could say the Buddha conducted an experiment he invites others to test (it's unbiased) with the evidence of their own senses (it's empirical) and prove for themselves (it's replicable). So the Buddhist outlook is highly scientific. And the neat thing is you don't need a rocket ship or atom-smasher. You can use yourself as the subject of your investigation. Your meditation is your laboratory. Instead of test tubes, arc lamps, and filter paper, you can utilize a bell, incense, and flowers.

Here are some of my lab notes, from the science of happiness: Buddhism, the joyous science.

New Physics and Ancient Eastern Thought

Buddhism is a very scientific method. And, like science, it has different schools of approach. Theravada takes a methodical manner of observation and inquiry. Doing this, we'll see such insight into such will produce thus-and-such. Zen emphasizes intuition, that *Eureka!* moment when a scientist makes a breakthrough to a new view. Pure Land emphasizes the relationship of the bounded human realm within the limitless cosmos. And Vajrayana is like Theravada in its emphasis on orderly, methodical process. It takes the molecule labeled (or mislabeled) "ego," previously analyzed under the vipassana electron microscope, and runs it through a particle accelerator.

To compress science and Buddhism into one chapter, let's divide our journey into three convenient stages: 1) the physical world (matter), 2) mind and matter, and 3) mind. Until recently, physical sciences were all there were. Up until 1900, science thought it had explained 99 percent of the universe. But it's that darned last 1 percent that's opened up a can of worms for scientists. Details! As microscopes zero in with greater and greater detail, more and more things are popping up on the invisible atomic and subatomic levels that contradict everything known up until now. And telescopes reaching farther and farther out are finding not only enigmatic black holes but also impenetrable "dark matter" suggesting that the visible world analyzed so far may comprise only 10 percent of the real universe. A scientific revolution is underway.

Holism: Keep Your Eye on the Doughnut AND the Hole

To begin, let me explain how a scientific revolution is underway. ("Scientists in berets are seizing control of the laboratory in the name of the people! Free cyclotrons for everyone!") It would be more accurate to call it a *paradigm shift*, a change in viewpoint. As Sir Arthur Eddington explained it, "We used to think that if we knew one, we knew two, because one and one are two. We are finding that we must learn a great deal more about 'and.'"

This Is

A paradigm is a framework of ideas and tools that make up a worldview, a mind-set, an exemplar of reality, a foundation and framework. If some reality isn't included in your paradigm, you won't see it until you shift your paradigm. If you've only walked and then learn to ride a bike, you'll see the world in a new way. A **paradigm shift** takes time to be realized and to resolve itself in society as a whole, affecting many walks of life as it does so.

It's important to realize how deeply our basic assumptions (paradigms) color our notions of reality. Was it coincidence that when science saw the universe as concentric spheres revolving around the earth, the model for society was a similar hierarchy, revolving around a king and his medieval court? Similarly, the same time as Newton described atoms with fixed properties, Western democracy was describing citizens as autonomous entities with inalienable rights.

We ourselves can only glimpse the paradigm of our era, and its shift, as it's so big we're intrinsically as caught up within it as fish within water. But we can get a glimpse. On the one hand, science has smashed the atom, and the nuclear family has been breaking down. No wonder people often find it hard to take things seriously. Our civilization's worldview, which does a good job at dividing things up, has broken reality down into so many bits that our world is as fragmented as shattered pottery, or a TV with 50,000 channels. Meanwhile, the paradigm is a-changing—from a *mechanistic* point of view that breaks everything down into parts and analyzes each separately, to a *holistic* view that looks at how parts interrelate to form wholes. Favoring process over product. *How*, over *what*. As it does so, it seems to move toward the Buddha's paradigm of life. As we've seen, Buddhism doesn't treat the universe as a collection of isolated, separate things but, rather, as interconnected events forming a web of karma, a multidimensional, interdependent network. Interacting and interbeing.

Hear and Now

"All concepts, such as causation, succession, atoms, primary elements ... are manifestations of the mind."
—Buddha

"Physical concepts are free creations of the human mind, and are not, however it may seem, uniquely determined by the external world."
—Einstein

As we'll see next, twentieth-century revolutions in Western science have had fascinating parallels with Buddhist thought. For example, Buddhism's grasp of the interpenetration of time as well as space anticipated the space-time continuum. When Einstein proposed that matter is energy, and energy is matter, he was echoing a Buddhist principle: "Form and phenomena have no unique identity beyond boundless energy; and boundless energy manifests itself to us as phenomena and form." No coincidence: Einstein had studied the Buddha's teachings, admiring his "covering both the material and spiritual … as a meaningful unity." Einstein was the first to crunch the numbers, so to speak.

Hear and Now

"If we ask … whether the position of the electron remains the same, we must say "no"; if we ask whether the electron's position changes with time, we must say "no"; if we ask whether the electron is at rest we must say "no"; if we ask whether it is in motion, we must say "no." The Buddha has given such answers when interrogated as to the conditions of a man's self after his death; but they are not familiar answers for the tradition of seventeenth- and eighteenth-century science."

—J. Robert Oppenheimer

Science soon came up against the limitations of its own vocabulary to describe what it saw as it advanced as far as the atomic and subatomic levels. For example, one test proved that light was composed of waves, and not particles, while another test proved that light was particles, not waves. (Paradigms, in action.) Physicists had to make up the word "complementarity" to discuss its being waves *and* particles (rather than call them "wavicles"; I guess they'd never heard of the Middle Way … much less a certain dessert topping that's also floor wax).

As they refined their tools, some saw the Buddha's footprints already traversing the terrain. Early Buddhists unequivocally stated the universe is made not only of particles but also *sub*atomic particles; to make this discovery, they required only observation of their own mind (and much free time). ("I." Am. A. Series. Of. Events. Divisible. Into. Sub-events. And. Sub-sub-events. E. Z.!) And their sense of the actual scale of sub-atomic levels coincide with science's measurements. Uncanny!

Another breakthrough in physics that reconfirmed what mystics had been saying for millennia is the *Uncertainty Principle*. Werner Heisenberg discovered that you can't measure both location and direction of a subatomic particle simultaneously, because the measuring tool enters into the equation. *Aha!* Interbeing in action: "This is be-cause that is." The electron's there because I'm over here. Observation affects func-tion. (Hence the need for Right View.)

How can we know the dancer from the dance? To the Buddha, that would be like try-ing to explain the origin of the universe. Yet now that scientists have taken on the challenge, measuring, some interesting spiritual implications are emerging. For instance, the beginning of the expanding universe is still beginning. Marvelous! Ten billion years later, as the universe fans out from the primordial foam or OM of origin, the expansion continues; its wavelength has increased a mere 2 millimeters. In your very own living room you can see the original photons of the Big Bang, on your TV screen. What great news for all beginners: The beginning itself is still beginning!

Hear and Now

"One finds in the realm of experience, essentially the same type of structure that one finds in the realm of elementary particle physics, namely a web structure, the smallest elements of which always reach out to other things and find their meaning and ground of being in these other things. Since this same type of structure is suitable both in the realm of mind and in the realm of matter, one is led to adopt it as the basis of an over-all world view."

—Henry Pierce Stapp

Newer breakthroughs in physics further reconfirm ancient Buddhist truths. For example, a *hologram* can create a 3-D mirage in midair; pretty neat! A sculpture made of light. Now, the really interesting thing is that if only half of the negative were used, you'd still see the full image, only a little dimmer. Using just a tiny corner, you'd still have the entire object, only dimmer still. That is, the entirety of information about the whole is distributed throughout the surface of the holographic negative. Remarkable. Any part leads to the whole.

To generalize our new paradigm, we might say it's the relation of matter and mind. Up until now science has been like a tree whose trunk is the study of physics ("This is a rock, you got a problem with that?"). Now the study of matter alone is no longer enough. We might paraphrase physicist Fritjof Capra in contrasting the old paradigm of building and taking apart substance, organizing life into *parts and particles,* substances and molecules—with the new paradigm of observing *interrelationships* within and between *patterns forming wholes.* The new trend is not to focus on stuff or parts but rather how they come to make living systems. The process rather than the product. How over what. This takes a network as its model rather than any static, fixed structure (such as ladder or chain). As the Buddha said:

> As a net is made up of a series of ties, so everything in this world is connected by a series of ties. If anyone thinks that the mesh of a net is an independent, isolated thing, he is mistaken. It is called a net because it is made up of a series of interconnected meshes, and each mesh has its place and responsibility in relation to other meshes.

There's interesting Buddhist convergence with science here. A mere fraction of a holograph projects the whole the way a bead on Indra's net of beads reflects all the other beads. One object or instant contains all others. Something as small as a hair tip contains millions of Buddha realms, each containing bazillions of subatomic Buddha realms, each a perfect pure land. We're each a body of light, whose innate radiance is reflecting and interpenetrating with each other in one vast, radiant 10-dimensional mandala of light (Indra's Net). (A still unproven but interesting avenue of note, too, is Superstring Theory, which holds that this is but 1 of 10 parallel universes. Stay tuned.)

As paradigms shift they can affect everything from art to "ego," from architecture to how you time your eggs. Here's a quick tour of three practical applications emerging from the new paradigm, each with a dash of Buddhist wisdom. Think: fuzzy, chaos, and complexity.

Middle-Way Logic, Fractal Buddhas, and Dharma Systems: Fuzzy, Chaos, and Complexity

With complementarity, Western science felt the limits of Aristotelian "either/or" logic. (Something's either this or that, but not both. For example, electricity's either on or off. Hence the Digital Revolution: all ones and zeros.) Toward the end of the last century, a new branch of science opened shop in the gray areas, appropriately called fuzzy logic. Fuzzy thinking is ready for questions like "Growing a beard—or just not shaving?"

Japan, a culture based more on the Buddha's Middle Way than on Aristotle's Either-Or, gained about a five-year lead on the West in exploring and applying fuzzy logic to actual product features. Today, fuzzy logic's programmed into some brands of camcorders, cars, and nuclear power plants. And scientists are discovering that fuzzy, gray areas can occur anywhere from 0 to 100 percent.

Chaos: There's a Method in the Madness

Another new science is called *chaos theory*, studying the orderly patterns of what previously seemed merely grainy, in between, pimply, pocky, seaweedy, wiggly, wispy, and wrinkled. (Sounds like they're studying my uncle Melvin!) For example, a formula for plotting the seemingly random pattern of the outline of clouds matches a formula for plotting the seemingly random pattern of coastlines. *Aha!* So how random is random, after all?

Chaos theory says, no, there are patterns to randomness, wildness, chaos. Such natural patternings (cloud shapes, coastlines, mountain outlines, broccoli, ferns, etc.) are mapped with a *fractal*, representing a fractional dimension, as between 1 and 2, or 2 and 3. This is interesting from a Buddhist perspective (the Middle Way). What was once thought to be chaos can really be quite orderly, like the "controlled accident" of Zen—the way gardens always have an odd number of stones or trees, because asymmetry looks more natural … or the way a teacup has a drip in its otherwise perfect glaze. Conversely, too high a degree of structure can ultimately look like goo; a warning to all control freaks.

Chaos theory upsets the paradigm of an orderly universe running like clockwork with perfect linear cause-effect relationships. Consider the Butterfly Effect, in which a single butterfly flapping its tiny wings in a Brazilian rain forest can cause a rainstorm in Texas. This is possible because the essentially chaotic motion of the earth's atmosphere can amplify small disturbances into long-range, long-term behavior. So a practical example of fractals is the realization that one outburst of anger, say, can ripple out in a whole domino effect, way beyond the seeming cause. Or a small act of generosity can spread to a similar extent.

And in showing us the underlying orderly patterns of seeming chaos, a fractal can reveal underlying orderliness of seemingly chaotic shapes in what's called their *self-similarity*. For instance, the jagged edge of just a chunk of cloud will be similar in shape to that of the entire cloud. A bud of a cauliflower has the same pattern as the whole veggie. The whole is similar to itself at varying levels of scale. And this is true for mountains as well as coastlines. Lightning and ferns. Fantastic. Touch one part deeply, and you see the whole. This reflects interbeing in action. Buddha nature is visibly coherent on all levels.

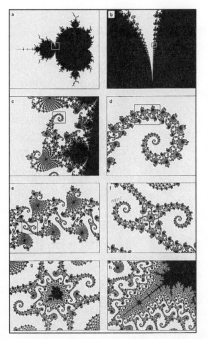

Start with a basic fractal pattern (upper left square), inherent throughout nature, called a Mandelbrot-set. A small sector of it is enlarged (b), revealing a new sublevel, varying the underlying pattern. Isolating fragments further (shown here, six more levels) reveals an infinite series, infinitely connected, self-similar on all levels.

From The Science of Fractal Images, *Heinz-Otto Peitgen and Dietmar Saupre, editors (Springer-Verlag, 1988).*

Now this middle way between order and chaos is called *complexity*. And it's here where you're most likely to find viable patterns for life.

Complexity: It's Basically Simple

Based on chaos study, *complexity theory* looks at living systems and their evolution as a process of interaction. The key word here is *inter*-action. Reaction only goes from A to B, whereas interaction represents ongoing communication between A and B (perhaps also with the environment C, plus factors D, E, and F).

Just as science finds chaos (nature) isn't at all random, it's finding complexity is composed of really simple things, but *organized* in ways that enable the diversity necessary to adapt to unpredictability and change, thus essential for all living systems). Self-organization is such a model. An example is Buddhism: created from the interaction of simple components, such as are enumerated on our Reference Page, dynamically evolving as a self-organizing complex system for each practitioner, and groups of practitioners (sangha), and their environments.

We've also seen how Buddhism maintains its integral core while evolving through interaction with various cultures *(self-similarity)*. And in our chapter on relationships, we've touched on the Buddhist principle of mutual interaction, complexity in action, with you at the center of the universe … interlinked with all of creation … everything and everyone else equally at the center of the universe … all moving toward unlimited freedom.

There seems to be an evolutionary trend in complexity, with what's called *emergent behavior* arising out of complexity, and which leads in turn to further diversity, complexity, and higher levels of emergent behavior. Indeed, the ultimate example of a complex system is life. Matter is an emergent behavior formed out of a diversity of subatomic particles. Some carbon comes in contact with a few, simple, basic ingredients, and *Shazam!* it's alive. (Watch it evolve!) As it develops in complexity, feelings emerge. Out of feelings emerges consciousness. Besides consciousness (which is nice), we've evolved the power of self-aware observation. As Wes Nisker puts it so well: "Mindfulness is the opposable thumb of consciousness."

So we come next to topics of scientific inquiry dealing with the nonphysical as well as the physical, such as "What is consciousness?" "Is there a mind-body connection?" and "Where'd I put my keys?"

Hear and Now

"Nothing novel can come from systems with high degrees of order and stability, such as crystals. On the other hand, completely chaotic systems, such as turbulent fluids or heated gasses, are too formless. Truly complex things—amoebas, bond traders, and the like—appear at the border between rigid order and randomness."

—John Horgan, *From Complexity to Perplexity*

Infinite Healing: Dr. Buddha

In the Buddha's day, medical knowledge was called *ayurveda*, meaning "life knowledge" (a very viable system still practiced today, Dr. Deepak Chopra being a well-known exponent). As a prince, he'd studied such medicine but chose not to be a specialist. Instead, he became a general practitioner, in the widest sense. Having seen how his teachings are good medicine, now we can better appreciate how his prescription might differ from what a general physician might prescribe. In a word, it's *holistic*.

Body Dharma: Healing the Whole Person

Interestingly, *medicine* and *meditation* come from the same Latin root (*mederi*, "to cure"). Traditional medicine favors a mechanistic model: compartmentalized and cause-and-effect. Have a headache? Here, take some aspirin. (Of course, eventually you'll need to take three instead of two, then extra-strength, and so on.) And you might have to see a gastroenterologist (stomach doctor) if aspirin causes you a stomachache. I'm exaggerating, slightly, but what if your headache was caused by posture? As the Buddha pointed out, if the roots of disease aren't addressed, illness will only reoccur in innumerable forms. (Commonly overheard patient's exclamation in a doctor's office: "But I thought we'd already taken care of that!")

Holistic medicine (also known as alternative, complementary, or integrative medicine), on the other hand, might begin by looking at underlying factors that cause headaches, such as posture, diet, stress, and escape valves from stress such as alcohol. And it would treat the whole person: body, spirit, and mind, equally. So for bad posture it would be appropriate to examine spiritual and emotional attitudes. Thus Dr. Dean Ornish, for example, has reversed incidents of heart disease with a regimen focusing on consciousness and behavior as well as diet.

It's interesting to note that in Greece, at around the same time as the Buddha taught, a man named Hippocrates (from whom we get medicine's Hippocratic Oath) seemed in tune with the Buddha when he trusted the body's innate powers of self-healing and defined health as a harmonious interaction of factors. And his oath, "Physician, heal thyself," echoes the Buddha's radical invitation for fellow seekers to investigate their findings using themselves as subjects.

Different Schools, But All Heal

Let's see how different Buddhist meditations can furnish good medicine. In some representations, the Buddha's bowl isn't for alms, but contains medicine; one for every human illness. Similarly, each school of practice has different emphases. Theravada literature recounts how the Buddha cured himself of severe illness during his final retreat. "With patience and without distress," it is said, he was mindfully aware of his painful physical sensations, and then they no longer occurred. That is, he noted the momentary nature of the painful sensations, breaking them down into segments, seeing the unsubstantial, impermanent, and nonseparate nature of each, and they went away. The primary sutra for practice here would be *The Four Establishments of Mindfulness*.

Mahasi Sayadaw has recorded cases of mindfulness leading to disintegration of tumors as well as elimination of arthritis and asthma. At the University of Massachusetts Medical Center (UMMC), a major American hospital, such teachings are simply called *stress reduction*. As with emotional intelligence, the traditional Buddhist form and vocabulary are removed. But as HH the Dalai Lama once said, "There are four billion people on the planet. One billion are Buddhists, but four billion are suffering.

The facts speak for themselves. The Mindfulness-Based Stress Reduction program (MBSR) which Dr. Jon Kabat-Zinn established at UMMC more than twenty years ago has been adopted by 240 other medical centers. Stress reduction (meditation) is being prescribed for all kinds of symptoms, many of which don't have easily identifiable sources, such as high blood pressure, heart disease, cancer, infertility, premenstrual syndrome, and psoriasis, as well as depression, hyperactivity, and attention-deficit disorder. The high records of success include not only positive changes in behavior normally believed unchangeable, but also positive physical changes. Less stress *is* best.

From a Mahayana perspective, the bodhisattva vow defines our own healing in terms of the healing of others. Here's one gatha for this you might try sometime: *Breathing in, I heal myself; breathing out, I heal others.*

Hear and Now

"These people have cancer, AIDS, chronic pain. If we think we can do something for them, we're in deep trouble. But if you switch frames of reference and entertain the notion that they may be able to do something for themselves if we put very powerful tools at their disposal, things shift extraordinarily."

—John Kabat-Zinn

A Zen approach identifies with neither illness nor health but the boundlessness and interpenetration of both. Zen patriarch Yun-men said, "Medicine and sickness mutually correspond. The whole universe is medicine. What is the self?" As Buddhist author Rick Fields said during his noble confrontation with cancer, "I don't have a life-threatening illness, I have a disease-threatening life." (Amen.) Visualizing a disease as being part of sunyata doesn't set up within the body the barbed wire of self versus other. Sometimes attacking a disease too violently causes only more damage. A Buddhist approach would be to continually recognize the interbeing of a disease and a host, and daily to politely invite it to leave.

Tibetan Buddhism has a large repertoire of healing techniques, including guided meditations and visualizations. A meditation called *tumo*, for example, enables Tibetans to generate warmth in zero-degree weather, at will.

Before we look deeper at mind-body connections we've been noticing here, let's round off our tour of healing with what's still often called mental health, or psychology. Like our bodies, our feelings have a mind of their own, to which we can give space to let be, understand, and appreciate mindfully.

Do Feelings Have a Mind of Their Own?: Buddhist Psychology

Just as Einstein transformed our view of the objective world, so Freud did likewise for the subjective realm. Our inner world, as it were. Actually, each broke objective and subjective down into interrelated components, inviting a spirit of inquiry into their interaction, that continues to this day. Anyway, it's interesting how the Buddha's spirit of inquiry anticipates psychology, and how they inform each other.

The Buddha was a people-oriented scientist. He taught self-inquiry as a means of finding harmony and thus true joy. Just his first truth, that life entails suffering, is noble for humans to realize, yet it can be a very big hurdle. It's easy to fool oneself, and ignore the harsh fact that one's not really tuned in to the present, even though this ignorance perpetuates a vicious cycle of suffering, leading to further withdrawal from the now, and so on. A therapy originating in Japan called Morita just focuses on enabling its patients to encounter their duhkha, in a supportive environment, so that they can accept it and begin to examine alternative outlooks. This underscores a basic assumption in both psychology and Buddhism: that pain is natural but suffering (depression) can be a self-perpetuating illusion. Our basic nature is to be happy.

Similarly, the Buddha's explanatory second truth echoes within the lingo of pop psychology: hang-ups. We hang on, rather than go with the flow, and so get hung up. It seems illogical that not only pain but pleasure can cause us suffering. Yet sometimes it takes the intervention of mindfulness or psychology to teach us that it's true.

> **Along the Path**
>
> "Hold evenly suspended attention."
> —Freud
> "Awaken the mind, without fixing it anywhere."
> —Hui Neng

Both psychology and Buddhism, as healing arts teach us to recognize our unrealistic views, dis-identify with them, and be in the moment. Our needless baggage (hang-ups) keeps us from being open and available to life's potentials. Baggage here might be thought of as a thick shell. It was needed for self-preservation, once, but has since been outgrown, such as a swaggering manner that paid off in the sandbox but doesn't cut it anymore in the world of grownups—or a thick scar over a wound now long gone, such as a childhood trauma. Now it blocks intimacy with life.

Of course, generalizations have limitations. For one thing, there are more schools of psychology than of Buddhism. Still, we can see Buddhism critiquing psychology in interesting ways. In childhood, we weren't necessarily aware of our feelings, lacking training in emotional intelligence. And so childhood experiences can set down patterns of behavior that today we might wish to change. Yet psychology can grow attached to a person's story, and thus to self. It asks, "How can this script be changed?" Buddha asks "Are scripts necessary? How can consciousness itself be transformed, beyond self?" A traumatic episode of the past no longer has control when it's recognized that the self of that situation (the person abused or denied or withheld) no longer exists. Buddhist psychoanalyst Dr. Mark Epstein points out, "There is no true self waiting in the wings to be released."

Ram Dass states, "Western psychotherapy rearranges the furniture in the room. Eastern techniques help you get out of the room." From this perspective, some contemporary psychologists seek to adjust the self to better adapt to the world, whereas the Buddhist says there is no self, no difference between self and world, no dualism ("me," in here; the world, "out there"—stimuli, out there, sensations, in here). "Show me your mind," as Bodhidharma replied to the question, "How can I quiet my mind?" It's all Buddha mind.

Nevertheless, when Buddhism sailed West, it caught the winds of psychology in its sails, also coming into its own at the same time. Seeing that it can be a mistake to view Buddhism as a therapeutic technology, a tool to be manipulated for predetermined ends, we recognize Buddhism and psychology as both responsible paths. Practiced in tandem, from time to time, they can re-check if either path is becoming a dead-end. On a psychological level, being Buddhist isn't a license to become passive, or walk away from feelings; and becoming attached to meditation can be another form of narcissism. Both practices offer the space for recognizing emotions and letting them be, without identifying with them. Just as the Buddhist learns being *in* the world, not *of* the world, the practitioner of psychology recognizes ego (visible personality) without identifying with it, seeing how to *have* an ego without *being* one, molding it for maximum benefit and happiness in this world.

No Matter, Never Mind: Mind/Body Connections

We've moved from the physical trunk of Western science to the nonmaterial, with dharma as our guide. Let's proceed by considering the interrelation between the non-material and the material. Mind and body, for example. To do so, let's pick up the thread of stress reduction (meditation) and its ability to affect the whole person and look deeper. We'll take a peek at two branches of human science at the forefront of the new paradigm: cognitive science and neuroimmunology.

Mapping the Ineffable: Cognitive Science

In 1967, A Harvard Medical School professor named Dr. Herbert Benson found bio-logical explanations for what meditators have been seeing firsthand for thousands of years. To do so, he snuck 36 meditators into his lab, under cover of night—and found that meditation lowered their heart rates by three beats a minute. They used 17 per-cent less oxygen. And their brainwaves showed more signs of theta activity, associated with entering sleep, though they remained awake. Three years later, he published his findings as a seminal book titled *The Relaxation Response*, opening the doors wide for further studies (conducted in broad daylight). More recent research, for instance, has found that the portion of the brain that responds to physical pain (the anterior cingu-lated cortex) also responds to emotional pain. So though the hurt feels different, the brain sounds the same alarm for emotional pain as for physical. As the first noble truth says, there *is* suffering.

Moreover, a new field called *cognitive studies* has opened up, with fascinating results. For example, using sophisticated imaging techniques, they're finding an interesting difference between the right and left prefrontal cortex (behind your lower forehead). Brain activity on the right prefrontal cortex is associated with depression and up-tightness; the left, on the other hand, is accompanied by happiness and relaxation. Guess whose left prefrontal cortex activity is at the top of the tests? Buddhist medita-tors, of course. Moreover, meditation seems to actually reshape the brain. There's a threshold or "set point" beyond which emotions get out of control. Meditation can reset the set point.

Gut Feelings: Neuroimmunology

Just as cognitive science is interdisciplinary, so too are other sciences springing up, now that physiological systems are studied in interaction rather than in isolation. One thing doesn't change without transforming another.

Recent studies are showing how meditation boosts immunity (increasing antibody response). But this is no surprise to another field opening up new mind-body connections; *neuroimmunology*. Now it's being discovered how emotions create chemicals which affect health, positively or negatively (cortisol, for example, is created under stress and is linked with depression). And health generates emotions (such as how exercise produces endorphins, a hormone inducing happiness). Health and emotions each create feedback loops between identity and well-being, mind and body. Indeed, our immune along with our endocrine system is being thought of as a parallel neurology, "a chemical brain," so to speak. So when we have a "gut feeling," we really might be thinking deeply. (Same with belly breathing meditation.) We also see here a little further how recitation and visualization, as in Pure Land or Tibetan Buddhism, can literally affect our entire body.

This Is

Immunology is one of physiology's newest chapters. Established in the 1950s, it studies the immune system which, among other things, defines and defends self from enemy. Now it's discovering that the immune system, the endocrine system (glands and hormones), and the nervous system behave more like a *network* than isolated systems. Thus, a new science of **neuroimmunology** has been born. Your health is bound up with your sense of who you are, mind and body mutually influencing each other.

Putting cognitive science and neuroimmunology side-by-side and standing back a little, Western science seems to be finally opening borders, such as between emotions (heart) and mind (head), a division which never occurred to the East. Starting with the brain, we seem to be moving towards the heart, which in the East is synonymous with the mind. And heart is a general location which can be seen to be outside as well as inside, as we say, for example "in the heart of the wild." So let's wrap up by re-re-asking the Buddhist question "Where is the mind?" in the light of the new scientific paradigm.

Imagine, Just Imagine: Mind to Mind (Heart to Heart)

Who are we, really? From the way I was taught science as a child, I remember imagining my skull as a small executive office with a big desk, equipped with a video monitor and speakers, at which the mind sat. Aside from the video and speakers, this was pretty much the model in vogue for about five centuries, ever since a French philosopher named René Descartes said "I think, therefore I am." But is our gray matter really the throne of our mind?

A more current definition of mind echoes the Buddhist definition, as that which is aware. Some scientists now say mind simply represents the process of knowing, *cognition*, and isn't necessarily confined to the brain. Consider the buddha flower by my window, exchanging ions with the atmosphere: It knows when it's dark and light, knows when I add soil fertilizer to its water, and has a preference for Mozart and Bach. It *minds* when I don't feed it. It is aware of its environment and responds to it in a cognitive way.

> **This Is**
>
> In the worldview of the Buddha's time, the heart was the seat of *prana* (energy), *ojas* (vitality), and *atman* (true self). Consciousness wasn't situated in the brain, but in the heart. Vedanta sage Ramana Maharshi located "the seat of the soul" in the sinoatrial node of the heart, which controls the heartbeat. In Buddhist texts, the heart is a sense organ, perceiving thought and feeling. We call that perception "mind," (*manas*, Hindi; meaning "heart"). It perceives dharma the way our nose perceives smell. Emotional balance occurs when we're in touch with our own emotions (heart) or the hearts of others. (So we don't exchange Valentine's Day cards with pictures of human brains on them, either.)

And science is discovering, as we'll see next, that mind may not be in just one place. This is coming closer to Buddhist definition of mind as formless. And it backs up a realization that's common in meditation: "Hey, I'm not in my head! Yet I'm still alive!!" (Until this point, some people might have a hard time with their breathing and attention; feeling, for example, like an oboist whose head's about to burst.) Moreover, it underlines the Buddha's advice not to grasp after a thing called self, nor any independent world outside such self that would thus come along with it. (A package deal.)

Indra's Net: A Scientific Paradigm for Mind

So the mechanistic model, with its image of a foreman with his gloved hands on the levers of some central control panel (and don't ask what that little red button does), is giving way to a more holistic model, more like a network of networks, all internetworked, operating autonomously through the checks and balances of feedback loops. (This is what the word "internet" means, of course: the internetworked network of networks. Thus, it's no surprise that humans should have invented it sooner or later; complexity theorists might call it emergent behavior.)

In the network model, there's no center, top, nor bottom. Any node is defined by its relation to all the others, its interactions. The network can survive failure of separate nodes because energy or information can reroute along the many alternative paths.

And when one node of the network attains a greater degree of knowing, the other nodes can bootstrap up, sharing that new complexity.

So our mind's not in our brain, but is rather part of a whole network of awareness—maybe we're not confined to our body at all. Let's go there ...

> ## Hear and Now
>
> "The big breakthrough is to see mind as a process, not a thing. And the process is called cognition, which has given birth to the interdisciplinary study of cognitive science. The idea is that there is a process of cognition which is essentially the same as the process of life and implies that all living organisms are cognitive systems, down to the simplest cell."
>
> —Fritjof Capra

Neither Here nor There: Nonlocal Phenomena

Physicist David Bohm (1917–1992) called the universe's underlying networked nature *implicate order*. His colleague A. J. Bell discovered an example of it when he separated two electrons across enormous distances and changed one. *Bingo!* The other one changed instantly, and with no time for a signal to pass between them—unless the signal traveled faster than the speed of light, which would disobey a basic law of physics. A current scientific word coined to categorize such events is *nonlocal*, because they operate outside the normal bounds of space and even time.

Dr. Karl Pribram, for example, believes that memory is nonlocal. It doesn't seem to live in any one lobe or part of the brain (selective brain damage doesn't erase specific memories), but is rather distributed throughout the network of our nerve cells much in the same way an image is equally dispersed throughout a hologram. Indeed, the universe is looking more and more like one big hologram, or a tenth-dimensional mandala light show played out on Indra's net. Ourselves included.

"Awakening your mind without fixing it anywhere" implies the mind is nonlocal. ("Show me your mind.") A few other neat nonlocal phenomena include animals finding their way across incredible obstacles and distances, twins developing similar idiosyncrasies even when raised separately, visualizing faraway objects ("remote viewing"), and ... prayer.

Doctors have conducted scientific experiments ("a controlled, prospective, matched double-blind study") on intercessionary prayer. In one, a group of people prayed for a group of cardiac patients. To make it scientific, they included a second group of cardiac patients not being prayed for. Neither group knew which was the object of prayer. Well, the group being prayed for responded as if they'd been given a miracle drug. And only they did so, not the others. By now, there have been at least 150 such tests, all positive. Of course, rabbis, priests, imams, and flocks of the faithful have known all along that prayer works. Only, now it's being scientifically proven. ("Nine out of ten doctors agree …") So when we Buddhists generate metta, now you know we're really generating metta! When you're sick, pray. For yourself and others. And when you're not sick, pray. For yourself and others. Dedicate a meditation session to the health of someone in need. Prayer works.

Mind is formless. Boundless. Timeless. Healing. And quite intelligent, too.

Hear and Now

"There is no matter as such! All matter originates and exists only by virtue of a force. We must assume behind this force the existence of a conscious and intelligent Mind. This Mind is the matrix of all matter."

—Max Planck, Nobel Prize–winning father of quantum theory

The Least You Need to Know

♦ The Buddha's mode of thought applied the scientific method. But whereas Western science has centered itself on studying the interrelationships of matter and matter, Buddhists have studied the interrelationships of matter and matter, mind and matter, and mind and mind.

♦ New scientific findings confirm facts Buddhists have known for millennia, casting them in a new light. As science changes its model, or paradigm, it comes closer to embracing Buddhism in its model.

♦ Some new branches of science that harmonize with and illuminate Buddhism are fuzzy logic, chaos, and complexity; holistic health; psychology; and nonlocal phenomena.

♦ Buddha's application of the scientific attitude was unique for using the human mind as both subject and laboratory. This can be seen to be a psychological process of analysis. Freud and the Buddha have thus shaken hands and begun to work together for mutual benefit.

♦ Sometimes the benefits of Buddhist techniques such as mindfulness meditation can become more easily and widely accepted when given a more generally descriptive name, such as "stress reduction" and "emotional intelligence."

Chapter 21

Happiness Is Not an Individual Matter: Engaged Buddhism

In This Chapter

- ◆ What is engaged Buddhism?
- ◆ Service
- ◆ Deep ecology
- ◆ Pluralism
- ◆ Peace

We might conveniently end where the previous chapter left off: prayer. But shall we leave everything to prayer? Prayer is but one of various options we have in the world. Having surveyed myriad applications of Buddhism in our daily life, as our final spot in our tour we'll explore application of Buddhism to the world itself, and of the world itself to Buddhism. It's a practice generically called *engaged Buddhism*, with a spectrum of interpretations. Whether or not you find it part of your calling, it's a vital aspect of Buddhism today worth exploring and understanding.

By now, I hope I've dispelled any misconceptions of Buddhism as bloodless, emotion-less, detached, otherworldly navel-gazing. Renouncing greed, fear, and illusion, the Buddhist doesn't walk away from the world of human relationships but, rather, joins a community of good friends heading in a common direction. Layperson or monastic, the Buddhist lives *in* this world without being attached *to* it.

Enlightenment is in this very world. And the world is just as much in need of enlight-enment as we are. (Here comes our final definition of idiot. Listening deeper, to its ancient Greek roots, it means private. Cut off from the world. So here are our notes about being a Buddhist … in public.) As you'll see, an apt place to conclude our tour because it's not only the most recent development within a 2,600-year-old tradition, but also one that calls up for review many core elements we've already seen.

What Is Engaged Buddhism?

Some critics have remarked that Buddhism has been around for over two millennia, yet the world doesn't seem to be any better off. Well, Buddhism's only been addressing the state of the world relatively recently. Its failure to keep its monasteries integrated with the rest of society only hastened its undoing in India. Traditionally, Buddhism has been largely monastic throughout the East. But now with its absorption into Western society, in primarily nonmonastic practice, Buddhism is proving a unique vehicle for the expression of democracy and freedom.

Engaged Buddhism draws on some cornerstones of Buddhism we've already seen. Right livelihood is engaged Buddhism, for example. Education and social work are ideal opportunities for extended practice of engaged Buddhism. The emphasis is on the precepts, beginning with the first, nonharm. So a vegetarian diet can be an engaged practice. Plus engaged practice extends the right action mode of the Eightfold Path.

This Is

Engaged Buddhism is any practice of Buddhism to effect change in the world in creative, life-affirming, transformative ways, howsoever small they may seem. World and individual are engaged as one. The phrase has been adopted by other creeds; *engaged spirituality* refers, similarly, to the drawing upon spiritual tradition in activities intended for peace, justice, compassion, and wholeness—and which involvement in social action reciprocally leads back to spirituality.

The wisdom here is the same insight as that regarding the self—that it's a composite construct, without any intrinsic, permanent identity. Except here the composite construct of self is seen mirrored in social constructs. They, too, bear the same three marks of existence, and are liable to the same three poisons that confound us all. Recognizing we're all one, there's no higher moral ground for the Buddhist. So on the one hand, I'm called to action, to an engaged practice, by compassion, out of the needless suffering of which I can't help but be aware. On the other hand, wishing to help by bringing reconciliation and peace to any situation of suffering, violence, or harm, I can't act against the welfare of anyone—even those who've caused others pain. There is no enemy. Good Guy versus Bad Guy doesn't apply. The awakened human heart can see all "sides" are acting out of their own wish for happiness. And I am as much responsible for the suffering as anyone else.

Hear and Now

"No man is an island, entire of itself ... / Any man's death diminishes me, because I am involved in mankind ... "

—John Donne

"All the happiness there is in this world comes from thinking about others, and all the suffering comes from preoccupation with yourself."

—Shantideva

An engaged practice is thus a continuation too of our entire chapter on relationships: Relation to a spouse can be an opportunity to practice engaged Buddhism. It's also an example of the bodhisattvic compassion for all beings. Yet there are Theravadins who practice engaged Buddhism, so it's not exclusive to Mahayana. There's Pure Land engaged practice, and Lotus Sutra engaged practice. Yet it's not a necessary feature of any practice. It's all up to how your own particular practice takes shape and life. In this chapter, I'll offer some key examples. What they all have in common ... is Buddhism. First, to ground ourselves in that essential fact, lest they superficially seem like other activities, let's get a little better grounding in how this leaf is now emerging out of the lotus.

Historical Engagement

Engaged Buddhism is a natural outgrowth of Western Buddhism's being primarily lay, rather than monastic, engagement in the world. Moreover, in its encounter with Western modernism, we can see a *secular Buddhism* emergent in the same way that a secular Christianity and secular Judaism emerged in the encounter with modernism (and as is now coming to fruition in Islam). Furthermore, Westerners who come to Buddhism from Judaism, Christianity, or Islam have roots in *prophetic* spirituality, each of those religions seeking the meaning behind and within historical process. Buddhism, on the other hand, is traditionally primarily a mystic spirituality (remember, for example, the Buddhist concept of the interdependence of the historical dimension and the transcendent dimension). Interfaith dialogue thus can be an opportunity for engagement.

Actually, the Buddha advocated activity in the political life of his day, to those householders who came to the Sangha. And his statements about economics evidence a compassion for the world's poor. The caste system also offended him deeply. And the strong evidence of his compassionate engagement in the world is what he did after enlightenment: going to wherever the path led, for the rest of his life, and teaching. That is, he could have stayed under the bodhi tree and just dug enlightenment. Instead, he set out and shaped a road—and the road shaped him.

There have been many ambassadors of engaged Buddhism. King Ashoka is an example. There's Dr. B. R. Ambedkhar, who opposed Gandhi's approval of the caste system, and is responsible for the Wheel of Dharma being on the flag of India today. Dr. A.T. Arayatne, a student of Gandhi's thought in Sri Lanka, has founded a movement called Sarvodaya, combining Buddhist spiritual practice with social service, whose extensive successes are being studied worldwide. Buddhadasa Bhikkhu and his mentor Sulak Sivaraksa have been very important in Thailand. The beginnings of Thailand's ecology movement, for example, began with what are now called "environmentalist monks," who ordain trees in endangered forests as members of the sangha. And His Holiness the Dalai Lama has evolved in exile an engaged Buddhist worldview studied internationally as a kind of global liberation theology.

Leaves from the Bodhi Tree

In the fifth century, Buddhaghosa, son of a brahmin family from India, became a Buddhist and studied in Ceylon (Sri Lanka). He left us a record of what he was taught, titled *Visuddhi Magga* (*Path of Purification*). It begins with these striking words: "There's the inner tangle and the outer tangle. This generation is entangled in a tangle. And so I ask of Gotama this question: 'Who can disentangle this tangle?'" Ask yourself are his words any less true today? How are your own tangle of self and tangle of world intertangled?

The phrase "engaged Buddhism" itself comes from Vietnam, largely through the work of Ven. Thich Nhat Hanh. His monastery preserved the tea ceremony while jet bombers strafed the skies. It became evident, though, that practice couldn't be confined by monastery walls. Monks and nuns practiced putting bodies into body bags while maintaining mindful awareness of their breath and feelings. If a child's parents had been killed, a helping hand needed to be outstretched. These occasions for the compassionate practice of selflessness weren't even considered matters of choice, but rather part of the practice.

Knowing a Better Way to Catch a Snake

Engaged Buddhists don't necessarily write angry letters to Powers That Be. An angry letter only creates more hurt, and who wants to read it, anyway? How about a love letter? Such a letter might instead begin acknowledging how wonderful it is to be a human being, and to hold office, and delegate power. (Do unto others …) An engaged Buddhist doesn't angrily shout slogans, but rather stands with others bearing witness. Being the whole situation itself, without judgment, with only naked awareness, bare attention, that healing might arise.

Here follows options for engaging the world … as meditation.

Service: One Big Circle of Giving

The Buddha began his path by renouncing, only to find out our freedom isn't independent of everybody else. There's no program to follow. (What a relief! And what a challenge!) Novelist and environmental author Peter Mathiessen has noted it's not New Year's resolutions; it's not politics. I'd say it's just looking out your window … going out your door … and following your nose. Old age, sickness, and death were "signs" that impelled Siddhartha to go out into the world to seek the ultimate meaning of life. Perhaps you might see similar signs in your life that do the same, or have but didn't notice that you have. See what needs to be done; ask, "How can I help?" And consider the opportunity as practice.

Whatever our faith, religious paths all point to leading a life bigger than ourselves alone. This fulfillment can come from family, from work, community service, working for the environment, culture, education.

Along the Path

Charity, in Greek (caritas), is another word for love. In Judaism, there is a concept of tikkun ha'olam, healing the world. God's creation was so energetic that it spun out of hand and so needs human beings to restore wholeness. Buddhism teaches the bodhisattva vow, taking refuge with all beings, affirming our interconnectedness. In the great Hindu epic, The Bhagavad Gita (The Celestial Song), Krishna speaks of karma yoga, a path to liberation practiced by using considered, intentional action for the benefit of others, unattached to any outcome. These all provide frameworks for engaged spirituality.

When I can, I volunteer at nonprofits whose cause I relate to. Small organizations that live low on the food chain can use all the help they can get, and miracle workers in adversity's doorway deserve our support. From a certain light, volunteering could be seen as selfish, because it can be a great boost for the person giving. In true service, there's a mutual relationship. There is no "helper," no "helped." Something larger and deeper is taking place. Buddhism grants us intimacy with life: with our own life, with the lives of those with whom we're in relation, and within the larger tapestry of life. Engaging the whole world. This tapestry's not a big fabric rectangle, though: It's a big living circle … with many threads.

Hear and Now

"It is my experience that the world itself has a role to play in our liberation. Its very pressures, pains, and risks can wake us up—release us from the bonds of ego and guide us home to our vast, true nature. For some of us, our love for the world is so passionate that we cannot ask it to wait until we are enlightened."

—Joanna Macy, *World as Lover, World as Self*

For example, consider the homeless (or, as Charles Dickens put it, "the houseless"). Rather than being given money, I've found it can be real important for a houseless person to have someone just stop and talk with them, nonjudgmentally bear witness. There's Buddha nature within all the grime. There but for fortune go you or I. As one homeless guy once said as I was walking away after giving him a quarter and talking with him: "Hey, thanks! The money's nice, but thanks for stopping—I was beginning to think I was on Mars!" And how could I thank *him*—for giving me an opportunity to practice compassion?!

Paradigm Shift: The Butterfly Effect

Remember the Butterfly Effect, from our previous chapter? A small action in a complex system can effectuate great change. If I practice tranquility and insight, that might have a subtle influence on the five or ten people who come in contact with me, and so that can snowball. Sometimes one thing leads to another, and individual service can open up into a bigger circle of mutual giving. If we happen to see a manifestation of this, the key is not to be attached to it, but rather to see if we can take the karma and make dharma out of it.

Consider: With or without a house or job, many people go hungry. A local soup kitchen is thus another occasion for engaged practice. Many people are involved. Ronna

Kabatznick, for example, is a Buddhist practitioner who volunteered at a local soup kitchen, feeding needy people in the community. She found it literally nourishing for herself, which led to her idea that this would be a good opportunity for people dealing with eating problems "to expand the ways in which they nourish themselves by practicing generosity and feeding hungry people," as she later recalled. She happened to be trained in these issues, having been a psychological consultant to Weight Watchers for nine years. Her experience at the soup kitchen (a lesson at a delicatessen) led to her forming an organization called Dieters Feed the Hungry, which eventually became a national movement, and included an infant formula drive.

Another example of the snowballing of service: In 1966, a Buddhist teacher, Venerable Master Cheng Yen, encouraged 30 Buddhist housewives in Taiwan to set aside a penny and a half of their grocery money every day to establish a charitable fund to assist the poor. During the first five years, they helped 31 elderly, ill, or poor people. Word spread, bringing more people into the program. The fund now has five million members worldwide (including 48 centers in the United States). Activities include international relief, medical care, environmental conservation, and community volunteers, yet the goals also are a heart filled with kindness, compassion, joy, and unselfish giving (the four immeasurable abodes). As Master Cheng Yen says, "Only by undergoing the trying lessons of human affairs do we become a strong person."

> **This Is** _____
>
> **Palliative care** brings relief to symptoms and pain for the terminally ill without hope of cure. A **hospice** provides interdisciplinary comfort and support outside of a hospital setting for the terminally ill and their relatives. This allows patient and family to focus on emotional and spiritual care, so that medical concerns don't dominate the experience of dying.

Living Dying: Service in Hospices

Yogi Berra once quipped that he went to everyone's funerals so he'd be sure they'd all come to his. Of course, it's not being dead but the dying that's difficult, doubly so when it's not part of our culture. But it's no surprise to see Buddha at the bedsides of the dying. A Buddhist was once voluntarily taking care of a dying man. One day, the dying man finally asked the Buddhist why he was always so cheerful at his duties, unpaid, and all for a perfect stranger. Without hesitation, the Buddhist smiled and replied, "I'm treating you the way I expect to be treated when my turn comes." (That's an engaged attitude.) Such impermanence meditation is becoming a bit more commonplace in our society through volunteering at a _hospice_.

The Buddha is depicted as lying down during his para-nirvana (literally, "final" or "total extinction"). Even then he continued to teach. It looks like it would be a real honor to sit by his bedside.

Paranirvana Buddha. *Sculpture by Loraine Capparell. Glazed ceramic. 54½″ × 43¼″ × 1½″.*

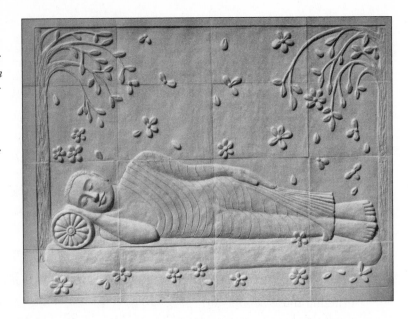

Awakening of mind can occur anytime, such as in counseling a client and family, often overwhelmed with an initial medical diagnosis. Or while lending a listening mind to a lonely voice, needing to be heard at least once in their life. Inquiring mind emerges in the silence of dying, as self dissolves, and true nature is recognized. In one hospice, a young volunteer asked each guest, "If you weren't here, where would you like to go?" Then, he'd visit that place—the local piano bar, say, if that's what the person said. He'd bring a small video recorder, and he'd say to the people there, "You know one of your regulars is staying at the hospice and she wishes she could be here at this piano bar right now. Is there anything you'd like to say to her?" Then, back at the hospice, being shown the video, the guest might recall and would talk about his or her whole life, and its whole meaning unfold.

Frank Osasteki, founder of Zen Hospice, says, "We take our elders and we shut them away in institutions, so that we won't have to bear witness to their pain or our ulti-mate destiny. What would it be like if we invited death in, if we offered it a cup of tea to get to know it better?" The motto at Zen Hospice is: Stay Close, Do Nothing. Zen priest Yvonne Rand suggests, "Just keep them company. Understand that sitting with a dying person is a great opportunity to stay with whatever you are accustomed to turn away from. It could be fear of pain, whatever. In being with the dying you meet your own edge." Hospice work is a wonderful way to engage your Buddhist practice in the world around you. And within you.

Doing Time: Prison Dharma

One place you might find Buddhist hospices now is in prisons. But Buddhist teacher Sakya Jetsun Chime Luding reminds us, "The Buddha himself said that the place of practice is your own mind. It's not a physical place." Suffering, and the cycle of violence, can be ended anywhere.

There are now national networks for the Buddhist practice groups forming within prisons, and your time might be well spent, depending on your experience with practice. (Be advised: Some inmates have a great deal to teach pen pals and visitors, as well as vice versa.) Volunteers are always needed to provide support: correspondence, visits, assistance in creation and leading of practice groups, and ex-convict employment. Just getting a prison to recognize a Buddhist practice or chaplain as legitimate can be an uphill trek.

Three inmates of San Francisco County Jail No. 7 begin a 10-day Vipassana session, up to 12 hours a day, giving up most of the daily privileges that typically define identity and dignity for prisoners. In a prison society where you have to always watch your back, just closing your eyes in a group setting can be a giant step.

Photo: Anthony Pidgeon

All schools of Buddhism are now taught in prisons as viable paths of self-rehabilitation. Pure Land's message to the lowliest rings loud and clear here. Heaven or hell can be just a second away. Namo Amitabha Buddha. The Buddha's compassion extends to everyone who sincerely asks. In the 1970s, Burmese Vipassana master S. N. Goenka taught prisoners in Tihar Jail, India's largest prison and one of the world's most dangerous; it was so successful that today there's a Vipassana center within Tihar, and similar programs have been tried out in America. For men and women accustomed to failure, just completing the rigorous training is a victory. While mindfulness can't transform a criminal overnight, it can furnish a crucial turning point, providing tools for understanding and transforming karma; taking responsibility; detoxifying the poisons of greed, anger, and ignorance; and offering a model for leading a peaceful, rewarding life upon release. And never going back.

Of course, not all crimes are nonviolent or victimless, though many are. Victims or families of victims haven't sought support from Buddhists ... as yet. But already the nonprison population is being affected. Geoffrey Shugen Arnold Sensei, for example, of Zen Mountain Monastery in the Catskills, teaches in New York's prisons. He recalls that when he'd first appear at a prison's gates, guards and staff were very skeptical. But after they began seeing positive changes amongst the inmates over time, they began taking a friendlier attitude towards him. As he sums it up so very well, "Nothing you do can be singularly about yourself, and once you see it that way, everything changes."

Seeing Like a River, Thinking Like a Tree: Deep Ecology

We come now to a worldly outlook virtually indistinguishable from Buddhism itself. *Ecology* (literally, "care for our house") studies relations between beings and their environment. But a common view of it is anthropomorphic, with humanity separate from nature, as if nature were a warehouse of goods or big park to play in. Looking deeper, we can speak of *deep ecology*. Both deep ecologists and Buddhists see we're an integral part of the park, inseparably embedded within a continuum of life. One Buddhist spin on deep ecology is called *Dharma Gaia*. Gaia (say "gaya") is the scientific theory (named after the Greek goddess of the earth) that the earth is a living organism, a sentient being, a self-regulating entity.

Hear and Now

"The entire range of living matter on Earth, from whales to viruses, and from oaks to algae, could be regarded as constituting a single living entity, capable of manipulating the Earth's atmosphere to suit its overall needs and endowed with faculties and powers far beyond those of its constituent parts."

—James Lovelock, on the Gaia hypothesis

So when our earth, our water, our air are threatened, working to stem the tide isn't necessarily an altruistic duty. That implies sacrificing separate Self, for the "higher" interests of Other. As activist Joanna Macy has put it, "It would not occur to me to plead with you, 'Oh, don't saw off your leg. That would be an act of violence.' It wouldn't occur to me because your leg is part of your body. Well, so are the trees in the Amazon rain basin. They are our external lungs. And we are beginning to realize that the world is our body."

Environmental actions thus must address systems-wide dysfunction at the roots. Taking refuge with all beings, the Buddhist vows to protect and preserve life in all forms, as one living thing. Statistics on any topic can be contested, so see for yourself.

For example, have you noticed changes in weather where you live? If so, have you investigated global warming to see if that might be contributory?

Deep ecology can be quite awakening, even for the city dweller. The migration of commuters is as timely as that of birds. Wherever we are, we can meditate on the voice of nature: the interbeing of the four elements within our bodies, the pull of the moon, the communion we make with our food.

Leaves from the Bodhi Tree

Here's a campfire game that Buddhist poet-ecologist Gary Snyder sometimes invites visitors to play with him when they visit his home in the wilderness of the Sierra Nevada Mountains (with wood stoves for heat and photovoltaic cells for electricity). Describe the location of your house without referring to anything manmade. *Think:* Basin, range, watershed, flows, drainages. *Hint:* Where does your water come from? Where does it go when you're through with it? Are you in the sun or the shady slope? What grows around you? What doesn't?

The spiritual and the natural are indivisible. As Buddhists have been saying for thousands of years, Buddha's body can be seen in the colors of the mountains; in the sound of water, we can hear Buddha's voice. (See?! Hear?!)

Wide Horizons: Humanity Is Our Sangha

Here are two more fields you might consider for engaged practice, touched on already as inevitable aspects of Buddhism in the West. However you might have considered them before, from a Buddhist perspective they might yield a new meaning for you.

Female Buddhas (Continued)

Let's resume two topics introduced in Chapter 3, beginning with women. With a growing body of Western women teachers and practitioners, women are asking questions and speaking up instead of conforming to the image that "good Buddhist girls" sit still and be quiet. Certainly this is a good thing, though still a long time in coming to fruition. For example, custom in ancient India called for a widow to immolate herself on her husband's pyre. The British outlawed the practice ("suttee") in 1829, yet cases still occur today.

We've noted as Buddhism adapts to different cultures, it's only natural for Western women to demand that Buddhism furnish the recognition they've come to expect.

And it's natural, too, that Western women will take up the cause of sisterhood across boundaries, whether the cause be restoration of the tradition of nuns in southeast Asia or the plight of Tibetan nuns ... the healing of the trauma of war widows ... the wholesale slavery of young girls recruited or kidnapped into the labyrinthine Asian sex industry ... or women's role in rebuilding war-shattered nations.

They say one man can make a difference. Well, one woman can, too. Consider Burmese Nobel Peace Prize laureate Daw Aung San Suu Kyi (pronounced *Dah Ohng Sahn Sue Chee*). In 1990, the political party she leads won the overwhelming majority vote, but the military wouldn't relinquish power over the throne. Despite threats to her life, she chose to remain inside her country, speaking out according to her conscience, rather than live in exile. Now, some critics of her Western supporters say, "Why pay so much attention to someone or something so far away?" Of course no one is an island. But another answer is that many Western Buddhists are aware of the debt they owe to the East, and the many ways they can be of service over there. So to answer the question with a question, can you drink from the well without putting back?

Hear and Now

"Political prisoners have known the most sublime moments of perfect communion with their highest ideals during periods when they were incarcerated in isolation, cut off from contact with all that was familiar and dear to them. From where do those resources spring, if not from an innate strength at our core, a spiritual strength that transcends material bounds? ... Nobody can take away from us the essential and ultimate freedom of choosing our priorities in life."
—Aung San Suu Kyi

Bringing it back home, I don't know why women are in the majority in Western sanghas. But it's interesting for me to be in the minority. And this engages me, extending my practice of the Fifth Precept out into my daily relations in the world. Whether you're a guy or a gal, you'll encounter gender gaps. ("Good girls don't." "Guys are wimps to do that.") They can be as simple as a random encounter in everyday traffic. Upon examination, you might often find a parallel between gender conditioning and ego: a construct we've accepted and identify with that keeps us from intimacy with our lives.

Along the Path

Molly Dwyers has catalogued male-female imbalances in terms of culture over nature, mind over body (or matter), life over death, the transcendent over the imminent, independence over dependence or interdependence, activity over passivity, order over chaos, objectivity over subjectivity, control over surrender, conscious design over spontaneous arising, clarity over mystery, reason over imagination, doing over being, competition over cooperation, work over play, private enterprise over public service, the professional over the amateur, the creative over the receptive, quantification over qualification, and the conscious over the unconscious, to name a few.

Buddhism offers generous helpings of what's typically defined as feminine traits: for example, emphasis on the feeling intuitive over the rational intellectual. The feminine has balanced the scales of Buddhism more than once. We've seen, for example, how the bodhisattva of compassion, Avalokiteshvara, manifested as a woman, Kwan Yin, in ancient China, and Tara in Mongolia and Tibet. Another example was the influence of Chabai, the wife of Kublai Khan, who helped the spread of Buddhism in Mongolia and who herself influenced Mongol rule; when Kublai conquered southern China, she was instrumental in preventing acts of vengeance.

When male-female interrelations get out of balance, other things can be affected. For example, in the densely woven *Woman and Nature*, Buddhist author Susan Griffin explores the interrelations between woman, nature, and culture, vs. male attitudes. Restoring balance, by definition, requires participation by men just as much as women. Nothing happens in a vacuum. This, too, is part of the Middle Way.

This life-size sculpture of Tara is the feminine aspect of Avalokit-shvara, embodiment of compassion. Tara originates in the Himalayan regions, and has 21 different forms. In her compassionate omniscience, the palms of her hands and the soles of her feet have eyes. Her actions (represented by her hands and feet) are informed by the wisdom (eye) of understanding, upon which true love is based.

(Sitatara. *White Tara; Mongolian, Caghan Dara Eke. Sculptor: Zanzabazar (1635–1723). Late seventeenth–early eighteenth century. Gilt bronze. Height: 27⅛" (68.9 cm) Diam.: 17⅝" (44.8 cm). (Museum of Fine Arts)*

Colors of Compassion: Dharma Pluralism

To understand what it means to be human, we're challenged by the question of how far we might widen the horizons of our definition of "family." This pertains to one of the latest topics of engaged Buddhism: race. The Buddha's paradigm provides invaluable means of getting through the tangles. Though more an immediate issue in America than elsewhere in the West, such questions are played out across the planet in terms of national identity—and, alas, sometimes violently. So the topic of pluralism is universal.

Of course, when you wake up in the morning, you probably aren't aware of how old you are, what race you are, or what your shoe size is. But what do you do when you're confronted by someone who labels you as a dreaded "Other"? Buddhism can help weather the storm. Buddhism nourishes understanding, dignity, and freedom from the bondage of that powerful poison, fear. And spiritual liberation coincides perfectly with a parallel goal of social liberation: freedom.

Along the Path

The Rabbi of Messervitch once asked his followers to define being awake. One person said it meant being able to see the lines in one's palm. The rabbi said that didn't mean awakening. Another said it was being able to determine if a silhouette on a hill was a goat and not a dog. The rabbi said that still wasn't awakening. So someone asked him what being awake meant. "You're truly awake," the rabbi replied, "when you recognize all men as your brother, and all women as your sister."

Similarly, Buddhism can teach us to understand when and how we might perpetuate subtle stereotypes, and see beyond their masks For people of European descent, Buddhism furnishes good tools for awakening to and uprooting roots of racism within and without, and the twisted effects it can have. Sitting in meditation for several days at a time, for example, can bring up many things, such as an awakened connection with one's ancestors. What happens when people of African heritage do so and make contact with the Middle Passage and the heritage of slavery? Or with internalized racism?

Note, this means making the invisible visible. It could be mistaken to expect persons of color to patiently explain to a white-skinned majority what's at stake or what's expected. At a seminal retreat for Buddhists of color, a recurrent refrain was, "I'm tired of having to explain." This is, rightfully, a white person's engaged homework rather than putting a person in the continued uncomfortable position of having to speak on behalf of a whole people. People would rather not keep repeating a story that's become a nightmare from which they'd rather wake up.

Like self, race is a construct. I am reminded of interbeing whenever called to consider race. Looking deeper, I realize nobody's purely just one race, be it black Irish, Italian-Irish (Friuli), Irish Mexican (like Anthony Quinn), Afro-Cuban, or Filipino (Asian-Hispanic). Most everyone's a walking column of interraciality. We inter-are.

Peace!

There are Buddhists who do go to war. But Buddhism is called "the gentlest religion" because no country ever went to war with another in the name of Buddhism. The Buddha descended from a warrior clan addicted to militarism, yet stated that hatred never ends hatred. Yes, it's possible to practice peace in time of war. The threads of the tapestry might seem all polarized, as if warp and woof were two separate, divided dimensions. In such conditions, the Middle Way furnishes a needful path to understanding. We can see it composed of peace as well as nonpeace elements. And should you know a time of peace, Dear Reader, remember to see how it is formed of non-peace as well as peace elements. Peace is every breath.

Look around you. What's happening? What would be good to help, and how can you help? Whatever draws your attention is a good opportunity to practice. You won't have to feel like a lonely "do-gooder," because you'll be practicing with all the others on this path, practicing peace for the sake of all beings. One big circle. One planet. One living being. One heart. One peace.

(*Note:* Dear Reader, I've learned a great deal writing this book. And learned yet more revising it for this new edition. Including how little I really know. Which could mean absolutely nothing except I have a hunch you've relearned a bit, too ... ... of all you'd always known ... and didn't know ... ... No end, no beginning. —*With palms joined.*)

The Least You Need to Know

- In our mutual relations, our engagement with the world can be a vital area of practice. As Buddhism addresses the conditions of the modern world, such practice is called "engaged Buddhism."

- Community services with growing Buddhist participation are the hospice movement and prisoner education.

- The Buddhist perspective toward conservation, environmentalism, and ecology is a profound consciousness of and reverence for the interpenetration of all life and place.

- Reawakening the feminine in our lives concerns us all, men and women. Issues of diversity can be understood, within ourselves and those around us, with compassion and healing.

- Engaged Buddhism is nonviolent, changing the means to change the ends. It's also nondualist, not dividing the world into enemies and friends. We're all responsible for the state of the world.

- Peace!

The Unfolding of the Lotus: A Chronology of the Timeless

The Early Years

c.7000–800 Vedas are "heard," memorized, and passed along orally by priests.   **c.3000** Small figurines of men in yogic meditation posture, in the Indus Valley.

1700–500 Basic Vedic texts written down.   **c.1600** Aryan invasion of India from North.   **c.1300** Moses announces the Ten Commandments to the Hebrews.   **c.900** Upanishads.

800–200 The Axial Age. Transitional period leading to civilization as we know it today, marked by a handful of figures: Buddha in India; Confucius and Lao-tzu in China; Zoroaster (Zarathrustra) in Persia; Solomon and the Hebrew prophets; King Numa in Rome; and classical age of Greek philosophy.

c.620 Emergence of Judaism as a monotheistic religion.   **c.604** Lao-tzu. **c.600** Ascetics rebel against Hindu doctrines.   **569** Establishment of Jainism.   **566–486** Buddha (traditional dates).   **550–470** Confucius. **460–377** Hippocrates.   **490–410** Buddha (according to recent research). **469–369** Socrates.   **410** First Buddhist Council.   **326** Alexander crosses the Indus and enters northwest India.   **325** Official schism within Buddhism over schools of practice.

273–231 Rule of King Ashoka. **c.245** Spread of Buddhism throughout Southeast Asia. **c.180** Brahman-led Hindu uprising almost extinguishes Buddhism in India.

The Common Era

c.24–26 Jesus begins ministry and builds a following. **67** Indian monks present *The Sutra of 42 Chapters* to China. **Second Century** Establishment of Nalanda, the first university. Rise of gnosticism and Eastern prophets in the West. **c.150** Nagarjuna founds Madhyamika school of Buddhism in India. An Shih-kao, Buddhist missionary, goes to China. **121–180** Marcus Aurelius (Roman emperor and stoic philosopher). **166** Buddha's teachings introduced at Luoyang Court, China. **179** Buddhist Prajna-paramita (wisdom literature: Diamond Sutra, Heart Sutra, etc.) translated into Chinese.

312 Roman Emperor Constantine (272–337) converts to Christianity. The first Christian monks practice their faith in remote regions of the Egyptian desert; their rules for conduct and meditation practices bear strong resemblances to the monastic traditions of Buddhism. **354–430** Saint Augustine. **320–400** Vasubandhu teaches in Nepal. **372** Spread of Buddhism from China to Korea. **399–414** Pilgrimage of Fa-hsien from China to Central Asia and India in search of sutras.

402 With the assistance of thousands of monks, Kumarajiva ushers in new level of translation of the Dharma into Chinese. **409–431** Buhddhaghosa translates and collates Sinhalese commentaries on Abidharma, Sri Lanka. **450–550** "White Huns" from the Steppes bring an end to the Gupta Dynasty in India, during which some kings had been Buddhist, some Hindu. **c.470–543** Bodhidharma (patriarch of Zen), brings Buddhism from India to China. **c.476–542** Tan-luan, Chinese patriarch of Pure Land. **504** Emperor Wu, south China, converts to Buddhism. **538–552** Korea introduces Mahayana Buddhism to Japan. **c.550** Queen of Sumatra converts to Buddhism.

570–632 Mohammed. **613–681** Shan-tao, Pure Land patriarch. **617–686** Wonhyo, Korean Buddhist patriarch. **618–907** T'ang Dynasty, Golden Age of China, and of Chinese Buddhism. **632** Ascension of Buddhism in Tibet. **638–713** Hui-neng (Sixth Zen Patriarch). **641** Chinese Buddhist princess is married to first king of Tibet. **690** Imperial Chinese decree favors Buddhism over Taoism. **c.700** Adi Shankaracharya, reformer and reviver of Hindu spirituality.

704–716 Pure Land Buddhist Ci-Min travels in India. **729** Chinese government begins census of Buddhists. **730** Tibet makes peace with China. **736** Kegon (Huayen) Buddhism introduced in Japan. **740–741** Tibet expels foreign monks during a plague. **750** Charlemagne. Padmasambhava. **791** Buddhism the official religion of Tibet. **835–841** Persecution of Buddhism in central Tibet. **843–846** Persecution of Buddhism in China. **972** Printing of Buddhist canon in China.

988–1069 Tilopa teaches tantra to Naropa in India.   **1100** First Crusade.
1016–1100 Naropa teaches Marpa in Tibet.   **1025–1135** Milarepa.   **1070** Neo-confucian attacks on Buddhism in China.   **1173–1206** Muslim conquest of India.
1133–1212 Honen founds Pure Land School (*Jodo Shu*).   **1141–1215** Esai, founder Rinzai (Lin-chi) Zen school.   **1173–1262** Shinran, disciple of Honen, founds True Pure Land School (*Jodo Shinshu*).   **1158–1210** Chinul, patriarch of Korean Ch'an.

1199 Destruction of Nalanda university, India.   **1200** Muslim General Qatab establishes a dynasty in Delhi, India; mosques built from columns of broken Buddhist monasteries and Hindu temples.   **1215** Magna Carta.   **1227** Soto Zen founded and brought to Japan from China by Dogen Zenji.   **1225–1274** St. Thomas Aquinas.   **1253** Nichiren founds Lotus Sutra school.   **1254** Interfaith dialogue between Buddhists, Christians, and Muslims in Karakorum, the Mongol Capital.   **1254–1324** Marco Polo.   **1260** Kublai Khan makes Vajrayana the national religion of Mongol Empire.

c.1300 Dante.   **c.1325** Aztec ascension in Mexico.   **1501** Portuguese soldiers land in Ceylon and massacre men, women, and children.   **1517** Martin Luther (1483–1531) publishes *95 Theses*.

1558–1616 Shakespeare.   **1625** Dutch settle New Amsterdam (New York).   **1686** Siamese King Narai sends noblemen and monks as ambassadors to the Portuguese King Don Pedro. But the boat shipwrecks and the expedition returns home.

1776 Thomas Jefferson modifies the inalienable human rights set forth in the American Declaration of Independence from "life, liberty, and property" to " life, liberty, and the pursuit of happiness ..."   **1783** William Jones, a fellow of the Royal Society, founds the Asiatick Society in Bengal, which publishes an influential journal, Asiatick Researches, read by many Westerners, including Thomas Jefferson.   **1784** Hannah Adams publishes an American survey of Christian sects and world religions which includes an 83-page appendix discussing Asian religions.

Modern Era

1789   French Revolution.

1803   Friedrich Schlegel coins the phrase "Oriental Renaissance," denoting the "discovery" of Asia and its heritage by the West.

c.1818   Arthur Schopenhauer begins studies of Buddhism, the first major German philosopher to do so.   N. A. Notovitch publishes *Unknown Life of Jesus*, describing 16 "missing years" of Jesus, during which he allegedly studied with brahmins and Buddhist monks in India.   **1844** Henry David Thoreau publishes a portion of his translation (from French) of The Lotus Sutra in *Dial*.   **1848** John Sutter discovers gold at his sawmill, north of San Francisco. Within a year, three hundred merchants arrive from China, the beginning of a vaster tide of Eastern immigrants. (By 1852, new arrivals would total 20,000.)

1853 The Sze Yup Company establishes the first temple in America, in San Francisco's Chinatown.   **1859** Darwin (1809–1882) publishes *Origin of Species*.   **1867** Chinese workers begin laying track for the Central Pacific Railroad, joining the east and west coasts of America.   **1875** Madam Helena Blavatsky and Henry Steel Olcott found the Theosophical Society, as a bridge between East and West.   **1879–1884** Blavatsky travels in India.   **1878** Edwin Arnold's *The Light of Asia* is published and will go through 80 editions.   **1881** Thomas W. Rhys David founds the Pali Text Society (still in existence). Henry Steel Olcott publishes *Buddhist Catechism*, ushering in a modernized Buddhism.   **1887** A printer named Veeterling publishes a magazine called *The Buddhist Ray*, under the name of Philangi Dasa, from the mountains of Santa Cruz, California.   **1888** Frederick Nietzsche publishes *The Anti-Christ*, which includes comparisons between Christianity and Buddhism. Van Gogh paints a self-portrait depicting himself as a Japanese Buddhist monk.

1893 The first World Parliament of Religions, part of the Chicago World's Fair, sparks major exposure of Eastern faiths in American media, through the presence of living teachers.   **1894** The first Jodo Shinshu mission is established in North America.   **1897** Discovery of the electron.   **1898** Founding of the Young Men's Buddhist Association in San Francisco for Japanese immigrants.   **1899** First Japanese Buddhist priests come to America. Hompa Hongwanji Temple founded in San Francisco. Branches open as Japanese American farmers settle in Sacramento, Fresno, and Vacaville, California.

The Twentieth Century

1900 Sigmund Freud publishes *The Interpretation of Dreams*. Paul Carus publishes the first book of D. T. Suzuki, *Ashvagosha's Discourse on the Awakening of Faith in the Majayana*. A Jodo Shinshu Temple of the Original Vow is established in Hawaii.
1915 Ezra Pound publishes *Cathay*, a watershed for the influence of Chinese culture on Modernism.   **1923** Alexandra David-Neel, well-versed in Sanskrit, disguises herself as a pilgrim and becomes the first European woman to enter Tibet's forbidden city of Lhasa. She stays in Tibet for 14 years. Upon her return she writes and publishes a few influential books about her pilgrimage.   **1924** Immigration to America is restricted by a quota system. In London, Christmas Humphreys founds the Buddhist Lodge of the Theosophical Society. Berliner Paul Dahlke establishes Buddha House, part hermitage, part monastery.   **1926** Establishment of first academic chair in

Buddhist Studies, in Paris.　**1927** Werner Heisenberg publishes his Uncertainty Principle. Niels Bohr proposes the concept of complementarity. Zenshuji, a Soto Zen temple, is established in Los Angeles, and acts as a bridge between Japanese and European Americans. D. T. Suzuki publishes *Essays in Zen Buddhism*. W. Y. Evans-Wentz publishes translation of *The Tibetan Book of the Dead*.

1931 Two monks, Nyogen Senzaki and Sokei-an, colleagues of Soen Shaku, teach Zen at a "floating zendo," in New York and Los Angeles.　**1932** Theodore Stcherbatsky publishes two-volume *Buddhist Logic*. After Christian missionary work in Asia, Dwight Goddard publishes *The Buddhist Bible*. Two years later, he establishes Followers of the Buddha, an American Buddhist monastic order.　**1941** Pearl Harbor attacked, December 7.　**1942** FDR signs Executive Order 9066; 110,000 Japanese in America are detained, "relocated," and interned in camps for the next three years, over half, Buddhists.　**1945** Following the tremendous upheaval of WWII upon Japanese culture, the Jodo Shinshu sangha is reorganized as Buddhist Churches of America.　**1946** Noted historian F.S.C. Northrop publishes *The Meeting of East and West*, establishing a benchmark for comparative philosophy in the English language. **1949** Three Englishmen are ordained in India, Osbert Moore (Nanamoli), Harold Musson (Nanavira), and Dennis Lingwood (Sangharakshita), each to be influential in the West.　**1950** Sri Lanka founds the World Fellowship of Buddhists.

1950–58 D. T. Suzuki offers free lectures on Zen at Columbia University. Princeton publishes the *I-Ching*; millions of copies sold since.　**1951** Peter Matthiessen journeys to the Himalayas and later records his journey in a diary, *Snow Leopard*. First publication in English of *Siddhartha* by Herman Hesse (1877–1962) by New Directions, a book now having sold over 40 editions.　**1952** Philip Kapleau journeys to Japan to study Zen, stays for 13 years. David Tudor performs John Cage's *4'33"* at a concert at Woodstock, New York.

1955 Rosa Parks is arrested in Montgomery, Alabama, after refusing to give up her seat and move to the back of the bus. Beat poetry reading at the Six Gallery by Gregory Corso, Allen Ginsberg, Philip Lamantia, Michael McClure, Gary Snyder, and Philip Whalen, all but two of whom are or would become Buddhist.　**1956** Gary Snyder voyages to Japan to study Zen; stays for ten years. *Chicago Review* publishes a special "Zen" issue.　**1958** One year after *On the Road*, Jack Kerouac publishes *Dharma Bums*.　**1959** Shunryu Suzuki comes to U.S. from Japan. Alan Watts publishes *Beat Zen, Square Zen*. Robert Aitken founds the Diamond Sangha in Hawaii. Tenzin Gyatso, the 14th Dalai Lama, leaves Tibet and goes into exile in India.

1962 Quarks are discovered. Tripitaka Master Hsuan Hua teaches in San Francisco's Chinatown. First gathering at Esalen, Big Sur, a site to become a watershed for East-West studies, new schools of psychology, and the Human Potential Movement.

1963 Seated in Buddhist meditation, Thich Quang Duc self-immolates in Saigon. Dr. Martin Luther King, Jr. delivers his "I Have a Dream" speech to more than 250,000 people at the Lincoln Memorial. Rachel Carson publishes *Silent Spring*.   **1963–74** Viet Nam War.   **1964** Vatican II opens ecumenical dialogue. Thomas Merton meets D. T. Suzuki. Judo is the first martial art accepted into the Olympics, in Tokyo. The International Karate Tournament is held in Long Beach, California, the first major demonstration of Asian martial arts in America.   **1965** The Immigration and Nationality Act dispenses with the quota system for immigrants.

1966 The Washington Buddhist Vihara establishes the first Theravada temple in America, in Washington, D.C. Thomas Merton meets Thich Nhat Hanh at Gethsemani Abbey. A "Be-In" is held in San Francisco, Alan Watts and Gary Snyder featured as speakers. Tassajara Zen Mountain Center, American Buddhism's first mountain home, is established. Philip Kapleau publishes *The Three Pillars of Zen*, following years of study in Japan. By including extensive transcripts of personal experiences of practitioners, it became a de facto do-it-yourself manual for over a million people wishing to study Zen.

1967 The first Earth Day. Tarthang Tulku founds the Nyingma Meditation Center, and Dharma Publishing Company. Master Hua establishes Gold Mountain Monastery in San Francisco. Sangharakshita establishes the Friends of the Western Buddhist Order (FWBO), in London.   **1968** Traveling in the East, Thomas Merton meets Chögyam Trungpa and the 14th Dalai Lama.   **1969** Chögyam Trungpa arrives in America, lectures in Boulder. Shambhala Booksellers opens on Telegraph Avenue, Berkeley, California. A publishing company is soon founded; the first title is *Meditation in Action*, by Trungpa Rinpoche. The same year, they publish *The Tassajara Bread Book*, a surprise bestseller.

1972 Korean Son master Seung Sahn arrives in America, gets started by repairing washing machines.   **1973** Trungpa Rinpoche establishes Vajradhatu, consolidating all of the American centers studying in his tradition.   **1974** Naropa Institute, America's first Buddhist university, offers B.A. and M.A. degrees in Buddhist Studies, Psychology and Performing Arts. Heng Ju, a monk from Gold Mountain Monastery, makes a pilgrimage from San Francisco to Seattle, bowing once every three steps.

1975 E. F. Schumacher publishes *Small is Beautiful*, with the concept of Buddhist economics. Physicist Fritjof Capra shows Shambhala Publications his manuscript, *The Tao of Physics*, which becomes an unexpected bestseller.   **1976** Dai Bosatsu, the first Japanese-style Zen monastery, is established in America. Sino-American Buddhist Association establishes the 237-acre City of Ten Thousand Buddhas in Ukiah. Joseph Goldstein, Jack Kornfield, and Sharon Salzburg establish Insight Meditation Center, in Barre, Massachusetts, in the Vipasanna tradition of Mahasi Syadaw.   **1977** Tarthang Tulku dedicates 900 acres of land along the Pacific Ocean in Sonoma County for a Nyingma community named Odiyan. Trungpa introduces the Shambahla Training. **1978** Establishment of the Buddhist Peace Fellowship, a grassroots engaged Buddhist network.   **1983** Ven. Dr. Henepola Gunaratna forms the Bhavana Society, with a 187-acre farm in West Virginia.

1985 Arnold Kotler, a longtime Zen practitioner and peace activist, establishes Parallax Press. He gathers and edits talks by Thich Nhat Hanh and publishes them as *Being Peace*.   **1987** Conference on World Buddhism is held in Ann Arbor. The International Association of Buddhism convenes at Bodhbgaya, India.   **1988** Hsi Lai ("she lye") Temple, a branch of the Taiwan-based Fo Kuang Temple, is established in the Hacienda Heights section of Los Angeles, the largest Buddhist monastic complex in America.

1989 The Nobel Peace Prize awarded to HH the Dalai Lama.   **1990** A delegation of American Jews visit the Dalai Lama in India.   **1991** Nobel Peace Price awarded to Aung San Suu Kyi.   **1992** Thailand replaces the hammer and sickle as its seal with Pha That Luang, its holiest Buddhist symbol.   **1997** Hsi Lai Temple hosts a dialogue between Theravadan, Mahayanan, and Vajrayanan Buddhists.   **1999** Power beads, a fashion craze inspired by Buddhism.   **2000** American Buddhist teachers meet for ecumenical symposia at Spirit Rock Meditation Center. Two years later, Spirit Rock sponsors a national symposia for Buddhists of color.   **2003** Inauguration of the multi-city International Buddhist Film Festival to sold-out houses at Los Angeles premiere.   **2004** Publication of completely revised, second edition of *The Complete Idiot's Guide to Understanding Buddhism*.

Tomorrow Today will only be yesterday. Please enjoy it.

Buddhism in a Nutshell: A Quick Reference

The Three Jewels

1. Buddha (The Awakened One)

2. Dharma (Buddha's teachings and all they pertain to)

3. Sangha (the practice, and the community of practice)

The Four Noble Truths

1. Life entails suffering (*duhkha*).

2. Suffering results from craving an illusion (*trishna*).

3. There's an end to suffering (*nirvana*).

4. The way to the end of suffering is the Path (*maggha*).

The Path

Wisdom	Ethics	Meditation
1. Right view	3. Right speech	6. Right effort
2. Right thought	4. Right action	7. Right mindfulness
	5. Right livelihood	8. Right concentration

The Precepts

1. Not killing
2. Not stealing
3. Not lying
4. No intoxicants
5. No sexual abuse

Karma (Universal Cause and Effect)

You are responsible for your actions, words, and thoughts.

Each results in a reciprocal action, word, or thought.

The Three Poisons

1. Greed
2. Hatred
3. Ignorance

The Three Marks of Existence (The Three Dharma Seals)

1. Impermanence
2. No abiding, separate self
3. Duhkha/nirvana

The Four Brahmaviharas (Immeasurable Abodes)

	Near Enemy	Far Enemy
Loving kindness (*metta*)	Selfishness	Hatred
Compassion (*karuna*)	Pity	Contempt
Sympathetic joy (*mudita*)	Boredom	Jealousy
Equanimity (*upekkha*)	Indifference	Aversion

The Four Bodhisattva Vows

Beings are numberless; I vow to awaken them.

Delusions are inexhaustible; I vow to end them.

Dharma gates are boundless; I vow to enter them.

Buddha's way is unsurpassable; I vow to become it.

The Present Moment Is a Wonderful Moment

Smile.   Breathe

The Vocabulary of Silence: A Glossary

arhat   "One worthy; worthy one." The ideal of arhatship in *Theravada* means having nothing more to learn, free of cravings and desires, having attained *nirvana*.

Atman   Hindu concept of a highest self, inherently one with the trans-personal, Eternal Self ("*Brahman*"). To Buddha the ultimate reality is "no self" ("*an-atman*").

bardo   The state in between death and rebirth.

Bhakti yoga   Union with the divine through devotional faith.

bhikku   Buddhist monk; literally means "beggar," as monks beg their meals from the lay community each day.

bhikkhunis   Buddhist nuns.

Bodhi tree   The historical tree (of the Indian *banyan* variety) under whose branches the Buddha sat and attained enlightenment.

bodhisattva   One who is ready for or who has even attained enlighten-ment yet has vowed to help all beings become enlightened.

Brahmaviharas   "Divine dwellings" or "immeasurable abodes": loving kindness (*metta*), compassion, joy, and equanimity.

Buddha   From the Sanskrit root *budh*, "to wake." The Fully Awakened One. Awake and capable of awakening others.

buddha nature   The capability of realizing buddhahood. Original nature, true nature, true self.

Buddhism   A way of life in accord with the teachings of the Buddha; in the East, often called Buddha Dharma, Way of the Buddha.

Buddhist   A person who studies, realizes, and lives the basic principles of the Buddha's teachings.

compassion   Universal sympathy, sometimes expressed as the sincere wish to end the needless suffering of all beings, born out of recognition of the oneness of all things. Commonly expressed by *bodhisattvas*. Often paired with *wisdom*.

concentration   Buddhism has many words analogous to concentration (much as Eskimos have many words for snow, because so much attention is paid to it). *Samatha*, stopping, or stillness, is a basis for concentration, and can yield tranquility. Used in conjunction with mindfulness and effort as part of the Eightfold Path, concentration is called *samadhi*, which is often translated as one-pointed concentration. In one-pointedness there's no duality between a mind and an object. This nondualistic state is the basis for meditation (or *dhyani*), which can further lead to what's often called self-realization, *kensho*, *satori*, enlightenment.

Dalai Lama   Dalai means "ocean," as in ocean of wisdom. The Dalai Lama is both a religious and a national ruler. Tibet was ruled by Dalai Lamas since the seventeenth century, until the sixteenth Dalai Lama fled into exile in Dharmsala, India, in 1959.

deep ecology   Ecology (literally, "care for our house") studies relations between beings and their environment. Deep ecology sees humanity as inseparably embedded within nature, part of a continuum of interbeing.

Dharma   The Buddha's teachings and the things to which they pertain (everything). Additional meanings: law, path, righteousness, phenomena, and reality, depending on the context.

dualism   Division of reality into oppositions, based on verbalization, conceptualization.

duhkha   (Sanskrit; literally, a wobbly axle.) Dissatisfaction, stress, suffering, anguish, pain, caused by craving or attachment to what is without a stable, separate identity.

emptiness   (Sanskrit: *sunyata*) The state of being empty of any separate, substantial, lasting existence. Rather than negative, it implies no boundary, fertile void, openness, transparency, infinite potentiality. *See also* suchness.

enlightenment   State of awakening (*see* satori); perhaps more usefully considered in terms of enlightened actions.

esoteric   Intended only for those sufficiently spiritually developed and properly initiated to grasp the true meaning.

gassho   Palms of hands joined together and held near the breast in greeting, gratitude, request, often accompanied by a bow. (*Namaskar/namastey*, Hindu; *añjali*, Sanskrit, *wai*, Thai.)

gatha   A short poem or meditation.

haiku   A short impressionist sketch in words.

hara   A node of energy (*chakra*) about the size of a quarter or a dime, three or four finger-widths below your navel, considered your true center—physically in posture, and spiritually as central repository of life-force (*prana, chi*). (*Dan tien*, Chinese.)

holistic   Pertaining to a whole, such as a whole system; taking into account interrelations of parts.

insight   Seeing deeply; penetrating into the true nature of things; gaining understanding and wisdom. *See also* Vipassana.

interbeing   The unimpeded interpenetration of all things; interdependence, interconnectedness.

karma   Universal law of cause and effect, not limited by time or space, it can imply reincarnation, rebirth, or, less figuratively, continual perpetuation, and the means of liberation from such repetition.

karma yoga   A path to liberation using action for the benefit of others.

koan   A Zen meditation on a question or story whose resolution goes beyond rational intellect and common logic, such as, "All things return to the One; what does the One return to?"

lamrim   Stages of the path in Tibetan Buddhism, leading to initiation into *tantra*.

Mahayana   Collection of Buddhist schools flourishing in northeast Asia, such as Pure Land, Zen, Vajrayana, and Nichiren.

mandala   Two- or three-dimensional diagram of cosmic forces, used for meditation; often depicts deities and their abodes.

mantra   Meditation practice using sound or syllables or words.

meditation   One of three components of the Buddhist way, along with wisdom and ethics. More than a relaxed state, it's an activity of nondualist, self-reflexive awareness, with various degrees of formal training available from a *teacher*, depending on the school. Meditation isn't confined to sitting on a cushion, but is also practiced walking, working, and so on.

metta   Loving kindness, friendliness, goodwill.

Middle Way   Harmoniously navigating between extremes, not choosing opposing positions. The Madhyamika School of Buddhism recognizes relative truth and absolute truth, the latter being *emptiness*.

mindfulness   Alert, sober attention; being aware of things as they are, in and of themselves, and nothing else.

mondo   (Japanese) Zen question and answer, similar to koan practice, with an immediate answer required.

mu   (Japanese) Nothing, not, nothingness, un-.

mudra   Postures and gestures often associated with a particular Buddha or an inner state of being; equivalent to speech, in preliterate cultures. In Vajrayana, they assist in visualization of a Buddha or deity.

mushin   ("No mind.") Innocence, nondualist awareness, no-thought, beyond skill.

nembutsu   In Pure Land Buddhism, recitation of the name of Amitabha Buddha (*Namo Amida Butsu*, Japanese; *Namo Amitofu*, Chinese, in which case recitation is called *nien fo*).

nirvana   Liberation; union with ultimate reality; state of perfection.

nonself   (Sanskrit *an-atman*) Absence of a permanent, unchanging self; selflessness. *See* atman.

noting   The mindful process of self-observation often used in *insight meditation*; observing whatever's passing through your body, feelings, thoughts, and consciousness, making a short mental note of it, and moving on.

Pali   Indian dialect derived from Sanskrit in which the canonical texts of Theravada are composed.

paranirvana   Nirvana before or after death.

precepts   Ethical guidelines for conscious conduct.

pure land   A field created by Buddha's enlightenment, in which he then dwells.

Pure Land Buddhist school (also known as Amidism)   Emphasizes faith in and devotion to Amida Buddha's compassionate bodhisattva vows.

refuge   Taking refuge means appreciating, trusting, and relying on something.

samsara   The world of endless cycles of rebirth into the same illusions, such as the illusion that true happiness consists in satisfying our ego.

samurai   The military elite who seized power from imperial aristocracy in feudal Japan, Kamakura era (1185–1333). As soldiers of fortune, the samurai appreciated and sponsored Zen for its fearlessness, irreverence, intuition, spontaneity, and strict discipline.

Sangha   "Assembly, crowd, host." Generally, a Buddhist community of practice, or practice itself; more specifically, the Buddhist monastic order, the oldest monastic order in the world.

Sanskrit   An ancient language of India, now used only for sacred or scholarly purposes.

satori   The experience of awakening or enlightenment. (Usually satori is reserved for the Buddha, and personal satori is called *kensho*.)

sesshin   "Touching mind; unifying mind; joining of mind to mind." A Zen retreat lasting from one to seven days.

shikantaza   Zen practice of sitting just to sit; choiceless awareness, without techniques.

skillful means   Teachings, techniques, methods designed to further spiritual practice (*upaya*, Sanskrit), varied according to the temperament of the practitioner.

store consciousness (*alaya vijnana*)   The Buddhist concept, akin to the unconscious, of the realm where karma accumulates, the soil where seeds of future energies and essences manifested in phenomena are nourished.

stupa   A burial mound. The architectural form of a Buddhist stupa stands for not only the Buddha but also his enlightenment. (*Pagoda*, China; *chorten*, Tibet.)

suchness   The immutable nature of things beyond all categories or concepts; their buddha nature, in which there is no boundary between perceiver and perceived; an outcome of *emptiness*.

sutra   Dialogues or discourses of the Buddha.

tantra   Originally a school of Hindu yoga which combined with Buddhism and native Tibetan beliefs. A distinguishing element of *Vajrayana Buddhism*, it's often characterized by its harnessing and transforming natural energies rather than suppressing them. The word can also refer to tantric teaching texts, which are called tantras instead of *sutras*.

Tao "The Way." The way of the universe and the way humanity can live in harmony with it. Shares affinities with *Zen*.

Theravada Blanket term for Buddhist schools flourishing in south and southeast Asia, the most popular one today being Vipassana (Insight Meditation). (Sometimes called Hinayana, which carries a disparaging connotation of "lesser, inferior.")

Three Jewels (or Triple Gem) *The Buddha, the Dharma, the Sangha.*

tonglen A meditation of exchanging self for others.

Tripitaka The Buddhist canon, recorded in *Pali*, including sutras, rules for discipline and conduct, and special teachings.

Vajrayana The Buddhist school predominating in Tibet, Mongolia, Ladakh, but also diffusing into China, Korea, and Japan. It embraces Theravadan and Mahayanan beliefs and adds *tantric* beliefs and practices, often with much symbolism and ritual, such as *mantra, mudra,* and visualization with *mandala.* A form of *esoteric* Buddhism.

Vipassana Mindfulness meditation practiced in the Theravadin schools. Often taught as *insight* meditation in the West. Insight into the impermanence and lack of abiding, separate, substantial identity of all things, leading to understanding of the true nature of reality.

visualization Picturing an image in the mind's eye. In Buddhist practice, uniting with the energy symbolized by a particular visualization; then realizing its essential *emptiness.*

wisdom (*Prajna,* Sanskrit) Often associated with enlightenment, wisdom can refer to insight into the true nature of reality, which is *emptiness.* Whereas the West often typifies wisdom as the result of an accumulation of knowledge, in the East it's often the result of the shedding of veils of ignorance. As in the Western sense of good judgment, it's largely intuitive. In terms of spiritual development, often paired with *compassion.*

yoga Literally "to yoke," or unite, such as yoking the mundane and the divine, integrating teachings and practice, learning and experience, and so on. (Note: The word "religion," similarly means to bind.) Specifically refers to particular Brahmanic practices in India, but can apply to any spiritual path. Its practitioner is called a yogi.

zazen Total concentration of body and mind in an upright, cross-legged sitting posture; seated meditation.

Zen A school of Buddhism emphasizing mind directly seeing into the nature of mind. The word derives from the Sanskrit for "meditation," with an added sense of the wisdom therefrom. *Dhyana; Chan* in China, where it mingled with Taoism; *Son* in Korea, and *Thien* in Vietnam.

Index

A

abhidharma, 25
abortion, 102
acculturation (Western Buddhism), 44-46
active verbs (Four Noble Truths), 81
addictions, 110
ahimsa, 100
alcohol consumption, 109-110
altars, 141-142
ambassadors, 342
Amidism, 31
Amitabha, 206-208
animism, 26
archery (samurais), 292
arhats, 20
Arnold, Sir Edwin, 42
arrangements, flowers, 287-289
art, 304
    Andrew Goldsworthy, 305
    Baroque paintings, 312
    contemporary spiritual, 306-307
    dualism, 312
    east Asian examples, 312
    expression, 305
    life art, 315
        Fluxus, 318
        happenings, 318
        music, 316-317
    modern, 305
    self-expression, 305
    spiritual practice, compared, 304
    Tibetan, 312
    Zen, 312-314
ascetic, 10
Ashoka, 21-22

Asia, 16
    east Asian examples, 312
    expansion of Buddhism
        China, 28-30
        Japan, 31
        Korea, 30-31
        Tibet, 32
        today, 33-34
        Vietnam, 32
    Further India, 25
Asian Classics Input Project, 282
atman, 123
attachment (cause of suffering), 76-77
Avalokiteshvara, 29
Avalokiteshvaras, 197
Avatamsaka, 221, 307
awakening, 4
awareness
    breathing, 161-162
    food, 265-266
Axial Age, 21
ayurveda, 329-331

B

Baroque paintings, 312
basic posture (meditation), 153
bearing witness, 106-108
Beatles, 38
beginner practice, 136-137
Bell, A.J., 336
bells (meditation), 142
Benson, Dr. Herbert, 333
bhikkhunis, 20
bhikkhus, 20
Blavatsky, Madame Helena, 40

Bodhidharma, 192-194
Bodhisattva Vow, 196-198
bodhisattvas, 22-23, 197
bodies
    language (meditation), 154-155
    scan meditation, 176-177
    Vajrayana, 232-233
Bohm, David, 336
Bon (Tibet), 32
books, printing, 29
bows, 154
Brahman, 123
Brahmavihara, 180
breathing (meditation), 157-158
    awareness, 161-162
    counting, 160
    nostrils, 159
    words, 160-161
breathing rooms, 140-141
Buddha. *See* Siddhartha
Buddhaghosa, 342
Buddhist films, 300-302
Buddhist math, 199
Burma, 26
Burmese Harp, The, 301
Butterfly Effect
    chaos theory, 327
    engaged Buddhism, 344-345

C

Cage, John, 316
calligraphy, 314
candles, 143
caste systems, 56
Ceylon, 25
chakras, 232
chanting, 295
chaos theory, 326-328
Chenrezigs, 197
chi, 157

Chief Flying Hawk, 65
children
    rites of passage, 253-254
    teaching Buddhism, 252
China
    Bodhidharma, 192-194
    Buddhism and Taoism interfaith, 57-59
    Buddhism expansion, 28-30
    Confucius, 28-29
    Hui Neng, 194-195
    Kwan Yin, 29
    Shaolin Temple, 290
    Taoism, 28-29
Christian followers, 59-61
circularity (life), 55
civil societies, 246
cognitive sciences, 333
comments, mental noting, 173
committed relationships, 248
common karma, 117
community. *See* sanghas
compassion
    practicing, 344
    Pure Land, 210-211
complexity theory, 328
concentration
    meditation, 171
    total, 96-97
Confucius, 28-29
consecutiveness (emptiness), 128
consumption, 109
    addictions, 110
    altered states/traits, 109
    media, 111
    mindful food consumption, 268
    self-help, 110
contemplation, 220-221
contemporary spiritual art, 306-307
cooking, 260
councils, 20
counting (breathing), 160
country 'n' eastern music, 296-297

cultures
  India, 28
  popular
    art. *See* art
    gardening, 286-290
    movies, 297-302
    music, 294-297
    physical, 290-294
  relationships, 246
cycles (emptiness), 128

D

Dalai Lama, 33
David-Neel, Alexandra, 40
Daw Aung San Suu Kyi, 350
death
  Buddha, 17
  relationships, 256-257
deep ecology, 348-349
deities
  Mahayana, 216
  overview, 215
  Pure Land, 216
  Tibetan Buddhism, 225-226
  Vajrayana, 236
deity yoga, 234
democracy, 46-47
Descartes, René, 334
detective novels, 308
dharma, 14
  abhidharma, 25
  defined, 70
  everyday life, 72-73
  Mahayana, 74
  parenting, 252
  Theravadins, 73
  three seals
    impermanence, 120-122
    nirvana, 124-125
    selflessness, 122-124
Dharma Door's online itinerary, 33

Dharma Gaia, 348
Diamond Abby, 282
didjeridus, 295
diet. *See* food
dokusan, 196
drug consumption, 109-110
dualism
  art, 312
  Jodo Shin-shu, 215
  Western Buddhism, 58
duhkha, 76
Dwyers, Molly, 351
Dzogchen, 226

E

east Asian art, 312
eating. *See also* food
  company, 264-265
  food awareness, 265-266
  food issues, 267
  health food, 269
  meat, 268-269
  mental noting during, 262-264
  mindful consumption, 268
  thanks for food, 261-262
ecology, deep, 348-349
ecumenism, 49-50
education. *See also* teachers
  bodhisattva, 22-23
  children (Buddhism), 252
  experience, 255-256
  first university, 22
  Mahayana, 23
  Nalanda University, 255
  schools of practice, 22
  student-teacher relationships, 255-256
  teachers, 255
  Theravada, 23
  Vajrayanaa, 24
  Western Buddhism living teachers, 41-42

Western Theravada, 24
effort
    practicing, 149
    proper, 94
egalitarianism, 17, 47
Eightfold Path, 86-87
    actions, 92-93
    concentration, 96-97
    effort, 94
    Four Noble Truths links, 87-89
    introducing, 14
    memorizing, 87
    mindfulness, 94-96
    right, 86
    skillful, 86
    speech, 93
    thoughts, 91-92
    views, 90
    work, 93-94
Einstein, 323
elements meditation, 178-179
Ely, Joe, 296
emergent behaviors, 328
emotional intelligence, 175, 253
empowerment (Vajrayana), 226, 230-231
emptiness
    consecutiveness, 128
    cycles, 128
    misconceptions, 128-129
    overview, 125-126
    spaciousness, 128
    suchness, 127
    Zen, 189-190
engaged Buddhism
    ambassadors, 342
    compassion, practicing, 344
    deep ecology, 348-349
    female Buddhists, 349-351
    male-female interrelations, 351
    mystic spirituality, 342
    origins, 342
    overview, 340-341

    peace, 353
    political activity, 342
    race, 352-353
    secular Buddhism, 341
    service, 343
        Butterfly Effect, 344-345
        hospices, 345-346
        nonprofits, 344
        prisons, 347-348
    witnessing, 343
engaged spirituality, 340
enlightenment
    Siddhartha, 11-12
    Zen, 198
enterprises, 280-282
ethical monastic conduct, 25
everyday life
    gardening
        flower arrangements, 287-289
        planting, 286-287
        sand, 289-290
    Jodo Shin-shu, 221
    movies, 297
        Buddhist films, 300-302
        watching, 297-300
    music, 294
        chanting, 295
        country 'n' eastern, 296-297
        wind instruments, 295-296
    physical culture
        martial arts, 290-291
        performance, 292-294
        samurais, 291-292
    Pure Land, 218
        contemplation, 220-221
        recitations, 219-220
    refuge, taking, 72-73
    Zen, 199
expansion (Buddhism)
    Asia today, 33-34
    Burma, 26
    China, 28-30

Further India, 25
Japan, 31
Korea, 30-31
Siam, 26
Silk Route, 26-27
Spice Route, 27
Sri Lanka, 25
Tibet, 32-33
Vietnam, 32
West. *See* Western Buddhism
experience, teaching through, 255-256

F

family meals, 264-265
family sangha, 252
female Buddhists, 349-351
    traits, 351
    Western, 350
female-male interrelations, 351
feminism, 46
fiction, Buddhist literature, 308-309
fine art, 304
    Andrew Goldsworthy, 305
    Baroque paintings, 312
    calligraphy, 314
    contemporary spiritual, 306-307
    dualism, 312
    east Asian, 312
    expression, 305
    life art, 315-318
    literature. *See* literature
    modern art, 305
    self-expression, 305
    spiritual culture, compared, 304
    Tibetan, 312
    Zen brush, 312-314
first university, 22
Flatlanders, 296
Flower Garland School, 119
flowers. *See* gardening
flutes (Japanese), 296

Fluxus, 318
food
    awareness, 265-266
    company, 264-265
    cooking, 260
    giving thanks for, 261-262
    health, 269
    issues, 267
    meat, 268-269
    mindful consumption, 268
    mindfully eating, 262-264
    produce, 266
    tea, 269-271
    whole grains, 266
foreign politics, 37
forest teachers, 9
four Brahmaviharas, 180-181
Four Establishments of Mindfulness, 96
Four Noble Truths, 75
    active verbs, 81
    attachment, 76-77
    Eightfold Path links, 87-89
    insight meditation, 171
    introducing, 14
    liberation, 78-80
    path to liberation, 80-81
    questions, 81
    scientific variation, 81
    self-inquiry, 82
    suffering, 76
Further India, 25
fuzzy logic, 326-328

G

gardening
    arrangements, 287-289
    planting, 286-287
    sand, 289-290
gathas, 161
Gautama. *See* Siddhartha
Gelug, 33

generosity, 103-104
Gilmore, Jimmy Dale, 296
Glass, Philip, 296
God, 53-54
Golden Rule, 52
Goldsworthy, Andrew, 305
grains, 266
Grandmaster Wong Kiew Kit, 290
Great Vehicle, 23
Greens Cookbook, The, 281
Greystone, 281
Groundhog Day, 301
Guan Yins, 197

H

haikus, 309-311
Hancock, Butch, 296
Hanh, Thich Nhat, 32
happenings, 318
healing of others, 330
health food, 269
heart character, 90
Heart Sutra, 307
Heisenberg, Werner, 324
Hellenism, 27
Hinduism, 24-25
    Buddhism influences, 55-56
    Buddhism, compared, 56-57
Hippocrates, 329
holistic medicine, 329
holistic outlooks, 89
holograms, 325
hospices, 345-346
houses (practice)
    altars, 141-142
    breathing rooms, 140-141
hsin tsung, 57
Hua Yen, 119
Hui Neng, 194-195

I

identities, searching, 56
immigration (Western Buddhism), 40
immunity (meditation), 334
immunology, 334
impermanence, 120-122, 180
implicate order, 336
incense, 143
India
    culture, 28
    decline of Buddhism, 24
indigenous peoples, Buddhism interfaith, 65
infinite openness
    consecutiveness, 128
    cycles, 128
    misconceptions, 128-129
    overview, 125-126
    spaciousness, 128
    suchness, 127
influences (Buddhism), 55-56
initiations (tantra), 230-231
insight meditation, 170
    body scan, 176-177
    concentration, 171
    elements, 178-179
    Four Noble Truths, 171
    impermanence, 180
    loving kindness, 181-184
    mental noting, 172-173
        comments, 173
        forcing, 174
        generic Post-it labels, 173
        internalizing, 174-175
        judgments, 173
        Three Dharma Seals, 174
        verbs, 174
    stopping, 170-171
intelligence, 175
interbeing, 117-120
    Flower Garland School, 119
    terminology, 119-120
    worldviews, 119

interconnected mindset (Eastern), 58
interfaith
 Buddhism and Taoism, 57-59
 Christian followers, 59-61
 deeper understandings, 61
 Golden Rule, 52
 Hinduism versus Buddhism, 56-57
 indigenous peoples, 65
 Jewish, 62-63
 Muslims, 64
 oneness, 52-53
International Buddhist Film Festival, 300
interrelations
 Buddha's family, 244-245
 civil societies, 246
 cube, 245
 cultures, 246
 death, 256-257
 love, 246-248
 male-female, 351
 marriages, 248
 parenting, 251
  Dharma, 252
  emotional intelligence, 253
  family meals, 264-265
  practicing, 251-252
  teaching children, 252
 rites of passage, 253-254
 sexuality, 249-250
 student-teacher relationships, 255-256
intuition, 200
It's a Wonderful Life, 301

J

Jackson, Phil, 293
Japan
 Buddhism expansion, 31
 Buddhist films, 301
 flower arrangements, 288
 Morita, 331
 rock gardens, 289-290
 shakuhachi, 296
 tanka poetry, 309
 tea ceremony, 270-271
Japanese Americans, 40
Jesus, 59
Jewish Buddhism, interfaith, 62-63
Jodo Shin-shu, 212-213
 dualism, 215
 enlightenment, 213
 everyday life, 221
 practice, 213
 recitation, 214
 reward, 212
 tariki, 213-214
Jukebox Mind, 82

K

Kabat-Zinn, Dr. Jon, 330
Kagyu, 33
karé-san-sui, 289-290
karma, 55
 categories, 116
 common, 117
 interbeing, 117-120
 meditations, 130-131
 merits, 208-210
 mutable, 117
 overview, 116-117
 personal, 117
 primary, 117
 secondary, 117
 simultaneous, 117
Kasyapa, 191-192
Kejawen, 64
kenosis, 60
King Ashoka, 21-22
Kitaro, 296
koans, 200-203
Korea, 30-31
Koryo, 31

Kuan-yin Temple, 39
kung fu, 291
Kwan Yin, 29
Kwannons, 197
kyudo, 292

L

lamrims, 227-228
Land of Pagodas, 26
landscape art, 314
Lao-tzu, 28
liberation
    overview, 78-80
    path to, 80-81
life
    art, 315
        Fluxus, 318
        happenings, 318
        music, 316-317
    circularity, 55
    reverence for, 100-102
light, 324
Light of Asia, The, 42
lineage (Zen), 191
    Bodhidharma, 192-194
    Hui Neng, 194-195
    Kasyapa, 191-192
    trees, 196
literature, 307
    detective novels, 308
    fiction, 308-309
    haikus, 309-311
    Shakespeare, 308
    sutras, 307
Little Buddha, 301
livelihood (work), 276-277
living teachers, 41-42
Lotus Sutra schools, 24, 221
love
    marriages, 248
    parenting, 251
        Dharma, 252
        emotional intelligence, 253

family meals, 264-265
    practicing, 251-252
    teaching children, 252
relationships, 246-248
sexuality, 249-250
loving kindness
    meditation, 181-184
    sublime states, 180-181
loving speech, 108-109
lying, 106
    bearing witness, 106-108
    loving speech, 108-109

M

Madhyamika, 10
Mahamaya, 5
Mahamudra, 226
Mahayana, 23
    Bodhisattva Vow, 196-198
    deities, 216
    medicine, 330
    Triple Gem, 74
Maimonides, Abraham, 63
male-female interrelations, 351
mandalas, 234
mantras, 160, 233
Manu Amida Butsu, 207
marga, 80-81
marriages, 248
martial arts, 290-291
Matrix, 301
matter, 323
MBSR (Mindfulness-Based Stress Reduction)
    program, 330
meat, eating, 268-269
media consumption, 111
medical knowledge, 329
    holistic medicine, 329
    Mahayana, 330
    Theravada, 330
    Tibetan Buddhism, 331
    Zen, 330

meditation. *See also* Zen
  body scan, 176-177
  breathing, 157-158
    awareness, 161-162
    counting, 160
    nostrils, 159
    words, 160-161
  Buddhist, 60
  candles, 143
  Christian, 60
  cognitive sciences, 333
  elements, 178-179
  immunity, 334
  impermanence, 180
  incense, 143
  insight, 170-171
  Jewish, 63
  karma, 130-131
  loving kindness, 181-184
  mental noting, 172-173
    comments, 173
    forcing, 174
    internalizing, 174-175
    judgments, 173
    Post-it labels, 173
    Three Dharma Seals, 174
    verbs, 174
  mindfulness, 112-113
  minds, quieting, 162-165
  pillows, 142
  posture, 152-155
    basic, 153
    body language, 154-155
    prostration, 155
  problems, 167-168
  relaxation, 155-156
  stress reduction, 330
  tools, 142
  tumo, 331
  Vajrayana, 232, 237
  walking, 165-167
  warm-up stretches, 156-157
  Zen retreats, 196

mental noting
  eating, 262-264
  insight meditation, 172-173
    comments, 173
    forcing, 174
    generic Post-it labels, 173
    internalizing, 174-175
    judgments, 173
    Three Dharma Seals, 174
    verbs, 174
mental snapshots, 138
merits, 208-210
Metcalf, Franz, 72
metta
  meditation, 181-184
  sublime states, 180-181
Middle Kingdom. *See* China
Middle Way, 10-11
mind/body interrelations, 333-334
mind/mind interrelations, 333
mind's eye, 236
mindfulness
  complete, 94, 96
  meditation, 112-113
  medicine, 330
Mindfulness-Based Stress Reduction program (MBSR), 330
minds
  mechanistic model, 335
  network model, 335
  nonlocal phenomena, 336-337
  quieting, 162-165
modern art, 305
Mon people (Siam), 26
monasteries
  forming, 20
  Korea, 31
  shutting down (China), 30
mondos, 203-204
Mongols, 23
monks, 20
Morita, 331

movies, 297
    Buddhist films, 300-302
    watching, 297-300
mudita, 181
mudras, 154-155, 233
music, 294
    chanting, 295
    country 'n' eastern, 296-297
    life art, 316-317
    wind instruments, 295-296
Muslim Buddhism interfaith, 64
mutable karma, 117
mutuality
    marriages, 248
    sangha, 245
mystic spirituality, 342

N

Nalanda University, 22, 255
Namo Adida Phat, 207
Namo Ami-to-fo, 207
namo/namu, 207
nembutsu, 207
neuroimmunology, 333-334
New School practice, 22
nien fo, 207
nirvana, 78-80, 124-125
nonlocal phenomena, 336-337
nostrils (breathing), 159
noting (mental)
    eating, 262-264
    insight meditation, 172-173
        comments, 173
        forcing, 174
        generic Post-it labels, 173
        internalizing, 174-175
        Three Dharma Seals, 174
        verbs, 174
novels, 308
nuns, 20
nutrition. *See* food
Nyingma, 33

O

Olcott, Colonel Henry Steel, 40
Old School practice, 22
oneness, 52-53
organic food, 269
other-power (Shin), 213

P

Packer, Toni, 45
Pagels, Elaine, 60
palliative care, 345
parables, 16
paradigm shifts, 323-325
parenting, 251
    Dharma, 252
    emotional intelligence, 253
    family meals, 264-265
    practicing, 251-252
    teaching children, 252
particles, 324
paths (Eightfold), 86-87
    actions, 92-93
    concentration, 96-97
    effort, 94
    Four Noble Truths links, 87-89
    memorizing, 87
    mindfulness, 94-96
    right, 86
    skillful, 86
    speech, 93
    thoughts, 91-92
    views, 90
    work, 93-94
peace, 353
performance (physical culture), 292-294
personal karma, 117
personalizing
    altars, 141
    precepts, 114
persuasiveness (Buddha), 15

physical cultures
  martial arts, 290-291
  performance, 292-294
  samurais, 291-292
physical sciences, 322
  holistic views, 323
  holograms, 325
  light, 324
  matter, 323
  paradigm shifts, 325-326
  particles, 324
  revolution, 322
  Uncertainity Principle, 324
pilgrims (Western), 40-41
pillows (meditation), 142
plants, 286-287
political activity, 342
popular culture
  art, 304
    Andrew Goldsworthy, 305
    Baroque paintings, 312
    contemporary spiritual, 306-307
    dualism, 312
    east Asian examples, 312
    expression, 305
    modern, 305
    self-expression, 305
    spiritual practice, compared, 304
    Tibetan, 312
    Zen, 314-314
  gardening
    arrangements, 287-289
    planting, 286-287
    sand, 289-290
  literature, 307
    detective novels, 308
    fiction, 308-309
    haikus, 309-311
    Shakespeare, 308
    sutras, 307
  movies, 297
    Buddhist films, 300-302
    watching, 297-300

music, 294
  chanting, 295
  country 'n' eastern, 296-297
  wind instruments, 295-296
physical
  martial arts, 290-291
  performance, 292-294
  samurais, 291-292
portable altars, 141
posture (meditation), 152
  basic, 153
  body language, 154-155
  prostration, 155
practice. *See* schools of practice
practicing
  beginner's mind, 136-137
  community, 143
  compassion, 344
  effort, 149
  houses, 140-142
  Jodo Shin-shu, 213
  parenting, 251-252
  precepts, 112
  Pure Land, 211
  selecting, 144-147
  time, 138-140
  tools, 142-143
  views, 147-149
prana, 157
prayers, 336
precepts
  consumption, 109-111
    addictions, 110
    altered states/traits, 109
    media, 111
    self-help, 110
  impossibility of killing, 112
  killing, 112
  lying, 106
    bearing witness, 106-108
    loving speech, 108-109
  mindfulness meditation, 112-113
  personalizing, 114

practicing, 112
reverence for life, 100-102
sexual restraint, 105-106
straightforward, 112
trustworthiness/generosity, 103-104
Pribram, Dr. Karl, 336
primary karma, 117
printing books, 29
prisons, 347-348
produce, 266
prostration (meditation), 155
Proust, Marcel, 90
psychedelic, 38
psychology, 331-332
Pure Land, 24
  compassion, 210-211
  deities, 216
  everyday life, 218
    contemplation, 220-221
    recitations, 219-220
  faith, 211
  Japan, 31
  merits, transferring, 208-210
  overview, 206
  practice, 211
  remembrance, 206-208
  sciences, 322
  Shinran Shonen, 212-213
    dualism, 215
    enlightenment, 213
    everyday life, 221
    practice, 213
    recitation, 214
    reward, 212
    tariki, 213-214
  T'ang Dynasty, 29
  universality, 217-218
  vows, 211
  Zen combination, 218

Q–R

questions (Four Noble Truths), 81
quieting minds, 162-165

race, 352-353
Rahula, 7
recitations
  Buddhist/Christian, 60
  Jodo Shin-shu, 214
  Pure Land, 219-220
  Vajrayana, 233
refuge (Triple Gem), 71
  everyday life, 72-73
  schools of practice, 73-74
  trees, 237
  unity, 74
reincarnation, 55
relationships
  Buddha's family, 244-245
  civil societies, 246
  cube, 245
  cultures, 246
  death, 256-257
  life art, 315-318
  love, 246-248
  marriages, 248
  parenting, 251
    Dhamra, 252
    emotional intelligence, 253
    family meals, 264-265
    practicing, 251-252
    teaching children, 252
  rites of passage, 253-254
  sexuality, 249-250
  student-teacher, 255-256
relativity, 129
relaxation, 155-156
Relaxation Response, The, 333
remembrance, 206-208
renunciation (Siddhartha), 8
restraint (sexual), 105-106

retreats, 139
reverence for life, 100
    abortion, 102
    negatives/positives, 101
    vegetarianism, 101-102
Riley, Terry, 297
rites of passage, 253-254
Roach, Geshe Michael, 282
rock gardens, 289-290
rosary beads, 60, 143

S

Sabbath, 62
Sakya, 33
Salzberg, Susan, 136
samatha, 170-171
Sambhava, Padma, 32
samurais, 31, 291-292
sand (gardening), 289-290
sanghas, 14, 20
    defined, 70
    ethical monastic conduct, 25
    everyday life, 73
    family, 252
    Mahayana, 74
    mutuality, 245
    practicing, 143
    selecting, 146-147
    Theravadins, 73
    Zen, 195-196
sanzen, 196
Satipatthana, 96
Sayadaw, Mahasi, 172
scholars (Western Buddhism), 43
schools of practice, 22
    Avatamsaka, 221
    Flower Garland, 119
    Gelug, 33
    Kagyu, 33
    Korea, 31

Lotus Sutra schools, 24, 221
Mahayana
    deities, 216
    medicine, 330
Nyingma, 33
Pure Land. *See* Pure Land
Sakya, 33
selecting, 144-146
Theravada
    medicine, 330
    sciences, 322
    vipassana. *See* vipassana
Tibetan Buddhism, 331
Triple Gem, 73-74
Vajrayana. *See* Vajrayana
Zen. *See* Zen
sciences
    Butterfly Effect, 327
    cognitive, 333
    fuzzy logic, 326-328
    medical knowledge, 329-331
    minds, 335-337
    neuroimmunology, 333-334
    paradigm shifts, 323
    physical, 322-325
        holistic views, 323
        holograms, 325
        light, 324
        matter, 323
        paradigm shifts, 325
        particles, 324
        revolution, 322
        Uncertainty Principle, 324
    prayer experiments, 336
    psychology, 331-332
    Pure Land, 322
    Theravada, 322
    Vajrayana, 322
scientific Four Noble Truths, 81
secondary karma, 117
secular Buddhism, 341
SEL (Social and Emotional Learning), 253

self-compassion, 165
self-expression, 305
self-inquiry, 82
self-similarity (chaotic shapes), 327
self-sufficiency, 280
selflessness, 122-124, 200
service, 343
    Butterfly Effect, 344-345
    hospices, 345-346
    nonprofits, 344
    prisons, 347-348
sesshin, 139, 196
sexual restraint, 105-106
sexuality
    relationships, 249-250
    Western, 249
shabbos, 62
Shakespeare, 308
shakuhachi, 296
Shakyamuni. *See* Siddhartha
shamanism, 31
Shaolin Temple, 290
Shen, Hu, 39
Shikibu, Lady Murasaki, 246
Shingon, 31
Shinran. *See* Shonen, Shinran
Shinto, 31
Shogunate, 31
Shonen, Shinran, 213
    dualism, 215
    enlightenment, 213
    everyday life, 221
    practice, 213
    Pure Land, 212
    recitation, 214
    reward, 212
    tariki, 213-214
Siam (Mon people), 26
Siddhartha
    birth, 5
    death, 17
    egalitarianism, 17

enlightenment, 11-12
everyday life, 72
family
    leaving, 8
    relationships, 244-245
forest teachers, 9
growing up, 6
Jesus, compared, 59
Mahayana, 74
Middle Way, 10-11
parables, 16
persuasiveness, 15
reality glimpses, 6-7
renunciation, 8
son, 7
silence, 16
teaching, 13-14
Theravadins, 73
"The Turning of the Wheel of Truth," 14
Siddhartha. *See also* Buddah, 5
silence, 16
Silk Route, 26-27
simultaneous karma, 117
skillful means, 237
snapshots (mental), 138
Social and Emotional Learning (SEL), 253
sounds, noticing, 164
spaciousness (emptiness), 128
speech
    loving, 108-109
    perfect, 93
    Vajrayana, 233
Spice Route, 27
spirituality
    engaged, 340
    mystic, 342
    work, 274-275
spontaneity, 200
sports, 292
Sri Lanka, 25
Star Wars, 301
stopping (samatha), 170-171

straightforward precepts, 112
stress
    reduction meditation, 330
    work, 275-276
student-teacher relationships, 255-256
sublime states, 180-181
suchness (emptiness), 127
suffering, 76-77
sunyata, 126
Suquamish Chief Seattle, 65
sutras, 15, 24, 307
swords (samurais), 292
symbolism, 238

T

T'ang Dynasty, 29
taking refuge (Triple Gem), 71-74
    everyday life, 72-73
    schools of practice, 73-74
    unity, 74
Tale of Genji, The, 246
tanka poetry, 309
tantra, 33, 226-227
    body, 232
    deities, 236
    deity yoga, 234
    initiations, 230-231
    mandalas, 234
    meditations, 232
    mind's eye, 236
    overview, 238-239
    refuge trees, 237
    rituals, 237
    sexuality, 250
    skillful means, 237
    speech, 233
    symbolism, 238
    visualization, 233, 236
Tao, 28
Tao Te Ching, 57
Taoism, 28-29, 57-59

Taras, 197
tariki, 213-214
Tassajara Bread Book, The, 280
tathata, 127
tea, 269-271
teachers. *See also* education
    experience, 255-256
    selecting, 145-146
    student-teacher relationships, 255-256
    Vajrayana, 228-229
temples
    Kuan-yin Temple, 39
    shutting down (China), 30
Thai Buddhism, 26
thanks for food, 261-262
Theosophical Society, 40
Theravada, 23
    medicine, 330
    sciences, 322
    Triple Gem, 73
    vipassana. *See* vipassana
    Western, 24
Thinker, The, 92
Thoreau, 42
three baskets, 25
Three Refuges. *See* Triple Gem
three seals of dharma
    impermanence, 120-122
    nirvana, 124-125
    selflessness, 122-124
Three Treasures. *See* Triple Gem
three-month retreats, 139
Tibetan art, 312
Tibetan Buddhism
    body, 232-233
    Buddhism expansion, 32-33
    deities, 225-226, 236
    deity yoga, 234
    Dzogchen, 226
    empowerment, 226, 230-231
    lamrims, 227-228
    mandalas, 234

medicine, 331
meditations, 232
mind's eye, 236
overview, 224-226, 238-239
refuge trees, 237
rituals, 237
sexuality, 250
skillful means, 237
speech, 233
symbolism, 238
tantra, 226-227
teachers, 228-229
visualization, 233, 236
time, 138-140
tonglen, 60, 228
tools, 142-143
Toynbee, Arnold, 36
tranquility, 170-171
transferring merits, 208-210
translations (Western Buddhism), 42-43
Tripitaka, 25
Triple Gem, 70-71
elements, 70
taking refuge, 71
everyday life, 72-73
schools of practice, 73-74
unity, 74
trishna, 75-77
True Pure Land School. *See* Jodo Shin-shu
trustworthiness, 103-104
tsingshas, 142
tso wang, 57
Tudor, David, 316
tumo meditation, 331
"The Turning of the Wheel of Truth," 14

U

Uncertainty Principle, 324
universe, 55
universities, 22
upaya kausalya, 237
upekkha, 181

V

Vajrayana, 24, 33
body, 232-233
deities, 225-226, 236
deity yoga, 234
empowerment, 226, 230-231
lamrims, 227-228
mandalas, 234
meditations, 232
mind's eye, 236
overview, 224-226, 238-239
refuge trees, 237
rituals, 237
sciences, 322
sexuality, 250
skillful means, 237
speech, 233
symbolism, 238
tantra, 226-227
teachers, 228-229
visualization, 233, 236
vegetarianism, 101-102
verbs, mental noting, 174
Vietnam, 32
views
perfect, 90
practicing, 147-149
universe, 55
vinaya, 25
vipassana, 24, 170
body scan, 176-177
concentration, 171
elements, 178-179
Four Noble Truths, 171
impermanence, 180
loving kindness, 181-184
mental noting, 172-173
comments, 173
forcing, 174
generic Post-it labels, 173
internalizing, 174-175

judgments, 173
  Three Dharma Seals, 174
  verbs, 174
 stopping, 170-171
visualization, 233, 236
Visuddhi Magga, 342
void, 126
vows
  Bodhisattva, 196-198
  Pure Land, 211

W

waking up, 4
walking (meditation), 165-167
warm-up stretches (meditation), 156-157
wealth, measuring, 278-280
Western Buddhism, 39
  1960s, 37-38
  acculturation, 44-46
  democracy, 46-47
  diversity, 48
  dualistic mindset, 58
  Eastern pilgrimages, 40-41
  ecumenism, 49-50
  egalitarianism, 47
  everyday life integration, 47
  feminism, 46
  first Buddhist clergy, 40
  foreign politics, 37
  immigration, 40
  Japanese Americans, 40
  living teachers, 41-42
  scholars, 43
  Theosophical Society, 40
  translations, 42-43
  World War II, 37
Western female Buddhists, 350
Western Theravada, 24
whole grains, 266
Why Has Bodhidharma Left for the East?, 300
Williams, Dr. William Carlos, 121

wind instruments, 295-296
women Buddhists, 349-351
Wonhyo, 30
Woods, Tiger, 293
words (breathing), 160-161
work
  enterprises, 281-282
  entrepreneurs, 280
  right livelihood, 276-277
  spiritual nature, 274-275
  stress, 275-276
  wealth, measuring, 278-280
  wholesome, 93-94
World of Parliament of Religions, 41
World War II
  Japanese Americans, 40
  Western Buddhism, 37
writing haikus, 311

X-Y-Z

yab yum, 250
yoga, 57
Yu, Lu, 269

zabutons, 142
zafus, 142
zazen, 190
Zen, 24. *See also* meditation
  art, 314
  authenticity, 199
  Bodhisattva Vow, 196-198
  brush art, 312-314
  calligraphy, 314
  China, 29
  completeness, 199
  dedication, 200
  emptiness, 189-190
  enlightenment, 198
  everyday life, 199
  happenings, 318
  immediacy, 199

intuition, 200
Japan, 31
koans, 200-203
Korea, 31
lineage, 191
    Bodhidharma, 192-194
    Hui Neng, 194-195
    Kasyapa, 191-192
medicine, 330
meditation retreats, 196
mondos, 203-204
performing, 190
Pure Land combination, 218
sanghas, 195-196
selflessness, 200
spontaneity, 200
zendos, 195
zendos, 195
zone (sports), 292